Scotland since 1707

Scotland since 1707

The Rise of an
Industrial Society

R. H. CAMPBELL

Second Edition

JOHN DONALD PUBLISHERS LTD
EDINBURGH

ISBN 0 85976 122 3

Exclusive distribution in the United States
of America and Canada by Humanities Press
Inc., Atlantic Highlands, NJ 07716, U.S.A.

First published 1965
Reprinted 1971
Second Edition 1985

Filmset by Burns & Harris Limited, Dundee
and printed in Great Britain by Bell & Bain Ltd., Glasgow

Preface to the Second Edition

In preparing the second edition I have become more aware than ever of the very large amount of excellent work which has been undertaken in the field since I wrote the first edition a quarter of a century ago. I owe a great deal to the scholarship of many. Recognition of some of the works on which I have drawn is in the bibliography. With so much available it would have been possible, and no doubt some will think preferable, to have written a totally different book, but a second edition with the same structure as the first and with recognition of new work seemed an effective way of meeting the demand which still exists for the book. I am grateful to Mr John Tuckwell of the publishers of the second edition for encouraging me to undertake the task.

To the acknowledgements in the first edition I wish to add my thanks to Dr M. W. Kirby, with whom I have discussed recent economic history but who must not be held responsible for my views, and to Miss Margaret Hendry, who produced a faultless typescript from a much corrected original.

I acknowledge permission from W. Green & Sons Ltd. to use in this edition material which I contributed to the *Juridical Review*.

The map is not reproduced in the second edition.

Preface to the First Edition (1965)

The present work is not a definitive study of Scottish economic history. Its aim is the more limited one of trying to provide a general introduction to the chief forces which have determined the growth of the industrial society that is modern Scotland. Inevitably, therefore, some selection of material has been made, and not all will agree with the choice. Two leading principles guided it. First, it was judged unnecessary to reproduce detailed discussions of aspects of economic history already published, even if in works not particularly concerned with Scotland. For this reason many technical developments, common to industries on both sides of the Border, have been considered only briefly. Second, especially in modern times, when assimilation of Scotland and England has been increased, mostly through the economic and social policies of the central government, greatest emphasis has been placed on those topics which still tend to be distinctively Scottish. For example, the growth of the welfare state is an aspect of British history, more appropriately considered in that context, but the exceptional nature of Scottish housing warrants an extended investigation in the present study. Selection has been determined, therefore, by a desire to produce a study in Scottish history with emphasis on its economic and social aspects, rather than a general economic history with special reference to Scotland. How far the aim has been achieved is another matter. The danger of this approach is that it can lead to an unbalanced analysis of economic growth because, for good or ill, Scottish economic development since 1707 cannot be considered apart from events in England. But the present approach seems legitimate, since to regard Scotland as only an economic appendage of England may present an equally unbalanced interpretation and, more important, may lead to a neglect of Scotland's unique, though not necessarily major, contributions to the development of British industrial society in the last two hundred and fifty years. Of these conditions Scots, and others, should be more aware than they are.

It is possible to write a book of this nature only by incurring extensive obligations to many people. The main sources used are listed in the bibliography, and I am particularly grateful to the custodians of unpublished collections for granting me access to them. Anyone who writes in any field of Scottish history soon comes to realize, however, that his main obligation is to the facilities provided by the Scottish Record Office in the Register House in Edinburgh. I owe much to the ungrudging help of all its officers, but especially to Mr J. Imrie, the Curator of Historical Records, whose assistance far exceeded his official obligations. The manuscript was read in whole or in part by Dr D. H. Aldcroft, Professor R. E. Cameron, Mr R. S. Campbell, Professor S. G. Checkland, Mr R. E. Cramond, Mr J. B. A. Dow (who also read the proofs), Mr M. Gaskin, and Dr P. L. Payne. All made helpful suggestions. Dr T. C. Smout not only read the entire manuscript, parts of it more than once, but in a variety of other ways has made it a much better book. I am grateful to Miss J. Clark for typing assistance and to Mr J. S. Keates and Miss Robertson of the Department of Geography in the University of Glasgow for preparing the map.

I acknowledge permission to use material already published from the Editors of *Business History, Economic History Review, Scottish Geographical Magazine, Scottish Journal of Political Economy*, and from William Collins Sons and Company, Ltd.

R. H. Campbell

Contents

Introduction

The evolution of the modern Scottish economy does not date from the Union of Parliaments in 1707. The search for improvement was present before the Union provided the political framework within which potential moved to achievement. Though there were solid and cumulative gains in the eighteenth century, progress was slow and often interrupted. Until towards its end at least, the economy was still based on agriculture and trade; its industry was more a portent of the future.

Industrial success became more widespread and lasting from the 1780s, first of all in the cotton industry and later in the coal and iron industries. The geological resources of Scotland then gave a unique basis for industrial success, and for around a century Scotland became an industrial power without rival in some fields. Though the society which then emerged was squalid and unstable, its economic foundations seemed so secure that they bred complacency and self-satisfaction, which contrasted with the efforts and struggles of the eighteenth century, and which served Scotland ill in later years.

The industrial successes persisted until 1914, but — to later generations if not to contemporaries — they became tarnished from the 1870s as Scotland experienced the pressures of international competition. The cotton industry suffered by the middle of the nineteenth century and the iron industry by its end, but any warnings of the need for change which were implied could remain unheeded in the resounding successes of the allied fields of steelmaking, shipbuilding and heavy engineering in the half-century before 1914. Their success ensured that Scottish industrial society remained prosperous until 1914. The reversal of their fortunes after 1918 gave much of the character to the needs and aspirations of Scotland thereafter. Since 1945 the stress of adjusting to the loss of the old industrial supremacy has dominated many aspects of its life.

Part One

Economic Struggle, 1707 to 1780s

CHAPTER I

A Changing Society

The consequences of Union

The parliamentary union of 1707 strengthened the close links which already existed between Scotland and England and gave them a particular form. It increased the opportunities for the larger and more powerful neighbour to influence, perhaps even to dictate, many aspects of the life of the smaller and in the interpretations of some to exploit it. As a result, historians of Scotland generally accord the Union of 1707 such a fundamental place in the country's history that it can be thought to be more important than it was. The tendency to do so has increased with the growth of political nationalism. The acceptance of the desirability of political self-determination, accompanied by the belief that governments can and should direct economic and social affairs, have led to attempts to devise an alternative political structure for Scotland. The current political discussion has an historical dimension. It has encouraged debate on whether the parliamentary union need have come about in 1707. Claims that the Union was politically wise and economically beneficial have been supported by more modern versions of an old historical interpretation which stressed its economic necessity. Another view suggests that the issue was much more open in 1707 and that acceptance of the Union was in doubt until the last moment. There is no necessary connection between interpretations of the making of the Union and of its benefits, but those who favour explanations involving a belief in its necessity obviously regard opposition as futile to some degree. They accept the political settlement more readily than those who regard its consummation as open and optional.

The rival interpretations have been presented with some degree of acrimony as mutually exclusive. A measure of reconciliation is possible. Some of the differences arise simply because each approaches the evidence from a different standpoint. Those who stress the inevitability of the Union usually examine the evidence from a long-term perspective. They identify trends, particularly of economic development, which, if not making an independent economic existence for Scotland impossible, implied that greater prosperity was available through union. The strength of the alternative approach is its short-term perspective, which emphasises the confusing variety of evidence which must be taken into account in explaining the immediate determinants of union. Its supporters stress that the Union need not have taken place at a particular time and that the outcome was uncertain until it actually happened. To accept that the long-run influences imply some degree of inevitability in the making of the Union does not involve denial of the short-run uncertainties, merely the acceptance of the operation of powerful trends which were bound to influence the decisions of those whose immediate short-term, even vascillating, attitudes contributed to the final outcome. The long-term trends were parameters which determined the range of practicable choice. Their influence, and the limits they placed on action, are evident in the economic policy which Scotland tried to follow before the Union.

The Restoration of 1660 saw an attempt to provide comprehensive legislation to encourage manufactures, even if it embodied few new principles. The objectives, repeated in several acts, were chiefly to reduce imports, to promote home-based production, and to devise a colonial policy to ensure markets overseas. The bias of the legislation, which can be paralleled in the records of the privy council, has been sufficient to earn condemnation because of the success of the attack on all forms of mercantilist restriction from the later eighteenth century. The basic assumption of the policy was the desirability of maintaining a closed economy and of exploiting its indigenous resources, an assumption that became anathema to later generations, who gained so much from the international division of labour. There were no comparable advantages in the seventeenth century. Even more important, the diplomatic principle, that political independence required economic independence, was as valid then as in other ages of international conflict. If defence was more important than opulence, economic policy had to aim primarily at supporting political power even at the sacrifice of economic growth. In Scotland in the later seventeenth century economic change was leading to greater co-operation with, even dependence on, England. In retrospect the trend may seem irreversible, and even one that the Scots would have welcomed if accompanied with acceptable, though unlikely, terms. If that were not possible, through English indifference as much as anything else, economic independence was essential for political and strategic needs.

The defence of the policy may seem untenable when the measures promoted were largely ineffective in spite of their frequent repetition. Their ineffectiveness arose from various causes. The first was that the provisions of the new economic policy were too advanced for a still largely primitive economy, and so a new measure was sometimes followed by exemptions or concessions which detracted from its effectiveness. The second was the ineffectiveness of much of the Scottish administration. Though the administration could maintain life and property in many parts of Scotland, with all the benefits that implies for economic growth, it did not have the resources or the competence to apply many of its economic policies. The third and most fundamental reason for the ineffectiveness was simply the absence of other necessary conditions for sustained economic growth, a limitation which was overcome only gradually in the eighteenth century. The measures should be interpreted as indicative of a country poised to promote new economic measures when other factors made that possible. The parliamentary union was such a factor. More than that, it was a prerequisite if it is accepted, first, and more important, that the Scots' desire for economic growth overrode any other aspirations to such an extent that it determined the form of political association with England, and, second, that the incorporating parliamentary union with England was the only one possible. Neither proposition can be accepted without qualification. The extent to which economic objectives determined the political connection can never be proved conclusively, and alternatives to the incorporating union were little considered. Such qualifications rule out any unequivocal assertion that economic causes made the Union inevitable, but the influence of economic aspirations on the political arrangements between Scotland and England was strengthened by mercantilist thought and, more mundanely, but no less potently, by the possibility that union seemed to offer to many the opportunity to escape from mere subsistence to share the more expansive life of the wealthier neighbour.

The legislative and administrative actions of parliament and privy council before the Union show how the rising aspirations of the Scots for economic progress required some form of political accommodation in the mercantilist world of the seventeenth century, with its tariffs and trading restrictions. The voting figures on the various articles of the Treaty of Union itself confirm that the Scots recognised its economic attractiveness. Article IV, which offered freedom of trade, was passed by 154 votes to 17, though the final vote on the Treaty as a whole was only 110 to 69 in favour. In the negotiations England was fully aware that economic concessions interested the Scots and, understandably, was unwilling to grant them unless in compensation for a guarantee of the Hanoverian succession. To ensure the succession England passed the Act of Settlement in 1701. The Scots responded with the Act of Security and Succession, given the royal assent eventually in 1704, which held that Scotland would follow the Hanoverian succession only on conditions guaranteeing greater political independence. The English answer included the passing of the Alien Act of 1705. Among its provisions was a threat to stop imports of linen and cattle from Scotland to England unless commissioners to negotiate for union were appointed by Christmas Day. The Act was a deliberate and direct economic blow at the Scots, who shared the desire of all men at all times to retain political independence with the freedom of action it implies, and at the same time gain the advantages of political association. Such a combined objective was impracticable and unrealistic. The only way of achieving economic concessions in a mercantilist world of economic warfare was by political union. In the short run, economic objectives may not have determined Scottish action, but the failure of much Scottish enterprise before 1707 suggests that in the long run they had to. In the short run a union seemed only one path to economic growth, and political independence an option which could be preferred; in the long run union was essential for the economic strength which was necessary for political survival, and there was no choice.

The trading and financial terms of the Treaty were benefits offered to the Scots to compensate for the loss of political independence. Among the short-term gains in trade were profits from selling in England goods imported in Scotland before duties were raised to the higher English rates, or from the inferior organisation of the Scottish customs enabling the Scots to be better smugglers; but the major contribution came from inclusion within the privileges of the Navigation Acts, which had previously barred Scottish trade with the English colonies. The Scots fully appreciated the benefits of the Acts' protection and in the negotiations before the Union tried to secure their privileges for the maximum number of ships. It was proposed that all vessels belonging even only in part to Scottish subjects, whether built at home or overseas, should be counted ships of Great Britain if registered within twelve months of the Treaty of Union. Against this all-embracing provision, which, especially through the possibilities of part-ownership, would have opened the closely preserved English trade to a multitude of outsiders, the English rebelled and insisted that only ships registered at the date of the Treaty, and wholly owned by Scots, should be included. Substantially the English had their way, except that the privileges of the Acts were extended to ships wholly owned by Scots at the date of the ratification of the Treaty.

The financial provisions of the Treaty of Union had more direct consequences. The equalisation of customs and excise duties in the two countries implied an increase of duties in Scotland, and that part of the revenue raised in Scotland after the Union would have to make a contribution to the servicing of the larger national debt which England had incurred before 1707. Compensation assumed two forms. First, Scotland received a payment of £398,085 10s., 'the Equivalent', the capitalised value of the existing revenue-yield which would help to service the English national debt, and, second, an 'Arising Equivalent', which could not be calculated at the time of the Union, but which was to be a continuous compensation from revenue raised in Scotland. The second, or Arising Equivalent, was to consist of the entire increase in Scotland's customs and excise revenue for the seven years after the Union and of such part of the increase as would be used to meet payments on the English debt thereafter. Article XV of the Treaty of Union stipulated that the various funds of the Equivalent were to be used for a variety of purposes — payment of Scotland's own national debt; provision of compensation for those who lost through standardising the coinage of the two countries and for investors in the Darien Company; lastly, assistance of £2,000 a year for the woollen industry and other economic projects.

Of the economic provisions, the removal of restrictions on trade from Scotland to England and its colonies was the more influential ultimately. A new pattern of trade was being established before 1707 in spite of the restrictions, but the Union made a difference sufficient to classify it as an epoch-making event in Scottish economic history. The difference lay in the means by which the emulation of English economic achievement, which was evident in so much economic policy before the Union, was to be achieved. It had two aspects, one external, the other internal. The external factor was the confirmation of the reorientation of Scotland's trading links from Europe to England, and so to America, and their increasing fruitfulness.[1] To some the attempts at re-establishing closer links with France through the rebellions of 1715 and 1745 were valiant endeavours to maintain Scotland's earlier independence from England; to the majority of Scots, especially to those promoting and profiting from the reorientation of economic contacts, the rebellions were unfortunate interruptions, the tragedy of which was not that they failed, but that they ever happened. The Union also brought about an internal change by ensuring that Scottish economic policy aimed at rivalling the achievements of the English economy through complementary rather than competitive action. Before 1707 the incomplete political union led in a mercantilist environment to attempts at competitive rivalry of a stronger economic power. Such efforts came to little unless supported by a protectionist policy; even high protection failed to save those ventures, especially fine cloth production, which were directly competitive with English manufactures. The industrial successes lay only in sectors, such as sugar refining, which were not competitive but complementary to the English economy. After 1707 political union ensured that, once and for all, attempts at economic development in Scotland had to follow complementary lines.

Though providing a new and potentially fruitful framework for economic growth, the parliamentary union of 1707 gave no guarantee that it would take place. It offered opportunities, but whether they gave rise to benefits or merely to exploitation by the more powerful partner depended on the internal response of the Scottish economy to the challenge. A society which meets the opportunities of a customs union by resisting change is unlikely to experience a successful economic transformation; it is more likely to suffer economic decay. In Scotland the new ideas and attitudes which gained currency from its rich and vigorous intellectual life of the eighteenth century encouraged a favourable response.

Some have suggested that earlier theological disputation failed to give Scotland the social stability needed for economic growth. Examples of alleged social disruption are varied: the Scots were theologically obsessed; insistence on the right to personal judgement in all matters ensured an almost total absence of social cohesion; even more extreme is the suggestion that Scotland became so introverted by her theological disputations that stimulating contacts with other societies, perhaps most of all in Europe, could not be maintained. Such criticisms ignore the extent to which large areas of Scotland were not affected by the troubles and how another more peaceful and more progressive state of Scotland co-existed with a more trouble-ridden one. In the later seventeenth century, a period when the Scottish parliament and privy council are sometimes portrayed as being concerned only with the extirpation of the Covenanters, they were also planning means of promoting industrial growth. Even if the plans were to prove abortive, they are indicative of the issues which were in the minds of contemporaries.

More positively, the possibility that the Scottish theological interests produced incentives which equipped the Scots for economic action can be derived from the suggestion, advanced particularly in recent years, that the qualities requisite for successful entrepreneurial action are more likely to be acquired in a society in which there is a strong motivation towards high achievement, and that they will be expressed in economic action wherever that motivation is directed towards economic ends. Scottish theology encouraged the individual to believe that, as one of the elect, he could find himself called to be a direct and active agent of God's will. In that way he was provided with a major incentive to the self-confidence and assurance in his actions which is necessary for a successful entrepreneur. The intellectual contribution of the eighteenth century was to take the qualities of mind, derived partly from the theological obsession of earlier years, and apply them to wholly secular affairs without loss of fervour. The change took place without those social tensions which retard economic enterprise. The intellectually revolutionary leaders of the secularisation of Scottish thought were politically and socially conservative. For them the political changes of 1688 and 1707 were sufficient, and they opposed those who perpetuated political dissension, particularly in the form of Jacobitism.

The revolutionary thinkers were not social iconoclasts, partly because those with political and social power became reformers too. The possession of political power in Scotland was the prerogative of the landowners. Parochial authority rested on a balance, not always clearly defined, between the kirk session and the heritors, the proprietors of land within the parish to the extent of at least £100 (Scots) of valued rent appearing in the land-tax books. Heritors were responsible for the upkeep of church, manse, school and schoolhouse and shared with the session the responsibilities for poor relief. The landed interest still maintained its authority in the wider spheres of county administration. The two chief bodies were the Justices of the Peace and the Commissioners of Supply. Justices were chosen by the sovereign but the office was confined in effect to landowners. Commissioners of Supply, appointed originally from among those paying the land tax, and charged with its collection, came to include most of the landed proprietors. Since the higher administration always remained rudimentary, neither body dislodged the parochial authorities. Scottish life centred on the parish.

The need for landowners to use the power and influence they possessed for the development of the Scottish economy was more necessary after 1707 than it had been before, because the abolition of the Scottish parliament and privy council meant the end of an effective Scottish administration. From 1709 to 1746 a third secretary was added to the United Kingdom's existing two, and charged with responsibility for Scottish affairs, but the office was frequently vacant. As a result there was no really effective Scottish administration from the Union until the institution of the Scottish Office in 1885. Under such conditions any failure by the landowners to encourage economic development could not have been made good easily. There was no such failure. The landowners discharged their responsibilities, especially when there was an infiltration into their ranks of new men, ready to use the privileges of their status to effect the social and economic transformation which Scotland required. In the

Highlands the ancient landowners retained their privileged position longer, but in the Lowlands successful bankers, lawyers and merchants were readily accepted as landed proprietors. They purchased their way into social position with a speed and completeness less easily achieved by their nineteenth-century counterparts. Assimilation was easy in the eighteenth century, when many of the successful were themselves scions of ancient landed families and so were returning to their heritage, and when many of the landowners participated in industrial enterprises so long as they remained subordinate to their normal rural activities. Until the nineteenth century there was no sharp distinction between the successful commercial men and the landowners, since the interests of both were complementary. The two groups moved easily together, as did both with the intellectuals. But the new landowners brought a unique contribution to the social and economic influence of their class in Scotland in the eighteenth century. They often acquired their possessions to obtain social prestige but used them for further commercial gain. The estate had to be a good investment, commercially as well as socially. All the economic opportunity implied in its possession, and the accompanying social prestige, were exploited, and the traditional power of the landowners, which could have been a restraining, if not an opposing force, supported social and economic reform in Scotland in the eighteenth century.

The ferment of social and intellectual change, with its underlying stability, both contributed to and gained from the provision and nature of education in Scotland. The laudable aims of Scotland's ecclesiastical and educational reformers are well known and easily stated: a school in every parish with opportunities for the more able to progress to the universities, which themselves increased from three to five after the Reformation. Education was neither compulsory nor free, but the kirk sessions were expected to ensure attendance by moral pressure and by assistance with the fees of the poorest. The early educational plans were not easily realised, chiefly through lack of the resources which were needed for their implementation. Defects and deficiencies appeared, and it is possible to present a less favourable interpretation of Scottish education in practice than in theory. Iconoclasm is often the easier approach because there is no obvious objective standard by which the educational provision may be judged, but, by the modest standards of what was being achieved elsewhere, the record — in lowland rural Scotland at least — is undeniable, whether tested by the extent of the provision or by the standard of instruction. Many of those who made the greatest contribution to the intellectual achievements of the eighteenth century were themselves the product of the educational system.

The most widely recognised educational legacy came from the universities. Their contribution has been assessed differently, both by contemporaries and by subsequent commentators. Reform was not the prerogative of the eighteenth century and can be traced back into the period of most frequently alleged reaction. The content of the curriculum changed, particularly in the introduction of Newtonian ideas in the teaching of physics; the regenting system, in which one tutor — the regent — took the student through the entire curriculum, and which was perhaps the greatest hindrance to intellectual improvement, was breaking finally in the early eighteenth century, from 1708 in Edinburgh and 1727 in Glasgow, though not at King's College, Aberdeen, until 1799. In the eighteenth century the greatest advance was in the encouragement in the universities of those intellectual attitudes most likely to produce a technical lead in industry. The origins of the achievements, especially the extent to which they lie in Scotland or not, may be various, but their intellectual characteristics are less questionable. Newtonian influences were supremely important. As Newton had been able to explain complicated natural phenomena on the basis of a single principle, so much Scottish thought in the eighteenth century was directed to the same end. Beauty was seen in order and in simplicity; the existence of any form of disorder provided an incentive to the mind to try to reduce complexity, which was not easily understood, to simplicity which was. The method adopted by the Scots was similar to that used successfully in the examination of the physical world; they applied it to social phenomena, to the study of man in society. The translation of the same methodology to a totally different range of phenomena was not straightforward and automatic because of the uncertainties inherent in the empirical observation of man in society, but that interest was extended to a whole range of intellectual disciplines, with the result that the bias of Scottish intellectual endeavour was towards the evolution of the social sciences and towards applied science. The latter was the key to technical leadership in industry, and was evident in the personal interest in the application of their abstract ideas by many Scottish scientists of the eighteenth century. William Cullen set the tone when he claimed that his second course of lectures at Glasgow in 1748 would be 'Chemical lectures and experiments directed chiefly to the Arts and Manufactures'. The chemists provided a long list of such interests. William Cullen tried to find an indigenous source of alkali for bleaching; Francis Home pointed out the possibilities of using vitriol, or sulphuric acid; John Roebuck pioneered the industrial manufacture of sulphuric acid. The Scottish contribution was not confined to bleaching. James Hutton and the 9th Earl of Dundonald demonstrated the possibilities of chemical extraction from coal.

The Scottish intellectual tradition's contribution to industry lies less in a series of specific inventions which had some industrial application and more in the emergence of a new methodology, a scientific method, which could perceive the advantages of new methods of production even when it was not always possible to provide convincing explanations of why that should be so. Whether Scottish thinkers succeeded in transferring to social phenomena the scientific method of the Newtonian approach to the physical world is a moot point, but they held firmly to the belief that it was possible, thereby producing explanations and understanding of the totality of any physical and social system. Rational explanation was called for, and on that basis appropriate courses of action could be determined. Such an approach, an acceptance and a rational evaluation of change, encouraged industrial improvement, but it was likely to encourage some industrial skills more than others. Though the methodological approach may properly be described as scientific, it was not one which led by itself to the emergence of skill in those industries which required a high level of abstract scientific knowledge. Scotland developed its chemical industry, and was able to exploit its scientific knowledge because of the proximity of the growing textile industries, but even more impressive than the more abstract scientific lead, as in chemicals, was the less abstract, more obviously applied industrial tradition, which was most evident in the growth of an engineering, or — to take an example from an entirely different field — a medical tradition. The beneficial effects of this tradition were evident in the eighteenth century, in the earlier phase of modern industrialisation. With the notable exception of the chemical industry, the mechanical arts made the main contribution to industrial change in Scotland. That was the field in which the Scots were skilled, and it was in that field that they continued to make their main contributions to industrial growth. The bias of the educational structure complemented the stability of society.

The people and their way of life

Though some of the intellectual changes were accorded international recognition, and their influence appeared in unexpected ways and places, they had only an indirect and often marginal effect on many Scots. The anonymous majority continued to lead their lives as their ancestors had done, and some of the changes which affected them can be identified only by an examination of their aggregates.

It is notoriously difficult to explain population trends before the modern system of vital statistics appeared. In England attempts to do so have been made from the information which may be culled from parish registers and bills of mortality. In Scotland it is difficult to do likewise. The compilation of the parochial registers of Scotland, now far from being all extant, was adversely affected by a stamp duty imposed from 1783 to 1794. Even earlier there were difficulties. The register of baptisms usually omitted those baptised privately at home, and the increasingly important group of seceders; the register of marriages was really one of the proclamation of banns, which could lead to duplication through recording in the parishes of both bride and bridegroom; lastly, the register of burials sometimes missed those buried outside their usual parish of residence and, most important of all, only those using the parish mortcloth, or pall, were included. Even in places where more detailed records were kept, such as Edinburgh or Glasgow, the information was similarly defective.

The first reasonably accurate estimate of the population of Scotland in the eighteenth century came from a census carried out by Alexander Webster, Minister of the Tolbooth, Edinburgh. Webster's figures compiled very shortly after 1755 drew on his wide experience and contacts in his work from 1743 in establishing a fund for ministers' widows. He reached a total of 1,265,380 persons. Webster also detailed the distribution of the population and its religious affiliation. His simple ecclesiastical census, distinguishing protestant from papist, showed a distribution of denominational affiliation since radically altered by Irish immigration. In contrast to the later position, Lanarkshire had only two Roman Catholics; Ayrshire and Wigtownshire had none. The distribution of the population among different counties also differed from later experience, as it was permanently altered shortly afterwards. In 1755 the population of Lanarkshire was exceeded by those of Aberdeenshire, Midlothian and Perthshire and almost equalled by that of Fife.

The disintegration of the old social structure influenced the movement of population from the countryside even before the massive changes caused by industrialisation. The sequence was conspicuous in the Highlands, where a conflict between two sets of ideas and customs appeared. On the one hand were those derived from the earlier society of the clan, when strategy rather than economy dominated Highland life. Hence came the recognition of the binding obligations of kinship, and the attachment of the Gael to the land. On the other hand were the new, primarily economic motives, acceptable in an industrial society but not in one ruled by custom. The new standards began to be applied in certain areas, notably on Campbell lands, even before the rebellion of 1745. Afterwards in all districts the landowners who remained in possession of their estates became more concerned with economy than with strategy. The ideological clash alone was sufficient to rend Highland society. Consequently, some of those who left the Highlands in the mid-eighteenth century, though departing unwillingly, sailed overseas, not because of economic failure, but in an attempt to maintain lost social prestige. In this category fell the tacksmen, generally kinsmen of the chief, who were an essential part of the old strategic system, and who were supported by the difference between the largely nominal rents they paid for the tracts of land they held on lease (tack) from the chief and the rents at which they let that land to sub-tenants. The tacksman's function had no part in the new society.

Since the initiation of such emigration came from changes in the social order, its explanation was frequently assumed to lie in the landlords' demands for higher rents, as they tried to raise their standard of living to conform with new conceptions of their status. Though the demand for higher rents was a common complaint of those who emigrated, the landlords were not only forwarding their own ends selfishly at the expense of the welfare of their tenants. Retaining everyone's younger sons on the land implied wretched tenantry. By about mid-century few landlords, or tenants, were willing to accept that implication any longer. Emigration was a means of avoiding it. By forcing him to emigrate a landlord was, therefore, frequently only forcing a tenant to act as he would have had to do eventually. Though in the long run there was probably no other alternative, and landlords, like tenants, were the victims of economic forces over which they had little control, they did not accept the position easily. The motives behind the landlords' attitudes towards tenants were various: feelings of kinship, humanitarian concern, a residual belief that greatness, personal or national, was ensured by retaining large numbers on the land — these were mixed with new economic motives. Modification of plans for improvement were often accepted because of a lingering acceptance of the old social structure by landlords, especially when the dispersal of tenants was at stake. Some landlords were as reluctant as their tenants to see that order disappear. Under such circumstances movement could not be extensive, and became so only later in the eighteenth, or, in some cases, only in the nineteenth century.

Though there are no adequate statistics, emigration seemed to increase from the 1770s and was then the consequence of more specifically economic influences. Movement from the Lowlands grew, especially when, following an example set at Wigtown in 1773, a number of associations were formed to provide assistance. Pamphlets describing the attractions of St John's Island (where leases were offered at rents rising during seven years from 2d. to 2s. an acre 'and never after to be raised') caused alarm among the landed proprietors of Ayrshire, who feared the information would encourage their tenantry to follow those who had already gone from Ulster and Argyll. To many landlords the restriction placed on emigration in 1775. — mainly in an effort to prevent accessions to the ranks of the rebels in America — was welcome. The movement from the Lowlands was encouraged by the adverse economic conditions of the early 1770s, and even more so by those of 1782 and 1783. In the Highlands at the same time economic forces reinforced the existing social tensions making for emigration, but their influence was more potent in later years, especially in the nineteenth century. One economic factor relevant in the Highlands before 1800 was the increasing openings offered in the Lowlands which led to movement within Scotland. Seasonal demand for agricultural labour and for special grades of industrial labour, as in the bleachfields of the Vale of Leven, was of long standing; to that seasonal demand a permanent demand was added as the growth of modern Scottish industry accelerated from the 1780s. Such economic opportunities in the Lowlands led to a greater exodus from the south and east of the Highland area, though one less dramatic than the emigrant ships which sailed from remote parts with those who could no longer be assimilated into Highland society. The emigration of the 1770s and 1780s from both Highlands and Lowlands is remarkable not by comparison with what was to follow, but only by comparison with what had gone before. The incentive, or compulsion, to move to countries overseas or to the towns of Scotland was to become yet greater. The balance of Scotland's population was not radically altered before the 1780s. Scotland was still a rural society, but one in which transformation was imminent.

In this predominantly rural society the towns were small. The parishes of Edinburgh, Canongate and St Cuthbert's, then Scotland's biggest conurbation, had only 47,570 inhabitants. By the early eighteenth century their housing had earned the reputation of being Europe's worst. The largest part of the population lived in high tenement stone buildings, as much as ten storeys high at the front and fourteen storeys at the rear. By each floor being let to a different family, Scotland followed a European tradition. Social distinctions were determined not by the part of a town in which one lived but by the layer of the tenement rented. In Edinburgh it was socially desirable to have a flat in the middle, about the fifth floor, while the higher and lower flats were let to those less elevated socially. Even with the end of the defensive reasons which had dictated its adoption, the old method of living continued until its attractions were outweighed by the appearance of a desire for more healthy living in the later eighteenth century. The classic instance of change was in Edinburgh. Geographical considerations, as well as the need for defence, forced building upwards within the old city walls. The Castle, Holyrood, the Nor' Loch and the Burgh Loch encircled the city except for a small piece of land to the south. In the long run the physical limitations proved beneficial. They forced the construction of the New Town, where the foundation-stone of the first house was laid in October 1767. James Craig's plan for the New Town of Edinburgh aimed at preventing some of the old difficulties and defects. An Act of 1771 limited the height of houses on the main streets to three storeys, inclusive of basement, and to two storeys in intermediate streets. The completion of Charlotte Square to Robert Adam's designs in 1800 marked the conclusion of this early essay in town planning, though one arrested and restricted by the difficulty of acquiring land from the Corporation, which was apprehensive of the falls in value in the old town. The overall effect of such building was slight. The magnificence and satisfactory construction of the New Town of Edinburgh were comparable with the contemporary seats of some of the nobility — Hopetoun, Mellerstain, Culzean — often built to the designs of the Adam family. The new edifices provided accommodation for only a fraction of the Scottish people. Until well beyond this period, until well into the age of industrialism, little was done to improve their lot.

Overcrowding and squalor were not confined to the towns. In the burghs considerations of defence, of geography, and of polity, sometimes forced building to take place within restricted limits; in the countryside, where it was physically possible to spread houses over wider areas, it was frequently financially impossible to do so. Construction was often solid, but was determined, as in any poor country, by the materials available locally. Bricks were uncommon and in the Highlands were unknown. In the country the usual cottage was built of undressed stones and divots; sometimes of mud walls; sometimes, especially in the Highlands, of turf only, with walls about five or six feet high. The roof was kept in position by branches of trees over which straw and turf were laid to try to keep the house watertight, a method which frequently meant only a reduction to drops of sooty water in wet weather and of worms in dry weather. Chimneys were uncommon and the smoke escaped, when it did, through a hole in the roof. A desire for heat, as potent a factor as poverty in deter-mining the construction of Scottish houses, militated against windows. Upper storeys were rare, so the family had only a damp soil floor on which to sleep. A few possessed a recess above the rafters, to which access was obtained by a ladder, and which provided the normal sleeping-place for the male members of the family. Families and cattle lived together, though some rural houses had a triple division, the byre being separated from the kitchen by a low partition of wattle and the kitchen from the spence, or parlour, generally by the box-beds, two of which were placed lengthwise from the walls. The outside door was often common to both man and beast, and the entrance and mud floor inside were so churned up that the laying of fresh turf was an unavailing task. Outside was the midden, a chief source of disease.

Higher up the social scale improvements in degree rather than in kind can be noted. In the laird's house conditions were cramped. The distinction between living-room and bedroom was neither exact nor rigid, understandably in the cramped quarters of the old town of Edinburgh, and in those parts of the Highlands where a large retinue of followers was still thought a mark of social distinction. The great hall of some West Highland castles became the sleeping-chamber of the gentlemen dependants of the family at night. Furniture was neither extensive nor beautiful. The previous century witnessed some notable improvements in its manufacture, but it was only later in the eighteenth century that the increasing wealth of the country led to the purchase of greater quantities of mahogany furniture and to the opening of shops in Edinburgh by London manufacturers. The record of the Countess Marischal's furniture in 1722 is a depressing catalogue of broken pieces. In all the household plenishings — in high and low estate — only linen was in ample supply.

The bad construction of Scottish housing was complemented by lack of sanitation. John Wesley could write feelingly in 1761: 'How long shall the capital city of Scotland, yea, and the chief street of it, stink worse than a common sewer? Will no lover of his country, or of decency and common sense, find a remedy for this?'[2] In Glasgow, then commended by many for its charm and beauty, a statute of 1696 failed to stop the throwing of filth out of windows by day or by night. As with improvements in housing, most of those in sanitation were also delayed until the later eighteenth century. The magistrates made some efforts to improve Edinburgh's unenviable reputation towards the end of the seventeenth century, but all types of penalties failed to secure adherence to the provisions. A major change in the public's attitude came only in the middle of the eighteenth century; in 1771 an Act was obtained for the cleansing of the southern suburbs and was extended later to the whole city. Probably no single factor was more important for better sanitation than an improvement in the water supply. The quantity was generally adequate at the public wells or conduits in the main streets, except in a town such as Edinburgh, with an increasing and concentrated population, or in a few places — Auchterarder was one — where the water supply frequently dried up in summer. Quality was much less satisfactory. Water had to be carried to most houses, a formidable task in tall tenements, as in Edinburgh, where water was brought to houses by full-time, but inefficient, caddies. Once again, improvements began in the second half of the century, when an increasing number of towns laid down metal water-pipes. Thereafter it was easier to have water led into houses, but the practice remained uncommon until well into the nineteenth century.

Under such conditions it is not surprising that Webster's calculations for the actuarial basis of annuity schemes showed the shortness of life and the extent of infant mortality. Less than 75 per cent of those born survived their first year; 50 per cent survived only to their tenth year; only 25 per cent survived beyond their forty-eighth year. Webster's conclusion on the high death rate of early years is confirmed by the mortality bills of a few Scottish towns. In the parish of Kettle in Fife there were 625 deaths in a period of over 20 years. Of these, 140 were of children under six. In Tranent, in East Lothian, during a period of 30 years, 586 deaths out of a total of 1,620 were of children under six. In Torthorwald, in Dumfriesshire, conditions were better, with an expectation of life at birth of 49.64 years and at age five of 54.69 years. In Kettle the expectation of life in infancy was 40.6 years.

The level of child mortality was the key to many social problems, especially in the large towns. In 1791, for instance, of 1,508 deaths recorded in the City Parish of Glasgow, 46 per cent were of children under two and 63 per cent of all deaths were of children under ten. Any large-scale improvement came only after the middle of the nineteenth century. In 1861, 54 per cent of all deaths in Glasgow were still of children under ten. If child mortality was a major factor ensuring the maintenance of a high death rate in the eighteenth century, two chief explanations of its fluctuations may be offered. The first, the adequacy of nutrition, became more favourable as agricultural improvements, in some cases from early in the eighteenth century and more generally from mid-century, removed the spectre of famine from Scotland for the first time. The lean years of the end of the previous century were still recalled with perhaps exaggerated horror in agricultural reports of the later eighteenth century, but they never recurred. There were still occasional years of scarcity, or periods of intense local shortage, especially in such areas as the Highlands, where the margin of subsistence was least, and where poor communications made the relief of local shortages less easy. There were years of want, as in 1740, 1756, 1762, 1772, 1782-3, 1793, 1799, when scarcity increased the death rate in some areas at least in what was still predominantly an agricultural society. Only by the end of the eighteenth century was it becoming increasingly evident that dearth, and its consequences, came to many Scots less through the direct effect of failure of food supplies than through a failure of industrial employment.

Epidemics were the second factor leading to variations in the death rate. They were not so terrifying as they became in the congested conditions of the towns. In the eighteenth century, if a Scotsman survived his childhood, he had a reasonable chance of living to a good age. Sir John Sinclair's adulation of the healthiness of the Scot rested on this assumption. When dealing with the medical history of adults, he could assert more truthfully that, 'excepting cold and rheumatism, occasioned by inattention, and often by poverty, there is no disease that can be called peculiar to Scotland; neither are the distempers, by which we are sometimes visited, more frequent, or more fatal and violent, than in other countries, which are esteemed highly salubrious'.[3] Rheumatism, which became increasingly prevalent throughout the eighteenth century, greatly decreased industrial and agricultural efficiency, and was the cause of much discomfort, but was not a major cause of death. That was the role of the 'distempers', which, as Sinclair stated, did not come to Scotland often, but, when they did come, came with disastrous effects.

Some of these more violent diseases did not take their tolls in the eighteenth century. The plague, for instance, had not reappeared in Scotland since the 1640s, but the greatest specifically identifiable scourge of the eighteenth century was smallpox which was the cause of about one-sixth of the deaths in bills of mortality. Sinclair was justified in putting it at the head of the diseases with which the country was then affected. Highland parishes suffered only intermittently, though devastatingly, but the disease was endemic in Edinburgh and also in Glasgow by the end of the century. Its effects fell most heavily on children aged between six months and two years, who accounted for 40 to 55 per cent of the deaths in some outbreaks. Around mid-century about ten per cent of all deaths in Edinburgh, and at the end of the century almost 19 per cent of all deaths in Glasgow, and more than half of those of children under five, were due to smallpox. The disease was first attacked with some success by inoculation, advocated in the 1720s, but used extensively only towards the middle of the century. In 1754 the College of Physicians of Edinburgh declared inoculation to be 'highly salubrious to the human race', but it was not accepted without severe criticism. Its early use in Aberdeenshire was discontinued because of fatalities; it was thought to tamper with divine laws; many parents objected to the temporary upset it caused to their children; some objected to the cost. The last objection led to the cost of inoculation sometimes being borne by the heritors or by the kirk session. Inoculation had one possible defect, though one not so readily recognised by those contemporaries who attributed much saving of life to the practice, and still subject to differences of opinion. Because those inoculated became carriers, smallpox, instead of occurring at long and relatively infrequent intervals, appeared frequently, especially, of course, among children. Its defeat had to await vaccination, which appeared only in the last few years of the eighteenth century.

Whatever was done to mitigate the ravages of smallpox, other diseases remained. Reports of 'fever' throughout the eighteenth century are frequent, but various types were not distinguished, in part because clinical diagnosis is not easy. Two diseases which showed a variation in incidence were ague or malaria, and tuberculosis. The ague was previously so common, especially in spring and summer, that it sometimes interfered with agricultural operations. By the end of the eighteenth century it had become much less frequent, not only because of enclosure and drainage of land, which was the explanation of contemporaries, but because the indigenous mosquito was attracted from its breeding ground in human habitations to cattle houses, which it prefers, by the increased survival of cattle in the winter-time. On the other hand an unfavourable change during the eighteenth century was the increasing incidence of consumption, though the term was used freely in the eighteenth century to cover much besides tuberculosis. The Western Isles, later to suffer severely from the scourge, were relatively immune throughout most of the eighteenth century. There were sufficient explanations for the independent increase in consumption, especially the effects of Scottish housing, without Sinclair's unhelpful suggestion that 'where the ague has ceased to exist, consumptions are apt to become prevalent in their room'.[4]

NOTES

1. See below, p. 38.
2. J. Wesley, *Journal* (Everyman Edition), vol. 3, p. 54.
3. Sir John Sinclair, *Analysis of the Statistical Account of Scotland* (Edinburgh, 1831), p. 120.
4. Sinclair, *Analysis of the Statistical Account*, p. 138.

CHAPTER II

Agriculture

The old system and its methods

In the eighteenth century many of the problems of Scottish farmers came from the physical influences of a harsh climate and a poor soil. Agricultural operations were frequently late and protracted, especially on the west coast, where rain fell on about two-thirds of the days of the year. Inadequately drained, sour soils prevented much early sowing; harvests were late, frequently lasting until November. Sometimes crops, rarely adequate even in the best of weather, were lost through rain, and even snow. The soil did not offset the adverse influence of climate. With few exceptions the hill land was uncultivated. The most barren area, then as now, was in the north and west, where the vagaries of climate were most fickle. Further south and east the adverse influence of the physical forces became only less pressing. Wresting a living from such an environment was difficult.

That it was as necessary as ever to do so was underlined in the middle of the eighteenth century when Scotland became a net importer of grain. In due course the rising population was supported by the exchange of industrial products for even greater imports of foodstuffs, but the earliest moves towards the industrial society which made such trade possible needed increased agricultural production. If more had to be imported because of bad harvests in the short run or because of the needs of the rising population in the long run, the possibility of consequential deficits on the balance of trade threatened the liquidity of the financial network and its ability to provide credit for the expanding industrial economy. Good harvests and the permanent increase of agricultural production were essential to support the rising population directly and also to do so indirectly by ensuring no interruptions to the industrial growth which became the means of providing for the expansion of imports on which the improvement of living standards in the nineteenth century was based.

The history of Scottish agriculture deals largely with attempts to achieve improvements by mitigating physical adversities. Drainage prevented the land from becoming sour; shelter belts of trees, and afforestation generally, mitigated the severity of winds; a greater variety of crops helped to stagger agricultural operations, increasing the probability of obtaining the benefit of good weather when most required; mechanisation speeded operations. The way for these improvements was paved through changes in land tenure, and through changes, sometimes but not always consequential, in methods of cultivation.

It is possible to suggest a model of land tenure which could be found in much of Scotland in the earlier eighteenth century.[1] It varied throughout the country and was constantly undergoing change, adaptation, and improvement before being finally swept away. A characteristic was that both tenanted and proprietary land were held in different rigs or strips, the system known as runrig. A farm was frequently leased to a number of tenants, who comprised the inhabitants of the very small rural villages, or ferme-touns, of the period. In some cases a number — perhaps members of the same family — held the land in a joint-tenancy, in which they leased and worked a farm together; in others they formed a multiple tenancy, when the farm was worked together but in which each paid a separate rent for a specific holding. Multiple tenancies have often been considered the usual, if not the only, form of tenure in Scotland before the agricultural improvements of the eighteenth century, but more recent work has drawn attention to the variety, and to the existence of substantial numbers of single tenants on some estates. In runrig the holdings of tenants were distributed and intermingled to ensure equality in their shares. They may have been re-allocated periodically with the same objective — mostly perhaps in the granting of new leases — though evidence is lacking to show that reallocation was common.

The system of tenure has to be distinguished from that of cultivation. Again with local variations, and with a constantly changing pattern over time, a general pattern may be suggested. In less fertile parts of the Lowlands and generally in the Highlands the ferme-toun had a greater supply of permanent pasture than in the more fertile parts of the Lowlands. The arable and meadow land were separated from hill pasture by the head-dyke, the remaining evidence of which indicates the limits to which cultivation was then driven in an effort to maintain the population. The basic characteristic of the cultivated land itself was its division into the infield and the outfield of the farm or township. The infield, the land adjacent to the farm steading, was under constant cultivation, and generally comprised about one-fifth of the total arable acreage. On it a rudimentary rotation was commonly followed. Each year one-third, which was given all the dung available, was sown with barley, or bere, and the rotation was completed by taking two unmanured crops of oats from it. Variations on the basic pattern were common. In more fertile areas, as in the Carse of Gowrie, or where the arable acreage was limited, the infield exceeded one-fifth of the land cultivated; more unusual rotations, often improvements on traditional practice, were found in more advanced agricultural districts, as in Ayrshire, where an occasional fallow year interrupted a rotation of oats, oats and barley; and, usually in less fertile regions, attempts were made to cultivate crops, no matter how poor, from the same plot of land for as many successive years as was possible without much, or any, manure.

Unlike the infield the larger outfield was not in continuous cultivation. Part was cropped, generally with oats, for a number of successive years, probably about four or five. When the return no longer justified the effort (and standards of judgement were low), the cultivation of a section was abandoned for a time and its place taken by another, which had regained some fertility through resting. Otherwise the outfield was given little attention. Local variations in its cultivation, mainly in manuring and in the number of successive crops, were less marked than in the infield. Even the best manuring practice of folding cattle on parts of the outfield for short periods, sometimes at night, sometimes during the middle of the day, was inadequate. The number of successive crops taken off the same part of the outfield varied according to the physical environment and to the degree of agricultural enlightenment: in the north-east sometimes five times as many were taken off a patch of the outfield as were taken from a similar piece of land in the south-west.

The implements used in cultivation were primitive and inefficient. The old Scots plough, a mouldboard plough, was about thirteen feet long and, apart from the share, coulter and bridle, which were of iron, was made entirely of wood. Because of its weight it was a useful implement for breaking up rough, and especially stony soil into a series of ridges and furrows, but it required considerable draught power. The common practice was to use a team of eight oxen, but again there were local variations. In Aberdeenshire as many as twelve oxen were used; in the Lowlands the team was frequently a combination of six oxen and two horses; in Ayrshire it was often formed entirely of horses. Such unwieldy power, linked to an unwieldy instrument, could be controlled only by a band of men, which the prevalence of joint or multiple tenancies provided. One man urged the animals forward; another, or sometimes a woman, removed stones; another ensured that the plough made a furrow of a correct depth; yet another followed behind to remedy the defects and deficiencies in the ploughing with a spade. Such effort ploughed perhaps half an acre in a day.

The plough left an indelible imprint in the ridges into which Scottish arable land was formed. Ridges were not unique to Scotland. Partly they were the result of ploughing from the centre to the outside; partly they were formed by design, because — of minor importance — in a system of intermixed strips an individual could then preserve his soil from spilling over to his neighbour's ridge, and — of major importance — because they provided a primitive form of drainage. The old Scots plough ensured that these ridges, sometimes five hundred yards or even more in length, were crooked. To guarantee straightness the head ridge would have had to be of enormous breadth to allow the huge plough team to turn, but a deflection at each end enabled the team to draw the plough out on a moderately broad head ridge. Whatever advantages the ridges possessed were outweighed by their disadvantages. It was difficult to apply modern methods of cultivation to land covered with ridges, which were 'almost universally broad, high, crooked and of unequal and irregular breadths, and frequently had strips of uncultivated land between them, named *baulks*, sometimes of considerable breadth, which were overgrown with brushwood and weeds, and filled with every kind of rubbish gathered from the cultivated land'.[2]

The use of the old Scots plough was wellnigh universal. Lighter ploughs were used mainly in the Highlands: the ristle, or restle, to break up ground prior to ploughing with the heavy plough; the better-known *cas chrom*, or foot plough, still used within the last century, to turn over patches of arable ground roughly. The implements used in subsequent agricultural occupations were equally primitive. Harrows, like most of the old Scots ploughs, were sometimes made of wood, especially in more backward areas, so that teeth were easily broken. Frequently they were tied to a horse's tail, and in some areas in the Highlands and Islands, even into the twentieth century, were man- or woman-handled. The sickle was used, again in some cases until the twentieth century, to reap the crops; the flail was a major means of threshing them.

'Under the system of management . . . even that part of the lands of Scotland which is capable of good cultivation, could produce but little in comparison of what it may be capable of producing.'[3] The writers on agricultural improvement at the end of the eighteenth century echoed Adam Smith's scandalised horror at the defects of the old system of Scottish agriculture. It had its merits, if judged by its ability to provide subsistence for as many as possible, but it was inefficient commercially. The range of crops was limited. Oats and barley were most commonly cultivated. The former was of two types: white or grey oats, which gradually gained ground in the Lowlands and in the better land in the Highlands, and inferior, small, grey or black oats, the cultivation of which persisted in some areas because its lightness withstood the ravages of wind and rain better than the heavier white oats. Bere, an inferior type of barley, was grown for the same reasons as the black oats. It thrived on land of poor quality, was less liable than barley to be affected adversely by wet weather, and it matured more quickly. The acreage sown with bere or barley was only about half that of oats. Other crops were of less importance. Rye was grown, sometimes as a mixture with oats, but not extensively, as it was considered an impoverishing crop, with only the compensating reputation of grinding more economically than oats. Wheat was cultivated in the best infield lands of the Lothians, the Merse, the Mearns, Ayrshire and elsewhere. Flax was grown generally only for domestic use. Though the potato was cultivated in Scottish gardens by the time of the Union, its major contribution came only later in the eighteenth and in the nineteenth centuries.

In the early eighteenth century an adequate supply of good pasture was as important as any crop. In many areas, especially where physical conditions of soil and climate were most adverse, as in the Highlands, agriculture depended more on the rearing of livestock than on arable cultivation. Beef cattle gave the greatest surplus for sale off the land; sheep ranked next, and in some areas, notably the southern uplands, they were the major agricultural product. Both suffered from undernourishment in winter, especially if there was much snow, and from disease. Sheep suffered most, because, as a means of combating maggots, the animals were smeared with a mixture of tar and butter which ensured that the wool was of a poor quality, as effectively as disease and inadequate feeding ensured the inferior quality and inadequacy of the mutton. In the long run the growth of arable and livestock production could not be separated. The maintenance of additional stock required improvements in arable cultivation. Some increase was always possible without improvement through the very old and international practice of transhumance, followed most extensively in the Highlands, by which a large part of the community moved with most of their animals to the shielings in the hills where there were plentiful supplies of summer grass. In the early eighteenth century the practice was essential for the growth of the cattle trade, especially in the Highlands, because winter keep was inadequate prior to the cultivation of artificial grasses to make hay. Until then the meadow land was often merely those parts which were so defective that they could not be used for arable cultivation. Swampy or stony ground produced little for grazing and less for hay, which was of the poorest quality. Survival was not easy in some areas even in summer unless the cattle were removed to more succulent hill pasture; in winter it was often impossible. Cattle existed, if at all, on straw, dry rushes or thistles, boiled chaff and similar non-nutritive foodstuffs. Estimates of mortality vary, partly because of regional differences, and in some areas it may have been as high as one in five; some of the animals which survived were in such a poor condition in the spring that they were hardly able to persist in the active search necessary to locate the scanty fodder available.

The improving movement

Though cultivation in Scotland was sometimes communal, the limits of an individual's ownership or tenancy were usually clear. An exception was on some of the grazing areas, especially the poorer hill land, where permanent pasture was owned by more than one proprietor, though the boundaries of each were not demarcated. An early legislative attempt to improve agriculture was an Act of 1647, which, with some exceptions, enabled a majority of proprietors to have the land divided to convert it from grazing to arable use. The Act was confined to Ayrshire, Lanarkshire and the Lothians and its effectiveness limited by the political unrest which accompanied its passing. Though revoked with others at the Restoration in 1661, it was one of several early but abortive attempts at agricultural improvement. By the late seventeenth century provision was still necessary to ensure the division of the commonties which existed, but more urgent was the need for legal provisions for the consolidation of strips held in runrig and for ensuring that enclosure fencing, hedging, or walling of land could be implemented without opposition from difficult proprietors.

Several major statutes at the end of the century provided for action. An Act of 1695 authorised the division of all commonties, except those belonging to the king or to royal burghs, by a process in the Court of Session even at the instigation of only one proprietor. Commonties, including mosses and peat bogs, were to be divided among proprietors in proportion to the valued rents of their existing holdings. A subsidiary provision recognised that owners of land adjacent to a commonty might have acquired rights to its use by custom. Though a legal process of rouming and souming could limit the number of animals which could be grazed (by reference to the land rents of the farms using the commonty and to the number of cattle which each could support with his own winter fodder), the right, if it had been exercised without dispute for forty years, was continued after division by the burden of it being placed on one proprietor who had his share increased accordingly. A second Act of 1695 authorised sheriffs to divide lands held in runrig, again even at the request of only one proprietor. As in the division of commonties, allocations had to be of land adjacent to the proprietor's dwelling-house. Though the effectiveness of the Act was limited by the exclusion from its provisions of the lands of incorporations, which included burghs, it was extended to cover intermixed holdings, even when they were not lying separately in rigs. Lastly, a series of Acts of 1661, 1669, and 1685 provided for the erection of fences along the boundaries of different holdings — for enclosure in the literal sense — by a process before the sheriff in which a proprietor could ensure that his neighbours paid half the cost of erecting fences, and that boundaries were straightened wherever necessary.

The legal provisions for division, consolidation and enclosure encouraged the introduction of new methods of agricultural production; the changes in implements, rotations and crops which were so notable in the eighteenth century. The old Scots plough was replaced chiefly by a light plough designed by a Berwickshire man, James Small, in the 1760s. Small's plough was the most notable innovation in farm implements in the eighteenth century, as it replaced the worst and most cumbersome of the old. Complementary to it were a variety of other improvements: iron teeth took the place of wooden ones in harrows generally; stone, and later cast-iron, rollers replaced mallets as a means of smoothing out rough patches on the ground; leather straps and iron chains replaced twisted hair or heather as harness; implements ceased to be attached to horses' tails. More radical in its effects, and comparable to the introduction of Small's plough, was the successful threshing machine of Andrew Meikle of 1786. The new implements were the means by which the ground was prepared in new ways — levelling, draining, manuring, liming — all preparatory to the introduction of new rotations. Throughout Scotland rotations varied, but the fourfold, turnips, barley, clover and wheat of Norfolk was usual, except that in Scotland oats generally replaced wheat. By the late eighteenth century grain alternated with grass and green crops on arable land throughout Scotland. Though oats remained the dominant crop, with the white oat increasingly displacing the grey oat except in the Highlands, the most characteristic crops of the new order were the turnip and the potato. Their contribution to Scottish agriculture differed. The turnip became the basis for the rearing of much fatstock, especially the higher-grade animals of the north-east and of other livestock-rearing areas. A poor season in 1782 encouraged its introduction, and also of many artificial grasses, in areas in the north which had resisted them longest. The potato, on the other hand, augmented human diet, especially in those regions where the margin of subsistence was low. It was suitable for areas of less generous natural endowments, because, as well as giving acceptable food, it could be grown easily. Though suited to drill cultivation, the potato, unlike the turnip, could also be grown by the 'lazy-bed' method, particularly appropriate in wet land. Its most important contribution was to the agriculture of the Highlands and, even more so, of the Islands, unsuited as they frequently were for the cultivation of almost anything else. The potato first reached the Islands at South Uist in 1743, and though initially planted in Lewis only in the mid-1750s, a decade later it was a staple item in the diet for over half the year.

Many of the improvements were adopted only later in the eighteenth century. Runrig was not brought to an end quickly, and, perhaps because its worst defects were mitigated by the permanent allocation of the strips, the system survived even in districts with improving lairds. As is evident in the *Old Statistical Account*, the system remained to be eliminated in many areas only during the Napoleonic Wars. Enclosure proceeded more slowly except where it was necessary for a change in agricultural production and was one of the later improvements to be carried out. It is important, therefore, not to stress the availability from the late seventeenth century of legal provision adequate to transform Scottish agriculture. Some of the Acts were less important in Scotland than they would have been in other countries. For example, the importance of the Act relating to the division of commonties was lessened by the rights of landowners and tenants being already clearly defined in Scotland, since the feuing movement established definitive, rather than customary, tenure in the sixteenth century,[4] and in the Highlands the retention of the military tenure of ward-holding until its abolition in 1747 prevented the evolution of a new structure. In the Lowlands and in parts of the Highlands, those on the land at the time of the Union were either tenants, with clearly defined rights and obligations, or owners, whose power, within the limits of any leases granted, was absolute. Difficulties arose only where a number of individual proprietors held strips in runrig, or where adjoining proprietors were unwilling to share the costs of enclosure. In both cases opposition could be overcome, in the first by the second Act of 1695, which gave power to sheriffs to divide land, and in the second by the Acts of 1661, 1669 and 1685, which required expenditure on enclosure to be shared.

Since the legal basis for many tenurial changes had existed even before the Union of 1707, such rural unrest as arose in the eighteenth century, though less than in England, cannot be traced to the appearance of new legal procedure. It was most noticeable in those areas where the type of agricultural production changed. A well-known example was in Galloway, where the rise in cattle prices after the Union encouraged the conversion of arable land to pasture. The proprietors' legal right to evict tenants to effect the change was not disputed, though in the 1720s the evicted tenants objected so vigorously to the landlord's moral right to do so, that they threw down the dykes built to retain the cattle. Better-known, though later, examples come from the Highlands, where the conversion of arable land to sheep-walks and, later still, to deer-forests, took place on the same legal basis, without any legal redress, but with the same social upheaval. When social unrest appeared in the Scottish countryside, it indicated change, usually drastic change, in the type of agricultural production, though the influence of this factor was limited in many parts of Scotland, apart from the Highlands and southern uplands, by arable cultivation remaining common and providing opportunities for rural employment.

Since the landlords already enjoyed a favourable position in law, the speed of change was increased when they were subjected in the later eighteenth century to the new influences which encouraged improvement. They accepted the new belief that man's relation to his environment was not chiefly theological but secular, that the individual, far from being unable to influence the environment, could understand and control it. The attempt to cast all knowledge into systematic form was as applicable to agriculture as to any sphere of human endeavour.

If the acceptance of an intellectual analysis of the physical and social world which no longer regarded the hazards of agricultural operations as divinely ordained was a prerequisite to the successful onslaught on the hazards of agricultural change, then it becomes possible to hold that the motivation for change was not economic necessity but patriotism, fashion, social control, factors which operated in a social environment which was uniquely Scottish, and which render Scottish experience less comparable with events elsewhere. It is doubtful if Scottish experience was so unique. At the deepest level economic factors were probably still the most important agents in change. That would be so if the fundamental motivation lay in the demand for higher rents, and there is evidence that it was so. The movement of the greater magnates to London increased their economic needs, and alone ensured that they became active promoters of agrarian change. Lavish living and political objectives required additional resources or led to increased debt. The need for increased rent of an absentee landlord may then have been the most powerful force making for agrarian change.

The burst of legislation at the end of the seventeenth century restricted their freedom in one way. A statute of 1685, which provided for estates to be entailed, placed additional impediments in the way of its improvements. An entailed estate could not be alienated from specified heirs; debt affecting the estate could not be contracted; the succession could not be altered. Contravention of the prohibitions was invalid and an heir who broke any forfeited his right to the estate. Over 500 deeds were recorded in the Register of Entails by the later 1760s. The number increased sharply thereafter. Adam Smith suggested that one-fifth, perhaps even more than one-third, of the land of Scotland was entailed in 1776. Sir John Sinclair confirmed about one-third in 1811. Smith, Kames and others were critical of the system, but the landlords' interest in perpetuating their successions inhibited radical change. A relatively minor alteration, but with a significant influence on agricultural improvement, came with a statute of 1770, which permitted actions to facilitate enclosure, such as the exchange of small parcels of land, and the granting of longer leases, contingent on the tenant agreeing to effect certain enclosures, and including an important provision to allow proprietors of entailed estates to charge to heirs three-quarters of the money spent on enclosure and other agricultural improvements.

The initiative for the improvement of Scottish agriculture in the eighteenth century came from relatively few landowners at all levels. The background of John Cockburn of Ormiston in East Lothian, who was perhaps the best-known of all, shows the formative influences common to many. The eldest son of a Lord Justice-Clerk, he represented the new element then being infused into the landed interest, and, as Member of Parliament for Haddington, had sufficient opportunity to observe the new practices of English agriculture. His improvements, more notable for scale than for their uniqueness, took the common form of long leases, enclosure, the planting of trees, the growing of new crops, such as barley (for which he considered East Lothian ideally suited), turnips (though he was probably not the first to introduce them to Scotland), artificial grasses, clover, potatoes, and so on. Cockburn's efforts were notable for extending from the introduction of several commendable but isolated improvements to an attempt to achieve a complete and radical reorganisation of his estate. This was the hallmark of the leading improver. He rebuilt the village of Ormiston and, combining industrial with agricultural improvement, tried to encourage the linen industry by importing skilled labour from Ireland and forming a bleachfield. Other improvers were of the same stamp. Sir Archibald Grant of Monymusk in Aberdeenshire was the son of a Senator of the College of Justice, Lord Cullen, who had purchased the estate in 1713, and so regretted the purchase that three years later he handed its management to his son, then aged twenty. When the son died in 1778, the estate had been transformed. Lord Kames was probably the most important improver among several in the College of Justice itself. His contribution was more interesting than many, because he carried out improvements in different environments; first in Berwickshire, where he probably introduced turnips in drills for feeding cattle and the cultivation of potatoes with the plough; second in Perthshire, at Blair Drummond, which he inherited through his wife, and where, though then aged seventy, he added to the usual improvements a major attempt to clear the Moss of Kincardine, a venture which could have been undertaken only by someone not requiring, or not demanding, an immediate capital return. In addition, Kames spread his knowledge by means of his writings in a way few other improvers did. Such improvers among the minor landed gentry, and especially among those of the first or second generation of those who had entered their ranks from the professions or merchanting, were found throughout Scotland except in the extreme north and west. In Kirkcudbrightshire was William Craik of Arbigland; also in the south-west at Arkland in Dumfriesshire worked Robert Maxwell; on the east coast were Robert Barclay of Urie in Kincardineshire, and Lord Gardenstone, another Senator of the College of Justice, at Laurencekirk. Beside the contributions of the lesser gentry must be set those of the greater lairds, whose influence also stretched throughout Scotland; from the estates of the Earl of Stair in the south-west, as well as in the Lothians, to those of the Earl of Marchmont and the Earl of Haddington in the south-east, and to those of the

Earl of Findlater, improved greatly by the sixth earl while still heir as Lord Deskford, in the north-east.

Two major impediments stood in the way of even the most dedicated improver: the cost of improvement and the continuing conservatism of many, especially among the tenants. Not all improvements were expensive; even more, not all had to be implemented on a large scale, but frequently the more expensive were also socially the more disruptive, and so were doubly unattractive, even when they held the greatest promise of increased productivity. The financial difficulties of extensive improvement are obvious in the emphasis in the *Agricultural Reports* of the 1790s on the continued need for action over enclosure, the abolition of runrig, and drainage. Since enclosure and drainage were costly operations, the responsibility for action fell heavily on the proprietors. The adequacy and generosity of their help may be questioned, and when capital was provided, some at least thought the rate of interest charged was excessive. The landlords were not without excuse. Their desire for higher rents indicated that their capital resources were often strained, and so they borrowed. The banks helped, particularly from the 1760s when landed estate was an acceptable form of security, but the help was often intermittent, varied and sometimes quite small.

Conservatism and resistance to new methods and ideas, especially among the tenants, were less easily overcome than similar resistance to new industrial methods. The virtual absence of any industrial base implied the existence of fewer prejudices to be broken than in agriculture, in which the bulk of the population worked according to customary routine and to practice not easily altered. The major limitation on radical and general agricultural improvement in the eighteenth century was that, even within the old system, considerable improvements were effected, such as intaking from the waste, so that dearth became much less common than it had been. The compulsion of necessity was lessened. In such circumstances many saw no need to follow the improvers in the more radical and more expensive work of enclosure, road-building and large-scale drainage. It was easy and correct to regard the new practices as expensive and not always profitable hobbies to be followed by those with outside incomes, but not to be emulated by other, not at least until the rise in prices in the later eighteenth century made them less risky ventures. Many writers were highly critical of the tenantry in the eighteenth century. One quotation of 1732 stands for all: 'Husbandry, till of late, was intirely managed in Scotland by the Vulgar, who, like Moles, blindly ran on in the Tract their Fathers had made before them'.[5] On their own estates proprietors found difficulty in obtaining fullest co-operation and emulation because of the opposition of many tenants to any alteration to customary practice. Even though the Duke of Argyll embodied all the favourable forces making for change, his estates provided an example of the problem. In 1737 Duncan Forbes visited the old Duart lands in Mull, Morvern, Coll and Tiree to eliminate the tacksmen and lease lands directly to the subtenants. The opposition was virtually complete. Eventually Forbes leased the lands directly, but victory was hollow. The increase in rents proved illusory as arrears accumulated. Consideration was given to the possibility of restoring the tacksmen, and sub-letting was permitted. Perhaps most interesting of all, while initially no special preference was given to Campbells, the '45 led to the modification of policies to ensure political loyalty. If Argyll modified his plans, even reviving sub-letting to avoid emigration, it is not surprising that others did likewise. When Grant changed land use, he encountered opposition similar to that experienced by the Galloway proprietors. At Monymusk objections that afforestation reduced the area available for grazing were so strong that tenants destroyed trees and fences. Though opposition could be combated in some cases by such compulsion as the insertion of restrictive clauses in new leases, or, by following the ways of Sir Alexander Grant, and using the powers of the Baron Court, a form of persuasion was necessary for the full benefits of the improvements to be dispersed throughout Scotland.

Three methods of persuasion were common. The first was to introduce Englishmen to teach new and better ways to the Scots, sometimes by using English materials. Grant of Monymusk had an English manager and used English horses and ploughs. Cockburn introduced English farmers to Ormiston and sent his tenants' sons south to learn English ways. Hutton, the geologist, also an important improver in Berwickshire, studied agriculture in Norfolk for a time and returned home with a Norfolk ploughman and English implements. The Earl of Findlater introduced an English manager. From such centres of enlightenment a cumulative influence spread in turn throughout Scotland. Sir James Hall of Dunglass sent three of his 'most knowing tenants to Ormiston where they have learned more of labouring and improving their grounds in two days than they have done in all their life'.[6]

The second method of persuasion was by placing in influential positions as factors and agents those converted to new ways and able to exploit them. From the middle of the eighteenth century their influence spread, supplementing the work of the lairds and often assuming an independent momentum. Some tenants fulfilled a similar role. A major effect of the changes in tenure was to give rise in many parts to a new type of full-time professional farmer, no longer completely absorbed in the everyday work of his employees, though engaged full-time in agriculture and wholly dependent on it for his livelihood. Many of the more successful lairds realised the importance of allowing such tenants to devise their own form of improvements. The possibilities of such co-operation were illustrated most strikingly by the progressive Wight family, tenants of Cockburn of Ormiston. Robert, who tenanted Muirhouse, first co-operated with Cockburn, but the partnership was strengthened greatly by his son Alexander, who maintained a correspondence with Cockburn when the latter was in London and, with Charles Bell, the gardener at Ormiston, who carried out many of the laird's ideas. Alexander's son, Andrew, later made a major contribution to the improvement of Scottish agriculture, and to our knowledge of it, when between 1778 and 1784, on Lord Kames' suggestion, he visited every county on the Scottish mainland, except Argyll, and wrote reports on improvements in their agriculture. Though such a family of tenants did make a major contribution to the improvement of Scottish agriculture, the social and legal structure of the period, with the initiative in the hands of the landed proprietors, and with the need for adequate financial resources to back improvements, meant that tenant farmers could achieve little on their own. Equally, since co-operation between laird and tenant was essential, the influence of tenants of the stamp of the Wights was as important as the influence of lairds of the stamp of Cockburn. In each area of successful improvement examples of co-operation similar to that of Cockburn and Wight can be cited. Successful improving lairds realised the need for such tenants by fixing long leases, often with the same, satisfactory family, and by taking smaller monetary rents in order to get an acceptable tenant. The Earl of Findlater leased one farm to a father and son for nearly a century, while Barclay of Urie once declared that he never acted more selfishly than when he refused a rent of £71 and chose instead to take one of £60 from someone he considered would be a good tenant, at the same time offering that tenant an interest-free loan of £200.

The third method of ensuring co-operation was by disseminating agricultural information at all levels, geographically and socially. The methods were various, but notable were the use of literature, local discussion groups, and national societies. Agricultural literature in the eighteenth century was of all kinds and came from all sources. Sometimes the writers were simply observant men with no practical experience of agriculture, sometimes they were improvers, and sometimes the inevitable armchair critics. The form of the literature differs before and after about 1770. Before then most writers were encouraging Scots to follow the ways of others. After about 1770 there were sufficient examples of improved practice in Scotland to show the way enlightened men should travel. In Scotland fifty years or so after the Union the new agriculture was no longer simply a theory but an established practice in some places among some people. When the literature could be compared with successful practice, its effect among tenants was greater. The agricultural discussion clubs had an equally varied influence. Many were never formally organised, many never kept records, fewer still of these records have survived. One of which the records do survive, the Farming Club at Gordon's Mill, was limited to fifteen members, and, since six of these were members of the University of Aberdeen, its influence was restricted. The Club met fortnightly outside Aberdeen, the members recording and discussing agricultural improvements, especially those in the neighbourhood. The great advantage of such a club was that it could sift the experience of other areas to find what was most applicable in a particular locality. In this way the local groups made the influence of the national bodies more effective. The first of the agricultural societies was a national one, The Honourable the Society of Improvers, founded in Edinburgh in July 1723. It lasted only until 1745 but had a major influence in propagating the new methods, especially since its three hundred members contained most of the peerage, the landed gentry and the leading professional men. An exceptionally active secretary, Robert Maxwell of Arkland, gave the necessary stimulus to realise its potential as an improving agent. The Society discussed all the innovations of the time and ensured their adoption by publication and encouragement. Local societies were founded to carry on its work. The local societies became more numerous in the second half of the century. The demise of the Society of Improvers did not end its work. In 1755 another society, formed from the Select Society founded a year earlier by Allan Ramsay, the painter, carried it on. Known as the Edinburgh Society, the new body encouraged the arts, sciences and manufactures in Scotland, and so included agriculture. It came to an end in 1764. For twenty years, until 1784, no similar body took its place, but in that year the Highland Society was formed. Its apparently more restricted concern is significant. By then improvements in agriculture had been introduced in many parts of the Lowlands, and a non-agricultural sector was rapidly growing in its economy. Conditions were different in the Highlands. Just as the Lowlands had started to emulate England successfully in the three-quarters of a century after the Union, so it was felt the Highlands should be encouraged to emulate the Lowlands.

The contribution of a few proprietors to the improving movement has been discussed and praised by many writers in studies of individual initiative. Examination of the impediments to agricultural change raises some doubt as to its extent. The two major impediments of social opposition from the tenantry and the need for capital expenditure limited improvement to areas where landowners had complete control and where relatively little capital expenditure was required: in effect to the policies and home farm, and no further. Stress on the impediments provides a possible explanation of why the powerful motivation of the Scottish improvers failed to achieve widespread agrarian change quickly. But the improvers may not have been so well endowed with the qualities requisite for agrarian change as is usually assumed. In particular the criticism of the recalcitrant tenantry by the landowners, and by later writers, may need qualification. The desire for higher rents, and some of the reasons behind it, show that the landowners themselves were not wholly enlightened.

Two critical appraisals of landlords' contributions are in the abstract reasoning of Adam Smith and in the more practical views of farmers and factors, such as of George Robertson. Smith considered that landowners, especially the larger among them, had the potential for improvement. They had greater capital than the tenant and so could afford to run the risks of experiment. But they suffered great defects. Specific legacies of feudalism were harmful; primogeniture, entails, modes of conveyancing, all retarded agriculture. Even their removal would not eliminate all the defects of the large proprietor, since he attended more 'to ornament which pleases his fancy, than to profit'. Hence 'it seldom happens . . . that a great proprietor is a great improver'.[7] Smith's judgement, based on philosophical principles, may seem extreme. The more practical view of George Robertson, advanced as late as 1829, was that 'the great mass of improvements arising from a better mode of tillage, and system of rotation in cropping, has been owing almost entirely to the farmers themselves, with very little example set them by the proprietors'. The reason was that agriculture required more 'attention, and so much laborious industry, that few men who are in the independent circumstances of an opulent landholder can bring themselves to dedicate to it their whole talents and time'.[8] Robertson limited his definition of an 'agricultural improver'. Many given the title did not engage in his narrowly defined practical agricultural activities. They concentrated on the administrative reorganisation of their estates, and on their policies and home farm. Whether the landowner was one of the great, as Argyll, or of lesser importance, as Monymusk, the same stream of instructions flowed out explaining what was required, the instructions being directed at some intermediary factor. Such a stream of orders can be accepted too readily as warrant for admission to the ranks of the improvers, but it should be accepted only as an endorsement of the much narrower view that 'supervision of estate management rather than the promotion of agricultural improvement was their characteristic contribution'.[9]

When to the impediments of social opposition and lack of capital is added the possibility that the landlords contributed only narrowly to the improving movement, it is not surprising that success was not easily achieved. For those landowners possessed of limited social prestige and power, or of limited financial resources, the need for capital expenditure spread over a period, lengthened by the time needed to overcome the resistance to social change, led frequently to strained and straitened resources at best, and, at worst, to bankruptcy. The best-known example of technical success and of private economic failure is John Cockburn of Ormiston. Those who survived, and earned a lasting reputation, did so often because they did not do too much too quickly. Some of the improvers operated on a minute scale, and the time-scale was protracted. Improvements at Monymusk lasted over four generations, and were completed only a century after they were started, when an absentee acting for an insane baronet first incurred claims against subsequent heirs under the provisions of the Entail Act, 1770, and drained with government aid.

The improving movement was far from being a general and widespread force in eighteenth-century Scotland, and agrarian change was not some automatic and common response to it. If the basic attraction to the improvers was the possibility of higher rents, then, since agrarian change involved many risks, the alternative of obtaining higher rents through limited action, if available, was attractive to many. Where the prospects of agrarian change were least favourable, as in areas of limited endowments and remote from markets, the attraction of limited action was greatest. Such was the case in the Highlands, and explains why change was often least when, as during the Napoleonic Wars, increased demand, prices and income were making conditions otherwise favourable to improvement. Even where hazards and impediments were less, they were adequate to limit the attractions of improvement until the risks of doing so were reduced by favourable market conditions, and this was not the case in Scotland until late in the eighteenth century, or early in the nineteenth.

The Highlands and the cattle trade

The social change which was a necessary prelude to the introduction of new methods of agricultural production in the Highlands was taking place in some areas before the rebellions of 1715 and 1745 and the abolition of heritable jurisdiction and wardholding in 1747. Earlier still, before the parliamentary union of 1707, large numbers of Scottish cattle were driven south, providing for some Highland areas virtually their only export to the Lowlands and to England. The trade to England was frequently interrupted by political factors. With the removal of such political hazards after 1707 the trade stood to gain; it gained much more from the rising demand for food in England and from the Navy's need of salted beef, especially during the series of wars in which Britain engaged throughout the eighteenth century. Prices rose with only minor interruptions until 1815. About the time of the Union the average price of cows in Scotland was about 20s. to 27s; in 1794 the average price of the animals sold at the Falkirk Tryst was £4.

These events lay behind Adam Smith's well-known assertion that:

> Had the Scotch cattle been always confined to the market of Scotland, in a country in which the quantity of land, which can be applied to no other purpose but the feeding of cattle, is so great in proportion to what can be applied to other purposes, it is scarce possible, perhaps, that their price could ever have risen so high as to render it profitable to cultivate land for the sake of feeding them. . . . Of all the commercial advantages . . . which Scotland has derived from the union with England, this rise in the price of cattle is, perhaps, the greatest. It has not only raised the value of all highland estates, but it has, perhaps, been the principal cause of the improvement of the low country.[10]

Two factors limited the growth of the cattle trade in the eighteenth century. The first was the difficulty of fattening cattle on unimproved pastures in Scotland so that Scotland was concerned more with cattle-breeding than with cattle-fattening. The second factor, a related one, was that the only method of transport available in the eighteenth century —making the animals walk — did not bring them to the consumer in the best possible condition. The Scottish system of cattle droving grew as a consequence. The drovers were not usually men of substance, though they sometimes worked in co-operation with those who were. Their transactions were frequently helped by the ease of obtaining credit in Scotland, particularly through the willingness of some banks to discount their bills freely. Owners parted with their cattle to the drovers in return for only a small payment in cash, taking the remainder in bills of exchange. Cattle from the Highlands were taken to the trysts, first at Crieff, then at Falkirk, while those from Galloway went to Dumfries. Because of the inadequacy of the pastures on which they had been fed, the cattle were in such poor condition that they were then driven further south, mostly to be sold in Norfolk for a period of fattening on English pastures before going finally to Smithfield. Estimates suggest that about 25,000 to 30,000 head went south annually before the Union. In the middle 1720s about 30,000 cattle were sold annually at the Crieff tryst, and by the end of the eighteenth century, when the trade gained from the price rise during the Napoleonic Wars, about 100,000 cattle were exported every year from Scotland.

These great sales had different effects in the Highlands and in the north-eastern counties. In the Highlands the rise in cattle prices in the eighteenth century, but particularly during the Revolutionary Wars, retarded change by enabling an anachronistic economy to continue to exist still longer. In the north-east cattle-raising, by the use of artificial as well as natural grazing, began to replace the old system of arable cultivation. Consumers preferred the cattle from the north-east and so the trade from Aberdeenshire, Moray and Angus grew more rapidly and grew from cattle-breeding into cattle-fattening. Complete success then required that the condition of cattle should not be allowed to deteriorate through having to walk to markets in the south. The north-east breeders were, therefore, ready to exploit to the full the advantage of better methods of transport when they appeared in the nineteenth century. The drovers' services came to an end eventually but not the cattle trade. A more efficient one appeared in the north-east. Its success combined with the new openings in sheep-farming to spell ruin to the cattle trade of the Highlands.

NOTES

1. For detailed information see Ian Whyte, *Agriculture and Society in Seventeenth Century Scotland* (Edinburgh, 1979).

2. Sinclair, *Analysis of the Statistical Account*, p.356.

3. A. Smith, *The Wealth of Nations* (1776) (eds. Campbell, Skinner and Todd, Oxford, 1976), I.xi.l.3, p. 239.

4. Margaret H. B. Sanderson, *Scottish Rural Society in the Sixteenth Century* (Edinburgh, 1982), esp. chap. 6.

5. *An Essay on the Husbandry of Scotland with a Proposal for the further Improvement thereof* (Edinburgh, 1732), p. 5.

6. Historical Manuscripts Commission, vol. 67. Polwarth MSS., vol. v, p. 208.

7. Smith, *Wealth of Nations*, III.ii.7, p. 385.

8. George Robertson, *Rural Recollections* (Irvine, 1829), p. 352.

9. H. J. Habakkuk, 'Economic Functions of English Landowners in the Seventeenth and Eighteenth Centuries', *Explorations in Entrepreneurial History*, vol. VI (1953). Reprinted in W. E. Minchinton, *Essays in Agrarian History* (Newton Abbot, 1968), p. 192.

10. Smith, *Wealth of Nations*, I.xi.l.2 and 3, pp. 237-40.

CHAPTER III

Trade and Transport

The Union and trade

The pattern of foreign trade in the century before the parliamentary union draws attention to the structure of the Scottish economy and to its deficiencies. Three major categories of imports reflected its weaknesses. The first were raw materials, essential for further industrial processing, but which could not be produced at home in adequate quantity or quality — supplies, often from the Baltic, of iron, copper, wood, pitch, tar, flax. Next were manufactured goods, such as fine-quality linen and woollen goods and metalware, the import of which reflected the inability of the Scots to compete in superior finished products usually against England and Holland. Lastly came the luxuries, the import of which was often criticised so severely by those worried about Scotland's balance of trade, and sometimes prohibited, though usually ineffectually — wines from France, and such exotic produce as sugar and tobacco from the West Indies and the English plantations in America. The exports were chiefly raw materials, or manufactured goods of coarse or inferior quality. Re-exports, to become so central to Scottish trade in the eighteenth century, were of slight account. In the later seventeenth century both exports and the markets to which they went changed. Grain exports fluctuated but increased to the old markets on the other side of the North Sea, Norway being a main destination of the increase. Baltic markets attracted herring, though exports declined during the Cromwellian interlude, when fishing off the east coast suffered heavily. Export of coal, which also suffered during the Interregnum, increased even more steeply in value than in volume thereafter, though its bulk required so much shipping capacity that in the 1680s almost half the ships sailing foreign from Scottish ports were freighted with coal. They were bound chiefly for Rotterdam, though their cargoes were usually for subsequent transshipment, with a localised trade from Ayrshire to Ireland in the 1680s, and even a small trade to London. Competition and protection closed markets after the Restoration. Imports of salted herring were forbidden in France in 1689. England kept them out too. Norway was self-sufficient. Holland was too competitive. The surplus grain of the later seventeenth century became more difficult to sell to Norway, both because of competition from Baltic producers and because of increased protection, while England, which had taken surplus Scottish grain earlier in the century, effectively closed her markets after the Restoration.

One feature stands out in the changing network of overseas trade, as much for political as economic reasons, and that was the growing importance of trade with England, notably in cattle and linen. Protective tariffs were more damaging and more likely to sour relations as dependence on English markets grew, but the potential for dissension was even greater when the Scots entered colonial trades which England had already established. The Scots tried to establish their own colonies throughout the seventeenth century, but the success, and so the attractions, of the English colonies were greater. The resentment of the Scots at any attempt by the English to keep them from trading with their colonies and from the wider benefits of their trade was evident in the response to the English Navigation Act of 1660 and subsequently. As both the Convention of Royal Burghs and the Privy Council recognised, the only remedy lay in the English Act being 'rescindit'.[1] Even if it was not, it was still possible to exploit the colonial trade. But such illicit activities were precarious, and, when they came into open conflict with English interests, as supremely over the Darien scheme, the consequences could be disastrous.

The trade with England was then of special importance before 1707 as well as after, and the English threat to stop imports of linen and cattle in the Alien Act of 1705 was an effective means of exerting economic pressure on Scotland. After 1707 the need to maintain the exports was not diminished. Rather emotively Patrick Lindsay pointed out in 1733 a further strain which became increasingly evident in the balance with England in the eighteenth century:

> To all this we have to add another very heavy Article against us, in the Balance of our Trade with *London*, our Expense there; that the Persons of Quality who have the best Estates here, live for the most part at *London* and have all their Rents sent thither in Specie, or by Bills of Exchange; and are there consumed.[2]

A more important reason for seeking a surplus with England after the Union was that it could be used to offset imports from other countries with which Scotland had a trading deficit, such as France. Triangular trade had been a feature of the Scottish economy before 1707. It remained so afterwards.

The removal of restrictions on trade with England and her colonies, especially through inclusion within the privileges of the Navigation Acts, was not completely responsible for the growth of Scottish trade as has sometimes been assumed. First, the Navigation Acts did not stop the growth of trade before 1707, because it was possible to comply with their terms by trading — as was done — through Whitehaven. Second, an illicit trade grew up, helped by the presence of many Scottish servants (exempt, with victuals and horses, from the restrictions of the Navigation Acts) in the plantations. This trade before 1707 helped to account for the first rise of the west of Scotland, and of Glasgow in particular, as a trading centre. Nor did the Union, and the consequential privileges of the Navigation Acts, immediately confirm the supremacy of the west of Scotland. It was not till about 1740, when Scottish imports of tobacco, then equal to about 20 per cent of total British imports, rose after some years of stagnation, that Glasgow began to achieve its final and complete triumph over Whitehaven, Liverpool and Bristol. The lag may be attributed simply to the time taken to break the rivalry of other ports, or until the others found the slave trade, in which Glasgow did not participate, more profitable; but the existence of the lag meant that the legal privileges of the Navigation Acts had to be supplemented by greater efficiency, or by a more favourable geographical situation, to give Glasgow the place it eventually occupied. Contemporary Scots did not look on the Union as having first opened up such trade to them. They had already traded, illicitly of course, with the English colonies, so after 1707 they were continuing an established practice. Legality helped especially in leading towards a more extensive trade, but alone it was not enough, and its benefits were certainly not immediate.

It is much more difficult to judge what effect the trade had on indigenous industrial development. One point, perhaps obvious, must be stressed. The trade which grew up successfully in Scotland was an entrepot trade, requiring relatively few Scottish products for export and requiring relatively few markets in Scotland for the disposal of its goods. In 1771, just before the interruption of the financial crisis of the following year, 47,250,000 lbs. of tobacco, the principal commodity of trade, were imported and 45,500,000 lbs, were re-exported, much, but by no means all, being sent to the Farmers-General of the French Customs. The vessels which carried the tobacco to Europe were then loaded with European manufactured goods, sometimes took wine on board at Madeira, and perhaps called at the West Indies for rum and sugar before returning to the North American colonies. Only a minority of ships went directly from Scotland to North America but not necessarily with Scottish products, because part of the demand from the colonies was met through the export of goods made in England. The connection can be tested by reference to the linen industry. Its progress was discouraged immediately after the Union by a new export duty on Scottish linen in 1711, which, since it did not affect goods sent to England, was probably less harmful than the duties imposed in 1715 on all printed linen and on imports to Ireland. But Scottish manufacturers had difficulty in meeting competition in colonial markets from German and Austrian cloth re-exported through London until after 1742, when bounties were paid on exports of British linen. Production of linen, which was stable at about 4,500,000 yards annually in the decade before 1742, doubled in the subsequent decade and fell only with the removal of the bounties between 1754 and 1756. The continuing competitive weakness of the industry was then confirmed by pleas that, if bounties were not received, no drawbacks should be given on foreign goods re-exported and duties on imported foreign yarn removed. Consequently, even from the mid-1750s, when information on Scottish exports first becomes available, until the mid-1770s, perhaps about 15 per cent of production was exported from Scottish ports. Unfortunately statistical inadequacies prevent any conclusive judgement on the effects of the Union in stimulating demand for Scottish products. After 1707 goods sent to England, whether for use there or sale overseas, were no longer included as exports, but the major benefit of the Union seems to have come from the opening of English markets. If allowance is made for such indirect exports, one estimate suggests that overseas markets took about one-third of Scottish production by the 1770s.

If the direct stimulus of the Union to trade and to the development of the

Scottish economy is minimised, the indirect effects of the Union on the pattern of Scottish trade cannot be. The Union's greatest contribution lay in providing a final confirmation of a change in Scotland's international relationships, a change which, without such final constitutional confirmation, could not have been as effective as it became. The reasons for the changing Scottish links with Europe were various. The importance of the French connection was declining for economic as well as cultural and religious reasons, but, whatever the explanation, its decline placed the Scottish economy in a better position to reap the gains from international trade. The connection with foreign markets, which the link with England ensured would be maintained, meant a link with continually growing foreign markets. Freer access to English markets was only the first and most evident outcome of the new connection, and the gains were in such fields as the cattle trade, where Scotland could exploit the opportunities offered without further developments — even though the exploitation was less efficient than it might have been. The Union provided a favourable environment for sales, an environment necessary for success when low cost production became characteristic of Scottish industry later in the eighteenth century. When after the 1780s the Scottish economy was resting on a basis laid by achievements apparently its own, it was resting in reality on a foundation established through union with England.

The tobacco trade

The success of the Scots in the tobacco trade has been attributed to many factors: by English merchants, displaced by Scottish successes, to fraudulent ways; by the Scots, to their greater frugality and efficiency. The Scottish trade had some characteristic features which increased its efficiency. In the early eighteenth century planters normally consigned their tobacco to British merchants. The planter retained ownership of the tobacco, though the merchant was completely responsible for the cargo after its arrival in Britain, for unloading, paying customs duties, warehousing and, ultimately and most important, for selling it. The merchant used the proceeds to purchase such manufactured goods as had been ordered by the planter and was remunerated by a percentage of the price obtained for the tobacco and by any profit he made on the goods exported. Generally the Scots did not adopt the consignment system for the large-scale expansion of trade. They first traded with America in a more primitive way, by a merchant either himself taking, or sending a supercargo with, a cargo of manufactured goods which were bartered for tobacco. The method of bartering was confined to the early days of the trade. As it grew, the merchants appointed resident factors, who purchased tobacco outright and sold goods exported from Scotland. Initially each merchant or firm had a single store but soon, especially with the rapid expansion of the trade in the middle of the eighteenth century, some firms, notably the Cunninghames and John Glassford, began to have several stores scattered throughout Virginia and Maryland. The merchants had suffered much criticism under the old consignment system; the new store or factoring system gave rise to much more. The merchants received all the opprobrium reserved for middlemen, especially when they tried, not always successfully because of the number of merchants engaged in the trade, to fix the prices at which the tobacco could be bought. The Scottish merchant became one of the most disliked members of colonial society, the man at whom non-importation agreements were aimed, and one cause of the Revolution.

The two systems differed in ways which favoured the Scots. First, the American planter was in chronic need of credit, at least seasonally, and frequently for much longer periods. Loans to American planters were rarely self-liquidating as the annual sale of the tobacco crop did not always pay the debts. Though, in theory at any rate, the consignment system should not have led to the granting of credit, it did so when planters bought more from merchants than they could pay for from the proceeds of the tobacco which they had for sale. In the store system the separation of the purchasing of tobacco and the sale of the goods imported led to a direct grant of credit, though one that had often to be paid for by the planters generally in the form of higher prices. The store system, therefore, required greater credit resources on the part of the merchants. The merchant had to be able to purchase the tobacco outright and carry stocks in his stores in the plantations. The Scottish merchants were better able to supply such capital because their intimate connection with some of the new banks in the west of Scotland gave them privileged access to financial resources, particularly through enabling them to draw more freely on the greater resources of the London capital market.

A second feature of the store system worked even more distinctly to the advantage of the Scots. Under the consignment system a merchant tended to have only a few customers in the colonies; under the storage system he had a large number. Consequently, though the total debt owed to the Scottish merchants was often considerable, it was usually composed of a large number of small accounts. One computation suggests that in the early 1770s about 31,000 individual accounts were due to 112 stores in Virginia belonging to 37 Glasgow firms. The disadvantage of numerous debtors — that some had frequently only limited resources — was more than outweighed by the overriding advantage that the total debt could be more easily reduced than under the consignment system. This was to prove important to the Scottish merchants at the Revolution of 1776.

The first signs of impending difficulties for the tobacco merchants came with the non-importation agreements, the settlers' way of meeting the Stamp Act, when the value of Scottish exports to North America fell from £270,548 in 1763 to £185,733 in 1765. In 1767 the value rose again to £274,610. The distribution of the population and the absence of large trading centres made enforcement difficult, and the presence in the colonies of the loyal factors in their stores ensured a continuation of imports, so that the effects of the non-importation agreements were less detrimental to the Scottish than to the English merchants.

The effects of the non-importation agreements, and of the restrictions on credit following the financial crisis of 1772, were less important than the crisis of 1776. The collapse of the tobacco trade in that year is well known. Imports of tobacco in 1775 were nearly 46,000,000 lbs; in 1776 they were almost 7,500,000 lbs; in 1777 they had fallen to less than 300,000 lbs. Re-exports fell too. In 1775 they were over 30,000,000 lbs; in 1776 nearly 23,500,000 lbs; in 1777, under 5,500,000 lbs; in 1778 about 2,300,000 lbs.

The merchants were not ruined because they did everything in their power to anticipate and minimise the effects of the revolution. From 1774 some factors were sending home warnings of possible insurrection. In 1775 the *Caledonian Mercury* was circulating reports — apparently false, but symptomatic of the feelings of the time — that the Navigation Acts were being openly infringed by vessels trading directly from Virginia to Dunkirk. In light of these warnings the Scots adopted two methods of cutting their prospective losses. First, they pressed the factors to obtain payment for all debts, the smallness of most of which, combined with the presence of the factors, made collection easier, though at the expense of losing any remaining popularity of the merchants among the settlers. Second, the factors were urged to try to buy as much tobacco as they could in the years immediately before the revolution, in expectation, which was realised, that the exceptionally heavy imports could be sold later at inflated prices. The average annual imports of about 44,000,000 lbs. were maintained from 1771 to 1775, though during the same period re-exports were falling. The Scottish tobacco merchants were therefore well organised when the blow, which they had expected and which they had anticipated, duly struck. The traders had to face the problem of replacing the system on which they had built their reputation. In the short run doing so was difficult, and the fortunes of Scottish traders fluctuated during the war. The colonists began to send their ships directly to Europe; the harvest was poor in 1777; in 1778 war with France precipitated a run on the banks. The result was a number of failures in the next two years, relieved only by both exports and imports rising from the low level to which they had fallen on the outbreak of the revolution. Then the Scots traders began to take measures for a revival of trade.

The success of the Glasgow tobacco trade has led to much stress being placed on its contribution, and indeed on that of foreign trade generally, to the development of the Scottish economy. The tobacco trade was an entrepot trade which the relatively backward Scottish economy was not always able to exploit to the full. Favourable effects were evident in some ways. By the middle of the eighteenth century many of the tobacco merchants were buying the bulk of their exports in Scotland and helping to finance new related industrial enterprises which were beginning to emerge in the west of Scotland — the ropeworks, the tanneries, the sugar houses. Some qualifications must be made, however, to the contribution of the merchants. The ships which went directly from Scotland to north America carried the variety of manufactured goods which the colonists required — linens, leather goods, pots, pans, axle bushes, hoes, shovels — but the more extensive expansion of Scottish industry later in the eighteenth century was not based on the demand for such commodities. The extensive industrial activities of the merchants were in the primitive industries; their contribution was less evident in the large-scale production of cotton and iron and has led to some questioning of the traditional belief in a major movement of resources from trade to industry, and especially to the nascent cotton industry. There were examples of significant involvement: James Dunlop, probably the greatest industrialist among the merchants, was a major coal and iron master; Robert Dunmore, a tobacco merchant and West Indian trader, and laird of Balindalloch and Ballikinrain, had an interest in the cotton mills at Balfron and in the Endrick printfield. The brothers James and William McDowall, both partners in the West Indian firm of Alexander Houston and Company, invested in a number of different textile enterprises. The investment did not, however, lead many to become primarily industrialists. The Glasgow tobacco lords' greatest contribution to the economic growth of Scotland was not by becoming industrialists.

The contribution of foreign trade to economic development is of a more general and indirect kind. First, merchants generally, but especially those engaged in foreign trade, were among the leading promoters of the new banks, especially in Glasgow. The Ship Bank was first floated under the title of Colin Dunlop, Alexander Houston and Company, names of tobacco lords. Second, foreign trade brought wealth to a few Scots, some of whom had gone to the colonies in lowly positions, but who returned to Scotland with sufficient wealth to set themselves up as landed gentry and, more occasionally, as industrialists. A notable example, who probably provided the prototype for Mr Cayenne in John Galt's *Annals of the Parish*, was Claud Alexander of Ballochmyle, whose settlement as a landed proprietor was matched by other successful merchants in the same district of central Ayrshire at the same time, such as the Hamiltons, in their various branches, of Bourtreehill, Pinmore, Sundrum, Rozelle and Belleisle. Alexander was notable for his industrial interests. On the other hand the number of Scots who made good in this way was not great. Many went out, few lived to come back at all, fewer still came back with adequate wealth, and of those who did succeed many were blood relations. Though the power and authority they enjoyed as landowners heightened their influence, it was still confined mainly to their lands, spreading only indirectly to other sectors of the economy.

An evaluation of the indirect contributions of merchants and foreign trade might simply confirm the fundamental importance of the direct effects. Scottish foreign trade did not absorb an overwhelming part of Scottish industrial production, and even the moderately successful linen industry required the removal of other limitations on the country's industrial growth before overseas demand had its main effect. But Scottish overseas trade still provided a continuing demand for Scottish goods, which, though not absorbing a large part of Scottish industrial production, was of crucial importance in some cases. It was probably so in the linen industry. It was certainly so with Carron Company: from the earliest days the Glasgow merchants were among its most important customers and such they remained, so that just before the American War no less than seventy-five Glasgow merchants were on the Carron books. In the eighteenth century Scottish overseas trade opened up a new demand for Scottish manufacture which the Scots could not satisfy entirely at once, but which was a necessary prerequisite for subsequent developments. Before it could be exploited fully, additional internal changes were necessary, towards which foreign trade made some contribution through the men and the finance it produced.

In looking for these additional contributions it is necessary to move from concentration on the activities of the merchants engaged in foreign trade to those who participated primarily in the country's frequently neglected domestic trade. The most important of this group were associated with the organisation of the linen industry and the maintenance of its external connections, either to obtain raw materials or to sell the finished product. Because of the domestic, dispersed, and, at least in the early years of the century, part-time nature of the various operations in the industry, a number of merchants emerged with some capital and, as important, with the ability to organise their workers. The need for such large-scale organisation did not arise from the new techniques of manufacture introduced later in the eighteenth century; it was only changed. These merchants, with their interests rooted primarily in domestic industry, rather than the foreign merchants, made the most direct contribution to the new industry which appeared after the 1780s. This is the contribution of trade which must be stressed.

Communications

Since few areas of Scotland are far from the sea, coastal shipping provided the means of communications for most internal trade, but, for access to the richer internal markets in the central belt, the attractions of a canal were recognised early. Topographically there are few more obvious locations for one, especially since the sea passage round the north coast is long, dangerous, and virtually impracticable for small vessels at certain times of the year. The first serious survey of the route, made in 1762, proposed a canal from the Yoker Burn to the river Carron at Abbotshaugh, about two miles from its junction with the Forth. The Board of Trustees for Fisheries and Manufactures was interested in the venture and commissioned John Smeaton to make another survey. In 1764 Smeaton reported on two possible routes. One, not seriously considered until the 1920s, was along the Forth for some miles above Stirling, then across to the Endrick into Loch Lomond, finally by the Leven into the Clyde at Dumbarton. The second route, which became the basis for future serious discussion, was 'from the River Carron, by way of the Bonny, through the Bog of Dolater into the Kelvin and from thence into the Clyde by way of the Yoker Burn'. Smeaton thought the first route would require only seventeen miles of artificial cuttings against twenty-seven miles for the second route. On the other hand the greater elevation of the first offset any economies through less artificial cutting. In any case, whichever method was going to be adopted, the canal would obviously be expensive. For one seven feet deep on the second route Smeaton estimated that the cost would be about £80,000.

The implications of the financial requirements must be appreciated to understand much of the subsequent discussion on the canal and the light it throws on the economic problems of contemporary Scotland. The resources required were so substantial that some assistance from public funds was thought necessary. There were precedents in road-building, in subventions to industry, and the Board of Trustees had been sufficiently interested to commission an early survey. Hope centred on the Commissioners for Forfeited (Annexed) Estates. When they refused funds, the need to raise the necessary capital by public subscription was recognised. To some the whole project was then seen in a different light and a lengthy debate ensued. Smeaton had suggested the route that was probably technically, perhaps in the long run even economically, superior, but his opponents were more concerned with what they considered to be the virtual impossibility of raising £80,000 privately in Scotland in the mid-1760s and with the location of the canal. Rivalry grew between interests in Glasgow and Edinburgh, the former campaigning for a smaller and, to their way of thinking, a more realistic canal, which came to the centre of Glasgow. Eventually a compromise was reached. An Act of 1768 authorised a seven-foot-deep canal from Grangemouth to Dalmuir (later altered to Bowling), with authorised capital of £150,000 and power to raise another £50,000 if necessary. There was still much opposition from the defeated Glasgow interests, especially from Samuel Garbett, who brought James Brindley, the engineer, to make a further survey in 1768, but to no effect. The Act of 1768 provided the basis on which the canal was built.

It is easy to criticise the Glasgow interests as short-sighted, but their fears of the possible recklessness of the financial proposals proved to rest on good grounds. The advocacy of a large canal, sufficient to accommodate subsequent developments, seemed to indicate vision and foresight; it also drew attention to its elaborate and capital-consuming nature. Such schemes frequently run into financial disaster. So it was with the Forth and Clyde canal.

Construction began at the east end in 1768, and reached Kirkintilloch in 1773 and Stockingfield in 1775. Expenditure exceeded estimates, so, though parliamentary sanction was sought for raising additional funds, work had to be stopped in July 1775. The Glasgow interests rescued the venture in part by raising sufficient funds to complete a cut in 1777 from Stockingfield to Hamilton Hill, which remained the Glasgow terminus until a larger basin, Port Dundas, was built in 1790. The financial implications of the venture, which had been so easily neglected, had to be tackled by appealing for support to the government, as the Glasgow interests had originally thought necessary. In the end the belief that such a venture was beyond the limits of private resources was proved correct. In 1784 an advance of £50,000 was authorised from the funds accumulated through the sale of the annexed estates to allow the canal to be completed in 1790.

The Glasgow interests may be complimented for their common sense, especially their financial common sense, rather than criticised for their lack of enthusiasm. On the other hand the Glasgow interests were concerned more with the expansion of international than interregional trade in the late eighteenth century and so were less anxious to establish contact with the east of Scotland. Apart from their obvious lack of interest in a canal which entered the Clyde only at Bowling, they did not see the waterway offering them all the prospects it might have done even a little earlier. By the time the construction of the canal was an actuality, their trade was firmly routed westwards. Of greater importance to them was the second main transport improvement in Scotland in the eighteenth century, the deepening and widening of the Clyde.

Though the Broomielaw was long used for loading and unloading small vessels, its first quay was built in 1663. Five years later, when it could acquire land at neither Greenock nor Dumbarton, Glasgow purchased land in the parish of Kilmacolm where Port Glasgow eventually appeared. Improvements began when John Smeaton reported on the possibilities of deepening the Clyde in 1755, and when an act of parliament was obtained in 1759. Subsequently John Golborne surveyed the river in 1768 and proposed building jetties at intervals to confine it to a narrower channel which could be deepened by dredging. From 1799 to 1806 the jetties were linked by parallel dykes to secure a continuous uniform channel. Since then improvements have been continuous. The Clyde was in the favourable position of having a bed which could be deepened. The success of this enterprise, especially when compared with the restricted achievements of the Forth and Clyde canal, confirmed the accuracy of the emphasis Glaswegians chose to place on transport developments at the time.

The desirability of better waterways was increased through the deficiencies of roads. Though a study of the maps of the *Military Survey of Scotland*, carried out by General Roy around 1755, might seem to indicate a fairly comprehensive network, most tracks did not have made surfaces and were unfit for wheeled vehicles. In areas west of the Great Glen roads were non-existent. Elsewhere they were inadequate, as, for instance, from Selkirk to Edinburgh, where the carrier sometimes found the channel of the Gala Water safer than the road. The statutory basis for the upkeep of roads was laid down in a series of acts, chiefly of the seventeenth century. In 1719, when another act completed the provision, Justices of the Peace and Commissioners of Supply were authorised to appoint overseers to ensure that the roads were properly maintained by six days' compulsory labour annually from tenants and others, while, to provide necessary funds, they were permitted to tax heritors to an amount not exceeding 10s. in the £100 Scots of value rent. The effectiveness of the provisions varied. In some counties, such as Ayrshire, Commissioners and Justices did not co-operate; in others, such as Lanarkshire, the Justices had to act alone. Heritors objected to paying any levies and tenants objected to the compulsory labour. Improvements could be made only in areas where a major landowner was able and willing to direct improvement, as in Banffshire under Lord Deskford, the father of the improving Earl of Findlater. Even there opposition continued. In any case, knowledge of road-making was so elementary that no lasting improvement of surfaces could be brought about until satisfactory road-making techniques were evolved through the work of several engineers, including John Loudon McAdam, who built a stretch of road from his own property to the highway in Ayrshire in 1787.

Improvements in roads and canals were limited fundamentally by the same reasons, especially by lack of funds. There was, however, one major difference between the two. The improvement of local roads, and minor bridge-building, could be undertaken on a much more restricted scale than was feasible in the construction of any waterways or major roads. In the eighteenth century many Scottish landowners engaged actively in such minor improvements as an effective means of bettering their estates. Sometimes they worked independently; at other times they tried to force their fellow Commissioners of Supply to take action. In 1754 Grant of Monymusk was endeavouring to 'rouz gentlemen to serious thought and application' to improvement at the next meeting of the local Commissioners.[3] But many in Scotland would not be roused, partly through the inadequacy of the resources at their disposal, partly because improved roads were, with some justification, not always considered of vital importance for many economic enterprises in Scotland in the eighteenth century. Since roads were built in Scotland only if some special factor brought extraordinary support for their construction, the co-ordination of action necessary to promote any major improvement could also be engendered only through the operation of exceptional circumstances. The influence of the improving movement on the landed interest led to effective private action only in restricted areas. Turnpike trusts enabled the trustees who constructed the roads to levy tolls at the gates, or turnpikes. The first turnpike act, for Midlothian, was passed in 1713, the next only in 1751. Their main contribution came with the use of better methods of road construction in the late eighteenth and early nineteenth centuries, but they had important effects from the 1770s. Most striking was the bridge-building in which some Commissioners of Supply displayed great interest in the 1770s. In Lanarkshire some fine bridges were built during the decade — Roberton reputedly in 1769, Hyndford in 1773, Thankerton in 1778 — all improving the access from Clydeside to the south. As construction of roads and bridges grew, even on the local level that was characteristic of most years of the eighteenth century, easier communication was brought to many places which had previously been accessible only by packhorses. Internal trade was facilitated and concentrated. In 1740 there were fifteen fairs in East Lothian; in 1796 there were only six.

A more striking, and co-ordinated, group of road improvements, though with much less economic significance, was carried out at the public expense chiefly in the Highlands, the result of the official policy of attempted pacification. They fell into two main phases. The first was between 1725 and 1737, when General Wade built about 250 miles of road and 40 bridges. The second was after the '45

Rebellion, when about 800 miles of roads and 1,000 bridges were built under the superintendence of the neglected Major William Caulfield. Direct military labour was used in these cases and the aim was frankly strategic. Only in the nineteenth century were attempts made to bring roads with more peaceful purposes to the Highlands at public expense.

NOTES

1. Register of the Privy Council of Scotland (RPC), third series, i (1661-64), 89, 98, 173.

2. P. Lindsay, *The Interest of Scotland* (Edinburgh, 1733), p. 102.

3. H. Hamilton, *Selections from the Monymusk Papers* (1713-55). Scottish History Society Publication, vol. xxxix (third series) (Edinburgh, 1945), p. 162.

CHAPTER IV

Industry and Finance

The linen industry

After 1707, as before, such industrial enterprises as Scotland possessed required a new basis of processes and products to equip them to rival producers elsewhere, above all in England; but such an industrial renovation required a level of capital investment for which Scotland did not have the resources until increased wealth, at a time of technical development for which Scotland was particularly suited, eventually provided a solution. Until around the 1780s Scottish industry was only struggling towards the successes that were to follow. When it is stressed that, in spite of the economic achievements of the seventy-five years after 1707, it was still the next three-quarters of a century which witnessed the main industrial developments in Scotland, then the rise of Scottish industry cannot be explained simply as the product of political union, delayed perhaps by rebellion. Shortly after 1707 such a proposition seemed self-evident to many who considered the Union led to the decline of some Scottish industries through the removal of Scottish protective barriers and the consequential freeing of trade with England. The belief was prejudiced. The only notable failure was of the cloth industry, which had survived with decreasing success even behind protective barriers. Exports of finer cloth declined before 1707, but the coarse cloth industry survived the Union even to the extent of being able to send some cloth to England to be finished in the 1720s. The industries which suffered were those which had been nurtured by the seventeenth-century economic policy of encouraging direct competition with superior English production. Such a policy could not survive a union. Its demise was not an example of a vindictive English policy towards a growing competitor — Scotland was far from being able to claim to be such — but was the final acceptance that Scotland could not continue to encourage industries, such as the manufacture of fine cloth, in which it had no comparative cost advantage, and had to concentrate instead on those in which it had. The Treaty of Union made a direct contribution to industrial growth by the stipulation in Article XV that part of the financial compensation it provided — the Equivalent — had to be used to encourage economic projects. They received little immediate benefit. A large part of the funds available was absorbed in meeting the various demands of Scottish aristocrats and high officials. The Scots assumed that the Equivalent would solve many of their pressing financial problems. It failed to do so. When Scottish revenue was insufficiently buoyant to provide the additional compensation anticipated under the Arising Equivalent, the English saw no reason why they should provide any subventions.

Payment of the Equivalent, no matter how tardy, was considered to have given the British parliament the right to tax Scotland as it wished, and the assertion of that right was at bottom the source of the most popular dissatisfaction with the Treaty of Union from 1707 to 1760.

Before 1707 Scottish finances were chaotic. The Union stopped further deterioration and in due course placed them on a sound footing. The imposition of any such financial discipline is always resented, more when it involved subjection to the techniques and expertise of English officials. After the Union the Scots were aware that they were not gaining the financial benefits they had anticipated; they were more conscious of the additional taxes they had to pay: the new export duty on the Scottish staple export of linen in 1711; the increased salt tax, disastrous to the Scottish fishing industry which relied on salt imported from overseas, in 1712; and, most controversial of all, the malt tax in 1713 and 1725. Though even such additional taxation failed to provide the increased revenue the Scots hoped for under the second, or Arising Equivalent, it is equally clear that lack of buoyancy in the revenue, not English domination, was the basic reason why it became necessary to impose additional taxation rather than provide additional expenditure after 1707.

Of the major sources of revenue only the land tax, or cess, which Article IX of the Treaty of Union made a fixed proportion of the English land tax in the ratio of about 40:1, produced a substantial remittance to London. Practically all raised in Scotland, apart from various allowances for the apprehension of deserters, was sent to Westminster. The land tax was the exception. The salt tax provided for only one small remittance, of over £1,500, in 1716. Of the customs revenue only about 5 per cent went south in the eight years from the Union until 1715. Thereafter nothing was sent until 1747-8 when irregular, but fairly small, remittances began. But it is the experience of the excise duties which is most interesting, because they included the more controversial, especially the malt tax. Immediately after the Union few charges against excise revenue in Scotland enabled considerable remittances to be made to London, but as the charges grew, especially the cost of maintaining the Scottish courts, the remittances declined and ended after 1717. In this decade, from the Union till 1717, the excise had a sufficient surplus to enable about 27 per cent of its gross produce, or 40 per cent of its net produce, to go south. The chief cause of the inability to meet the higher expenditure in Scotland and maintain remittances to Westminster was the failure of the malt tax. Its net produce to the Scottish Exchequer in 1717-18, the year in which remittances south ended, was less than £1,500. In 1724-5 its net produce was negative. In this situation Walpole's decision to levy a tax of 6d. a barrel on ale may be understood, but it certainly was not by the Scots. To them it was the ultimate indignity to be inflicted by the Union, and the opposition was so strong that Walpole abandoned a tax on ale and substituted a duty of 3d. on every bushel of malt with the additional assurance, regarded by many contemporaries as 'a blind to make the tax go down',[1] that any revenue in excess of £20,000 would be used for the encouragement of Scottish manufactures. Until 1737-8 the malt duties provided the £20,000 for remittance to London, as had been planned, with a small surplus available for expenditure in Scotland. Thereafter, as its net yield fell below that level for some years, so did remittances. When yield recovered, so did they. Both were roughly similar until 1760. Until 1760, then, during the period when most disputes were over taxation, remittances to the Exchequer at Westminster were provided mainly by the land tax and the malt tax. They ensured that for fifty years after the Union about 15 to 20 per cent (but very rarely any more) of revenue raised in Scotland went south. In spite of all the objections made to the higher taxation which emerged in Scotland after 1707, the Union was not such an expensive political venture that it prevented a solution of the financial problems which restricted Scotland's ability to exploit to the full the opportunities it provided. Worse still, it was blamed for the financial discipline which it introduced to avoid the impending bankruptcy of the Scottish Exchequer.

The Union helped towards a solution in two ways at least. First, it gave readier access to capital in the richer south. Little moved north until political confidence was engendered by the Union, and later by the defeat of the Jacobite rebellions. Not only private English capital came to Scotland. The Scottish banks used London agents as lenders of last resort and so had to hold less extensive liquid reserves in Scotland, a privilege which in later years proved a source of much annoyance to English financial interests. Second, and more immediately, the policy of complementary development was officially sponsored after the Union. Before 1707 such official aid as was given was directed, consistently and purposely, towards competitive rivalry with England; after 1707 it was continued but directed to more complementary aims. Confirmation is found in the records of expenditure from the Scottish Exchequer from the revenue from customs and excise. A large proportion of the revenue raised was, of course, absorbed by the costs of doing so. Thereafter almost all the customs revenue was used to meet various bounties or debentures. (The only major exception began shortly after 1715 when allowances were granted to the Equivalent Company, into which the holders of various obligations which should have been met by the Equivalent had been incorporated.) Excise revenue was used for more varied purposes. The largest single item of expenditure was for the maintenance of the courts and other civil purposes. In addition excise duties financed a steady stream of assistance for economic projects complementary to English efforts: bounties for fish and flesh exported, which, as one contemporary remarked, 'is an encouragement for exporting the product of the Country not known before the union';[2] grants to the Society in Scotland for Propagating Christian Knowledge, concerned with propagating educational and economic, as well as Christian, knowledge; and, from 1727 throughout the century, a steady income, especially in some years, from any surplus of the malt tax above £20,000, was given to the Board of Trustees for Fisheries and Manufactures for economic development. Its policy provides the best example of economic action after the Union, and was probably the Union's most beneficial, though delayed, consequence. It was active in the development of the linen industry.

Before 1707 linen production was so successful that exports to England were sufficiently important for their threatened exclusion by the Alien Act of 1705 to be an effective means of exerting economic pressure on Scotland. Though output grew with increasing inputs of labour during the eighteenth century, the industry had still much need for improvement: possibilities appeared at all stages: at one end the flax, frequently a by-product of unimproved agriculture, was of poor quality; at the other end part-time efforts of spinners and weavers could not ensure good finished cloth. So long as the production of Scottish linen remained subsidiary to agriculture and was aimed primarily at supplying a highly localised market, frequently indeed only family needs, the limitations of inferior workmanship were hardly restrictive. They became so only with attempts to expand sales in wider markets in England or overseas. Then the linen industry had to reform its manufacturing processes. It was ineffective to urge, as did the Convention of Royal Burghs, that parliament should try to enforce higher standards of production. Such attempts were unlikely to succeed when the Union had deprived Scotland of her indigenous administration. The only body which could have taken action on a national level was the Convention of Royal Burghs itself, but it represented only a small group of vested interests, frequently more interested in the preservation of existing rights and privileges than in branching into new ventures. The creation of the Board of Trustees for Fisheries and Manufactures in 1727 was a more effective agency. Since the Board was unattached to any particular vested interests, though its members generally included more enlightened landowners, it was better able than the Convention to venture into new areas. Its willingness to pioneer new methods contributed to the renovation of the linen industry as much as the limited financial aid it could provide. Of the £6,000 available from the Board's expenditure in its first year, £2,600 each was earmarked for the linen industry and for the herring industry and £700 for the woollen manufacture. The linen, and not the woollen, industry was the favoured sector.

Precept and example became the Board's chief weapons to effect improvement. Direct encouragement of technical improvement took various forms. First, distinguished Scottish scientists, such as Francis Home, Professor of Materia Medica at Edinburgh, were encouraged to investigate the industry's problems. Second, the Board tried to introduce superior foreign skill and knowledge to Scotland in the hope that the natives would be taught better ways. Dutch bleachers and French cambric weavers were attracted to Scotland, the latter setting up their school in Edinburgh in 1729. Third, the Board sent representatives overseas to learn secrets there, probably the most important instance being in 1729, when in one of its earliest actions the Board despatched a Scot to the Continent to study the difficult processes of scutching and heckling. From his experience he was able to invent a scutching machine which was adapted for water power at Bonnington Mills, Edinburgh. Technical ability was improved at a difficult juncture in flax preparation. Indirectly the scutching machine made an even more radical contribution to industrial change by beginning the break from the domestic, and frequently part-time, nature of the industry. After the success of Bonnington Mills similar lint mills appeared throughout the country. By 1772 there were 252, stretching from Caithness to Dumfries, in which scutching was carried out by specialists. General implementation of the examples so provided was encouraged by spreading knowledge of new discoveries and by financial reward. At the Board's behest Home gave a course of lectures on the chemistry of bleaching; subsidies of 15s. an acre were granted to growers of flax willing to follow the Board's instructions on its cultivation; prizes were awarded for all sorts of special performances; more expensive processes were given special aid, as in the offer of £50 an acre to those who laid out bleachfields up to 40 acres in extent.

The success of these various efforts to improve the quality of the product was limited by the cost of diffusing its message of better methods. In 1743 the Board of Trustees had to come to the help of the French cambric weavers by advancing £845, arranging supplies of yarn at prime cost, and by fitting up additional looms, but in 1755 it reported that its attempts to establish the manufacture of French cambric in Edinburgh had failed. One of the lessons of the Bonnington Mills was that more efficient means of production required more expensive methods, machines and buildings. Even under the traditional methods and organisation of production certain processes were skimped or neglected, not wholly by choice but because of the financial burden of implementing them properly. Bleaching was a case in point, as bleachfields absorbed considerable capital. The undoubtedly fashionable nature of the spinning schools, or the high social evaluation of the ability to spin, could break the general technical incompetence only by encouraging an influx of capital and finance to the industry.

The Board never had sufficient funds to make a contribution to ease such financial stringency. In 1752 the diminution in the revenue of the malt tax, any surplus of which over £20,000 went to the Board, forced a reduction of salary on many of its officers. Some critics queried whether such expenditure as the Board made was always in ways that were most effective. The prizes were often simply rewards for special, but not typical, performances, which left little permanent legacy. The subsidy to the growers of flax was certainly misconceived, because, as one pertinent commentator put it, 'we do not want to raise flax so much as we want to raise good flax'.[3] Whatever the validity of the criticisms, they confirmed the financial needs of the industry's renovation and expansion.

One important contribution towards the provision of more adequate credit came in 1742 with the foundation of the British Linen Company, which in due course became the British Linen Bank. At first the Company, which had a nominal capital of £100,000, did not conduct banking business but provided credit to the dispersed spinners and weavers then engaged in the industry. The Company's activities were various. To quote one observer:

> they import flax from abroad, the best lint-seed, pot and weedashes for bleaching, and sell them on credit to proper hands, then buy the yarn and linen all at reasonable

prices; which linen, particularly the sort corresponding to Osnaburghs, etc., fit for America and the West Indies, they keep in large ware-houses, both here and at London, where they are sold for exportation.[4]

In these ways the British Linen Company performed the function which was later to be assumed by individuals whose leadership was vitally important in the growth of Scottish industry. The British Linen Company was their precursor.

The Board of Trustees recognised that its efforts were not immediately and notably successful. The Trustees asserted, a decade after their first appointment, that their method of encouraging renovation in the industry would achieve lasting success only slowly. An indication that the delay in the appearance of a large increase in output was due to factors not easily surmounted was the inability of the Scots to break German and Austrian competition in the plantations, which, with their important contingent of Scottish-born residents, were potentially the most likely markets for Scottish linen products. Such competition was possible because in the early eighteenth century German and Austrian cloth was allowed a drawback on most of the import duty which had been paid on it when re-exported through London by British merchants. To the Scots this was a scandal, and throughout the 1730s petitions for help poured into parliament from Scotland. Eventually in 1742 the Bounty Act subsidised exports and provided a stimulus to increased output. Its contribution was confirmed on the cessation of the bounty in 1754, when the Board of Trustees recorded a drop in the linen produced — 'by much the greatest alteration to the worse that has happened at any period since his Majesty was graciously pleased to take the Linen Manufacture under his Royal Care'.[5]

Though the industry was, therefore, still vulnerable, especially to competition from other producers, its lack of security compared unfavourably only with the secure international standing Scottish industry acquired in the late eighteenth century. Compared with the failures of earlier years, improvements were steady, especially after the 1740s. In 1728 output was 2,200,000 yards; in 1742, the year of the Bounty Act, it was 4,500,000 yards; in 1750, 7,575,000 yards; in 1760, 11,750,000 yards; in 1770, 13,050,000 yards. In addition an unrecorded quantity was produced for domestic consumption. Weaving was concentrated in Lanark, Renfrew, Ayr, Fife and Perth, but their supplies of yarn came from a much wider area. Coarse cloth was produced chiefly in the east of Scotland, which retained leadership in the manufacture of the coarser fabrics, until the industry gave way, except in Dunfermline, to concentration on more specialised lines: to jute in Dundee and to linoleum in Kirkcaldy. The more valuable production of fine-quality goods was in the west, where, though the Board of Trustees recorded improvement in some years, notably in 1742, expansion was less marked until the mid-eighteenth century. By the 1770s fine linen production accounted for one-tenth of the volume but over one-fifth of the value of total Scottish production. A reputation for the manufacture of fine linen fabrics was represented most strikingly by the introduction of the manufacture of silk gauze to Paisley in 1759. Though this interest was only temporary, the Paisley weavers quickly rivalled those of Spitalfields, whose products they displaced even in foreign markets. A more permanent specialisation came from attempts to imitate French lawns and cambrics. Doing so required imports of French and Flemish yarns because of two continuing defects in the Scottish linen industry. First, though scutching and heckling became specialised processes in the various lint mills and heckleries which appeared in the later eighteenth century, and though many of the mills were engaged in processing flax which was imported from Europe, the dressed flax remained of an inferior quality. Second, the increased supply of dressed flax was often spun incompetently, so the yarn was inferior in quality, and was also inadequate in quantity to allow a rapid expansion of weaving. Though weaving became a man's job and a full-time occupation, spinning remained the concern of women and still a part-time activity, interspersed with others, both domestic and agricultural. Imports of flax and yarn helped to offset the restrictions of an inadequate supply of flax and of inferior spinning, but the greatest success of the achievements in weaving in the west of Scotland came only when the technological changes in textile production later in the eighteenth century removed them.[6]

The iron industry

Though the foundation of the modern iron industry in Scotland is frequently identified with the foundation of the Carron ironworks in 1759, iron was manufactured in Scotland before then. For long it had been smelted in primitive conditions, but an early modern blast furnace in Scotland was at Invergarry. The works there, founded in 1727 and first in operation in 1729, could more properly be regarded as an offshoot or outpost of the iron industry of England than as indigenous to Scotland. They were founded and directly controlled by a Lancashire concern, the Backbarrow Company, which was attracted to the west of Scotland because of the difficulties in which the English iron industry found itself as supplies of timber suitable for making charcoal, then required to smelt the iron, became increasingly limited in the iron-producing areas, if not throughout the country. Smelting and refining were forced to go to the timber necessary for charcoal. That was the reason which led to the foundation of the works at Invergarry. At Backbarrow the cost of charcoal in the production of one ton of pig iron was 50s. 3d; at Invergarry it was 28s. 9d. Practically all other considerations warranted a different location. The ore, brought from Lancashire to Corpach mainly by vessels going on to the Baltic, was then taken along a road constructed by the Company to Loch Lochy, at the north end of which it again traversed a new road to the furnace. The result was that the cost of the ore at the furnace offset the savings on the charcoal. At Backbarrow it was 27s. 10d. per ton of iron produced; at Invergarry it was 54s. 6d. Desperately, but unsuccessfully, the Company looked for local resources, not only on the mainland but in Islay and Jura. Other costs tended to be higher in Scotland too.

Skilled labour had to be imported from England and charcoal burners from Ireland, while the local labour did not always prove suitable even for unskilled tasks. Finally, the pig iron was not consumed locally but was sent south. In spite of the additional costs, the quality of the Scottish iron was so inferior that, while Furness iron sold at £8 a ton, it sold at only £5 10s. a ton. In these circumstances it is not surprising that the life of the Invergarry works was unsuccessful and short. It came to an end in 1736.

The background to other concerns was comparable. The York Building Company's ironworks at Abernethy which began about 1730 used ore brought by pack-horse from Tomintoul about twenty miles away, but lasted for only a few years. The Bonawe or Taynuilt furnace, built in 1753, was first in the hands of Richard Ford and Company and later belonged to Harrison, Ainslie and Company, both Lancashire concerns. Another Lancashire concern, the Duddon Company, built a furnace at Inverleckan, later renamed Furnace, on Loch Fyneside in 1755. The latter furnace remained in blast until towards the end of the Napoleonic Wars. The Bonawe furnace was more successful and lasted until the 1870s. As at Invergarry, both works imported their ore, sent most of their pig iron to the parent concern in England, and both suffered from similar problems. The reduction in charcoal costs which they experienced was counterbalanced by an increase in the cost of ore. At Richard Ford and Company's English works charcoal and ore costs were respectively 66 per cent and 12 per cent of total costs of production of iron; at Bonawe they were 33 per cent and 30 per cent respectively. The use of native ores did not offer an easy solution. The successful exploitation of Scottish natural resources was first pioneered only at the Carron ironworks.

Carron Company differed from the others in size and in the technical processes adopted. When it was founded, the existing ironworks in Scotland were only small charcoal-burning ventures. But an early memorandum detailing the projected size of the Carron works listed four blast furnaces, plus ancillary equipment, a forge of three fineries and hammers, a boring mill, a slit mill and at least four air furnaces. A works of this magnitude was constructed at the outset and quickly earned the reputation of being the chief foundry in Europe. In its methods of production too Carron Company was revolutionary, not only in succeeding, where the Abernethy works had failed, in the use of native ore, but in its decision to be the first concern in Scotland to smelt with coke, a process first used successfully fifty years earlier but not widely adopted.

Unlike the earlier ironworks, Carron Company was dependent on the natural resources which later provided the basis for the success of Scottish iron production, but initially it was plagued with difficulties both technological and financial. So long as the Company confined itself to the casting of simpler goods — pots, girdles, axle bushes and so on — it was successful. Tributes to the usefulness of these soon came from customers overseas as well as from those at home. The difficulties began with more advanced work, notably with ordnance, the Company's most famous product. Skilled gunfounders were introduced from Sussex, and in 1761 the first gun was cast from a pattern taken at

Edinburgh Castle. Then in 1764, by a sharp and risky price cut, the Company obtained orders from the Board of Ordnance against opposition from the usual suppliers in Sussex. Success was fleeting. In 1771 the Board of Ordnance objected that the number of Carron guns bursting was excessive, and, in spite of a worried search for remedies (and excuses), the unfavourable trend continued. After two proofs at Woolwich in May 1773, when 36 of 133 Carron guns failed to pass, the Company was peremptorily ordered to cease casting guns for the Board, the removal of Carron guns from all naval ships was ordered, and the Board's original suppliers, whom Carron Company had supplanted with its sharp price cut, stepped once more into their previous position.

The basic fault was that Carron Company could not guarantee absolute precision, a fault of increasing consequence in the new industry. So in the new industrial structure, of which Carron Company so obviously was trying to be a part, the Company was at a severe disadvantage. Its cylinders could not compete against those from Coalbrookdale when used for the older type of engine; they could not provide James Watt, as he found to his cost, with sufficiently precise work for his early experiments with the steam engine, and later, when he and Matthew Boulton found that John Wilkinson could give them the precision they wanted, Boulton always refused to allow Carron Company to bore any cylinders, even for the Company's own steam engine. The technical problems were not insurmountable, but their removal involved additional cost. The builders of the furnaces, the skilled men to operate furnace and forge, colliers, nailmakers, and others, were brought from England. Again, in common with the experience of other works, Carron products were not immediately superior to those of rivals in the south, so the prices that could be obtained for them were no higher either. Profits proved elusive and technical difficulties were frequently outweighed by financial. The original contract of co-partnery provided for a capital of £12,000 with provision for its increase to £24,000, an amount soon shown to be inadequate. Ten years after the foundation over £150,000 had been spent on the works, so much more than the partners had envisaged that two of the three founders became bankrupt, and the other had to surrender other important interests to support Carron Company. Assistance was gratefully taken from any source. Like so many concerns in late eighteenth-century Scotland, the Company was on a precarious financial footing, so that any interruption to the flow of funds was liable to arrest its growth.

In the nineteenth century other concerns were as successful as Carron Company became after the introduction of its famous product, the carronade, in 1778, but for a time it remained unique. Since Carron Company consumed its own pig iron in foundry and forge, and since the west-coast furnaces sent most of their produce south, the growth of the production of pig iron in Scotland provided little stimulus to the foundation of either foundries or malleable ironworks to process iron further. Imported bar iron from Sweden and Russia was used in the two most extensive malleable ironworks, Smithfield and Dalnotter in and near Glasgow, and even Carron Company imported for use in its forge and in its slitting-mill at Cramond. Since there was no immediate growth of dependent or rival concerns, Carron Company remained the outstanding economic enterprise in Scotland for some time, but its early tribulations were not unusual. Until the 1780s most Scottish industry was still striving towards the success and security it later achieved. Even official help as in the linen industry, or dynamic entrepreneurship as in the case of Carron Company, were inadequate to ensure prosperity. The industrial renovation that was required was known by some, the difficulty was in persuading others that it was absolutely necessary. The problem was not simply one of propaganda. Even those who were convinced of the need often found the financial implications of such renovation onerous. Scotland's traditional poverty exerted its influence strongly once more.

Banking and finance

Virtually all eighteenth-century commentators accepted the fact of the poverty of Scotland, and an appreciation of the problem, even if not an acceptance of its overriding importance, led many subsequent commentators to stress the prominence of Scottish banking and the form of its development.

The foundation of the Bank of Scotland in 1695 marked the beginnings of the framework of Scottish banking. The Bank was given a monopoly of public banking in Scotland for twenty-one years, which was broken in 1727 with the foundation of the Royal Bank of Scotland. The Royal Bank's origins were peculiar. Among the many claims which the Equivalent was to meet were the payment of the Scottish national debt, deferred pay and pensions. Since most of the Equivalent was used for other purposes, debentures were issued to these creditors, but, in spite of prolonged efforts by their holders, the debentures were not repaid. As many of the debentures were eventually sold to English speculators, the holders found difficulty in collecting the interest, which was payable in Edinburgh, and so formed themselves into the Society of the Subscribed Equivalent Debt, the chief object of which was to purchase Equivalent debentures, receive the interest in one sum, and divide it among its members. A similar society for Scotland was founded in Edinburgh shortly afterwards. After extending their activities to making loans to members and others on the security of debentures and other stocks, and to speculating in lottery tickets, the Societies tried to obtain full banking powers. They were frustrated in England by the opposition of the Bank of England, while in Scotland the Bank of Scotland looked with disfavour on a proposed amalgamation with them. In 1724 the holders of Equivalent debentures were incorporated as the Equivalent Company, the Society of the Subscribed Equivalent debt subscribing its holding, as did others with the exception of those holding debentures to the value of £1,474, which remained unclaimed. The possibility of conducting banking operations in Scotland was soon raised, but the directors, in doubt whether they were formed as an English or a Scottish corporation, were uncertain of their powers. Though convinced that banking business was certainly prohibited only in England, they made their position sure in 1727 by obtaining a separate charter, carefully vetted by the law officers, and granted under the Great Seal of Scotland, permitting members of the Equivalent Company to subscribe their stock to the Royal Bank of Scotland. One of the first deposits was the payment by the government of the £20,000 which was to provide the income for the encouragement of industry and fishing by the Board of Trustees. It is fruitless to speculate on whether or not the Jacobite proclivities of the Bank of Scotland facilitated the granting of this charter to the Royal Bank and so the break in the Old Bank's monopoly, but the New Bank's foundation led Scottish banking to build a structure which contrasted with that in England, where the Bank of England long and actively maintained its exclusive privileges. No breach of principle was involved when the British Linen Company, incorporated in 1746 'to do everything that may conduce to the promoting and carrying on of the linen manufacture', spread its activities to banking, though nominally authorised to do so only in 1849. The incorporation of the three banks became a privilege envied by others, especially as their charters, since they contained no provision to the contrary, were deemed to confer limited liability.

A second identifiable group of banking institutions were the private banks, simple partnerships located in Edinburgh, which maintained close links with the capital's chartered banks. One modern estimate suggests they accounted for almost one-quarter of the total banking facilities of some £329,000 in 1744. The origins of such bankers were diverse, and many first entered banking only incidentally from other pursuits. The form of development is shown in the origins of John Coutts and Company of Edinburgh, which became Sir William Forbes, J. Hunter and Company in 1773. Coutts laid the foundations of his fortunes as a merchant in Edinburgh, but the firm's connections widened and, even before his death, one of his sons was connected with a Rotterdam merchant house, which supplied tea, spirits, and other goods for smugglers on the east and north coasts of Scotland. The corn dealings, which had been the basis of the Coutts family fortunes even in the seventeenth century, led to widespread connections. They acquired an agent in Northumberland, who also made purchases in Berwickshire; agents in Dundee, Aberdeen and Portsoy who purchased from the Mearns to the Moray Firth; and landed proprietors who made joint purchases for them at Toftingall in Caithness and Rosehall in Sutherland. The trade was not confined to Scotland. Shipments came from Yarm and Stockton in north-east England; from King's Lynn, Fakenham and Yarmouth in East Anglia; from Haverfordwest in South Wales; from Drogheda and Belfast in Ireland; and from Dantzig and Königsberg. These transactions involved the negotiation of bills of exchange on Holland, France, Italy, Spain and Portugal, as well as on London. The need was not met by the chartered banks in the early eighteenth century, since the Bank of Scotland, after an early and unsatisfactory venture, had temporarily deserted the field. The way was left open for merchant houses which required the service to provide it for themselves and for some to specialise in doing so. Other early private bankers had a similar background to

Coutts: among them were Adam and Thomas Fairholme; Fordyce, Malcolm and Company; Arbuthnot and Guthrie; Gibson and Hogg. In the middle of the eighteenth century some firms were formed specifically for such monetary transactions, though sometimes in combination with other trading activities. The two most permanent of this group were Mansfield and Company and William Cumming, firms which originated from a draper's and from a cloth shop respectively. Others included Seton and Houston, who originally manufactured woollen goods; Thomas Kinnear, originally an insurance broker before his sons started their banking business; and William Alexander and Sons who were chiefly employed as purchasers of tobacco for the Farmers-General of the French customs.

A third group of banking institutions is more difficult to identify. It is the remainder, but in practical terms chiefly the banking companies which emerged in the later eighteenth century and which can be distinguished from the national joint-stock banks which came to dominate the banking scene in the nineteenth century. These provincial banking companies provided many parts of Scotland with their only banking services. It has been estimated[7] that in 1772 the provincial banking companies, other than the exceptional Ayr Bank, accounted for 25 per cent of the total liabilities of the banking system, only slightly more than the 21 per cent share of the public banks and the 14 per cent share of the private bankers. The Ayr Bank accounted for the remainder.

In contrast to the structure of English banking, dominated by the Bank of England at the top and with a host of smaller private banks beneath, the structure of Scottish banking consisted in due course of a few large joint-stock banks with branches. The growth of branches was not extensive until the later eighteenth and early nineteenth centuries. The Bank of Scotland was quickly, though only temporarily, in the field. In 1696 it had branches at Glasgow, Aberdeen, Dundee and Montrose, but they lasted for only a year. In 1731 the attempt was repeated though not at Montrose, and the branches lasted for two years. In 1774 a third and successful attempt was made by the Bank of Scotland at Dumfries and Kelso, a year later at Ayr, then at Kilmarnock, Inverness, Aberdeen and Stirling. In 1802 it appointed Gilbert Hamilton, who had acted as correspondent in Glasgow, as its agent there. The Royal Bank had a greater role in Glasgow. In 1783 it opened a branch, with David Dale as joint-agent with Robert Scott Moncrieff, but concentrated on strengthening links with other banking companies instead of actively promoting branch banking until after the failure of the Western Bank of Scotland in 1857, when it took over many of its agents and branches. The peculiar origin and organisation of the British Linen Bank enabled it to convert some of its agencies to branches. But the British Linen Company only gradually became a bank. In 1765, when commercial operations were finally given up, its banking business was more akin to that of the private bankers. Even taken together, these efforts added up to very little. Until after the Napoleonic Wars branch banking remained unimportant, and so the extension of banking facilities in the mid-eighteenth century was not provided on a large scale by the older chartered banks. It was left to the

Commercial Bank of Scotland to pioneer extensive branch banking among its many other revolutionary ideas in the decade from 1815 to 1825, though its activities were then matched by those of the British Linen Bank. This aspect of Scottish banking was chiefly a phenomenon of the nineteenth century and was the work of some of the critics of the existing structure. The Commercial Bank pioneered the new conception of national instead of local banking, and that is the key to any successful prosecution of branch banking. Only later did others follow its lead.

The concentration of financial services, especially those of the chartered banks, in Edinburgh may have led to failure to provide adequate facilities elsewhere, especially in Glasgow. In 1749 both the Banking Company of Aberdeen and Glasgow's Ship Bank were started, the latter helped by credits from the Bank of Scotland. In 1750 the Royal Bank encouraged the foundation of the Glasgow Arms Bank. The Edinburgh banks encouraged these ventures to forge connections with the Glasgow merchants, who were the leading projectors of the banks, but the merchants' policies soon became too independent, and there appeared a divergence of policy, which was to reappear frequently as a dispute between Glasgow and Edinburgh. Independence of policy could not be tolerated, whether in Glasgow or in Aberdeen. In Aberdeen an agent had been employed by the Edinburgh banks to try to collect the notes of the Aberdeen Banking Company and by presenting them at the bank's office to embarass it through its lack of coin. In 1735 the Aberdeen Bank succumbed to the pressure. Similar action was adopted in Glasgow later in the 1750s, but in this case even the withdrawal of the credits granted by the Bank of Scotland and the Royal Bank a few years earlier, and refusal to accept notes, failed to lead to a stoppage of business. The resources of the Glasgow banks were greater and both survived: the Ship Bank until it amalgamated with the Glasgow Banking Company in 1836 as the Glasgow and Ship Bank, becoming part of the Glasgow Union Bank in 1843, and the Arms Bank until its failure in 1793.

The suspicion of banking enterprises outside Edinburgh, and the failure to provide facilities, lies behind much of the criticism that the public or chartered banks failed to provide adequate financial assistance to the developing economy. Since the surviving records of the banks do not provide systematic evidence of how they lent either by sector or region, the justness of the criticism can never be assessed satisfactorily. It may simply represent the dissatisfaction which accompanies any unsatisfied demand for credit. Since credit was usually granted by discounting bills of exchange rather than by advances, commercial interests could more easily obtain legitimate accommodation than industrial interests. A possible solution for those thwarted in their search for credit was to issue accommodation bills, that is bills which purported to represent some transaction in trade, but which were fictitious and passed between two people who had agreed to operate the system. It is easy to argue that the system was reprehensible, because it was often an attempt to bolster faltering credit or was started under unwarranted expectations of future profits. Not all banks were willing to discount the bills, certainly not those banks whose conservative lending policies were partly responsible for the more widespread adoption of the system. Such was the background which produced the Ayr Bank (Douglas, Heron and Company), the history of which epitomised the criticism against the established conservative order. To quote Smith,

> In the midst of this clamour and distress, a new bank was established in Scotland for the express purpose of relieving the distress of the country. The design was generous; but the execution was imprudent, and the nature and causes of the distress which it meant to relieve, were not, perhaps, well understood. This bank was more liberal than any other had ever been, both in granting cash accounts, and in discounting bills of exchange. With regard to the latter, it seems to have made scarce any distinction between real and circulating bills, but to have discounted all equally.[8]

The Ayr Bank engaged in a system which had a cumulative effect on speculation. Yet its wealthy shareholders — among the first rank of landed proprietors of the south-west of Scotland — assured those who held its notes and the bills it discounted that they could rely on obligations being met, and so the bank was able to expand rapidly.

The frequent and generous issue of paper money was another way of meeting the need for credit, one exploited so fully that it was the only aspect of Scottish banking subjected to legislative enactment before 1844. A common criticism from Smith and many others was the simple one that the note issue was excessive. Two factors aggravated the situation. The first was the issue of notes for very small denominations, a practice frequently adopted by firms to pay their employees, and one encouraged by scarcity of coin in the country. The issue of small notes in itself was not a pernicious practice; it became so only if they could not be honoured. That was the basis of Sir Walter Scott's famous defence of the Scottish note. At this point the second aggravating factor became relevant. A way of enabling banks, or any person who issued notes, to avoid the disastrous effects of over-issue was to insert what was known as the 'optional clause', first adopted by the Bank of Scotland in 1730. The 'optional clause' provided for the payment of a banknote either on demand or, at the option of the issuer, after a period, usually of six months. It enabled a bank to stave off any exceptional, and sometimes irrational, pressure, as well as providing a long-term precaution against the drain of bullion to England which at times followed deficits on Scotland's balance of payments. In spite of such justifications, the system was open to abuse, especially when adopted by less reputable institutions, which were issuing notes, particularly of small denominations, by the third quarter of the eighteenth century. The problem became pressing in the early 1760s, when the withdrawal of funds to England forced a deflationary policy on the Scottish banks and led many borrowers, deprived of their assistance, to accept more risky ways of raising capital, such as drawing bills or issuing notes. The Bank of Scotland and the Royal Bank encouraged the passing of an Act prohibiting the 'optional clause' from 1766 and the issue of notes of less than £1 from 1765. Thereafter those seeking easy credit in Scotland had to rely still more on the drawing and redrawing of bills, and so the practice increased in the late 1760s, culminating in the activities of the Ayr Bank from 1769 to 1772.

In 1752 David Hume pointed out that in a country where poverty made the issue of paper money attractive, then, in modern terms, there was a likelihood of over-issue and so of an inflationary tendency, which could lead to a deficit on the balance of payments. On this count Hume doubted some of the supposed advantages of the Scottish banking system. This fear of Hume's was confirmed in the next twenty years during which Scotland experienced two important financial crises. Both showed the insecure financial basis of so much of the country's industrial growth. The first was in 1762. Towards the end of the previous year funds had been withdrawn from Scotland for speculation in government securities. Partly these were English funds (one contemporary estimate was that Englishmen had invested about £500,000 in Scotland at that time); but they were also partly Scottish. At this time an important firm of private bankers in Edinburgh, the Fairholmes, became heavily involved in speculation in London and its partners afterwards became bankrupt. In consequence the exchange moved against Scotland, so that by the end of 1761 some of the Scottish banks were experiencing difficulty in maintaining an adequate cash reserve. Restriction of credit was the only solution to some, while others adopted the 'optional clause' on their notes. The banks weathered their immediate difficulties, but the fundamental danger of the inflationary pressure led to a continuation of the chronic scarcity of bullion to 1765. The problem remained and was greater in 1772 when the downfall of the Ayr Bank precipitated the collapse of a number of concerns connected with it directly or indirectly. The details of the career of the Ayr Bank are of less importance than its collapse in 1772. By then it was in an impossible position: almost half of its liabilities were in drafts on London correspondents and its assets included over £400,000 in bills of exchange and twice as much in advances, about half of which were to its shareholders. The whole superstructure of credit began to crash with the failure of the London banking house of Neale, James, Fordyce and Downe and at once spread to others, including the London correspondent of the Ayr Bank. The failure of Fordyce, a successful Aberdonian, precipitated a run on the Ayr Bank, which was quickly forced to suspend payment. Attempts to save the bank proved fruitless, even though some of the leading landed proprietors who had been its supporters, notably the Dukes of Buccleuch and Queensberry, announced their continued backing and approached the Bank of England for further help. Since the Bank of England held £150,000 of the Ayr Bank's notes, it is not surprising that the appeal was unsuccessful. The Ayr Bank was never again in business, though eventually its debts were paid in full, with great strain on some of those who had to do so. The Ayr Bank was not alone in its failure. The three chartered institutions, the Bank of Scotland, the Royal Bank and the British Linen Bank, all survived, but the ranks of the private banks of Edinburgh were grievously thinned. Thirteen private bankers in Edinburgh failed, but others, notably in Glasgow, survived. Hence some have judged that the crisis of 1793 was more harmful to the Scottish economy than that of 1772. The importance of the crisis of 1772 lay especially in its impact on financial practices. To some it provided confirmation of the wisdom of the older banks' plea for stable policies; to others it gave confirmation of these banks' failure to provide for expansion. Both sides in the discussion, then and since, often failed to realise that two advantages claimed for the Scottish banking system — stability of the banking structure and easy lending facilities — cannot always be reconciled. Stability of the banking structure prevented the worst cumulative effects of financial collapse, which were more common in England. But stability is more obviously beneficial in the long run, and especially in retrospect. In the short run, and to contemporaries, the quest for stability was not necessarily the more desirable policy for the time, because it lessened the provision of risk capital, which, in a country such as Scotland then was, could arrest economic growth. Care must therefore be exercised in discussing the contribution of the banks and the criticism made of it. The banks' own argument, that their greatest contribution lay in ensuring financial stability, forgets two important points. First, financial collapse was not completely avoided in Scotland, though it may be suggested that it would have been if the policies advocated by the chartered and private banks had been followed whenever any difference of opinion arose. Second, and probably of greater relevance, stability was much less necessary in Scotland then than now. The basic defect in any commendation of the policy of the established banks is that it judges the merits of the two possible strands of banking policy from a modern standpoint. Financial crises were less likely to arrest industrial growth in eighteenth-century Scotland than the country's need for capital, especially for capital willing to run risks. The consequences of even the well-known crisis of 1772 were confined mainly to the commercial and banking world of Edinburgh. It had little effect on Glasgow, and the city's growing commerce continued virtually without interruption. If a commercial panic did not have widespread adverse repercussions, it was not so with the need for capital. Stability of the banking structure was not necessarily of unquestionable benefit to the country's economic growth, if stability could be achieved only by following more conservative lending policies than were desirable for the country to exploit fully the industrial and commercial opportunities then appearing. This was the nub of the criticism against the policy of the established banks.

NOTES

1. Robert Wodrow, *Analecta* (ed. Maitland Club, 1842), vol. ii, p. 281.
2. Scottish Record Office, GD 18/2703, *Clerk of Penicuik Muniments*.
3. Lindsay, *Interest of Scotland*, p. 171.
4. M. Postlethwaite, *The Universal Dictionary of Trade and Commerce* (fourth edition, London, 1774), vol. ii. Article on Scotland.

5. Scottish Record Office, NG 1/14. Records of the Board of Trustees, *States of the Annual Progress of the Linen Manufacture, 1727 to 1754*, p. 135.

6. See Chapter 6.

7. S. G. Checkland, *Scottish Banking: History 1695-1973* (Glasgow, 1975), p. 237.

8. Smith, *Wealth of Nations*, II.ii.73, p. 313.

Part Two

Economic Success, 1780s to 1870s

CHAPTER V

Trade and Transport

The overseas links

Trade with the independent United States of America was quickly established after the War of Independence but not to the detriment of the expanding links with the West Indies. Before the war more than four times as many ships entered Port Glasgow and Greenock from North America as from the West Indies. By 1790 the number from each region was similar. More significant than simple geographical change was the changing nature of the trade. About one-third of the value of total exports to North America before 1776 was re-exports; re-exports to the West Indies were less important. Scottish products — plain linen, haberdashery, and fish, the last of which accounted for over 20 per cent of total exports and re-exports to the West Indies in 1777-8 — were its basis. This link between foreign trade and domestic production grew to support much subsequent industrial expansion.[1]

Scottish enterprise overseas widened in the nineteenth century. Financial and shipping interests were added to the established trading ventures, and direct industrial investment overseas took place. In 1837 the Illinois Investment Company pioneered real estate companies which invested in the United States and in Australia. The pioneers were not imitated extensively until the 1870s when Dundee assumed the lead. Robert Fleming formed the Scottish American Trust Company in 1873, chiefly to invest in railway mortgage bonds. At the same time the Scottish American Investment Company and the Scottish American Mortgage Company were registered in Edinburgh to concentrate on stock market securities and on real estate respectively. Between them, Dundee and Edinburgh supplied eight of the eleven British joint-stock ventures formed between 1880 and 1885 for cattle-ranching in Texas, and a contemporary estimate suggested that three-quarters of the foreign investment in ranching in America at the time came from Scotland. When the City of Glasgow Bank failed in 1878 it had considerable property interests in Australia and New Zealand and had financed much of the Western Union Railroad which ran from Lake Michigan to the Mississippi.

Shipping connections were as widespread as financial. The activities of P. Henderson and Company, founded by four brothers who came from Pittenweem to Glasgow, show their ramifications. Henderson's chartering and shipbroking department was a clearing house for the Glasgow tramp owners in the years before 1914. The firm also provided new shipping services in a complex system of shared ownership. Attempts to enter the Australian trade in the 1850s or the trade of the river Plate in the 1880s did not succeed, but three notable efforts did: the trade to New Zealand, carried out by the Albion Line from 1864 until its amalgamation with the Shaw Savill in 1882; the service to Burma by the British and Burmah Steam Navigation Company and the Burmah Steam Ship Company; and the trade on the Irrawaddy by the Irrawaddy Flotilla Company. Five of the major lines offering regular passenger services in the later nineteenth century grew on the Clyde from the 1850s. The Allan, Anchor, and Donaldson Lines sailed mainly on various routes across the Atlantic; the City Line plied to India and the Clan Line of Cayzer, Irvine to South Africa as well.

Industrial development overseas had more direct effects on the Scottish economy. The most obviously beneficial, indeed necessary, investment overseas was to obtain raw materials which the Scots needed to support their industrial production, but which they could not obtain at home either because they had exhausted local supplies or did not possess them at all. The pyritic ore mines at Tharsis in Spain and the mining of hematite ore in Spain and Scandinavia are examples. In other instances the industrial investment overseas was an extension of activities for which there was only limited potential at home and so the overseas investment soon achieved such a degree of independence that its links with Scotland quickly became comparable to those of the great merchant houses or shipping lines. In such cases there was no alternative to exploiting the resources overseas. The outcome was very different when future competition was encouraged directly, as in investment by Dundee jute interests in mills in India or the extension of J. & P. Coats' thread production throughout the world.

In many cases the switch of investment overseas represented a gradual progression of interests, essential for the growth of the firm even if leading to the ultimate eclipse of its Scottish interests. James Finlay and Company's origins lay in the early phase of the modern cotton industry in Scotland. It expanded its manufacture nearer its sources of supply of raw materials in India and increased its range of interests. Cotton manufacture in Scotland came to an end after a protracted decline. In retaining its administrative headquarters in Glasgow, James Finlay was unusual. Unfortunately for Scotland the move of head offices to London if not overseas became common among the various enterprises which had their origins in Scotland but operated mainly overseas. The headquarters of merchant houses could be retained least easily. They needed the assurance of sources of supply and of points of export. As Scotland ceased to offer these as in the past, the firms left. Their needs and problems were probably not appreciated at home as they might have been. The home-based industrialist, not the overseas merchant, was the central figure of economic life in the nineteenth century.

The growth of trade was facilitated by the appearance of more efficient trading agencies and services. Of direct importance were the increasing port facilities, notably on the Clyde. The success of steam navigation enabled Glasgow to become a leading port, and in 1840 an Act authorised a scheme for a three-hundred-foot channel with a minimum depth of twenty feet. Further progress was delayed when the channel reached solid rock in 1854. In 1869 the expensive expedient of underwater blasting gave a channel of fourteen-feet depth. In consequence the plan authorised in 1840 was realised only in 1886. At the same time demand for more berthage grew as Glasgow attracted trade from Port Glasgow and Greenock, where the construction of the James Watt Dock and the Great Harbour in the 1880s and 1890s represented a fruitless attempt to retain trade. Though a wet dock was authorised at Glasgow in 1840, the construction of timber, and later masonry, wharves downstream proved easier; by the 1870s the wharves extended to the Kelvin on the north and to Govan on the south, with only Kingston Dock, opened in 1867, providing some relief. The wharves then so encroached on the shipyards that many of the latter moved to new sites, paving the way for further development in the harbour. In 1870 an Act authorised the construction of Queen's Dock and ushered in the period of construction of harbour facilities on the Clyde in the last quarter of the nineteenth century.

Improvements on the Clyde were accompanied by the more formal organisation of the commercial fraternity in Glasgow. The West Indian interests were associated even before their rise to prominence after 1776, and Glasgow merchants had always gathered as a group for discussion of common problems, as when they met to consider proposals for trade with Ireland in 1778. It was an easy step to meet the growing importance of the merchants in Glasgow, and of the need for consultation, by founding the city's Chamber of Commerce in 1783. Though the Chamber became as concerned with the problems of manufacturers as with those of merchants, its interests, as reflected in the surviving minutes, bear witness to the influence of the latter, especially of the West Indian interest, in its counsels. Their domination continued throughout most of the nineteenth century, understandably so as long as the cotton industry, with its reliance on foreign trade for both the supply of its raw materials and the sale of its products, was the leading industry in the west of Scotland. Later the heavy industries, which relied on exports of pig iron, were aided by a new race of merchants who specialised in dealings in iron ore on the Glasgow Pig Iron Market, the prices on which were accepted as the standard international prices for pig iron.

Scottish trade, finance and shipping increased Scottish economic influence through the world. They provided opportunities for emigration, not for the massive movements which were also characteristic of the nineteenth century, but for movements of key personnel, many of whom never settled abroad but returned ultimately to Scotland. Nevertheless many of the ventures with which they were associated had only a marginal influence on Scotland's economic evolution. Even the activities of many of the merchants and traders who are among the better-known representatives of the Scot abroad were of little consequence in Scotland. So it was with the firm of Jardine, Matheson and Company, which pioneered British trade with China and the east. Its history shows the vital importance of the family links of Scots in the expansion of trade, and how they gave opportunities for many to move to positions of responsibility, influence and profit overseas, while making only marginal contributions to the growth of the Scottish economy. In the late eighteenth and in the nineteenth centuries this aspect of Scottish enterprise was overshadowed by its importance in ensuring adequate sales of Scottish products overseas. Until the growth of the coal and iron industries gained momentum in the later 1830s, textile goods were an overwhelming part of Scottish exports.[2] The proportion of the output of the heavy industries which was exported was never so high, but throughout the middle decades of the nineteenth century more than half the production of pig iron left Scotland.[3] When the demand for such early industrial products was faltering, that for the skilled engineering output which gave much of the character to the success of the Scottish economy in the later nineteenth century was maintained, though subject to increasing difficulties, until the 1950s.

One direct consequence of the overseas activities was the demand of the shipping lines, especially for steamships which required the skills of engineers as well as of shipbuilders. Proximity of head office to shipbuilding yard did not mean the assurance of orders, but proximity helped. It helped William Denny and Brothers of Dumbarton, who built many ships for Burma and the east because of their interest in shipping firms and especially in P. Henderson and Company. Other shipbuilding yards had similar connections, and a large proportion of the steam locomotives built in Glasgow also went overseas. Imports rose to match the growth in exports. The West Indian trade expanded through Scotland's need to import raw cotton, which rose rapidly to about 2,750,000 lbs. by 1790. The jute industry had similar requirements for a non-indigenous raw material. Until the 1840s the raw material was imported through London or Liverpool, but by the 1860s the imports of jute to Dundee were about 65,000 tons annually. Finally, the continuing inadequacy of home supplies of flax forced the less important linen industry to rely on overseas supplies too. On the other hand the natural resources of coal and ironstone were so abundant that Scottish supplies were adequate until the rise of the special demand for hematite ores for steel-making in the later 1870s. With the increasing variety of Scottish production, numerous other commodities had to be imported: Swedish pulp, esparto grass, and rags for paper mills; South American guano and nitrates, mineral phosphates from America for agricultural fertilisers; Cuban and West Indian sugar for the refineries.

Whatever the connection in earlier years, Scottish external trade and internal economic development were closely linked from around the 1780s, as the full potential of worldwide markets, which the Union of 1707 had first opened, was fully realised. An economic community, more closely knit than in the past, appeared. It was strengthened still further by the financial contribution of the merchants towards industrial growth in the nineteenth century. They continued their earlier support of Scottish banks and helped indirectly to finance the manufacturers. The merchants to whom the manufacturer consigned his goods generally issued a bill against them. The number of such bills increased, especially in the West Indian trade, with the growth of trade and of discount facilities in the late eighteenth century, and banks, as well as many business houses, became accustomed to holding a considerable quantity of West Indian paper. The system was double-edged. It was a means of obtaining credit for the Scottish manufacturers, but much of the West Indian paper then circulating in London and Edinburgh had been drawn to finance the rapid exploitation of West Indian islands, and so was subject to many speculative influences. Earlier the lesser importance of manufacturing and its greater independence of merchanting meant that any such speculation in one section (and it was always most notable in foreign trade) could continue without a drastic effect on the entire Scottish economy. So it had been in 1772 and in 1776. It was so no longer. That was the debit side of the closer alliance of the different sectors of the economy.

Because of the greater integration of Scotland in the world economy from the 1780s, the country's prosperity was determined to a considerable degree by external influences, though the successes in textiles, and later in the heavy industries, were so great that foreign competition was either absent or able to effect only little damage. If the Scottish economy had to face few problems of international economic competition, it could not avoid international economic fluctuations. While Scottish experience had many exceptional features in 1762, 1771 and 1776, the pattern of the financial crisis of 1793 in Scotland did not differ significantly from elsewhere. The textile industries suffered widespread distress, but stocks were quickly reduced and the industries revived. In the first decade of the nineteenth century, war and its attendant restrictions retarded the increase in the crucial cotton exports, culminating in the crisis of 1812 when the dependence of manufacturer on merchant was clear. In 1825 the Scottish economy's experience was again, though for the last time, similar to that of other textile districts. By the crisis of 1836 the industrial structure was undergoing a fundamental change, as the iron industry began to overshadow textiles. The links with foreign markets remained. The iron industry's low costs enabled it to pass through the troubles of 1836 largely unscathed, but less so in the crisis of 1848. Home demand passed its peak in 1845, but the continuation of strong overseas demand postponed serious dislocation until 1848. The trend continued. In 1857 the failure of cotton merchants led to the closure of the Western Bank of Scotland, with subsequent mercantile and manufacturing distress, and in 1872 all industries, but especially the then dominant iron industry, enjoyed short-lived but very high profits, principally on the basis of foreign demand. Whatever the difficulties raised by such fluctuations, they were small compared with what came later. Until the 1870s the comparative cost of much industrial production in Scotland was so favourable that the economy rested on an apparently sure foundation of buoyant foreign demand.

Roads and canals

The expansion of trade also required better internal means of transport. Some of the most striking improvements, when judged by a technical or engineering criterion, made relatively little contribution to the country's need for economic growth. They were most notable in the Highlands, where the need for military roads declined in the eighteenth century with the increasing pacification of the region. With the restoration of the annexed estates in 1784, and the transfer of responsibility for the maintenance of the military roads to local funds, the roads would have fallen into disuse through inadequate finance for their maintenance. They had other deficiencies, which became increasingly evident by contrast with the improvements then taking place in the Lowlands. Virtually none spread beyond the Great Glen, and as the Corrieyairack, rising to two and a half thousand feet, demonstrated, they failed to follow what were technically the best routes. By the end of the eighteenth century a completely new road system was required in the Highlands, but, because of the insufficiency of local funds, it could be obtained only through the provision of more direct government encouragement than had been given to the construction of military roads. The adoption of such a policy was encouraged at the end of the eighteenth century by the first appearance of a suggestion, much repeated subsequently, that one way of arresting emigration from the Highlands was by providing the area with better communications. In these circumstances George Dempster of Skibo encouraged Pitt to commission Thomas Telford to survey Highland roads in 1801 and again in the following year.

Telford interpreted his remit widely. His reports were not concerned simply with the problems of surveying or road construction. He recognised the symptoms, even if he failed to provide an accurate diagnosis of the changed conditions of Highland life. 'The Lairds have transferred their affections from the people to flocks of sheep and the people have lost their veneration for the Lairds . . . It is not a pleasant change.' Telford considered he was commissioned not simply to suggest how the best roads could be built in the Highlands but to suggest how emigration could be stopped. To him the solution was simple: crofting and fishing should be encouraged instead of sheep-farming, and for their successful operation they required a foundation of good communications, a canal through the Great Glen, a network of roads and bridges, and better harbours. Eventually, two official commissions — one for Highland Roads and Bridges and the other for the Caledonian Canal — were appointed with Telford as engineer to both. The state was to pay half the cost of any roads constructed; landowners had to raise the remainder, either voluntarily or by assessment. There followed an immense achievement in civil engineering and, for a time, a striking example of government aid. The Commissioners for Highland Roads and Bridges constructed a total of 920 miles of new roads and 1,117 bridges, notably those of the Dee, Tay, Beauly, Conon and Spey, at a cost of over £500,000, £267,000 of which was contributed by the government. Piers and harbours were also improved by the Commissioners, who contributed about half the total cost of approximately £110,000 from funds which arose from the return of the annexed estates. In 1813 the remaining military roads were assigned to their care, by then only about 300 miles in length — with an annual grant of £5,000 for maintenance. The grant was continued, even when the state's contribution of 50 per cent of the cost of constructional work was withdrawn, until 1862, when the remaining responsibilities of the Commission for Highland Roads and Bridges were transferred to the Commissioners of Supply.

In Telford's view the roads had to be supplemented by the Caledonian Canal. It was advocated for some time before it was constructed. James Watt first surveyed the line in 1773, but its costly nature caused the project to languish. In the early years of the nineteenth century during the French Wars Telford's views received additional support. The construction of the Canal offered the strategic advantage of a safer route for vessels, apart from the economic benefit of making it no longer necessary for ships trading from the Baltic to the west of Scotland, or perhaps to Liverpool, to go north about through the Pentland Firth. The construction of the Canal was financed almost wholly by the state, which had to shoulder a growing burden as unexpected technical difficulties, including damage by floods, and the continual necessity of increasing its size to accommodate larger vessels required additional expenditure, most of it during a period of rising prices. Telford's original estimate of £350,000 for a canal 20 feet deep, increased by the consultant engineer William Jessop to £474,000, was surpassed, as costs eventually soared beyond £1,000,000. The construction of the Crinan Canal bore many similar features. Initially its construction was in private hands but the capital expenditure involved necessitated the acceptance of state aid to enable the Canal to be opened, though unfinished, in 1801. Subsequent difficulties in operation led to further subventions and eventually to the Canal passing under the management of the Commissioners for the Caledonian Canal.

The importance of the work of the two Commissions appointed in 1803 to improve Highland communications cannot be gainsaid, if judged by the sheer magnitude of the work involved, or by the state's contribution to it. The successes were mainly technical and are less striking if judged by other criteria. Telford had set himself the problem of devising ways and means of diminishing Highland emigration, but the construction of roads, bridges and canals failed to provide a solution. The condition of the Highlands did show some improvement in the mid-nineteenth century, and was one factor causing parliament to withdraw its special grant towards road maintenance in 1862, but the Highland problem remained. It was much more complex than Telford imagined. The failure of the Caledonian Canal was the most striking illustration of his miscalculation. Not only was its cost of construction substantially above his estimate; when it was officially opened in 1822, the Napoleonic Wars were over and the strategic reasons which had encouraged its construction no longer applied. Even its supposed economic advantages were less evident. The trade from the Baltic to the west coast, which the Canal was supposed to assist, had never been of major importance, and, in any case, a passage through the Pentland Firth became less hazardous with the growing adoption of steam propulsion and the installation of better systems of navigational lights along the coast. The irony of the Caledonian Canal was that, as its cost of construction increased, so its contribution to the economic life of Scotland diminished.

The transport improvements which had greater economic effect lay south of the Highland Line. In the late eighteenth and early nineteenth centuries the contribution of improvements in roads should not be underestimated because canals were never of much consequence in many parts of Scotland, and railways made their contribution only later in the nineteenth century. Though many turnpike trusts were authorised between the 1750s and the 1780s, they first contributed to road improvement in some areas only in the nineteenth century. Even in Banffshire, where road-making was undertaken under Lord Deskford early in the eighteenth century, the first turnpike trust came only in 1804. In Ayrshire, which had John Loudon McAdam as one of its road trustees, the effectiveness of the first Turnpike Act of 1766 was limited by the inability of the trustees to borrow on the security of the tolls, but, even when that was remedied in a second Act of 1774, work proceeded slowly. The first turnpike road in the parish of Ardrossan was constructed under the 1766 Act only in 1779; the inland road from Girvan to Ballantrae, constructed under the 1774 Act, was completed only in 1791. In central Scotland, soon to be the centre of much industrial development for which good communications were indispensable, improvements also appeared, especially in the last decade of the eighteenth century, when two new roads (one through Stepps, Falkirk and Linlithgow; the other through Airdrie and Bathgate) joined Glasgow and Edinburgh. The beneficial effects of many of the early roads were limited both by imperfect knowledge of road-making, which, according to McAdam, was worse in Scotland than in England, and by levying so many tolls on the roads (there were ten on the thirty-four miles from Glasgow to Ayr) that traffic was sometimes driven off them. Consequently, though the first mail-coach from London reached Glasgow in 1788, the necessary improvement of the road it had to take from Carlisle exceeded local capabilities, both financial and technical. Financial aid came with a parliamentary grant of £50,000; technical aid came from Telford, from whose labours in Lanarkshire more than the Glasgow to Carlisle road benefited. He engineered the branch through Lanark to Cumbernauld; the road which joins the old Edinburgh to Glasgow road from the Calders across Garrion bridge (built in 1818) to the Ayrshire border at Loudon Hill; and, the most memorable legacy of all, left a series of fine bridges, built from 1818 to 1830.

When the surfaces of the newer roads benefited from the work of McAdam and others, they were far more suitable for fast wheeled vehicles than were those built earlier in the eighteenth century. It is easy to see how frequently the two ministers who contributed to the first and second statistical accounts of one parish both recorded major advances in road construction. Those who wrote in the 1780s and 1790s saw only the beginning of the work of the turnpike trusts; those who wrote in the 1840s saw its completion and the extension of minor roads by heritors and others. By then the major network of roads had been built in many parts of Scotland, frequently only their surfacing and alignment being changed in later years, until an Act of 1878, which became effective no later than 1883, finally abolished the old system of statute labour (compulsorily commuted to money payments in 1845) and any turnpike trusts that remained.

Thereafter all roads and bridges within a county were administered by the County Road Board, the executive agency of the County Road Trustees, who included Commissioners of Supply and representatives of ratepayers and town councils. In 1889 the newly formed County Councils assumed responsibility for the roads and provided the members of the County Road Board.

The contribution of road improvements was overshadowed where canals were constructed, but Scottish canals were never extensive and, apart from the Forth and Clyde and the Caledonian Canals, were of local importance. In another respect the Forth and Clyde and the Caledonian Canals differed from the others: the former was first envisaged as providing more convenient access for west-coast merchants to Europe, the latter was conceived as a means of preventing emigration from the Highlands; the other canals of any economic importance were intended to assist in the exploitation of the natural resources of Scotland. Of these the Monkland Canal was the most important. It opened the landlocked coalfield of north Lanarkshire to provide additional supplies to meet the expanding industrial and domestic demand of Glasgow — estimated by James Watt to be about 70,000 tons annually around 1770 — and so to break the monopoly of the Glasgow coal merchants, who were thought to be charging extortionate prices because of the increased demand. James Watt was commissioned to survey a possible route in 1769, and, as Smeaton did when he surveyed for the Forth and Clyde Canal, Watt suggested two possibilities. One brought the canal right into Glasgow, but required a series of locks near the city, and so would have cost over £20,000. Watt favoured a cheaper scheme, costing only about half as much, but in which the canal terminated just where the locks began on the first scheme. The route into the city was then completed by means of a waggonway down a steep slope. The assumption that the less expensive venture should be accepted reflected the financial stringency in contemporary Scotland, and possibly also the same conservative Glasgow interests which had actively advocated a less elaborate Forth and Clyde Canal. An Act was obtained for the canal in 1770, but even the restricted scheme which had been adopted proved excessively optimistic for Scotland, then embroiled in the financial crisis of 1772, and the project came to a halt until 1784. By then a large part of the shares were held by the partners of the firm of William Stirling and Company. Its head from 1777, Andrew Stirling, had a direct interest in the development of the Monklands through the purchase of the estate of Drumpellier. In 1786 the Stirlings became the sole proprietors of the canal, which they completed and extended to join the Forth and Clyde Canal at Port Dundas in 1790, the same year in which the Forth and Clyde itself gained access to the sea at Bowling. A third canal, the Union, completed the framework which had been laid by the Forth and Clyde and Monklands Canals for the exploitation of the natural resources of central Scotland. Its aim was to provide a direct link by water between Glasgow and Edinburgh, and more especially, to enable Edinburgh, and indeed much of Midlothian, to gain from the increased supplies of coal, which, it was hoped, would be encouraged through the junction of the Forth and Clyde and Monkland Canals. Though the idea of the canal was accepted, disputes on the most desirable route delayed its authorisation for nearly a quarter of a century. An Act was obtained only in 1817, and the canal, which ran from lock 16 on the Forth and Clyde Canal to Edinburgh, was finally opened in 1822. With the network provided by the three canals, coal could be sent from the Monkland parishes to Port Dundas on the west or to Port Hopetoun in the east. Glasgow and Edinburgh could be served directly from the coalfields of central Scotland.

A number of other canals were projected towards the end of the eighteenth century, but not all came to full fruition. The most notable was the Glasgow, Paisley and Ardrossan Canal, part of the Earl of Eglinton's plan to transform Ardrossan into a major port for the increasing shipping traffic from the west of Scotland. The cost exceeded Telford's estimate of nearly £135,000, and by 1811 the canal reached its limit of eleven miles from Glasgow to Johnstone. Later a connection to Ardrossan was made by rail. Ardrossan never displaced Port Glasgow and Greenock, or Glasgow itself, but it is impossible to guess what might have happened if the canal had been completed earlier, before the railways rendered the project obsolete. The only other canal of any importance in Scotland was a cut of eighteen miles from Aberdeen to Inverurie, but, since it had a large number of locks, its cost, both in construction and operation, was high. Even its local importance, considerable as it was, was diminished.

Railways

Waggonways, the ancestors of modern railways, emerged to take the coal short distances from collieries in the late eighteenth century. Originally the rails were of wood; later they were plated with iron, and later still they were made entirely of iron. Sometimes, in the most rudimentary instances, waggonways were constructed with a slope sufficient to allow the waggons to run along them on their own momentum. More frequently, waggons were horse-drawn until the development of the steam engine. Examples were to be found throughout central Scotland, with an isolated example at Brora, though only about 60 miles of line had been built by the end of the Napoleonic Wars. If the possession of an act of parliament is the test of the transition from a waggonway to a railway, the Kilmarnock to Troon's claim to be the first railway in Scotland is substantiated. It had other claims to pre-eminence. Its ten miles had cost about £60,000 by 1814 — almost double the estimate — but the first dividend of 5 per cent in 1817 was often bettered in subsequent years. Though built chiefly for the transport of coal, it carried much other commercial traffic as well as passengers, though not specifically authorised to do so. It also experimented with steam power.

The change to recognisably modern railways came only after the power of the steam locomotive was firmly established in the early 1830s. The earliest of them were also concerned mainly with transporting coal, for which the need had been intensified in the late eighteenth century by the demand from Glasgow and from the growing iron industry for the resources of Lanarkshire. The first of the modern group was the Monkland and Kirkintilloch Railway, which, authorised in 1824 and opened in 1826, gave access from Old Monkland to the Forth and Clyde Canal, and enabled coal to go to Port Dundas on the west, to Grangemouth on the east, and, by means of the Union Canal, direct to Edinburgh. The fears of the Town Council of Glasgow and others that the benefits of cheap coal, made possible by the railway, might be enjoyed by Edinburgh rather than by Glasgow, were apparently justified, especially whenever prices in the west were low. The possibility increased when the Ballochney Railway, approved in 1826 and opened in 1828, connected New Monkland to the Monkland and Kirkintilloch Railway.

The Garnkirk and Glasgow, opened in 1831, stood apart from all the early railways. It aimed, as had the Monkland Canal, at breaking the monopoly of the coal masters whose power was not diminished because of the continued expansion of demand in Glasgow and district in the 1820s, but its importance arose from various factors, all of which indicated the acceptance of new ways and methods. The Garnkirk and Glasgow Railway used steam locomotives from the start, important for the passenger traffic it soon built up in spite of being primarily a coal line. Most other early railways were integrated into the canal system, and were supplementary to it; the Garnkirk and Glasgow Railway was directly competitive with the canals, following the line of the Monkland Canal. Two other early railways also contributed to the exploitation of the resources of central Scotland. First, the Wishaw and Coltness Railway, projected in 1829 and opened in 1833, ran from the Monkland and Kirkintilloch Railway southwards to within a mile of the Omoa ironworks, opened up the area between Holytown and Hamilton, the future site of Carnbroe and Coltness ironworks, and made possible the use of a large field of ironstone which had been found in the coal measures some time previously but which had been neglected until the railway was built, and had been 'an object scarcely worthy of attention'.[4] Second, the Slamannan Railway, towards which the Ballochney Railway contributed half the capital, gave an outlet from the coal and iron districts of north Lanarkshire to the east without the necessity of using the Forth and Clyde Canal. The line, projected in 1835 and completely opened in August 1840, ran from Ballochney, where it joined the Ballochney Railway, to the Union Canal. Though the railway gave direct access from Lanarkshire to the east by rail, the Union Canal was still necessary for contact with Edinburgh. In 1848 all three, the Monkland and Kirkintilloch, the Ballochney, and the Slamannan Railways amalgamated to form the Monkland Railways, later absorbed by the Edinburgh and Glasgow Railway and in turn by the North British Railway.

As with the waggonways, so the railways constructed before the later 1820s were concentrated in the centre and west of Scotland, apart from a group from Dundee through Newtyle to Coupar Angus and Glamis and from Dunfermline to Charlestown. They were projected chiefly to reduce the cost of transporting coal and gained from the emergence of the buoyant demand from the ironworks, which came only after the earliest lines had started. Even then forecasts of the costs of construction and operation, and of the revenue, erred as with so many early engineering ventures, and the financial returns of the lines were overestimated. The Monkland and Kirkintilloch and the Ballochney were the most profitable, though less so in the mid-1840s. By the time they amalgamated in 1848, the former had paid an average of 5½ per cent over 22 years and the latter 7½ per cent over 20 years. On the other hand the Slamannan Railway paid only one dividend, in 1841, before it merged with the two more successful lines. Even the Garnkirk and Glasgow Railway, for all its other claims to recognition, was unprofitable initially. The wider economic benefits it conferred show how the narrow conception of private profitability may underestimate the contribution of a railway to the development of a region. It succeeded in its objective of reducing the cost of carrying coal to Glasgow, giving a saving — claimed at the opening — of about 1s. a ton. Though the Garnkirk and Glasgow relied on mineral traffic, it carried passengers from the start, in company with the even more unprofitable Dundee and Newtyle. In its early years it had almost 40 per cent of the non-road passenger traffic to the east of Glasgow, almost as much as travelled by the Forth and Clyde Canal. Even if unprofitable at the outset, the Garnkirk and Glasgow showed the way forward.

The promotion of the early railways was undertaken chiefly by merchants and by coalmasters, some of whom became leading figures in the iron industry. Among them were Alexander Baird, father of the brothers who founded the ironworks, James Merry and William Dixon, all directors of the Garnkirk and Glasgow Railway. James Merry and William Dixon were on the board of the Monkland and Kirkintilloch Railway and Dixon on that of the Wishaw and Coltness. They were also often the major customers of the early railways. Almost 16 per cent of the traffic on the Wishaw and Coltness in 1843 was for the Bairds and almost 10 per cent for James Merry. Apart from the Monkland and Kirkintilloch Railway, most of the directors of which were coal merchants, promotion and direction was spread more widely among Glasgow merchants and manufacturers such as Charles Tennant. One notable absentee from the group of railway promoters was Kirkman Finlay, who never became fully convinced of the superiority of railways to canals.

In Scotland the railway boom of the mid-1830s saw the construction of railways geared mainly to carrying coal, though some, among them the Dundee and Newtyle, had to exploit the passenger trade for lack of an alternative; others, notably the Garnkirk and Glasgow, found passengers unexpectedly profitable. Some of the projects which were completed from the later 1830s originated in the boom, but by then the expansion of the railway network had more varied objectives. In some areas it was still aimed at the exploitation of natural advantages. In Ayrshire, where the coal and iron ore were exploited extensively only from the late 1830s, the basis of communications was the abortive plan for the canal from Glasgow to Ardrossan. The canal had not progressed beyond Johnstone, and in 1827 the canal company was authorised to complete the route by railway. The track, starting this time from the coast, reached only Kilwinning, though the line had some useful branches. In 1837 the Glasgow, Paisley, Kilmarnock and Ayr Railway was authorised, the five-mile stretch between Ardrossan and Kilwinning was amalgamated into it, the line to Ayr opened completely in 1840 and the branch from Dalry to Kilmarnock in 1843. Later the bed of the moribund canal from Johnstone to Glasgow was filled in to give an alternative line. The Glasgow, Paisley and Greenock line, authorised on the same day in 1837, and sharing seven miles of track from Glasgow to Paisley, was opened in 1841. By the time of the railway mania the south-west had its main system of communications complete. At the same time a network appeared in the east, around Edinburgh and Dundee, which, for obvious reasons, had few of the mineral lines of the west of Scotland. In Edinburgh the railway network began with the Edinburgh and Dalkeith Railway, opened in 1831 and using horse-drawn waggons until absorbed by the North British in 1846. It was followed by the promotion in 1836 of the potentially useful but actually disastrous Edinburgh, Leith and Newhaven Railway. In Dundee a start was made with the Dundee and Newtyle Railway, authorised in 1826 and opened in 1832, on part of which locomotives were used in spite of steep inclines. Extensions to Coupar Angus and Glamis were authorised in 1835. They were followed quickly by the Dundee and Arbroath and the Arbroath and Forfar lines, which were opened in 1838 and 1839. By then Angus had an effective railway network.

The change which the railway mania of the 1840s brought was not so much the projection but the completion of a system of trunk lines distinct from the local networks which had appeared in the earlier years. With their appearance the Scottish railway system became no longer only concerned with the exploitation of the country's mineral resources. It carried passengers and provided the means of communication between different parts of Scotland and England, so necessary for the exploitation of foreign demand on which the country's industrial expansion was increasingly dependent.

The potential of the trunk lines was first demonstrated before the railway mania by the Edinburgh and Glasgow Railway, which can be regarded as part of a local network or the foundation of a wider, even of a national system, linking Scotland to the rest of the United Kingdom. The Edinburgh and Glasgow Railway was a direct challenge to the Forth and Clyde Canal. Surveys were made from the 1820s, the Act authorising the line was obtained in 1838, and the line opened in 1842. It was followed later in the 1840s by the first appearance of the main railway lines between Scotland and England. Suggestions for them were of long-standing. In 1833 a railway from England to Scotland was first mooted along a line from Newcastle through Jedburgh and Melrose to Edinburgh, with a branch from Melrose to Peebles, Lanark and Glasgow, a route never followed exactly. In 1841 when two commissioners (Smith and Barlow) reported, among other matters, on routes across the border, they identified sixteen possibilities, though the choice soon narrowed to one of three, each of which became the line of one of the main railway companies which dominated Scottish railway history in the later nineteenth century. These were the east-coast route through Berwick and Dunbar, the line of the North British Railway Company; the Annandale route, the line of the Caledonian Railway Company; and the Nithsdale route, the line of the Glasgow and South Western Railway Company.

The first line across the border was the North British, east-coast route from Edinburgh to Berwick, opened in 1846. Previously George Stephenson had surveyed two routes from Newcastle to Edinburgh and had favoured the east coast, but the scheme lay dormant until revived in an alliance with George Hudson in the 1840s. Hudson's energy and influence may well have been responsible for the success of the venture. His Newcastle and Berwick Railway provided the necessary link with the south and he invested £50,000 in the North British Railway, shares which were later transferred to the York and North Midland Railway. Parliamentary authorisation came in 1844. At the same time the Grand Junction Railway wanted to extend its interests to the north on the west coast. In 1835 Joseph Locke surveyed two possible routes from Carlisle to Glasgow, one through Nithsdale and the other through Annandale. Because of inclines involved in crossing Beattock summit, Locke chose the former, a preference which seemed even more reasonable when the Glasgow to Kilmarnock Railway was incorporated in 1837 and so held out the prospect of a line being constructed part of the way from Glasgow towards Nithsdale. At this stage the Annandale route might have been neglected but for the enterprise of local landowners. They could stress in its support that Beattock provided only a difficult, not an insurmountable, barrier; that the Annandale route, by leading into Clydesdale, gave access to the developing industrial areas of north Lanarkshire; and that the Annandale line, unlike that through Nithsdale, offered communications to both Glasgow and Edinburgh. A further survey by Locke seemed to show that he was undecided between the two. The Smith-Barlow report clarified many of the issues without leading to a firm conclusion. On the assumption that there would be only one line across the border, which was all the commissioners felt was justified by the existing traffic, they recommended the Annandale route, with the addition of a branch to Edinburgh from Symington or Thankerton. If they had deemed two lines feasible, they would have favoured the east-coast route and, since the Annandale's attraction of a link to Edinburgh as well as to Glasgow would no longer be a major attraction, the choice between it and the more easily engineered line along Nithsdale would have been more open. When the east-coast route was authorised, some of the priority in the claims of the Annandale scheme were removed, but, in spite of opposition from those who favoured Nithsdale, and from the Edinburgh and Glasgow Railway which was already associated with the North British Railway, the route was authorised as the Caledonian Railway in 1845 and completed in 1848. Construction of the Nithsdale route was authorised in 1846. On its completion in 1850 it was amalgamated with the Glasgow, Paisley, Kilmarnock and Ayr Railway to form the Glasgow and South Western Railway. By the end of the railway boom one railway had crossed the border and two others had been authorised.

The 1840s witnessed expansion to the north. The Scottish Central Railway reached Perth, and the North Eastern Railway completed the Scottish Midland's line from Forfar to Aberdeen. Eventually they became part of the Caledonian Railway. The following decade, the 1850s, saw the beginning of lines which were ultimately to comprise the two other companies which joined the North British, the Caledonian, and the Glasgow and South Western to form the five great Scottish railway companies. The oldest section of the Great North of Scotland Railway, which was located in the north-east, was the Elgin to Lossiemouth line opened in 1852, and the oldest section of the Highland Railway, which eventually stretched to Thurso, was the line from Inverness to Nairn, opened in 1855. The Scottish railway network was virtually completed in the later nineteenth century by the expansion of the existing companies through amalgamation and through new construction. Of the latter, the work of the North British Railway was most dramatic as it bridged the Tay, first and disastrously in 1878, secondly in 1887, and the Forth in 1890, and at the end of the century carried the railway westwards to Fort William in 1897 (the year in which the Highland Railway completed the ten miles from Strome Ferry to Kyle of Lochalsh) and Mallaig in 1901.

The expansion of the later nineteenth century provided Scotland with some of its memorable feats of railway engineering, but its economic influence was not comparable to the construction of the 1840s. The railway mania of the 1840s gave Scotland the nucleus of its railway system. In later years expansion was frequently of branch lines or in rural districts. By the middle of the nineteenth century most of those required for the general exploitation of the country's economic potential had been built. Most important of all, the link provided with England in the later 1840s, helped by access to English capital, was the greatest step towards economic integration since 1707.

NOTES

1. See pp. 69-70.
2. See Chapter 7.
3. See Chapter 8.
4. Hamilton Muniments. Memorandum of William Paterson, 19 January 1831.

CHAPTER VI

The Textile Industries

The cotton industry

By the late eighteenth century technical change was beginning to overcome the deficiencies in both the quantity and quality of yarn which had restricted the growth of the linen industry. New methods of spinning gradually became more effective and more common between the invention of the spinning jenny in the 1760s and of the mule in 1779. Though a power loom was developed by Edmund Cartwright in 1784, a similar revolution in weaving was delayed. The innovations in both spinning and weaving were complemented by the mechanical adaptations which followed Watt's invention of the steam engine, among them being Watt's own devices to connect the linear motion of the steam engine into rotary movement. Such developments provided the basis for a transformation in the manufacture of all textiles, but especially of cotton, as the fibre was more suited to the early machines than flax or wool. Yet the new technology is rather the immediate explanation or the occasion of the appearance of the new type of industry in Scotland. It provided the renovation which Scottish industry needed but found so difficult to achieve, but to explain the rise of the industry solely on the basis of the new technology misses the point. Its successful application, especially in the west of Scotland, depended on the favourable environment already formed in the linen industry through the special skills and abilities, particularly in finer fabrics, of the linen weavers and through the commercial acumen of the merchants who organised the industry.

The barrier placed by the inadequacies in the supply of yarn on a full exploitation of the skill of the linen weavers of the west of Scotland was only gradually removed by the new technology. The yarn spun by the spinning jenny was soft and suitable only for the weft; that spun on the water frame was sufficiently strong for the warp but too soft for finer fabrics and was suitable only for cheap cotton calicoes. In spite of its deficiencies the yarn was used for finer fabrics wherever possible, and in the late 1760s the weavers of Anderston and Paisley began to use cotton for the weft in an effort to produce muslins. James Monteith imported some 'bird-nest' Indian yarn and had the first webs of muslin woven in Scotland. The textile industry of the west of Scotland never shifted from its specialisation in high-quality fine products. Consequently, the full exploitation of the particular abilities the industry had first evolved in the manufacture of linen could be deployed in manufacturing cotton only in the 1780s when Crompton's mule enabled yarn to be spun sufficiently strong and fine for both weft and warp in high-quality cotton cloth. Thereafter the finest muslins could be woven in Scotland. The new technology gave the Scottish weavers the opportunity they had been seeking.

The growth of the cotton industry required that the skills and abilities brought by the weavers from the linen industry be complemented by the commercial acumen of the linen merchant, or manufacturer, as he was called indiscriminately. His contribution grew as the industry lost its domestic character and its dependence on localised raw materials, labour and markets. Spinners were scattered throughout the country; full-time weavers were concentrated towards the commercial centres of the industry, chiefly in Glasgow, Paisley, and, to a lesser extent, in Dundee; raw materials came increasingly from overseas and finished products went there. Unity was given to the varied industrial complex by merchants, who had resources adequate to finance the extended process of production and who sometimes owned the lint mills or the expensive bleachfields. The establishment of the cotton industry required men with capital, with commercial experience, and with an ability to organise their workers in new places and with new techniques. As it provided the weavers for the cotton industry, so too the linen industry provided the entrepreneurs.

What is reputed to have been Scotland's first cotton mill was built at Penicuik in 1778 and was followed by a more successful one at Rothesay, which, though long disused as a cotton mill, was destroyed by fire only in 1955. The Penicuik and Rothesay mills were exceptional. Renfrewshire and Lanarkshire were the areas of development even in the earliest phase of the industry's growth. In 1787, 19 mills driven by water were listed in Scotland: four each were in Lanarkshire and Renfrewshire, three in Perthshire, two in Midlothian and six in other places, but there were probably more. Paisley's existing reputation as a textile centre was confirmed, though the first modern cotton mill in Renfrewshire, and probably the third in Scotland, was just beyond the Paisley parochial boundary, in the parish of Neilston, where an old corn mill, driven by the river Levern, was converted to cotton-spinning in 1780. The first mill in Lanarkshire was founded in 1783 at East Kilbride, and was followed by another at North Woodside, Glasgow, in 1784. The period of busiest construction of cotton mills followed, lasting from the foundation of the Deanston mills in 1785 to the outbreak of the French Wars in 1793, a period of expansion rivalled in Scotland's industrial history by the growth of the iron industry in the 1830s. Until about 1790, relatively few mills were built, but most were of considerable size and remained the major enterprises of the industry in Scotland; in 1793 New Lanark and Catrine between them consumed 20 per cent of the imports of raw cotton into Scotland. A period of extensive construction of small mills began after 1790. There were also changes in location. The mills built in the early 1790s were distributed throughout the country, with two notable centres: one was on the east coast around Dundee, though mills spread southwards to Kinghorn and Dunbar; another, and more important, cluster was in the west, in north Ayrshire and the adjacent lowlands of Renfrewshire. When the attractions of some areas diminished in the early nineteenth century through the use of steam rather than water power, the erection of new mills nearer the main centre for importing the raw materials was feasible, and so construction became more concentrated in the west of Scotland, particularly in Glasgow, where new mills were built in Govan and Bridgeton. In 1833, 74 of the total of 134 mills were mostly in the city; Renfrewshire had 41 and with Lanarkshire had over three-quarters of Scotland's spindles. The concentration was accompanied by a slackening in construction. After the boom of 1825, though expansion was still undertaken when required by improvements in machinery, new spinning-mills were generally offshoots of new weaving establishments. The adoption of power-loom instead of hand-loom weaving led some merchants, previously concerned only with the organisation of hand-loom weavers, to become power-loom manufacturers and at the same time to build spinning-mills to supply their own power looms with yarn.

The construction of the large mills was usually the work of a few individuals, frequently linen merchants. Notable among them was David Dale, better known, perhaps, for his philanthropic than for his industrial interests. From being a weaver, Dale became one of Glasgow's most important importers of fine foreign yarn for the linen weavers and controlled a large number of weavers working domestically throughout the west of Scotland. Dale's partnerships and associations show the widespread interest in the new possibilities of spinning from which he was able to draw support. Richard Arkwright was associated with his decision to build at New Lanark; at Blantyre he combined with James Monteith, the pioneer of the manufacture of muslins in Glasgow, who had similar industrial interests, mainly in Anderston; at Catrine his partner was Claud Alexander of Ballochmyle, a laird home from the east with capital to spare and with land near a good supply of water; at his far-flung ventures at Spinningdale in Sutherland and at Newton Stewart in Wigtownshire, he was in partnership with, among others, George Dempster and Sir William Douglas respectively. Dale's chief rival, the Buchanan family, had a similar background. Like Dale, they imported the fine yarn the Scottish weavers required, and so, when the new technology provided the opportunity, were also able to move easily to cotton-spinning. In 1785 they built the Deanston works in Perthshire and a few years later, in partnership with Robert Dunmore, sometime a Virginian merchant but by then laird of Ballindalloch and Ballikinrain, they built the Ballindalloch works near Balfron. The smaller mills which appeared after 1790 often continued a tradition of local enterprise, evident from the first days of the new technology. The larger ventures were located on sites which offered special advantages of water power as at New Lanark, Deanston, Catrine, and Blantyre, but the smaller mills were located in a particular area simply because their projectors lived there. They ranged in size and activities from small workshops, in which a number of hand-operated spinning jennies were gathered, to water twist mills. The more primitive establishments had a limited life and few survived long, but the smaller water twist mills did continue, though primarily only in those areas which had such special advantages for cotton production that they brought the founders of the larger mills to the same district.

Though larger mills — Deanston, Catrine, New Lanark and others — were individually the most evident illustrations of the new Scottish cotton industry, the numerous smaller mills were more representative of its development. Many, if not most, of the smaller mills were buildings converted from other uses, a process which was not always cheap. One estimate, for example, shows that between £3,000 and £4,000 was required for the conversion of an old sugar house of seven storeys to house about 9,360 spindles. The old mill at Neilston was a conversion of this kind. The spinning of cotton began in 1780 in what had been originally an old corn mill at Dovecothall on the banks of the Levern. The old mill was 54 feet long and 24 feet broad and had three storeys, each 8 feet high. In 1800 another mill, 123 feet long and 32½ feet broad, with five storeys, was added, and in 1834 yet another, 113 feet long and 40 feet broad, until in this way a unit of considerable size was gradually erected. Its success led to the construction of others: Gateside in 1786; Broadlie in 1790; Arthurlie in 1791; Crofthead in 1792; and Graham's mill in 1801. The experience of the parish of Lochwinnoch, on the other side of the Cart Valley, was similar. In the *New Statistical Account*, the parish minister reported that the old mill, built about 1788, had five storeys with 8,140 spindles, while the new mill, again with five storeys, had 25,224 spindles. In addition there were two small mills, one of which, where the jennies were worked by hand, did not last long; the other was burnt down in 1813. The experiences of these two parishes were common to many in Lanarkshire, Renfrewshire and Ayrshire, indeed wherever there were adequate water supplies. They were transformed by the mills, of whatever type, bringing new activities, and new ways of life, into what had been rural parishes, though with a number of the inhabitants already engaged in textile production. Even before the development of cotton-spinning, Lochwinnoch had a linen mill, thread mills and, because of its good water supply, a number of bleachfields, as well as a large number of weavers working for Glasgow merchants on linen cloths, silk gauze, and, from the 1780s, on muslins. The importance of all was eclipsed by the cotton mills.

A mill converted to other uses in an old community never had the same dramatic effect as a completely new construction or settlement, but of these early major enterprises so little now remains that it is difficult to envisage what they meant to contemporaries. In Glasgow even names have been lost in development as with Carding Lane and Warp Lane, which used to run from Stobcross Street to Argyle Street near Anderston Cross. At Blantyre more substantial evidence remains, especially through the preservation, as the centre of the David Livingstone Memorial, of a good example of the tenements in which the cotton operatives lived. At New Lanark the complete transformation wrought on virgin sites is still evident and gives excellent visual evidence of a planned industrial village. The proposal for a cotton mill at New Lanark may have originated with either Dale or Arkwright, as the latter visited Scotland in 1783; but in the following year Dale feued a low-lying and marshy stretch of land, with the supreme advantage of access to ample supplies of water from the Clyde. The barrenness of the site, combined with the difficulty of securing adequate supplies of labour, required the construction of a completely new settlement. Since the building area was limited, the dwelling-houses had of necessity to be built upwards, much higher than was common in most of the textile areas of Scotland at the time, and more in keeping with the traditions of building in some of the older Scottish towns and in the new and overcrowded cities. The first mill started spinning in 1786 and expansion continued in spite of the setback of fire, so common in many of the early mills. The history of Catrine is similar. It was not such a barren site as was New Lanark. Its general attraction was that Claud Alexander, with his fortune made in the service of the East India Company, lived at adjacent Ballochmyle; its specific attraction, as at New Lanark, was the presence of an adequate supply of water from the river Ayr. Again as with New Lanark, Catrine was an ideal example of a planned factory town. The local quarries supplied the red sandstone with which the town was built in a regular pattern. Subsidiary roads led into a main street, down which flowed the lade from the mill, a massive five-storeyed building with attics, containing 5,240 spindles and standing in the centre of a square. This pattern remained virtually untouched for many years.

The increased output of yarn from the new spinning-mills transferred the bottleneck in production from spinning to weaving. The widespread use of the power loom came only slowly, partly because it required adjustment and improvement, partly because of the general lack of capital investment at the time. As improved by Horrocks and Radcliffe, it was used successfully at Catrine in 1807; and after the end of the war, and especially in the boom of 1825, investment in the cotton industry was mainly in power-weaving. By 1831 about 15,000 power looms were working in over 60 establishments. The existence from the 1780s to 1800, and even later, of a bottleneck in weaving gave a temporary boost to demand for the services of the hand-loom weavers, who, while mostly still working domestically, were employed full-time. Consequently, numerous villages in Renfrewshire, Stirlingshire, Ayrshire and Lanarkshire, which until then had been only agricultural hamlets clustering round a parish church, began to acquire additional housing. The cottages, sometimes of two storeys (or one and an attic), or sometimes with a common close between them and a weaver's shed in the garden, have mostly been demolished, though at Kilbarchan some weavers' cottages have been preserved. These were primarily the villages which often acquired a few larger buildings, long since converted to other uses, in which small-scale establishments carried on spinning and weaving. In some of these a few hand looms, probably only about six, were gathered together and the weavers employed by a master, in contrast to the majority of their fellows who operated independently on commission for merchants or large manufacturers.

Success and decline in the cotton industry

In the nineteenth century a new generation soon dominated the cotton industry. Of this second generation perhaps the best known was David Dale's son-in-law

D

Robert Owen. A more permanent contribution to the growth of the Scottish cotton industry in the nineteenth century came from Kirkman Finlay, the background of whose father, James Finlay, was similar to those of Dale and the Buchanans. The father's firm, James Finlay and Company, specialised in exporting textile goods to the Continent, and from this position Kirkman Finlay easily acquired control of a major part of the Scottish cotton industry. By entering into partnership with the Buchanans he gained a share of Deanston, and later added to his interests the mills at Catrine in 1822, and in 1825 those at Ballindalloch which the Buchanans had sold when they entered the partnership with Finlay. James Finlay and Company thus became, and remained, the major concern in the Scottish cotton industry.

Imports of raw cotton rose sharply at the end of the eighteenth century: in 1778, over 200,000 lbs; in 1788, over 1,500,000 lbs; in 1798, over 2,800,000 lbs; in 1801, nearly 7,550,000 lbs. The confidence of the period of rapid mill construction from the 1780s to the early nineteenth century continued, and the industry withstood the interruptions of the outbreak of war and years of declining demand as in 1788, 1789, 1803 and 1810. In evidence before the Select Committee on Manufactures, Commerce and Shipping in 1833, Kirkman Finlay explained the resilience of the industry by the absence of foreign competition, an accurate general evaluation, if one that erred in some particulars:

> When I first entered into business extensively, which was in 1792, there was no manufacture of cotton of any importance in any part out of Great Britain. There were, perhaps, some domestic cotton manufactures carried on abroad, but there were no finer fabrics of any kind. I believe my house was amongst the first that ever exported cotton manufactures of fine fabrics generally to the continent of Europe, to Germany, to Italy, to France, and to Switzerland. In those times there was no cotton manufacture in France at all; none in Switzerland worth speaking of; none in any part of Germany. Then the practice came to export cotton twist; and I think it was about the year 1794 or 1795 when we first began to export a good deal of cotton twist. At that time there was no cotton twist spun in any part of Germany.[1]

To the favourable environment of little effective foreign competition, the industry made its own contribution towards success by maintaining the cheapness of its products. The new technology enabled the cotton industry to reduce prices even with higher labour and raw materials costs during the war. At the end of the eighteenth century the fall in raw material prices following the introduction of the cotton gin in the United States also helped to keep costs down.

Recent calculations of the amount of capital invested in the industry differ, but, being a new demand on limited resources, the expansion of the industry could be sustained only with the support of landowners and others with capital to spare. The industry, and especially the growth of its export trade, was encouraged still further by the willingness of the Scottish banks to provide ready finance for exports. Goods were sent overseas on consignment and bills drawn on the purchaser were discounted more readily by banks in Glasgow than by those in Manchester or London. In addition, while in England bills were generally not discountable unless drawn for goods sold, the Scottish banks were willing to discount bills issued to cover intermediate transactions, as, for instance, those granted by manufacturers to spinners for yarn. Still more generously, they discounted what were virtually accommodation bills, provided the drawer and the endorser were of good credit standing. The export trade depended on this extended credit base, but a corollary was the resulting difficulty of maintaining exports when monetary derangements supervened, even when Scottish banks continued ready to grant discounts though losing heavily on some of them. An example came in 1812. Initially the embargoes and restrictions which culminated in the Continental System in 1810 were circumvented and new markets exploited, as in South America. Recovery, which began in 1808, was halted only with the stringent restrictions of 1810. With the collapse of many of their markets, especially in South America, exporting merchants could not meet bills due to manufacturers, while the banks, many of which had given credit on them, were unable to increase their advances when the bills returned on the manufacturers. The structure of credit in Glasgow collapsed in a series of bankruptcies in the summer of 1812, with repercussions beyond the cotton industry, especially when for a time the banks adopted a more stringent policy towards all advances. Recovery on the basis of a revival of exports to the United States was interrupted by the outbreak of war with America. At the end of 1816 Glasgow was reported to be suffering from unparalleled distress, relieved only by general charitable subscriptions, while the manager of Catrine held that profits in the previous seven years had failed to provide an adequate return on capital. The Scottish cotton industry had reached the end of its phase of unqualified successful development. Thereafter it faced increased competition from both home and foreign producers.

Once again Kirkman Finlay was able to give a striking picture of the changed conditions which faced the industry after the end of the war in 1815:

> Now there is not a single country in which there is not a great manufacture of cotton carried on. There is a very extensive spinning carried on in Switzerland; there is a very extensive spinning carried on in Austria, and a large cotton manufacture carried on there. By the recent accounts it appears that the Government has relaxed a little the prohibition against cotton twist, and that it may be introduced in future on the payment of a moderate duty. Their manufacture has, in my recollection, entirely grown up. The French manufacture, which did not exist at all at the period I first spoke of, in 1792, and which was very inconsiderable at the conclusion of the peace in 1814, when I was in France, and saw it, has become of late very formidable; and by the means that are taken, as I understand, by the regulation of the drawback, by which the manufacturer receives more amount of drawback than he pays of duty, there is a very formidable advantage given to the French manufacturer by that fiscal regulation.[2]

In general Finlay was right. The undermining of the favourable comparative cost position of the Scottish cotton industry through the development of native industries was bound to have adverse repercussions on large sectors of the Scottish industry which depended on export markets. Two other changes confirmed the weakness and insecurity of the Scottish position. First, competition arose from some of the new producers entering markets in other countries which did not yet have domestic production, but which had previously been Scottish preserves. A Glasgow cotton spinner, William Graham, discussing this in 1833, showed the spread of such competition from the United States:

> In Mexico for the last five or six years largely; to the Brazils considerably, Buenos Ayres and Cape Horn also considerably, and at Valparaiso; I think their imports of the stouter manufactures are larger than ours; and in Manilla and in Singapore they have also made their appearance. Also from St. Domingo, where we have done considerable business, we have lately had letters, expressing great surprise tnat the Americans should be competing with us.[3]

Second, and perhaps even more serious for the industry's long-term prospects, were signs of declining competitiveness within Great Britain. In such circumstances increasing competition in foreign markets brought even greater losses to the Scots than to the Lancashire producers. To some, including Kirkman Finlay, Lancashire was superior only in those branches of cotton production in which it had also specialised, but, even if Finlay's interpretation was true, and so Scottish failures in one field could be offset by successes in others, problems were still liable to emerge in the long run if demand for the special products of Scotland proved less stable. Others, among them Henry Houldsworth, a Mancunian long resident in Glasgow, were much less self-satisfied and held that Lancashire led in all fields. Perhaps Finlay and Houldsworth were prejudiced in their respective ways, but others, among them some of the operatives who gave evidence to various parliamentary commissioners on their conditions of employment, believed that by the 1830s the rate of profit was lower in Scotland than in England. Lastly, in the introduction of mechanised and improved methods of production the Scots quickly became dependent on Manchester. Lancashire gained a lead which it surrendered only to the United States.

The only period after the Napoleonic Wars when the Scottish cotton industry was as buoyant as ever before was in the boom of 1825. A slight increase in economic activity in 1818 only arrested the downward movement in prices, which had been evident since the end of the war. The speculation of 1825 led to a rapid expansion of industrial capacity, most notably in the number of power looms, which increased throughout the 1820s from 2,000 to 10,000, and was sufficient in some minds to lead to excess capacity in the industry. Kirkman Finlay shared the opinion and characterised the period as 'one of great extension, of a rapid sale and activity, but making very moderate returns of profit'; 'stocks on hand are inconsiderable; the payments are good'. While his large, well-established firm was in good shape, others with limited capital resources found survival less easy as profit margins lessened. The industry never regained the prosperity, speculative as it was, of 1825. It shared in the boom which began in 1833 and which lasted until 1836, but much less so in that of 1845; from 1845 it stagnated. In 1831, 1,652 bales of raw cotton were used weekly in Scotland; in 1835, 2,035 bales were used; in 1840 consumption was 2,364 bales.[4] Thereafter the trend, though it fluctuated until the American Civil War, was stable. An apparent resurgence of production came in 1866, after the war, when 2,500 bales of raw cotton were used weekly in Scotland, but the quantity fell to 1,700 bales in the following year. For the next decade the average weekly consumption in Scotland varied from 1,500 to 2,000 bales. Stocks of raw cotton in Glasgow in the 1830s were normally over 20,000 packets, but were twice as much in the 1840s, touching 80,000 packets in 1845; they collapsed in the mid-1850s and were never again of any significance. Scotland obtained all the cotton it required from Liverpool. As it stagnated, the industry became more concentrated. In 1838, 198 cotton mills employed over 35,500 people; in 1850, 168 mills, with 1,683,000 spindles and over 23,500 power looms, employed 36,325 people; in 1856, 152 mills, with over 2,041,000 spindles and over 21,000 power looms, employed 34,698 people; in 1861, 163 mills, with nearly 1,915,400 spindles and over 30,100 power looms, employed 41,287 people. After 1861 the number of mills decreased still further. Lanarkshire and Renfrewshire continued to be the most important centres of the industry. In 1838, of the 198 mills Lanarkshire had 111 and Renfrewshire had 60. In 1861 Lanarkshire had 96 and Renfrewshire 44 of the 163 mills.

The expansion of the cotton industry in the early nineteenth century marked a change from its origins. Initially it had specialised in the production of finer quality goods. The increasing output of the early nineteenth century was chiefly of printed calicoes and coarser fabrics. By 1818 heavier fabrics were about 80 per cent of the value of cotton exports; a quarter of a century earlier fine muslins had accounted for about two-thirds of their value. The move proved unwise in the long run. As the Scottish product became less differentiated, the Scots encountered direct competition from Lancashire, Europe, and the United States.

With the emergence of foreign competition in the market for coarser cloths in the 1820s, the Scots responded by trying to increase production at lower cost. The move was unsuccessful. Increased production merely led to still lower profit margins, with adverse effects on the industry's technical performance. Funds for investment were limited, and the lack of an adequate home market restricted the production of textile machinery in Scotland. Much of the machinery then installed for the manufacture of coarse and medium-grade yarns was not of Scottish design. The inability to maintain technical leadership forced the industry to rely increasingly on the support of cheap labour, which it was enabled to do in the second quarter of the nineteenth century through the use of the plentiful supply of Irish and other migrants and by a major confrontation with the Cotton Operatives' Union over substantial wage reductions in the 1830s. When the Union was finally broken with the transportation of its leaders, the cotton industry — for good or ill — experienced a phase of tranquillity in its labour relations and was based firmly on low wages. Any possibility of its future prosperity resting on technical achievement had been surrendered and prosperity depended on the support of the availability of cheap labour. Greater competitiveness was not achieved in the long run. In the 1830s, when the industry was still expanding, Kirkman Finlay's complaints about the extent of competition were underlined when some producers left the industry. The increased production of less specialised goods was shown to be a move in a direction which was not likely to hold out prospects of any permanent relief from international competitive pressure. It was only a remedy of despair.

The intense competition encountered in the move led the Scots to return from the 1840s in part to the production of more specialised lines, though not to return to the same high-quality products on which the Scottish cotton industry had been originally built. Power-weaving grew in Scotland from the 1840s to the 1860s to allow the production of better quality calicoes which had become totally uneconomic for the handloom weavers as the Lancashire producers moved into that sphere. The move towards a higher quality product provided only a temporary reprieve from the growing competition. The weakness of the industry in these circumstances was soon revealed. The need for credit in an expanding but insecurely based industry is not surprising. With credit extended to some firms, as by the Western Bank, any collapse in the financial arrangements had disastrous repercussions for their creditors. That was the position in 1857, when the Western Bank failed. Its experience is a reflection of the state of the industry rather than the cause of the industry's collapse. The cotton industry was in straitened circumstances even before the 1857 crisis or the cotton famine which marked the American Civil War. These two external events, which have often been used to explain the end of the industry's prosperity, were more the public occasions when its private difficulties were revealed. The 1857 crisis is the more significant. The cotton famine was bound to have a harmful effect, at least temporarily, on the cotton industry, no matter how profitable its production, and from it recovery was possible. The 1857 financial crisis showed the speculative and unstable nature of much recent expansion in the cotton industry.

It is easier to explain than to justify the collapse of the Scottish cotton industry. Was it inevitable? Could it have been avoided? Were the Scots to blame? Such questions were frequently avoided, because the rise of the heavy industries prevented the decline of the cotton industry from having obviously detrimental effects on the Scottish economy overall and so gave the impression merely of industrial displacement. But one factor is evident. The Scottish cotton manufacturers themselves did not transfer to the new and developing industries, with the partial exception of the Houldsworths. If they had done so, no accusation of lack of enterprise could have been levelled against them. Their actions would have demonstrated a high degree of resilience. Of course the Scottish cotton manufacturers, unlike their rivals in Lancashire, suffered from competition for labour and capital from the newer industries, but it is impossible to say that such competition for resources from the heavy industries accounts for the failure, and ultimate collapse, of the cotton industry in Scotland. It is possible that the growth of the heavy industries in the west of Scotland made a certain lack of enterprise on the part of the cotton manufacturers less evident. Scottish producers were slower to adopt newer mechanised methods and frequently depended on Lancashire for the machinery they used. Such factors were of minor importance. The industry could never regain its international leadership.

Other textile industries

The cotton industry encouraged the further growth of the ancillary activities in textile manufacture of bleaching, printing and embroidery. In addition in the nineteenth century the ancient woollen industry developed its own specialisation and the jute industry was established.

Bleaching was concentrated in the Vale of Leven in Dunbartonshire and in the Cart Valley in Renfrewshire. Both had adequate supplies of lime-free water, and the Vale of Leven was especially fortunate in being able to draw from Loch Lomond. The Vale of Leven had the additional advantage of having a ready supply of labour from the Highlands, from which many came during the summer as seasonal migrants and some of whom settled there. The greatest drawback to the satisfactory bleaching of cloth was its expense. The Board of Trustees assisted notably by grants of £50 an acre for the laying out of fields for bleaching by the more labour-intensive Dutch method, but its aid made only a marginal contribution. Bleaching required large areas of land, which had to be laid out and suitably watered; the process was lengthy, the cloth requiring about eight months' exposure, reduced later to only about four months; it was a seasonal occupation only, which required a large temporary labour force. Fortunately, before the large-scale expansion of cotton manufacturing, new methods of bleaching by chemical processes were devised. James Watt is reputed to have suggested the first use of Berthollet's method of chlorine bleaching at the Clober bleachfield in Dunbartonshire in 1787, but a further improvement came in 1799 through the introduction by Charles Tennant of the method of bleaching by chloride of lime. Coinciding as it did with the expansion of the cotton industry, the process was quickly adopted, until, shortly after the beginning of the nineteenth century, the west of Scotland had about sixty bleachworks using the chloride of lime method. As a corollary to the development of the new methods of bleaching, the growth of the chemical industry in Scotland was fostered. Charles Tennant founded the St. Rollox works beside the Monkland Canal to manufacture his bleaching powder (chloride of lime), and in due course St. Rollox became the largest chemical works in Europe.

The growth of bleaching was partnered by that of printing, the branch of the textile industries to which, more perhaps than to any other, Glasgow merchants made their greatest direct contribution. It was encouraged after 1707 by a prohibition on the import and use of Eastern prints, but suffered from the imposition in 1712 of an excise duty of 3s. a square yard, which was doubled two years later. Because the continued popularity of printed calicoes was thought to threaten ruin for the wool and silk industries, linen alone could be printed from the 1720s until 1736 when mixed goods were allowed. Even under such conditions printing was introduced to Scotland, as in the foundation of a large works at Pollokshaws in 1742, and it gained from the growth of cotton production, the removal of any remaining prohibitions on printing in 1774 (though the excise duty remained until 1831), and the increased technical efficiency of the industry following the invention of cylinder printing by Thomas Bell of Glasgow in 1785. Once again Renfrewshire and the Vale of Leven had the advantages of adequate supplies of water and of labour cheaper than could be obtained nearer Glasgow, and so the printworks moved there. In the 1730s William Stirling moved from Dalsholm on the Kelvin to Cordale in the Vale of Leven and the Crums from the Gallowgate in Glasgow to Renfrewshire.

Dyeing was the third subsidiary industry which expanded in line with the growth of cotton production. Glasgow and Manchester both claimed the distinction of being first in Britain to introduce Turkey Red dyeing, but both acknowledged French assistance. At Manchester Louis Borelle received a government grant of £2,500. Shortly afterwards another Frenchman, P. J. Papillon, went to Glasgow and, with George Macintosh, father of Charles, was more successful. Colour could be applied only to yarn and thread until yet another Frenchman devised a way of dyeing the cloth in 1810. Whatever its origins, Scotland soon secured a monopoly of Turkey Red dyeing. As was to be expected, the process was most quickly and permanently established in the bleaching-fields of the Vale of Leven, where it was first used successfully at Croftingea in 1827. Its use spread. Production was soon concentrated in the nineteenth century, and most of the Vale of Leven's industry came to be concentrated in eleven works controlled by nine firms.

The growth of the textile industries encouraged two more specialised products: first, sewed muslin, embroidery or tambouring, as the process was sometimes called, after the circular frames on which the cloth was stretched for embroidery, and, second, the Paisley shawl. The former proved exceptionally profitable when sewed muslin became an acceptable substitute for lace at the end of the eighteenth century. When the outlines of the patterns to be sewn were imprinted by blocks, the cost of manufacturing limited the range of designs, but after 1837 printing by the lithographic press increased the variety. Exports of sewed muslin rose especially between 1845 and 1857. Even earlier a few Glasgow firms gave out work to be done by women in their own homes, mainly in Ayrshire, where schools were set up for the sewers, and where the end of domestic spinning gave a ready supply of female labour. Cheaper Irish domestic workers were also employed, but the rapid expansion of demand for sewed muslin in the second quarter of the nineteenth century meant little unemployment for any, and there was never any tendency for the headquarters of the trade to shift from Glasgow. Indeed one Donaghadee firm, which first introduced the lithographic process of printing the designs, moved its headquarters to Glasgow during the period of most rapid expansion. The break in prosperity came in the financial crisis of 1857. Expansion was probably too rapid and unwise after 1845, when cheap domestic labour in Ireland enabled muslin to be sewn there more cheaply than ever before. The leading firm in the industry, D. and J. McDonald, though supported in its increased activities by the Western Bank, was eventually forced to adopt a variety of dubious expedients to maintain its credit, but to no avail. In the autumn of 1857 McDonald's collapsed, carrying the Western Bank with it. Widespread unemployment among muslin sewers in both Ayrshire and the north of Ireland followed. The Scottish sewed muslin trade never recovered. The manufacture of the Paisley shawl, a similar fashionable product, was established in the early years of the nineteenth century among Paisley's highly skilled weavers, who found in this occupation a temporary remedy for their displacement by the power loom. Though first made of cotton, the finer shawls were latterly made of spun silk and were, therefore, so subject to fluctuations of trade and fashion that one local historian estimated that in the depression of the early 1840s more than half of the manufacturing concerns in the burgh collapsed.

Though overshadowed by the cotton industry in the earlier nineteenth century, jute and woollen manufacture survived more successfully than cotton into the twentieth century. Earlier textile production in Dundee and district was limited by the absence of water power, but by the beginning of the nineteenth century steam-driven mills were established and started to spin tow, the waste produced when flax was dressed, instead of flax. Subsequently hemp spinning was introduced, and in the 1830s depression led the industry into the use of jute, helped especially when Dundee obtained the benefit of a reduction in the price of jute following direct trade with India in 1839. Technical changes also encouraged the transfer to the newer fibre. In 1848 James Aytoun of Kirkcaldy devised a method which enabled jute yarns to be woven without sizing, and a new method of carding was invented in 1853. When the Crimean and American Civil Wars both provided the stimulus of a sharp increase in demand, Dundee had almost a complete monopoly of world production. In 1875 it imported nearly 114,000 tons of jute, 22,500 tons of flax and 6,500 tons of tow. The expansion of imports was matched by an increase in capacity, especially in the boom of the early 1870s. In 1870 there were 94,520 spindles and 3,744 looms in the Scottish jute industry, virtually all of them in Dundee; in 1874 there were 185,419 spindles and 8,325 looms. During the same period the employment in the industry more than doubled from almost 15,000 to almost 38,000. The industry's expansion had then reached its peak.

The woollen industry's origins were ancient. Its growth had been encouraged before the parliamentary union and, though less favoured than the linen industry, the Board of Trustees devoted some effort and finance to its improvement in the eighteenth century. Its transformation came in the nineteenth century when it was able to specialise successfully in higher quality production, notably in three branches: the manufacture of tweeds, hosiery and carpets. The growth of the Border tweed industry, centred especially on Galashiels, was helped by the coincidence in time of the use of the power loom in the manufacture of narrow cloths, the exploitation of fashionable demand through the use of different patterns, and the availability of supplies of wool from Australia, New Zealand and South America. Consequently, many of the Border mills were built in the middle of the nineteenth century. In 1851, 72 tweed factories used 329 power looms and 225 sets of carding engines; in 1862, 82 mills used 1,069 power looms and 305 sets of carding engines. Hosiery work was less prominent. It played an important part in the local economies of Hawick, where the stocking frame was probably first introduced to Scotland, and, to a lesser extent, of Dumfries. Once again, the increase of the industry was concentrated in the early nineteenth century. In 1791 Hawick had twelve knitting frames; by 1844 it had about 1,200. The manufacture of carpets grew from the work of Thomas Morton of Kilmarnock, and later of James Templeton of Glasgow, and also received encouragement from the Board of Trustees for Manufacturers, when by the early nineteenth century it was turning its attention from the linen industry to other branches of the economy. By granting various premiums the Board facilitated the introduction into Scotland of the manufacture of carpets comparable to Brussels and Turkish make. Kilmarnock was quickly established as the centre of the industry, and by 1839 carpet manufacturing in the town employed about 1,200 persons, who produced goods valued at about £150,000.

NOTES

1. *Select Committee on Manufactures, Commerce and Shipping*, 1833. Q. 652. British Parliamentary Papers. 1833. VI.

2. *Select Committee on Manufactures, Commerce and Shipping*, 1833. Q. 652.

3. *Select Committee on Manufactures, Commerce and Shipping*, 1833, Q. 5451.

4. With the end of the Scottish Board of Customs, separate information on imports of cotton wool to Scotland cease. The figures used in this paragraph come from the Clyde Sugar Market Reports in the Mitchell Library, Glasgow. The terms 'bales' and 'packets' are not satisfactorily explained, but were used consistently, and so give a reasonable indication of relative movements.

CHAPTER VII

The Heavy Industries

The rise of the iron industry

The dominating influence of the heavy industries, which became an accepted feature of Scottish economic life, emerged only in the later nineteenth century. Structural changes in the economy, starting around 1830, ushered in the new era.

The modern Scottish iron industry was pioneered by Carron Company when it was founded in 1759 to smelt with coke and use both the coal and ironstone of Scotland. Though its revolutionary methods were not followed immediately, its influence on subsequent efforts was soon evident. The Scottish iron industry's first expansion owed much to Thomas Edington, sometime traveller with Carron Company and later manager of the slitting-mill at Cramond. Edington helped to promote iron-smelting ventures, first, in 1786 at the Clyde ironworks in partnership with William Cadell and, second, in 1787 at Muirkirk, where he was associated, though in a subordinate way, with partners of the established Dalnotter and Smithfield works. Muirkirk was practically a co-operative venture by Scotland's leading ironmasters, a form of enterprise which was to have a conspicuous, though not wholly successful, record in the Scottish iron industry in the nineteenth century. Though Carron, Clyde and Muirkirk provided the nucleus from which all branches of the Scottish iron industry grew, they had certain features not typical of later developments. Unlike many later firms, they produced more than pig iron. From its inception Carron Company was basically a firm of ironfounders and had forges for the production of bar and malleable iron; Clyde was formed by Edington partly to try to obviate Carron's need to import bar iron from Sweden and Russia; Muirkirk quickly became the Scottish ironworks which specialised most of all in the manufacture of bar iron for sale. Its produce, according to the almost certainly biased report of the parish minister, was 'little if at all inferior to the best Swedish iron'.[1] Four other ironworks, all less successful, date from the same period of development: Wilsontown (1779), Cleland or Omoa (1789), Devon (1792), and Glenbuck (1795). After a short interval Calder, Shotts and Markinch followed at the turn of the century. During the Napoleonic Wars many of these works found themselves in difficulties. Glenbuck, Wilsontown and Markinch became bankrupt, while at Muirkirk a strong effort was made to sell the works to the landlord on moderate terms. Some of these ironworks operated under disadvantageous conditions. The location of Wilsontown was determined by the availability of coal and ironstone, but its inaccessible position required iron to be taken on horse-drawn carts to Bo'ness and to Glasgow. Failures of the period were not always permanent. Though the Wilsontown works were deserted from 1812 to 1821, Dixon of Govan and Calder continued them thereafter until 1842, during which period the manager, John Condie, made the first satisfactory water-cooled tuyère, an advance necessary for the fullest exploitation of the hot-blast. In spite of such qualifications, the relative lack of prosperity of much of the Scottish iron industry cannot be denied. The contrast with conditions in England was striking, even more so with the resounding successes then being demonstrated at Carron, the one highly successful Scottish concern. After the war, at the peak of the boom of 1825, when the iron industry elsewhere in Britain was expanding, the only developments in Scotland were the flotation of the Shotts ironworks as a joint-stock company and the start of the erection of furnaces at Chapelhall by the Monkland Steel Company.

The major defect of the Scottish iron industry lay in its high fuel costs. In 1829 the cost of production of one ton of pig iron at Clyde was 82s; at Calder it was 78s. J. B. Neilson could argue that 'unless as much as £6 per ton could be obtained for iron no profit was realised, on account of the heavy expenses attending the furnaces'.[2] Success lay in lowering production costs or in developing specialised finished products such as those on which the success of Carron Company had been built. For a variety of reasons, the second alternative was difficult and was not to happen. The production of pig iron, and not further processing, was the basis of the modern Scottish iron industry.

The necessary reduction in costs came through the exploitation of the west of Scotland's natural resources of coal and ironstone. Since their discovery by David Mushet in 1801, the rich and low-rented fields of blackband ironstone had been little used except at Calder and later at Clyde, where, however, the blackband was mixed with other ores. At first the use of the blackband ironstone led to little saving, since its advantages were considerably offset by the difficulty of smelting it when using cold air in the small furnaces which were then common. Making possible the profitable, indeed the highly profitable, use of this was the great work of the hot-blast, patented by J. B. Neilson in 1828. The hot-blast and the blackband ironstone provided respectively the technical and the geological bases for the low production costs of the Scottish iron industry. With the introduction of the hot-blast, coal consumption was cut by at least 50 per cent and costs fell rapidly, especially when from 1831 it became general practice to substitute raw coal, especially non-caking splint coal, for coke. At Muirkirk, coal consumption fell from 7¼ to 2¼ tons per ton of iron produced, and at the works of the Monkland Company it fell from 7½ to 2 tons. This major reduction in fuel costs was helped still further by two other factors operating at the same time. First, mineral royalties were low, since, like many others, the landlords of the west of Scotland failed at first to appreciate the immense economic importance of their ironstone fields and in the early days leased them to the ironmasters for what was later to seem only a nominal royalty. A common lordship for the smaller fields of ironstone was from 1s. to 2s. per calcined ton of 22½ cwt. with a very low annual rental of £100 to £200 in the years when the field was being worked. Second, the price of labour was low.

In Scotland many Irishmen and Highlanders were available to keep wages down. Since labour and mineral royalties were the chief components of the prime costs of iron production, it is not surprising that Scottish firms at this time were reputedly producing at 27s. 6d. a ton. At Muirkirk pig iron was once produced at 25s. per ton, though there the cost of minerals was unusually small, the lordship on coal being only 1d. per ton and that on ironstone only 3d. per ton. A more representative comparison may be made with conditions at Clyde and Calder. In 1833 at Clyde the normal cost of production was 49s. 6d. per ton; at Calder it was 47s. 6d., coal accounting for only 20 per cent of the total cost, a fall of about 40 per cent from 1829.

On the basis of such favourable natural endowments the iron industry was able to exploit the buoyant demand of the mid-eighteenth century. In Scotland the engineering firms and the foundries, working in many cases for overseas customers, provided a ready market. In addition, throughout England engineers bought Scottish hot-blast iron for the first time and were satisfied. Previously Scotch pig iron had always been priced higher than Welsh in the Liverpool market, but after the introduction of the hot-blast it was priced lower, and rose to be the market's most important feature. At Liverpool in July 1833 it was quoted at £4 15s. a ton while Staffordshire iron sold at £6. In Sheffield its quality was found to be 'exceedingly good' and the price, even with transport costs added, was so low that at the end of April 1834 the Yorkshire and Derbyshire ironmasters were forced to reduce No. 1 pig iron by 10s. per ton and Nos. 2 and 3 by 7s. 6d. Some criticism appeared. Hot-blast iron was held to be insufficiently strong, especially for large castings, and was disliked by marine engineers. Some specifications, including government ordnance, excluded its use. But those who were doubtful of its strength were convinced by its price. At Muirkirk in 1839, because of complaints about the hot-blast, 221 tons of cold-blast iron were made; Robert Napier took 54 tons and two other customers 29 tons between them, but the rest had to be used in the works itself for malleable iron and castings. At a price which was 30s. a ton higher than the hot-blast iron, it was unsaleable. With its outlook and prospects thus changed, the Scottish iron trade moved forward from stagnation towards prosperity and expansion. By the invention of the hot-blast the trade was 'saved from certain ruin'.[3] More positively, the foundation was then laid for the subsequent rapid expansion of the iron industry. The number of furnaces increased from 27 in 1830 to over 100 in 1844 and the output of pig iron from 37,500 tons to just under 400,000 tons. In the early 1860s the number of furnaces in Scotland reached its peak, though output continued to follow its almost continuous ascent until the record production for the nineteenth century of over 1,200,000 tons in 1870. More strikingly, the increase was not shared by the iron industry of Britain as a whole. Scottish output rose from 5 per cent of the total British output in 1830 to over 25 per cent in the middle 1840s, above which proportion it stayed, almost without a break, for two decades.

The leading pioneers of the iron industry's growth were the Bairds of Gartsherrie. Their first furnace went into blast in May 1830 and produced 3,100 tons of pig iron in the first year. They built a second furnace in September 1832, and a third in April 1834, when they decided to build four more. They also 'purchased every foot of ground which they can obtain in the neighbourhood and have likewise taken leases of what could not be bought'.[4] The Bairds became the leading Scottish producers, making 25 per cent of the total output. They took the greatest risk in exploiting the innovation and, as it was successful, made large profits, almost £270,000 between 1832 and 1840. In 1856 an American described them as 'princely proprietors . . . the richest manufacturers in the world'.[5] By the 1870s they were reputed to be earning £750,000 a year, while in size Gartsherrie was second only to Dowlais. Two other works, both involved in early experiments with blackband ironstone, were also active in the first phase of the expansion. Calder had four furnaces in 1830; Chapelhall (the Monkland Iron and Steel Company) had two. These successes encouraged others to extend their capacity. In 1831 the Monkland Iron and Steel Company built a third furnace at Chapelhall; in 1833 Colin Dunlop from Clyde and John Wilson started Dundyvan, which was to be Gartsherrie's rival in size, and took a large area near Coatbridge to work for minerals; Wilsontown, which had had a chequered career and disappointed many hopes, was re-opened in April 1834 by Dixon of Calder, who had purchased it some years previously, but had soon closed it down. Omoa, 'which had been a scene of desolation for a number of years',[6] was restarted at the beginning of 1833. In June of that year six furnaces were being built in Scotland by established producers, three at Gartsherrie and one each at Calder, Dundyvan and Calderbank. In November the Shotts Iron Company resolved to build a second furnace but postponed its operation for two years through a shortage of minerals. The blackband ironstone was leased equally rapidly. On the Hamilton Estates in north Lanarkshire almost all the ironmasters were eagerly prospecting for it, while in central Scotland three pieces of land, which the Duke of Hamilton thought of adding to his possessions, exceeded any price his representative considered worth offering, mainly because of competition from the ironmasters, Dixon and the Houldsworths.

Even a fall in prices and a gradual decline into depression between 1837 and 1843 did not stop the capital investment in the industry, which, on one estimate, almost doubled from 1836 to over £6,000,000 in 1840 in blast furnaces and other equipment. The established producers expanded their operations. The Bairds built two furnaces in 1837, and in 1839 decided to add eight new furnaces to their existing eight. Four were in blast by 1840, three were started in 1841, and the last in 1843. Firms of lesser importance also expanded. In 1837 one more furnace appeared at Calderbank; in 1838 there was another at Calderbank and one at Dundyvan, and the Shotts Iron Company started a new ironworks at Castlehill; in 1839 one furnace more was added to the existing two at Shotts itself; in 1840 two more appeared at Calder and at Calderbank and three at Dundyvan; another furnace was erected at Dundyvan in 1841. The increases characteristic of the period were among the new producers or at the new works. In 1836 Summerlee was established and by 1842 had six furnaces. Coltness, started in the same year, had six by 1845. In 1838 Alexander Alison and James Merry began at Carnboe and had built six furnaces by 1843. In 1839 Dixon started at Govan, meaning to build eight furnaces, but by the end of 1843 had only five and added only one more. The foundation stone of the Blair ironworks was laid in August 1839 and three furnaces were built by December 1843. William Galloway bought the estate of Househill at Paisley for £45,000 in February and had two furnaces by 1843. At the end of the year the Cessnock Works were established near Galston and by 1843 had two furnaces. In the summer of 1840 the Glasgow and Ayrshire Iron Company was floated to take over Muirkirk. In the same year operations began at Glengarnock and three furnaces were soon built, the works being taken over by Merry and Cunninghame in 1842. Langloan, opened in 1841, acquired three furnaces in the depression years and the Garscube ironworks two. In 1842 no new works were started but the existing ones still expanded. By the time of the railway boom of the 1840s the Scottish iron industry was well established to take advantage of the rising demand for iron.

The disposal of the iron

The rapid expansion of the industry was encouraged and sustained by British demand for iron rising rapidly in the 1830s and 1840s. Two main methods of disposal of the increased output were possible: to use the pig iron within Scotland, perhaps to produce goods for sale elsewhere, or to export the pig iron without any further processing. Around 1830 the heavy industries of Scotland could not absorb the increased output. There were two reasons to expect that home consumption would increase at least in the long run. First, supplies of fuel, especially in Lanarkshire, were adequate for the further processing of iron. Second, before 1830 Carron had earned an international reputation through the sale of finished goods. Even such favourable influences failed to stimulate sufficient demand to absorb the pig iron produced at home, and the disparate rate of growth between the production of pig iron and its use in iron manufacture became one of the most striking features, and failures, of the iron industry in Scotland. The finishing trade grew, but consumed only from between 30 per cent and 50 per cent of the output of the Scottish furnaces.

The foundries provided a ready market for pig iron. Though small, they were numerous — about twenty operating in the environs of Glasgow alone in 1830 — and when they increased all over Scotland, in number more than in size, the quantity of pig iron used in them grew accordingly. By 1846, the first year for which any statistics are available, they consumed almost 200,000 tons. The surprising failure was in the production of malleable iron by the puddling process, in which early attempts, at Clyde, Muirkirk and elsewhere, had been slight. When smelting increased under the impetus of the hot-blast, puddling still lagged behind. In 1834 the Frenchman Dufrénoy, on his tour of the Scottish ironworks, could report without exception that 'in the works near

Glasgow, they make iron for the foundry'.[7] Only in 1836 was puddling properly introduced, but until 1839, though many of the ironworks had foundries attached to them, as at Shotts or at Devon, little bar iron was produced by anyone. Even after the introduction of the hot-blast Muirkirk still remained the exception, but produced only up to 100 tons a week.

Attempts to increase the output of malleable iron on a comparatively extensive scale came only in the depression years of the late 1830s and early 1840s. The Monkland Iron and Steel Company abandoned the making of about 100 tons of steel annually at Calderbank and in 1840 had mills and forges capable of producing about 220 tons of malleable iron a week. Dixon, who had previously started but abandoned the manufacture of malleable iron at St. Rollox, built a bar-iron plant at Govan with 42 puddling furnaces, capable of producing about 200 tons a week. The malleable ironworks at Dundyvan, which also went into operation in 1840, was capable of producing about 300 tons a week. Apart from two small forges, one at Lancefield and one at Gartness, where they puddled a little white iron, there were no other malleable operations in Scotland. Total production could not have been more than about 40,000 tons a year. Yet it is doubtful if at this time such a large quantity was being produced, because Muirkirk was working at less than 50 per cent of its possible capacity. Another burst of investment came towards the end of the 1840s. In 1840 Neilson founded Mossend, capable of producing about 80 to 100 tons, and by 1845 total Scottish malleable iron production, of about 40,000 to 50,000 annually, probably consumed the output of only about 15 furnaces. The new and rising demand for railway iron generated more interest in malleable iron production in the 1840s than at any other period, and in the middle of the decade three malleable iron companies were floated. They differed from the earlier Scottish practice by not being integrated with blast furnaces. They aimed at manufacturing pig iron produced by the blast furnaces in the localities after which the companies took their names: the West of Scotland, the East of Scotland and Ayrshire. The ventures seemed bound to succeed. When Scotland's malleable ironworks absorbed such a small proportion of the output of the country's increasing number of blast furnaces, expansion seemed desirable; their location guaranteed plentiful supplies of pig iron; most important of all, the malleable ironworks were owned and directed by the leading Scottish ironmasters. The high hopes they engendered were doomed to disappointment. The lives of all three companies were short. The first to fall was the Ayrshire Iron Company in 1847; the West of Scotland Malleable Iron Company closed its works in 1848; the East of Scotland Malleable Iron Company did likewise in the following year.

The reasons for such failure in face of apparently good prospects are difficult to determine. Two may be suggested. The first was the nature and composition of Scotch pig iron, which was suitable for the foundry but not for the forge. The Scottish producers had almost a monopoly of the trade in foundry iron and in some works, Gartsherrie for instance, forge pig iron was rarely made. On the other hand the suitability of Scotch pig iron in the foundry meant that it was less suitable for the forge, where it had frequently to be mixed with other brands, as was done, for instance, in South Wales and in the United States. The second reason was that the two phases of relatively unsuccessful investment in Scottish malleable ironworks, from the late 1830s to the early 1840s and the late 1840s, were periods of depression. Scottish ironmasters turned their attention to the possibilities of manufacturing iron only when profits from the earlier process of iron manufacture declined. During the 1840s Scottish ironmasters saw others making large profits by producing railway iron; worse still, these profits were sometimes earned through the importation of Scotch pig iron, even though it was then mixed with other brands to be made into railway iron. So long as they were able to sell pig iron at high prices, the Scots do not seem to have been greatly alarmed by this state of affairs. When prices fell, they felt able to augment declining profits by producing malleable iron. Investment in malleable ironworks during years of relative depression was hardly the way to achieve profitable production. When the timing of the investment is combined with the comparatively unsuitable nature of the pig iron, the failure of the early attempts at malleable iron production are perhaps explicable, or it could be held that, if the Scots had combined the production of malleable iron with that of pig iron from the early days of the industry, their chances of success would have been greater. They might still have been forced to import pig iron from England and Wales to use with their native iron but would have retained part of the malleable trade in their hands.

The unsuccessful efforts at malleable iron production ended large-scale attempts by Scottish ironmasters to emulate the ironworks of England and Wales. Scottish production of malleable iron remained comparatively small. Some individual forges, such as Parkhead and Lancefield, were large and famous, but they used only a proportion of Scotch pig iron to mix with other brands and consequently failed to provide a major outlet for the produce of Scottish furnaces. Some forges were located in Scotland primarily to be near markets in the shipyards rather than to be near the raw material. Their reputation was gained by their skill in such work rather than by the cheapness of their products. Home demand for pig iron did not rise as many anticipated. Neither foundries nor malleable ironworks consumed a major part of the pig iron produced in Scotland. When the first satisfactory statistics became available in 1866, the foundries took 300,000 tons and the malleable ironworks nearly 200,000 tons of pig iron. In 1873, reflecting the increasing competition the Scottish pig-iron industry was experiencing, the foundries took only 230,000 tons and the malleable ironworks 143,000 tons.

Since domestic consumption did not absorb even half of Scottish production, the industry quickly relied on sales to external markets. Although those in England and Wales were nearest, the proximity of the Scottish ironworks to the sea enabled iron to be despatched abroad with comparative ease. Statistics of shipments, foreign and coastwise, reflect the relative importance of the two groups, although, since some coastwise shipments went overseas later, the figures for foreign shipments must be regarded as a minimum. In 1846, the first year for which reliable statistics are available, 119,000 tons or 21 per cent of Scottish production was shipped foreign and 257,000 tons or 46 per cent of production was shipped coastwise. By 1873 the position of the two markets had been reversed. In that year nearly 400,000 tons went foreign (though as much as 617,000 tons had gone overseas in 1872) and nearly 300,000 tons, almost the same as the year before, went coastwise. Though England and Wales provided ready markets for the industry's output in the early days of its expansion, foreign markets soon became as important, sometimes even more so. In the period of the industry's great prosperity, from the 1830s to the 1870s, roughly one-third was absorbed by each of the three main groups considered. But it was in foreign exports that the Scottish achievement relative to other British producers was most clearly demonstrated. From 1848, when Scottish pig-iron exports increased in the face of falling British exports, until 1843, Scotland sent abroad more than 90 per cent of the total United Kingdom exports of pig iron. The proportion fell thereafter. In 1855 it was 84 per cent and then — except for 1859 when it was 80 per cent — it never rose above 75 per cent of the total. The decline was caused by the increased competition Scotland experienced from the iron industry of the north-east of England, which, after the mid-1850s, encroached on Scottish markets at home and overseas. From the 1850s began the end of the Scots' international commercial supremacy in pig-iron production, but a more certain end came only later through competition from producers overseas. Until after the 1870s that could be ignored. Until then the Scots were simply building up the industrial potential of their future competition.

The coal industry

As with the iron industry, so the coal industry had ancient antecedents in Scotland, but it too was transformed in the nineteenth century.

Before the rapid industrial expansion which began in the 1780s, the coal industry found difficulty in meeting an increasing demand from domestic and industrial consumers because of its exceptional problems of increasing supply within the existing organisation of the industry. Two difficulties arose: first, the problem, general to all countries, of ensuring better drainage; and, second, the problem, unique to Scotland, of improving the supply of labour. To deal with the first, mechanical means to lift water from pits were used increasingly instead of drainage by the gravity flow of the day-level, and so the depth of mining was correspondingly extended. Water engines and horse gins used different means of power for the same technique of turning a wheel, which, by various methods, propelled an endless chain of buckets up and down a pit shaft. From the end of the eighteenth century these were supplemented, and later supplanted, by steam-powered vertical-cylinder beam engines.

Some aspects of the second problem, of improving the supply of labour, were peculiar to Scotland, where the conditions of serfdom of the Scottish colliers made the occupation repellent to most people.[8] Carron Company tried to resolve the problem by introducing English colliers, who had the added attraction of being reputed to be more industrious and sober than the Scots, and by recruiting pauper children as 'apprentice' miners. More generally, ironworks offered special inducements to attract the colliers they required, rousing great indignation among the established coalmasters who felt themselves unfairly treated. One writer, probably the ninth Earl of Dundonald, complained that

> the very *great profits* they now make on the manufacture of iron, exclusive of an extensive consumption and handsome profit on their coal and minerals, enables them at present to give or rather to promise, such wages to colliers, etc. etc. as coal-owners cannot afford to give.[9]

The root of the problem was that no one in Scotland was interested in becoming a collier, an attitude which lasted even after final emancipation in 1799, and gave the Irish immigrants their opportunity.

The industry finally broke away from the restrictions on supply when the growth of the heavy industries made the older methods of production no longer feasible. Increasing demand was noted around the Forth in the late eighteenth century, especially since Carron, then the leading ironworks, drew its supply from that area. During the French Wars its consumption increased sharply, and so too in many of those works which appeared in the fifteen years after the foundation of Wilsontown and which, in contrast to those which appeared after 1830, frequently depended for their coal on the production of the Forth basin. Since it was suggested that each furnace consumed, directly or indirectly, about 9,000 tons of coal annually, the cause of the concern of contemporaries is clear and went some way to justifying the suggestion by one alarmist that 'the ironworks and foundries of Carron and Clyde alone consume as many coals as all the inhabitants of Edinburgh'.[10] Alarm was only over the difficulties of increasing supply adequately to meet the demand. There were no fears of the absolute exhaustion of mineral supplies which were to be expressed by the 1870s. In the late eighteenth century all saw adequate coal resources simply awaiting efficient exploitation.

The first fear of exhaustion arose from the great demand from the ironworks after 1830, when the iron industry consumed about 170,000 tons of coal. This time demand was concentrated in the west, which, until the rise of the iron industry, supplied primarily domestic consumption and the export trade, especially to the West Indies, America and Ireland, with which the Ayrshire collieries maintained traditional links. Before the 1830s the only industrial demand in the west, though an increasing one, arose from the growing use of steam engines in the industrial establishments around Glasgow. By contrast in the east, though the collieries around the Forth shipped much of their coal elsewhere, they also met a varied industrial demand from ironworks, distilleries, glassworks and limeworks; the output from the Lothians was absorbed by the domestic and industrial demand of Edinburgh and district. By the late eighteenth century the eastern coalmasters could not meet the increasing demand, and the deficiency was offset by imports of English coal, especially after 1793, when Henry Dundas ensured the removal of a tax on coal shipped coastwise. The relative position of the producers in the east deteriorated, when transport improvements, especially the opening of the Union Canal in 1822, helped the movement of coal from the west. In 1824 a group of 'West Country Gentlemen' were reported to be planning to bring 60,000 tons of coal to Edinburgh, and until the mid-1830s, whenever the price of coal in Edinburgh rose slightly above that in Glasgow, more coal than ever moved east. Thereafter the prosperity of the industry in the west, as it met the demand of the expanding iron industry, limited the competition for some years.

The growth of the iron industry changed the form of much of Scottish coal production. Previously pits had been generally small, though not necessarily shallow, and, in spite of technical advances, many still worked along an outcrop until drainage difficulties caused them to be abandoned. The advent of the ironmasters as coalmasters did not always lead quickly to a new type of colliery; it did introduce a new type of organisation to the industry, something much bigger than anything previously known in Scotland. By the 1870s William Baird and Company and Merry and Cunninghame each had more than twice the number of collieries of any other company and, since they were concentrated in the iron-producing districts, their influence on colliery organisation and management was great. As the importance of the ironmasters in the coal industry grew, so the importance of noble coalmasters, who had frequently determined the industry's growth in the eighteenth century, declined. Consequently, the aims and actions of the ironmasters helped to produce the environment typical initially of the west of Scotland but ultimately of the industry throughout Scotland in the nineteenth century.

Unfortunately statistics of coal production are not available before 1854, by which time the proportion of total coal output consumed by the ironworks had probably declined, but it was still approximately one-third of Scotland's production of 7,448,000 tons. Though the ironworks were undoubtedly the most important single consumer, the consumption of other industrial users, and of domestic demand, remained important. Nevertheless, since the rapid expansion of the coal industry had been brought about by the ironmasters, any lack of buoyancy in their demand posed special problems to the industry. By the 1870s the stagnation could not be denied. In 1873 only about 16 per cent of Scotland's coal production of almost 16,855,000 tons was used in the ironworks. The reason behind this changing relationship was the increasing competition which the iron industry was beginning to experience especially after 1866. In the late 1860s the coal industry's difficulties first became evident. They increased when a number of pits, sunk in the years of prosperity, only then came into operation, and were more evident when the ironmasters began selling their own coal. The appearance of the ironmasters as salesmasters gave rise to a dichotomy of interests within the trade, and one not easily resolved.

The basic requirement of the coal industry from the late 1860s was to obtain new markets to offset the declining consumption of the furnaces. The proportion of total production absorbed by overseas demand doubled between 1854 and the early 1870s but was only partial compensation. The position of the coal industry in the 1870s was, therefore, similar to that of the iron industry. In the boom which culminated in 1872 and 1873 it was very profitable, but inadequate transport facilities on the railways and deliberate restriction of output led to a fall in production in the face of high prices. At the end of the boom the uncertain position of the coal industry was demonstrated. The most important consumer of coal in Scotland was finding difficulty in meeting international competition. The coal industry could not easily find a substitute.

NOTES

1. *New Statistical Account*, vol. 5, p. 155.

2. J. B. Neilson, 'On the construction of hot-blast ovens for iron furnaces', quoted in T. B. Mackenzie, *Life of J. B. Neilson* (Glasgow, 1929), p. 13.

3. M. Dufrénoy, 'Report on the use of heated air in the Iron Works of Scotland and England' (Paris, 1834). Translated in *Journal of the Franklin Institute*, vol. xv (N.S.), p. 212.

4. *The Glasgow Herald*, 28 April 1834.

5. *On the Statistics and Geography of the Production of Iron*. Reprint of anonymous pamphlet in Glasgow University Library.

6. *Glasgow Saturday Post*, 26 April 1834.

7. Dufrénoy, *Report on . . . heated air*, p. 419.

8. For details of serfdom see below, pp. 142-3.

9. *Description of the Estate of Culross, particularly of the Mineral and Coal Property* (Edinburgh, 1793), p. 63.

10. *Considerations on the Present Scarcity and High Price of Coals in Scotland* (Edinburgh, 1793), p. 20.

CHAPTER VIII

Finance

Banking policy

The financial crises of the eighteenth century were usually linked to difficulties on the balance of payments of Scotland, as far as it can be determined. Any deficiency in exports and particularly any increased need of imports, most often because of inadequate harvests, led to deficits on the balance of payments, which required a transfer of bullion or other reserves out of the country and so reduced the liquid resources of the banks. The consequences were restrictions on credit which impeded agricultural and industrial growth. Such strains were diminished through agricultural improvements lessening the need for imports and through industrial improvements encouraging new and more extensive exports. The economic successes after the 1780s were then likely to protect the growing financial network from some of the external strains of the eighteenth century and so enable the banking system to aid the country's developing economy more readily. The significance of its contribution is lessened, however, if the economic successes from the 1780s rested only slightly on the provision of a ready supply of finance. If other factors, such as plentiful supplies of appropriate natural resources or of labour, contributed significantly to the successes, the banks may have had a less influential role than has often been attributed to them. There is no doubt that the Scottish banks pioneered many banking practices and achieved international recognition by doing so, but their role in the expansion of the domestic economy may have been only secondary or supplementary.

Their practices became internationally recognised in the eighteenth century. The collapse of the Ayr bank in the financial crisis of 1772 was interpreted as providing confirmation of the wisdom of the policies of the more conservative bankers, especially of the three public banks and their close allies among the private bankers of Edinburgh. The crisis eliminated some of the more reckless elements in Scottish banking, but tranquillity was not without interruption after 1772. A minor factor which contributed to greater stability was changes in the Scottish law of bankruptcy. It became less necessary or desirable for any one person to precipitate the bankruptcies always made imminent by any financial crisis and which had an adverse effect on banks, when the failure of anyone with an obligation to one could so easily cause a run on them. In the early eighteenth century the law enabled any creditor who arrested the effects of his debtor to secure for himself the value of the property thus attached to the exclusion of other creditors, even if their arrestments should follow at once. Under this procedure some debtors helped creditors, with whom they were on intimate terms, by informing them privately of an impending bankruptcy, so enabling the favoured creditor to arrest the goods. Apart from the advantages of such advance information, creditors living close to a debtor always had a better chance of making the first arrestments than those living at a distance. In 1754 the Court of Session first made an order that all arrestments laid within thirty days of the bankruptcy should be of equal effect, but it was not renewed after seven years. A complete change came only in June 1772 when an Act authorised an equal distribution of a debtor's effects among the creditors. The new provision removed a factor which frequently precipitated bankruptcies, and may have helped to mitigate the repercussions of the crisis of 1772, but did nothing to remove the fundamental causes which led to them.

Important changes in the Scottish economy meant that these fundamental causes had taken on a very different form by the time of the next financial crisis of 1793, which followed some years of credit expansion and inflow of funds from England. A major difference was that the industrial importance of the west of Scotland had greatly increased, and Glasgow and the west of Scotland suffered much more noticeably in 1793 than two decades earlier. Two financial failures heightened the distress. The effects of the first, of the Glasgow Arms Bank, were lessened by the bank having been struggling for some years; the second, a week later, was more important. It was of James Dunlop, whose reputation and credit were second to none, but who, after the collapse of the tobacco trade in 1776, had moved extensively into landed and industrial ventures, which he could not maintain after the outbreak of the French Wars in 1793. In Edinburgh, in contrast to 1772, only one bank — Bertram, Gardner and Company — failed, though the survivors experienced difficulties. Sir W. Forbes, J. Hunter and Company found that, while under normal circumstances in their business the amount received about equalled the amount paid out, in the winter of 1792 to 1793 more was being paid out, increasing to an unfavourable balance of nearly £53,000 in March 1793 and to over £105,000 in April 1793. The contrast between east and west was evident in the different experiences of the two old public banks. Its limited interests in Glasgow freed the Bank of Scotland from the immediate cause of distress, but the Royal Bank's loans to Glasgow manufacturers placed it in a precarious position. The issue of Exchequer bills to businesses thought to be sound defused the crisis. Of the £405,000 issued in Scotland, Glasgow and Paisley received £350,000.

The problems of 1793 were increased in 1797, when the government had to take even more drastic action to abate the financial panic by authorising the Bank of England to suspend cash payments. Representatives of the three Scottish chartered banks and of Sir William Forbes' bank met and agreed that they too would suspend the convertibility of notes into gold, a joint action which became increasingly common. Their decision was supported by the leading inhabitants of Edinburgh and elsewhere and, though there was a popular demand for assistance, and some real hardship through the inadequacy of small change, especially for the payment of wages, the crisis was more easily survived than were those of 1772 and 1793. The system of mutual support, rather than

the wisdom of other policies, began to be the key to the success and stability of
the Scottish banking system. Such consultation reflected a subtle, if not openly
recognised, change in the organisation of Scottish banking towards the end of
the eighteenth and the beginning of the nineteenth centuries, a period when
private and local banking declined before an advancing system of national
banking. Before their decay, indeed partly its cause, the private banks became
increasingly associated with the chartered banks. Together they followed
policies which stimulated such criticism that new banks appeared to rival them.
In the early nineteenth century two interpretations of banking practice, similar
to those of the mid-eighteenth century were evident: the conservative policy
advocated stability; the radical criticism advocated expansion. Consequently,
the period of boom in the short peace of 1802 was one when, among many
indices of economic activity in Scotland, the appearance of a number of banks
was among the more notable. Even the two senior banks, the Bank of Scotland
and the Royal Bank, increased their authorised capitals to £1,500,000 each, but
more symptomatic of the economic state of the country was the creation,
especially in 1802, of a number of new institutions outside Edinburgh, in Fife,
Renfrew, Falkirk, and elsewhere, leading to twenty-four provincial banking
companies by 1810. The fate of some of these banks was unfortunate, most
notorious of all being the Fife Banking Company, which collapsed in 1795,
leaving its shareholders with a liability of £5,500 each. Its experience was
exceptional, but none of these new banks could easily rival the success of their
older competitors, partly because the longer-established banks had more stable
and more profitable connections while the newer institutions were often left
with the riskier types of business, partly because the older banks did not tolerate
the appearance of the new banks lightly and tried to arrest their progress, as, for
instance, by refusing to accept their notes. Both groups could argue that they
were entitled to adopt the policies they did. The older banks felt they should
refuse the notes because the institutions issuing them were unsound and often
insolvent; the newer banks felt that by doing so the older banks were trying to
maintain their privileged position and were thus stifling legitimate aspirations in
banking. Who was correct? This was the key issue to banking disputes and
policy in the first half of the nineteenth century.

Two criticisms of the existing system were advanced: first, of the organisation
of the banks, and, in particular, of the relationship between the private and the
chartered banks; second, of the type of lending policy followed.

The source of the unique relationship between the chartered and the private
banks lay in the difference between the early activities of the two groups. In
contrast to the chartered banks, the private banks entered banking by gradually
providing the banking services which as customers they could not easily obtain.
The private banks were, therefore, always in the most direct contact with those
who wanted banking services; not so the chartered banks. By the beginning of
the nineteenth century this dichotomy between the two groups was becoming
more rigid. By then an individual usually obtained finance only from a private
banker, who in turn went to a chartered bank for any assistance he required.

Apart from anything else the public paid higher charges through this system. In addition, its growth led to the private bankers having large shareholdings in the public banks and to their senior partners being consulted on matters of policy. The links were advantageous to both. The chartered banks avoided bearing considerable risks and many of the detailed difficulties involved in small deposits and discounts; the private bankers were assured of custom they might have lost. That the customer paid more was irrelevant to both sides so long as they seemed secure in its practice. The additional cost would have been less oppressive if the private bankers had acted with vision and foresight. They could have given greater attention to the individual needs of their customers than the chartered banks, especially since the latter's branch system was not extensively developed until later in the nineteenth century. But the private bankers did not operate in that way. They occupied a very low place in the public's esteem. To Lord Cockburn:

> no men were more devoid of spirit, and even of the proper spirit of their trade, than our old Edinburgh bankers. Respectable men they were, but without talent, general knowledge, or any liberal objects, they were the conspicuous sycophants of existing power.[1]

Even the favour of a private banker was insufficient to ensure a ready loan because of the lending policies followed by the Scottish banks. This was the second, and more vital, ground of objection to the banking establishment of Scotland. Branch banking reduced the variety of policies, while the concentration of control in Edinburgh made for consultation and so for joint action. The organisation of banking made the implementation of common policies easy and yet more difficult to breach. The objection to the common lending policy was not only that it was determined largely in Edinburgh but that adequate funds were not available for the growing demands for industrial investment, chiefly because the greater part of the banks' loanable funds was absorbed in the discounting of bills and investment in government securities. The more conservative nature of the policies of the chartered banks is evident in the distribution of their assets between advances on the one hand and investments and liquid assets on the other.[2] In 1802 they were 53 and 35 per cent respectively in the chartered banks and 52 and 46 per cent in the private banks but 87 and 10 per cent in all other banking companies; in 1825 63 and 34 per cent for the chartered banks, 65 and 33 per cent for private bankers, 81 and 17 per cent for all banking companies and 83 and 16 per cent for the new joint-stock banks which were appearing; in 1850 the percentages were 58 and 36 for the chartered banks, 73 and 26 for the banking companies, and 76 and 22 for the joint-stock banks.

Recent quantitative estimates of the extent of capital formation, especially in the developing Scottish cotton and iron industries,[3] and the extent to which it was financed by the banks, need to be accepted only with considerable qualifications, but, even if the total fixed capital represented a limited claim on resources and the banks made only a limited contribution to meeting it, the individual borrower, especially if disappointed in his application, complained vociferously and left a permanent record of his objections. Scotland, and especially the west of Scotland, was at a stage of development when it had a higher proportion of such projectors than in earlier years. Their disappointment lay behind the objections. It cannot be dismissed as uninfluential or insignificant even though it may seem unjustified in retrospect.

In the eighteenth century, the chief means of advancing funds in Scotland was by the discounting of bills, though cash credits steadily became more widely used in the first half of the nineteenth century. The system was largely the same as in England, except that in Scotland the need for banks to rediscount bills lessened as the system of branch banking grew. Then the bill-brokers' importance declined and it became easier to control the rediscount of fictitious bills. Nevertheless, any concentration on bill discounting as a means of supplying the necessary funds for business in the late eighteenth century gave many with a legitimate demand the finance they required. So long as the demand for assistance came predominantly from commerce rather than from industry, most potential borrowers held the necessary trade bills. Concentration on the discounting of bills led others to devise less reputable means of gaining assistance by the method and was almost certainly one factor forcing the growth of the issue of accommodation bills.[4] In the nineteenth century the appearance of increasing demands for finance for industrial development produced a group without the accepted security. Sometimes advances could be obtained on the security of heritable property, or, as with the pig-iron warrant, a security similar to a trade bill was devised, but often demands for aid could not be easily backed by acceptable securities. The bankers' objections to meeting them had some validity. The unsatisfied requests were often for finance for fixed capital formation. Advances on the security of trade bills and pig-iron warrants were in a different category. The new industrialists could not readily accept this argument. It seemed to them that the bankers were simply ignoring a new, but legitimate, demand for accommodation through adherence to outmoded lending policies.

The industrialists' argument was reinforced by the importance of the second outlet for much of the banks' funds, the purchase of government securities. The chartered banks first invested heavily in them during the Napoleonic Wars, when the funds were standing at considerably below par. Investing gave a good return and, when prices rose, capital gains, which were not generally realised. The banks continued to hold an amount equal to between one-third and one-quarter of their total deposits in Exchequer bills or government stock. The chartered banks went even further and held that this ratio of liquid assets should be maintained by all in order to meet any emergencies. Some were willing to support legislation to do so. Even when it was admitted that the chartered banks' distribution of assets ensured a high degree of liquidity, and so of stability, it was not admitted, as the chartered banks frequently suggested, that any other policy was irresponsible and bound to lead to financial disaster. In complete contrast to the attitudes of the chartered banks, some argued that it was not entirely foolhardy for a bank to use all its resources in granting cash credits, or in discounting bills of exchange, especially since some very respectable and important English bankers considered ordinary bills of exchange as good security as Exchequer bills. Some Scottish country bankers who followed the Edinburgh policy agreed with the critics. Whatever the merits of the case, new banks found great difficulty in following the precepts of the chartered banks after the Napoleonic Wars. Owing to its increased price, government stock gave a comparatively low return. What had proved profitable to the older banks would, in the changed circumstances, have ruined a new one.

The root cause of the objections to the relationship between the private and chartered banks and to their lending policies was that both diminished the funds available for advances to trade and industry. The objections were most vigorous in the first half of the nineteenth century, especially in the earlier period, before many successful attempts to meet them. The first attempt, and so the first major attack on the old organisation, came with the foundation of the Commercial Banking Company of Scotland in 1810. Its name was significant. Though the Commercial Bank was not established by public authority, its aim of providing a national service was characteristic of the new era of banking in Scotland. The private bankers began to decline, especially after the financial crisis of 1825, and were displaced by the large joint-stock banks which set out to serve the whole country and which in due course absorbed the older provincial banking companies and partnerships. After the Napoleonic Wars there was a decline in local institutions. The Commercial Bank had itself aimed effective blows at the private bankers and at their close connections with the chartered banks by ruling that no private banker could become one of its directors. It also tried to meet the other main objection to the Scottish banking system by trying to ensure a greater flow of funds to commerce and industry. The Commercial Bank's example was followed as new institutions appeared, especially during the period of extensive flotation of joint-stock companies in 1825. The year 1825 saw the start of the Aberdeen Town and County Bank, the Arbroath Banking Company, the Dundee Commercial Bank, and, most important of them all, the National Bank of Scotland, which followed the example of the Commercial Bank by being formed on a national basis.

The protests of the Commercial Bank, and to a lesser extent of the National Bank, against the organisation and policies of the older Scottish banks had much success. The relationship between private and chartered banks was broken, and the final decline of the private banks inaugurated. The two banks, following their avowed national coverage, encouraged the growth of branch banking and forced others to follow. Their policies, as much as those of the older banks, led to the evolution of some of the features most commonly associated with Scottish banking. But neither the Commercial nor the National Bank was as revolutionary as some institutions which appeared later, and soon each accepted some of the policies of the older banks and worked closely with them. In 1831 both received royal charters, though they were granted with the liability of shareholders unlimited, in contrast to the position of the older banks, and remained so until the two banks were registered under the Companies Act of 1879. In the 1830s representatives of the five chartered banks and generally a representative of Sir William Forbes and Company held regular meetings to agree on interest rates for both deposits and discounts. A new criticism, similar to that voiced earlier, then began to be heard, because by about 1830 the lending policies of the Commercial and National Banks were similar to those of the three oldest institutions. By then all five held that all banks should invest a large part of their assets in government securities. Moreover, to others the agreed rates allowed by them on deposits were so low that the banks' prosperity was notorious. Much of the competitive spirit of earlier years had apparently gone.

This background led to a further phase of attempted reform. It came from the west of Scotland and may be taken to reflect injured local sentiment as much as an objection to banking policy. It provided the most striking illustration of the two interpretations of the development of Scottish banking.

A burst of new activity came in the 1830s. The Ayrshire Banking Company and the Glasgow Union Banking Company were founded in 1830, the latter growing rapidly through amalgamation to become the Union Bank of Scotland in 1843. In 1834 the Central Bank of Scotland appeared in Perth, in 1836 the North of Scotland Banking Company in Aberdeen, and in 1838 the Clydesdale Bank in Glasgow. The two most notable institutions to appear in the decade were the Western Bank of Scotland in 1832 and the City of Glasgow Bank in 1839. Both actively opposed the chartered banks in Edinburgh before they came to disastrous ends in 1857 and 1878 respectively. The new banks, especially the Western Bank, tried to break the restrictive arrangements imposed on Scottish banking through the system of mutual consultation among the chartered banks with head offices in Edinburgh. The aggressive approach influenced interest policy, previously determined jointly by the Edinburgh banks. By 1841 even the Bank of Scotland, much against its will, was forced to follow the others and raised its rate on deposit to 3½ per cent. The public benefited. They received a higher return for deposits and paid lower rates for discounts. If the Western and its followers had been forced to invest at least a quarter of their deposits in low-yielding government stock, as the Edinburgh banks advocated, they would have been unable to afford such benefits to the public. The old rule of Edinburgh might have been completely re-established. Not surprisingly, when the Western Bank opposed the Edinburgh view of the proportion of assets which should be invested in government stock, it did so with such consistency and strength that it forgot the large element of wisdom in the policy. When the Western Bank employed a large part of its resources in discounting ordinary trade bills, it placed itself in a highly dangerous position. Any sudden pressure for funds, perhaps through the failure of some of its clients, was liable to strain the Western's reserves. Nevertheless the bank seemed to prosper. It had twenty-six branches within a decade of its foundation, within another, seventy-three, and, by the time of its failure in 1857, over a hundred. At that time it had the second largest note circulations of any Scottish bank; its paid-up capital of £1,500,000 was also the second largest in Scotland and its deposits were over £5,000,000.

The extensive system of branches, as well as late-night openings in Glasgow, attracted even more when the Western Bank (as well as the City of Glasgow Bank) gave depositors ½ per cent more on deposits than the other Scottish banks. The result was that by 1857, of the 42,000 depositors with the Western Bank, 26,000 were for amounts of under £50. The Bank also had the wealthiest of the western industrialists among its proprietors, clients and directors. In 1857 the Baird family (of the Gartsherrie ironworks) held 1,886 shares between them, and from 1839 onwards at least one of the brothers was among the directors. Many other well-known Glasgow men sat with them. Western Bank shares were quoted at a considerable premium on the Glasgow Stock Exchange but rarely entered the market as few of its 1,200 and more shareholders ever wanted to sell. As the failure approached, the desire to hold was strengthened when in 1856 the dividend was raised to 9 per cent. The following year, although profits fell by £20,000, to about £146,000, the rate was maintained and almost £11,000 was carried forward to the reserve.

When firms heavily in debt to the Western Bank collapsed in the crisis of 1857, and so precipitated its downfall, the apprehension and warnings of the Edinburgh banks seemed at last to be fully justified. Nevertheless much criticism was made of the Edinburgh banks' attitude at the time. With its strong and influential connection in the west of Scotland it is possible that, had the bank been helped over the 1857 crisis, its future might have been bright. Wider considerations, too, reinforced the desirability of keeping the bank going if possible. The failure of any Scottish bank, but especially that of a major institution such as the Western, was certain to play into the hands of the opponents of Scottish banking and its privileges, particularly of its note issue. Moreover, a failure of such magnitude was bound to spread distrust and difficulty through the whole Scottish economy. It might have been expected that the Edinburgh banks would have tried to support the Western. They did not do so, and the Western Bank closed its doors in November 1857.

It is difficult to form a straightforward opinion on the part played by Edinburgh bankers in the history of the Western Bank. Undoubtedly the two followed different paths. If the Edinburgh bankers were too conservative, the Western Bank was foolhardy. Much of the dispute hinged round the proportion of assets which should be invested in government stock. The Edinburgh ratio of one-third to one-quarter may have given the Scottish banking system its high reputation for stability, especially in an age when cash reserves were low. But other equally stable banks did not adopt this distribution. In Scotland many believed that the chartered banks had adopted it in the first place for no other reason than that it was profitable and that insistence on the rule was a means of restricting competition. It is also possible that the policy led the Edinburgh banks to neglect the wider interests involved in the economic development of Scotland. The belief that their emphasis on stability was so excessive that quite legitimate demands from industry and trade, though perhaps of a more risky character, were ignored was a major factor in the origin of the Western Bank and the cause of constant disputes later. The position of the Edinburgh banks is justifiable; but some retardation of economic growth may result if, because of such a policy, adequate advances are not made to trade and industry. Evidence that this view was not fully appreciated by the Edinburgh banks came less than a year before the stoppage of the Western Bank. When the Scottish banks were asked for their opinion on the Bank Act of 1845, the Edinburgh banks generally gave their approval to the measure. The Glasgow banks objected strongly, contending that the restriction placed on their note issues by the Act prevented a legitimate extension of operations to meet the expanding needs of industry and trade. When the Glasgow banks objected to the difficulties they experienced through not being incorporated, the Edinburgh banks did not support their appeals. In the years after 1830 the newer banks had broken much of the control of Edinburgh and its seems that, though the older banks were interested in maintaining the stability of Scottish banking, they were as interested in holding their dominant position in it. When some of the Edinburgh banks suggested in a letter to the Select Committee on the Bank Act of 1857 that it was advisable to prevent a repetition of the competition that had taken place between banks in Scotland before 1844, they displayed a fear that still more competition might dislodge them entirely from their leading position.

The episode illustrates, as did the failure of the Ayr Bank in the eighteenth century, that the Edinburgh banks did not fully appreciate the desires and aspirations that lay behind the Western Bank. It was perhaps inevitable that the extent of industrial investment in the west of Scotland at that time should lead to excessive demands on the banking system, but it is doubtful if the leading Scottish banks were always as ready to meet these aspirations of the west of Scotland as they might have been. Had they done so sooner, much misunderstanding and difficulty might have been avoided.

The collapse of the City of Glasgow Bank in 1878 was in a different category from that of the Western Bank. There were similarities between them. Though both were critics of the policies of the older banks, both were successful. The City of Glasgow Bank's reputation, like that of the Western, was not of the highest, but again as with the Western, the substantial resources of its shareholders allayed any fear in the minds of the public. The same kind of mismanagement brought the two banks to a similar position; the difference was that the leading officials and the directors of the City of Glasgow Bank covered their actions by systematic falsification of the balance sheets and tried to boost its standing on the Stock Exchange by purchasing the shares of the bank. Their action brought the directors of the City of Glasgow Bank to prison and led the shareholders to meet a deficit of over £5,000,000. On this occasion, however, the Edinburgh banks continued to accept City of Glasgow notes.

The failure of the City of Glasgow Bank was the last of the three great failures in modern Scottish banking. Its elements of fraud marked it out from those of the Ayr and Western Banks, but in origin and action all three banks represented a criticism of Scottish banking policy. That the critics had such dramatic failures among their ranks does not necessarily mean that they were completely erroneous in their views. The line of banking policy most typically represented by the chartered banks was conservative and needed the constant criticism of others.

Amalgamation and assimilation

The failure of the City of Glasgow Bank marked the end of one phase of the history of Scottish banking. Thereafter amalgamations within Scotland led to a more modern, less uniquely national banking structure and to assimilation to English ways. The amalgamations took place mainly before the last quarter of the century. The best example is in the history of the appropriately named Union Bank of Scotland. The Glasgow Union Bank absorbed the Thistle Bank in 1836 and two years later, in 1838, the Paisley Union Bank Company, and began to merge with Sir William Forbes and Company. In 1843 the designation, Union Bank of Scotland, was adopted and later in the year it took over Hunters' and Company (which had merged with the Kilmarnock Banking Company in 1821) and the Glasgow and Ship Bank (which was formed by the fusion of the Glasgow Bank Company and the Ship Bank in 1837). Two other accessions came to the Union Bank in the middle of the nineteenth century: in 1849 the Banking Company of Aberdeen and in 1857 the Perth Banking Company, which had carried on the business of the Perth United Banking Company after its dissolution in 1787. The classic example of the Union Bank was followed by other banks, though to a lesser degree: the Clydesdale Bank took over the Edinburgh and Glasgow Bank in 1858 and the Eastern Bank of Scotland in 1863; in 1864 the Royal Bank amalgamated with the Dundee Banking Company. At the same time others increased their capital stock. In 1844, the National Bank doubled its paid-up capital to £1,000,000; in 1850 the British Linen Bank did likewise; in two stages, in 1859 and in 1864, the Commercial Bank increased its capital by £400,000 to £1,000,000; in 1864 the City of Glasgow Bank increased its capital to £850,000. The amalgamations slackened in the later nineteenth century. There were no more from 1868, when the Bank of Scotland absorbed the Central Bank of Scotland, until 1907, when the Caledonian Banking Company merged with the Bank of Scotland. Less than a year later two banks, the North of Scotland and the Town and County Bank, both with head offices in Aberdeen, also merged, and the number of institutions was thus reduced to eight, at which number it remained until after the Second World War.

Between the wars amalgamations, or more accurately, affiliations led a number of Scottish banks to become associated with English counterparts. The first instance was in 1918, before the end of the war, when Lloyds Bank assumed control of the National Bank. Similar arrangements were effected the following year by Barclays Bank over the British Linen Bank and by the Midland Bank over the Clydesdale Bank, while the Midland Bank extended its control to the North of Scotland Bank in 1923. In such ways the Scottish banks were brought increasingly within the orbit of English banking and under

English control. Only in one case was the role reversed in the 1930s, when the Royal Bank gained control of the English institutions of Williams Deacon's and Glyn, Mills'. By then the trend was irresistible. For all its past Scottish banking was losing its distinctive characteristics.

By the second half of the nineteenth century signs of the imminence of such assimilation were unmistakable. The growth of Scottish banking was much less in real terms from the mid-1880s and particularly so from 1900. It was overshadowed increasingly by all the financial services of London. A minor indicator of the increasing subjection of the Scottish banks was in 1863 when the Scottish banks jointly instructed their branches to follow changes in Bank Rate immediately. In some ways, however, the increasing similarity of banking on both sides of the border reflected the increasing approximation of English to Scottish practice, particularly when the amalgamation movement in English banking gave rise to a structure of a few large joint-stock banks with branches, similar to that long established in Scotland. Some legal changes were aimed at forcing the Scots to approximate to English practice, even to what the Scots considered its less desirable or erroneous banking principles. The first important attempt was the proposal in 1826 to abolish banknotes of under £5, an attempt which produced such an outcry that the proposal to apply the prohibition to Scotland was never implemented. Whatever the provision's merits in England, Scots were so used to small banknotes, and had such justification for their confidence in their convertibility, that the prohibition was irrelevant in Scotland. Future governments avoided causing similar offence. In 1845 the Bank Act for Scotland left the nineteen issuing banks in Scotland with a legal circulation, determined in the same way as in England, of £3,087,000. The maximum country issue in England was £8,632,000. In other ways the Scots gained over the English. They were allowed to increase their note issue indefinitely against gold and silver held in their head offices, a privilege restricted in the south to the Bank of England, and amalgamations did not affect rights to issue notes in Scotland, though no new banks of issue were permitted. Although the opposition of 1826 was, therefore, sufficiently strong to allow the Scottish banks to remain relatively privileged under the legislation of the 1840s, the note issue did not pass uncriticised. When a bill was introduced into parliament in 1864 to divide the Western Bank's note issue among other Scottish banks in proportion to their existing issues, Gladstone indicated that, while willing to consider the merits of the application on various grounds, he was unwilling to admit it as a legal right. The matter of the note issue arose more dramatically some years later, when the Scottish banks began to open branches in England. The amalgamation movement in Scottish banking was accompanied by an extension of branches, especially when some, notably the Royal Bank, took over many of the branches of the Western Bank. After the crisis of 1866 the expansion was especially rapid. In 1873 the number was about 900, 300 more than in 1866; in 1878 there were about 950 branches. The most important repercussions of this expansion came when the branches were in England.

The first move into England was made by the National Bank when it opened a

London office in 1864. Others followed, to the indignation of English country bankers who could have taken such action only by losing their note-issuing rights. Eventually all major Scottish banks opened offices in London, the last to do so being the Commercial Bank in 1883. Opposition increased in 1874, when the Clydesdale Bank opened three branches in Cumberland, and a much more widespread invasion of England was feared. The excursion to the south cannot be regarded as a victory for the Scots, because the opposition of the English, bankers and politicians, halted it before much had been achieved. That the chief reason for the opposition was jealousy of the note-issuing powers was shown by three different attempts to limit the Scots' activities. The first was in 1875 when Goschen introduced a bill to prohibit the Scottish banks from opening offices in England, a direct attempt to limit the new line of expansion; the second, in 1879, was even more to the point when the bill to grant limited liability to banks at first excluded from its scope any bank of issue which had offices in a part of the United Kingdom other than that in which its head office was situated; finally, in 1881 the Bank of Scotland, the Royal Bank and the British Linen Bank promoted private bills to enable them to adopt the principle of 'reserve liability', but the government effectively blocked the bills by trying to use them as a means of bargaining over the banks' rights to issue notes.

Though the opposition in England was sufficient to stop the Scots' activities, it was not wholly unanimous. The country bankers were more apprehensive than those in London. They were more likely to feel the effect of the new competition and resented it because the Scots were able to retain their note-issuing privileges with offices in London. The country bankers themselves were not unanimous. Some, especially those in areas less likely to be affected by Scottish competition, were apprehensive of opposition to the Scots being pushed to such limits that there would be a general review of the whole position of banks of issue, a possibility which interested the politicians, none more so than Gladstone. In short the note issue was the topic of greatest interest to all. Their fear of losing their highly prized right led the Scottish banks to withdraw from any action which might have jeopardised it. Though the opposition to their entry to England did not lead to any interference with their note-issuing rights, for which some of their opponents hoped, it did effectively end the movement south. Had there not been such opposition, the Scots would probably have become more firmly established there. If they had done so, their more concentrated structure might have enabled them to gain considerably in the amalgamation movement in English banking which soon followed.

NOTES

1. Henry Cockburn, *Memorials of His Own Time* (edition by H. A. Cockburn, Edinburgh, 1910), pp. 238-9.
2. Checkland, *Scottish Banking*, pp. 240, 424, 426.

E

3. John Butt, 'The Scottish cotton industry during the industrial revolution, 1780-1840', in L. M. Cullen and T. C. Smout (eds.), *Comparative Aspects of Scottish and Irish Economic and Social History, 1600-1900* (Edinburgh, 1977), p. 120-3 and 'Capital and Enterprise in the Scottish Iron Industry, 1780-1840', in John Butt and J. T. Ward (eds.), *Scottish Themes* (Edinburgh, 1976), pp. 68-74.

4. See pp. 60-1.

CHAPTER IX

Agriculture

Prices and production

The process of agricultural change was well-established in the eighteenth century, but its effects were patchy. The cost of improved methods and the time before some of their benefits were evident deterred many from adopting them until the higher prices of the Napoleonic Wars gave a stimulus to general agricultural reform. Its effects differed in the Lowlands and in the Highlands, especially in the far west and north. While the benefits of the high prices of wartime encouraged and assisted the pace of agricultural change and improvement in the Lowlands, they postponed it in the Highlands. The contrasting response may be explained by differences in natural resources and human initiative, but the implications were far-reaching.

During the wars the experience of agriculture in the Lowlands resembled that of parts of England. The increasing proportion of the population concentrated in urban areas and in industrial employment provided a ready market, but wartime harvests were generally inadequate in spite of the improvements of the pre-war years. Though regional variations make any generalisations misleading, possibly about two out of every three of the wartime harvests were deficient. Imports of grain became continuous from the mid-1780s. The consequential rise in agricultural prices is evident in the fiars prices for different grains, fixed annually in Scottish counties and used for the conversion of obligations in kind to cash and for other purposes.[1] The prices in £s Scots (equal to 1s. 8d. sterling) for oatmeal at Lanark show the fluctuations, especially under wartime conditions, of a major item of consumption in a populous area:

	£	s.		£	s.		£	s.
1793	9	6	1800	22	16	1810	12	18
1794	9		1801	10	16	1811	14	2
1795	11	2	1802	10	16	1812	18	12
1796	9	6	1803	10	16	1813	13	16
1797	7	16	1804	11	2	1814	9	18
1798	9	6	1805	12		1815	8	8
1799	18	12	1806	12	12			
			1807	16	4			
			1808	15				
			1809	15	6			

In 1740, the year of the first notably poor harvest since the 1690s, the price was £10, which was not exceeded until the £10 16s. of 1782. With 1795 and 1799, they were the only years of the eighteenth century when a price of £10 or over was recorded. The increase at the turn of the century and its continued high level in the nineteenth century is obvious.

The rising prices led to increased rents and property values so that the rental of Scotland at the end of the war was thought to stand eight times higher than in the middle of the eighteenth century. High rents were charged and paid as the current prosperity seemed soundly based. The reality behind the prosperity was not the exceptional increase in demand in wartime but the growing demand of the urban population, which remained the basis for prosperity until improved transport enabled it to be met by greater imports from overseas later in the century. When Adam Smith pointed out how the country's poverty restricted the widespread application of better ways, the need for capital to effect agricultural improvement was general except in those areas under the control of a wealthy and influential individual. The restriction was raised during the wars, though not wholly removed. By 1815, while the Lothians and Berwickshire were still most advanced, the north and west of the Highlands were the only areas where agriculture remained largely in traditional ways. Elsewhere the new and efficient methods were adopted generally, so that the Napoleonic Wars marked the completion of the improving movement in Scottish agriculture. By 1815 agriculture, except in the unimproved remote north and west, was on a modern basis prepared to meet the post-war challenge.

The increases in price for different commodities, and the responses they engendered, varied. The fluctuations in the price of wheat reflected its production and consumption in England. In spite of an extension of the acreage under wheat, oats still remained the more important crop in Scotland, and its price exceeded that of earlier years less frequently. Since the prices of the special products of Lowland agriculture did not rise so sharply during the war, the inflationary gains accruing to its farmers were less than to their counterparts in the south of England or in the Highlands, where the inflation of incomes by the sharp rise in the prices of their typical products — of wheat in England and of cattle and kelp in the Highlands — gave many landowners and tenants false impressions of permanent prosperity. The same delusions of grandeur, and especially the assumption of its permanence, were not possible in the Lowlands, except in the wheat-growing areas of the Lothians, where during the wars the younger farmers began to follow a more expensive way of life than had many of their predecessors.

The rise in the price of wheat during the war gave an incentive to grow more wheat, even in areas considered unsuitable for its cultivation. The high prices offset the natural disadvantages of more northerly regions, but the natural determinants remained, so that, when the end of the war and later the repeal of the corn laws removed the exceptional opportunities of protected home markets, the tendency to expand agricultural enterprises for which Scotland was less suited was removed and a pattern of production more appropriate to the natural resources of the country was re-established. Lack of specialisation, particularly in the production of wheat, prevented Scotland from gaining the full benefits of its high price, but after 1815 the mixed nature of Scottish farming was an advantage. The main fall in prices was concentrated, as was the rise, in wheat. English farmers, many of whom had leased additional lands at high rents, and often on borrowed capital, found they frequently had difficulty in meeting their commitments. Their Scottish counterparts were more favourably placed. The trend, though interrupted, continued in the middle of the nineteenth century, especially when in the 1850s the price of wheat fell absolutely and relatively to oats and barley. When the continuous series of agricultural statistics became available in Scotland in 1866, 8.2 per cent of the acreage under grain was in wheat, 16.0 per cent in barley, and 75.2 per cent in oats; in 1876 the percentages were 5.7 per cent under wheat, 19.6 per cent in barley, and 72.8 per cent in oats. By then only the Lothians retained wheat in a normal rotation, though to a diminished extent.

The prevalence of mixed farming eased the transition between agricultural enterprises as their profitability varied. Only the grazing farms of the Highlands and of the Southern Uplands and a restricted arable belt in the Lothians and in the Merse of Berwickshire were highly specialised. Elsewhere, in the south-west and in the north-east, a switch from the cultivation of grain, especially wheat, to relatively more profitable livestock husbandry was a feature of the nineteenth century. In these areas the move to growing turnips and especially to improving grass for better pastures contributed to more efficient stock rearing. Both areas also gained from the improved transport offered by railways and steamships. In the south-west the prosperous urban markets of the Clyde Valley absorbed the dairy produce of the region, and steamships helped convey the cattle and sheep of Galloway to Liverpool and other English markets as well. The farmers of the south-west made their own contribution by developing Ayrshire cattle, which, apart from the unimportant Shetland, is Scotland's only dairy breed. It came from a cross between carefully chosen cattle, imported mainly from England and sometimes from overseas; it could survive damp; it needed little nourishment; it produced much milk. The Ayrshire cow became the basis of the success of the dairy farmers of the south-west and of other parts of Scotland.

The north-east's pattern of agricultural production was more varied and was divided into two distinct areas lying roughly on each side of the Buchan Ness. West along the shore of the Moray Firth the land rises quickly to the hills in the south, and the latitude is northerly, but the shelter from the east winds, and the full benefit of such sunshine as there was, made the narrow coastal strip suitable for the production of grain of the hardier varieties. Some of the surplus was exported to the south, but a large part was consumed locally in the nearby Highlands, in the fishing areas along the coast, and in the distilleries. Though the fertile areas, such as the Black Isle, Ferintosh and the Laigh o' Moray, were few and somewhat isolated, they complemented the encircling hill areas by providing good pasture for the fattening of cattle. By contrast, the lands of Aberdeenshire to the south of the Buchan Ness were exposed to the east winds, and, being unsuitable for arable cultivation, were used for cattle-rearing. The specialisation was encouraged by the transport improvements of the nineteenth century. Aberdeenshire breeders could then exploit wider markets without incurring the deterioration in the condition of animals which accompanied the traditional method of walking to market. They pioneered scientific breeding, especially when the use of bone meal increased the cultivation of turnips and so provided adequate winter feeding. As early as 1779 Udny of Udny was reported to have an English 'shorthorned' bull on his farm, one of the vanguard of many improved English animals to be introduced to Scotland. Then throughout the 1840s and 1850s two brothers, the Cruickshanks of Sittyton, tried to breed a bull which, when crossed with native cattle, would produce an animal which would fatten quickly and so be suitable for the London market. They succeeded with the beef Shorthorn, which became popular in America as breeding stock. More characteristic of the area, and probably better known, was its own breed, the Aberdeen-Angus. Its first success came at the Smithfield Show in 1829 with animals from the herd of a Coupar Angus farmer, Hugh Wilson. William McCombie of Tillyfour continued Watson's work successfully until by about 1870 his animals were achieving both national and international success and the Aberdeen-Angus had joined the beef Shorthorn and the Hereford as the world's leading beef breeds.

Other causes influenced the response to the challenge and opportunities of changing markets. One was the reduction in rents. Even when nominal rents were not reduced, effective rents were through the simple expedient of tenants not paying. The adjustment of rents downwards removed the assumption, so easily encouraged by a long period of inflation, that rents should only be adjustable upwards. Thereafter the movement of rent was linked to that of prices, sometimes explicitly, as in the Lothians, where the adoption of 'corn rents' ensured that rents depended on the price of corn. Such flexibility encouraged a similar flexibility, or adaptability, among the various enterprises in the mixed farming of Scotland. The transition in agriculture was facilitated still further in Scotland through the country's different poor law. Scotland avoided the heavy burden of poor rates and other local burdens, which fell on some English agriculturists, especially in the south, through the adoption of the Speenhamland system of supplementing labourers' wages. In Scotland the heritors had to support the poor, but, even with an assessment which was not universal, the burden was not grievous though a fertile source of frequent and acrimonious complaint. Nor did the Scottish system lead to the same demoralisation of the labour force as took place elsewhere; labour never became so cheap as in southern England.

The benefits of flexible rents and a lighter poor law favoured all Scottish farmers. Two more strictly technical developments in Scottish agriculture in the nineteenth century were the practice of putting land down to temporary leys, of which Scottish agriculture had a higher proportion than English, and the use of under-drainage, especially on heavier soils.

In much of Scotland the maintenance of fertility required that the land be laid down to grass for some years. The mixtures of artificial grasses then sown —

combinations of rye-grass and the clovers were most popular — were not always the most suitable, but their increasing use in temporary leys in the early nineteenth century introduced rotations in which temporary grasses played an important part. Temporary leys not only conserved the pasture, they encouraged the move to a form of husbandry for which these areas were more suited. Ayrshire is a case in point. When the cultivation of wheat became unprofitable, land was laid down to temporary grass, helping the breeding of dairy cattle and the production of milk, butter and cheese. In a farm report from Ayrshire about 1830 a seed mixture of cocksfoot, timothy and rib-grass was recommended, something far in advance of the customary rye-grass and clovers. Though not all were as far-sighted, and though not all mixtures were so suitable, the increasing use of temporary leys led Scottish farmers generally to realise that they were not rivals, or even alternatives, to arable cultivation but complementary to it.

The increasing use of under-drainage helped those districts which remained chiefly arable, and which had fewer advantages than competitive areas in the south. Whatever their disadvantages, the old ridges provided a primitive form of drainage. With their removal substitutes became essential except on sloping ground which had reasonable natural drainage. By the late eighteenth century they were appearing. Sometimes they were channels formed by small stones; sometimes flat stones were inverted against each other to form a channel; sometimes stones formed a box for the drain; but none was satisfactory on heavy land where surface water was retained. A major advance came with the work of James Smith, who began to farm Deanston in Perthshire in 1823 and who transformed it into a productive unit by his various drainage schemes. Smith's success rested on a combination of two methods. First, following a technique used successfully in Essex, he laid drains of different depths leading into a main drain at the lowest level. Second, Smith realised that such an elaborate system would be effective only if the water could penetrate the subsoil. To that end Smith devised his subsoil plough, which followed in the furrow made by an ordinary plough. In the 1830s his methods spread throughout Scotland, though their application was limited by their cost. Even with the utmost economy, drainage was expensive in Scotland, where it frequently required larger pipes though they were not placed at the same depth as in England. The cost of drainage schemes, and the probability that they would benefit areas greater than one farm, normally placed the responsibility for them on the landlords, who were encouraged to undertake improvements by government grants of £4,000,000 in the 1840s and by the authorisation of private companies for land drainage.

By about 1870 agriculture in some parts of Scotland at least was dependent on the success of livestock husbandry, which in turn depended on arable successes, notably the provision of adequate supplies of turnips and oat straw as supplements to oilcake and oats for winter fodder. They guaranteed the more rapid fattening of animals, and sometimes of much younger ones. But the arable successes and the expansion of livestock production needed better transport by road, rail and steamship. Lime and artificial manures, which were being used increasingly, could then be distributed more widely; sheep could be sent for wintering, and all animals despatched to market in better condition. Arable successes and transport improvements enabled the potentialities of livestock production to be fully exploited, but the fundamental cause of the specialisation was quite simply that, as always, Scotland was naturally more suited for it. Since the concentration on livestock production in Scotland was a reflection of the country's comparative advantages, Scottish agriculture, except for a few areas, notably the south-east, stood to suffer much less by international competition in grain. Many districts in Scotland were attracted to the production of grain only by the exceptional circumstances of war and protection, and, once these exceptional circumstances were removed, they reverted to the production of commodities for which they were naturally more suited.

Landlord and tenant

The changes in agricultural production in the middle of the nineteenth century were accompanied by the emergence of a relationship between landlord and tenant which lasted until the First World War. Sinclair stated what was expected at the beginning of the nineteenth century:

> There are various improvements . . . which in a peculiar manner are in the province of proprietors . . . The erection of substantial and convenient farm-houses and offices is of this description. The making of extensive drains, which reach over a variety of farms, cannot, and ought not to be executed by tenants. Embankments, and straightening of rivers are of the same nature . . . Inclosing, planting, trenching and clearing the land of stones and rubbish, as well as reclaiming moors and mosses, are all operations, more appropriate to a landlord, than to a tenant.[2]

Such responsibilities for expensive and long-term improvement placed a barrier between landlords and others. Improvements were more easily discharged by landlords who had greater capital resources and readier access to bank credit, even when their estates were entailed. Tenant farmers were regarded as much poorer credit risks. Ostentatious living, including the construction of large houses and of decorative parks, was a rival to agricultural improvement, but the demand for resources for industrial investment was a less pressing claimant on the landlord's capital resources in the nineteenth century. Although in the early nineteenth century industrial growth rested greatly on the exploitation of natural resources, which were frequently in the possession of the landed interest, many landlords differed from their predecessors in the eighteenth century by showing little interest in developing them independently. The willingness of the landlords to devote their resources to agriculture gave an opportunity to men of ability but little capital to become tenants. The relationship was subject to strain. It was evident in the control of agricultural operations. Some tenants resented restrictions on cropping or on the sale of crops off the farm, though such restrictions could usually be justified as means of keeping the land in good condition. More serious were some of the consequences which continued to arise from the social power and assumptions of the landlords when their basis was being challenged increasingly in the nineteenth century.

Two legal examples were in the game laws and the law of hypothec. The modern distinction between the possession or cultivation of land and the rights to the game on it was developed in Scotland from the seventeenth century and from an Act of 1772 statutes became concerned chiefly with ensuring protection from indiscriminate killing. Some restraint was placed on the possession of shooting rights, for example by the recognition of a tenant's right to compensation for an excessive increase in game since the date of a lease if the landlord had failed to keep the game down, but the drift of legislation from the eighteenth to the early nineteenth centuries to preserve game for the proprietor led to increased resentment at the ensuing damage to crops, especially by rabbits, and to the sympathy already felt for tenants being extended to poachers.

The right of hypothec was a peculiarly Scottish legal doctrine which gave a landlord a general right over a tenant's moveable property as security of payment of the rent, the general right being converted by a legal process into a real right over certain goods, which could then be realised for payment of rent. Opposition to the law grew in the nineteenth century: merchants, who were supplying increasing quantities of manures and feeding stuffs, objected to the landlords' privilege as preferred creditors and to their right to the security of crops which had been sold off the farm, perhaps to agricultural merchants; established farmers complained that the security provided by the right encouraged landlords to accept excessively high rents from those anxious to enter farming. Supporters argued in defence that the security of the law encouraged the landlord to risk letting to those of limited resources and to continue the Scottish practice whereby rents became due for payment eighteen months or more after first entry to a farm. In 1867 this right over land held for agricultural purposes was restricted and in 1880 it was virtually abolished. Two other causes of strain were of more general social origin: the Disruption in 1843 and the growth of Liberalism. Few landlords joined the Free Church in 1843 and some actively disapproved of those of their tenants who did, especially when the Free Church became the landlords' critic. The growth of Liberalism was suspect for the same reason. It represented the political criticism, which complemented the ecclesiastical criticism of the Free Church, of the established rights of property and patronage.

The social gulf between landlord and tenant was repeated between tenant and farm labourer. A tenant, no matter how lowly, was at least on the ladder of social promotion, even if he might never ascend far. Though the availability of farms to let and the provision of credit facilities offered the prospects of social and economic progress to the farm labourer, some tenant farmers drew a social distinction between themselves and their workers as rigid as that drawn by the landlords between themselves and their tenants. Neither was easily breached. The more responsible farm worker, the grieve or manager, was normally employed only by the larger tenant farmers and was himself likely to become at best a small-scale tenant. If he had been employed by a man of similar standing before the transformation, the change would have been less drastic, even imperceptible, and the difference between the two social groups less.

The rigidity of social distinctions varied throughout the country. It was strongest in areas of high specialisation where farms were large and found its classic exposition in the grain-growing districts of the Lothians. There the key farm labourer was the hind, who provided the stable element in rural society in the Lothians and, through the efforts of his wife and family, or of a female servant who lived in his cottage, he was able to supply much of the seasonal labour required. By guaranteeing his employer a supply of labour adequate for permanent and seasonal needs, the hind relieved the farmer of one of the more intractable problems of agricultural operations. Some benefit fell to the hind too, because, since he had a tied house, and received about two-thirds of his income in kind, he escaped the repercussion of many fluctuations of employment and income. By contrast the other main group of agricultural employees in the Lothians, the regular agricultural labourer, suffered from these uncertainties. The labourer gained from wartime conditions when, in spite of inflation, his real income increased, but after 1815 he could maintain a reasonable standard of living only when in continuous employment. When they were so employed, some of the labourers were able to maintain standards only slightly less than that of the hinds; when they were not, and especially where there were relatively few opportunities for non-agricultural employment, the labourers sank into squalor.

The structure of rural society in the Lothians in the nineteenth century provided a basic pattern by which other areas were frequently judged, but, since farms were generally neither so large nor so specialised elsewhere, ownership, agricultural practice, and employment varied. Wherever the family unit was important, as in the dairying south-west, the hired labourer was less important than in the Lothians, especially since any increase in demand for hired labour through a particular specialisation, as for potato lifting in Ayrshire, was generally only seasonal and could be met by Highland labour, or, in the south-west, by an increase in its long-standing use of seasonal labour from Ireland. When a labourer was permanently employed on a family farm, he was frequently a farmer's son, preparing himself, technically and financially, to become a tenant farmer. Social distinctions between the tenants and their few employees were less in such areas, and were even further obliterated through the existence of many small-scale proprietors, who were active workers on their land, and could not readily be distinguished from the tenants on the larger estates. If the south-west represented one extreme, and the Lothians another, east and central Scotland — from Fife and the Howe of the Mearns through Strathmore and Strathearn to Menteith — illustrated a variety of social patterns, which reflected its variety of agricultural activities. The larger units required a supply of labour similar to that in the Lothians, but the system never operated successfully in other areas. In central Scotland the young unmarried ploughman was the grade of labour most commonly used. Another factor distinguished its labour supply. Since hinds were not employed, there was no reserve of seasonal labour from hinds' families, nor was the area favoured, as was the south-west, by close proximity to Ireland, but it had a number of smallholders, given pieces of land generally to enable them to grow potatoes, in return for help when required on the larger farms.

Whatever the exact position of the various ranks of rural society, the new methods of agricultural production made novel demands on it and, though alternative opportunities were appearing in other sectors of the economy, the supply of rural labourers remained sufficiently ample to provide a continuing inducement to retain labour-consuming methods of production on some farms even when alternatives were being pioneered. Meikle's threshing machine, first produced in 1786, was more commonly used in Scotland than in England in its early days, but the most successful implement in this period was the reaper, devised in Scotland by a divinity student, Patrick Bell, in the late 1820s. Since it was manufactured inefficiently by country blacksmiths, few were used. The American, McCormick, invented his reaper on the same principles as Bell's in the following decade, but neither was exploited until the 1850s, when improved models combining the best of both were produced.

The new order was evident in the farm buildings. A typical transformation to the old structure began by making the barn a separate building, running at right angles to the original house, and so forming two sides of a square. The stack yard was placed behind it. The next stage was to add a third side to the square, with a line of cattle-houses running from the other side of the dwelling-house, and so opposite the barn, but, perhaps as a sign that the transformation was not complete, the midden remained in the middle of the square which was being formed. Later improvements made the whole steading bigger, as, for example, by adding a fourth side to the buildings, but, because the midden frequently remained in the square, the house was set down away from it with its front facing the garden and with its back, with as few windows as possible, facing the steading.

Such structural changes affected the provision of housing for the new groups of agricultural workers. Wherever the new order produced a dominance of family farms, as in much of the south-west, the change was not drastic. There the majority of agriculturists continued to live in the new farm steading much as they had lived in the old, and the need to supply new types of housing for the employed labourers was less important. The need for new housing was greatest in the large, specialised, and mainly arable farms of the Lothians and of central and east Scotland. Where the married worker was employed, some form of housing had to be provided, though it varied greatly from farm to farm and at different times. During wartime prosperity some improvements were made, but the deterioration in the hind's position after 1815 was most obvious in his housing. The tenant had no money to spare on its improvement and was reluctant to press his landlord to do so at a time when he was often seeking expenditure in other directions and sometimes a reduction in rent. Though housing conditions deteriorated, something had to be provided and, as many of the other payments he received were in kind, the hind became an isolated element in an economy increasingly on a cash basis. Then the increasing commutation of his payments in kind led him to consider the possibilities of other occupations. No matter how bad the housing of the hinds, the social degradation of the Scottish agricultural worker was most evident in the bothies, which were found only in those parts of eastern Scotland where young unmarried workers were employed extensively. In the bothies the labourers were normally left to look after themselves, in whatever conditions of squalor they wished, though sometimes they were accommodated and fed in the farmhouse.

The Highlands

The fortunes of the Highland economy contrasted with those of the rest of Scotland between the 1780s and the 1870s. As population grew and agricultural efficiency was increasingly the aim of the landlords, the grinding poverty which already existed was not relieved. In such circumstances emigration on a scale not so far witnessed in the Highlands was inevitable but was postponed by the economic effects of the French Wars until later in the nineteenth century. By that time the split in the Highland economy was clear. In the north and west lay the root of the gravest poverty. In the south and east some approach to a new and revived economy had been achieved. Social stress emerged when the small tenants, tenaciously regarding the land as inalienably theirs, could not meet the landlords' demands for higher rents and so had to submit to new forms of land use, which, whatever merits they may have had, ran counter to the rights the tenants assumed were theirs. The old order could have been maintained and the landlords' demands met only by action in two different ways. First, an increase in the subsistence from the land would have released some of the limited cash income available to Highland tenantry from purchasing necessary imports to meet higher rent payments. Second, an increase in cash income from non-agricultural sources would have provided a means of meeting the landlords' demands directly. The disintegration of the Highland economy was arrested temporarily in both directions.

Subsistence from the land was increased through the introduction of the potato, which was generally accepted by 1800 and which became the major crop on some holdings. The potato was one of the few crops suitable for Highland weather, and the plentiful supply of labour available for its cultivation helped to ensure high yields. The dangers of monoculture appeared only with the potato famine in the 1840s. Until 1815 the only effect was the benefit of increased subsistence. Additional cash income came, as often in the earlier eighteenth century, from seasonal employment in the Lowlands and from such indigenous activities as linen manufacture, distilling, fishing, and from kelp-making.

Linen manufacture was unimportant in the Highlands in spite of the efforts of the Board of Trustees and others after 1745. It was more successful in the east, though primarily only for the diminishing number who lived on the inland straths, but not for those in the problem areas of the west and north. Whatever linen manufacture there was in the Highlands remained dependent on the economic life of the Lowlands. Linen merchants from the south brought the flax to the Highlands to have it spun, and took the yarn back to the Lowlands for weaving. The occupation never interfered with any other activities but remained mainly a part-time activity. It was not an indigenous, independent, industrial growth.

A second source of cash income, though important only locally, lay in distilling whisky, an activity not confined to the Highlands but one with a greater influence in a region with few satisfactory alternatives. In the eighteenth century, when the demand for whisky was rising, Lowland distillers complained that they were losing local markets to Highland producers, which forced them to seek outlets in England, where Highland whisky was sold too. The importance of such markets was confirmed by legal exports, which rose from 34,000 gallons in the year 1779-80 to over 195,000 gallons in 1788-9, an increase made possible by importing barley from England, almost 100,000 quarters being brought into the country in 1781-2.[3] The official figures of exports are minimum quantities. A large quantity of whisky was distilled illicitly, not only for domestic consumption, but for sale. In 1782, 1,211 illicit stills were seized in the Highlands and 819 in the Lowlands; in 1796, apparently another active year by excisemen, 799 were condemned in the Highlands and 464 in the Lowlands. Illicit distillation was the result of a heavy taxation policy, which dated from increases in the malt tax and which became more onerous by additional duties levied in the 1780s. The most significant change came with the imposition of a tax on the licensing of stills in 1786 — initially at 20s. a gallon of capacity in the Highlands and 30s. in the Lowlands, but with sharp increases subsequently — and with a prohibition, which lasted until 1816, on sending Highland whisky to the Lowlands. At the same time small stills below 40 gallons capacity were made illegal. This penal taxation at a time of rising demand simply drove whisky distilling underground in the Highlands. When it was modified after 1816, the volume of spirits paying tax more than doubled in two years. Radical reform of the excise laws and their implementation in the 1820s, combined with such requirements as the insistence on allowing whisky to mature before being passed for human consumption, removed the industry from being a part-time, and often illegal, occupation to a full-time and legal activity. It continued to be a useful source of employment in the Highlands and Islands, especially in certain areas such as Islay and Glenlivet, but it did not remain a universal supplement to either subsistence or cash income throughout the region.

Fishing provided a third, and more fruitful, though intermittent and uncertain, source of additional cash income. White fishing was more stable than herring fishing. It was not seasonal, was not a rival occupation to agriculture, and experienced fewer difficulties in curing its catch or in establishing contact with the main markets of the Lowlands. Its contribution to cash income remained small even in those few locations around the Minch, notably in Barra, where it was concentrated. The contribution of herring fishing was more important but its expansion was limited. The capital required to fit out a fishing boat, though small, was beyond the resources of most Highlanders; the salt laws hindered curing, because, though drawbacks could be obtained on salt used for curing, they were difficult to collect from the dispersed customs houses in the Highlands; finally, the commercial barriers to sending the herring to markets in the south, essential to obtain cash income, were insuperable. Marketing fell into the hands of Lowland merchants, who ensured that the centre of the industry was located in the Clyde and that the greatest benefit from any expansion in demand accrued to those fishing in the lochs opening from the Firth, especially Loch Fyne. Further north the irregularity of maintaining the necessary commercial contacts prevented any consistent growth of herring fishing beyond whatever was required to meet limited local demand.

Attempts to help the fisheries took various forms. Fishing villages were constructed in the late eighteenth and early nineteenth centuries in attempts — sometimes by landlords, sometimes by private companies — to provide the necessary centres for commercial activities. Among them were Torridon, Gairloch, Rodel, Lochinver, Plockton and Dornie. In 1786 a more general effort was made to encourage fishing, especially as a means of reviving the Highlands, in the formation of a joint-stock company, the British Fisheries Society. The Society flourished for over a decade, but is remembered primarily because of the failure of its settlements on the west coast, at Lochbay, Tobermory and Ullapool, abandoned in 1837, 1844 and 1848 respectively. It succeeded at Pulteneytown (now part of Wick), where a settlement was already growing before the Society gave further assistance. External factors did not encourage the Society's growth: the Napoleonic Wars brought enemy interference with shipping and rising prices for raw materials; the west coast, where the failure was more notable, suffered when the centre of the herring fishing moved from the Minch to the Moray Firth, especially after 1797, and when European demand began to displace the older West Indian demand for herring. In spite of the failure of its settlements, the Society had a wider influence by obtaining some amelioration of the restrictive salt laws and by providing a pattern for official action under the Fishery Act of 1808, which brought into being an official organisation for the industry with resident Fishery Officers.

The Act was not the first government aid. It had existed for some time in the form of bounties towards the fitting out of vessels above a certain minimum tonnage. The Highlanders had inadequate resources for such ventures and gained from state aid only in 1787, when the restriction on bounties was altered and all vessels, of whatever size, received them on the basis of the number of barrels caught. Once again the Clyde ports gained. The direct repercussions on Highland fishings of the larger vessels then sent north varied. An unfavourable effect was the ability of the southern boats to follow the herring in the various lochs of the west and north, which reduced part of the benefit which the erratic movements of the herring brought to particular areas from time to time. A favourable effect, though until 1787 an illegal one, was that these ships frequently bought the catches of local fishermen and so provided them with the commercial contact with the south which they needed.

The fourth, and most important, addition to cash income came from the manufacture of kelp, an extraction of an alkaline ash from seaweed, which was used in various industrial processes, particularly in the making of soap and glass. Industrial demand grew during the latter half of the eighteenth century, then, especially during the wars, the interruption to the supply of such foreign substitutes as barilla, and the taxation of salt, which became the basis of the alkali industry in the nineteenth century, all contributed to maintain the rising demand. Prices, though fluctuating, rose sharply, from £2 a ton in the middle of the eighteenth century to a peak of £20 a ton in 1810. Production responded and rose during the Napoleonic Wars. In North Uist in 1770 it was about 400 tons; in 1810 it was about 1,500 tons. Though kelp manufacture was introduced to the Orkneys and to the east coast as early as the 1730s, the great increase in production in the late eighteenth century was concentrated in the areas of greatest poverty on the west coast and in the Islands. It was one of the few industrial commodities which such areas of poor natural endowments could produce. The rise in kelp prices was, however, only the most dramatic illustration of the effect of the wartime price rise. The Highlands gained more generally through the prices of such exports as cattle and wool increasing more than that of grain, the most important import. Cash income increased even from traditional products.

The most notable effect of the price rise was a substantial increase in rentals. In 1774 the total rental of Breadalbane was £4,194; in 1815 it was £23,000. Initially some kelping rights were let on reasonable terms, which allowed the tacksmen or tenants to make some profit, but, as the profits from the manufacture increased, the landlords leased land on the understanding that they would obtain high rents. At the same time the wages paid to labourers remained fairly steady. It was then an easy step for the organisation of the trade to fall into the hands of the landlords or their representatives. The quantity produced and sold on the account of some became very high. Clanranald, who owned the Uists, sold annually about 1,000 tons during the peak of wartime prices. In 1809 he had a gross income from his kelp manufacture of £13,277, leaving a net income of £10,047 on a land rental, increased by kelping rights, of £7,500. Early in the eighteenth century his land rental had been less than £1,000.

The appropriation of the surplus cash income by the landlords was less reprehensible than was their failure to put it to productive use. More attention should be directed to their action at this time rather than at the time of the clearances. Perhaps the clearances could never have been avoided, but any opportunity to do so came during the Napoleonic Wars. Instead, the landlords encouraged more people to settle in the already overcrowded kelping areas, an action as culpable as later attempts to clear them. Placing more people in areas with resources already inadequate for subsistence exacerbated an already grave social problem, which became acute when kelp prices and profits collapsed. In short, the economy of the kelping regions became precariously dependent on the continuation of certain favourable conditions which could only be temporary. The greatest tragedy of the period was the ignorance of the landlords, and indeed of most of the people, that their prosperity represented only a respite from the problems which had faced them throughout the eighteenth century. Frequently landlords thought the rise in rents to be the outcome of their own improvements rather than of impersonal, and passing, market forces. More expensive ways became not only increasingly attractive but increasingly practicable, so, in spite of rising cash income, debts accumulated. Clanranald's debts were £52,289 in 1797; in 1811 they were £71,280; in 1812 they were over £100,000. The decisive break in the prosperity came with falling prices, especially after 1815. The effect was worst in the peculiarly vulnerable kelping districts. The price of kelp fell before the fall in the prices of agricultural products generally, from a peak of £20 a ton in 1810 to £10 a ton, at which level it remained, though generally drifting down, until the excise duty on salt was abolished in 1825. In 1824 the price was £8 a ton; in 1825 it was £7; in 1828 it was £4 15s; and in 1834 it was £3 a ton. Since costs of production were around £5 a ton, production fell drastically. In 1827 even Clanranald stopped production for the season.

The drop in kelp prices, and the failure of the Highlands to gain any benefit from the expansion of the herring fishing in the Moray Firth, reduced the cash income of the Highlands sharply and substantially. The landlord had then either to reduce rents or increase his tenants' indebtedness. Eviction was no solution, except as part of the reorganisation of estates, because all tenants were similarly placed. As they had often done before, Highland landlords permitted indebtedness to grow, first that of their tenants, then of themselves. The only solution became the desperate one of selling the estates. Clanranald sold part in the 1820s. In the 1830s his debts began to accumulate once more and the whole estate was sold in 1838.

Such sales represented the final break-up of the old order which had stressed the needs of the family and of military strategy rather than economy in the administration of the land. The gulf between smaller and larger owners widened. On the other hand the landless did not grow proportionately. Where they did, as cottars, the scarcity of any form of employment placed them in a precarious position, though the crofters were little better off because of the pitiful size of their holdings. Lack of capital, intensified by the fall in money incomes after the war, inhibited improvement, and a high correlation may be postulated between the extent to which internal reforms in various districts met the challenge and the lesser degree of emigration from them. The greatest contribution to emigration came from the problem area of the north and west, where natural endowments were inferior and population pressure greater. The area was placed in a fundamentally difficult and dangerous position. Increasing population alone led to a worsening of the balance of trade between the Highlands and other regions. Imports of meal were continuous and the need for supplementary cash income grew. As cash income dropped, and cultivation remained poor and primitive, only dependence on the potato enabled the increasing population of the Highlands to be maintained. In the 1840s this last remaining barrier to change collapsed. The population of many Highland areas reached its peak at the 1841 census. In 1845, and more so in 1846, blight in the potato removed the major source of subsistence. A transformation of the Highland economy could no longer be averted.

The disintegration of the economy encouraged the extension of sheep-rearing in the Highlands. Sheep-farming as a specialised occupation was introduced to the central Highlands by men from the Southern Uplands in the 1760s until by about 1800 the counties just north of the Highland line were well stocked and the spread into the remoter parts of the west and north began. After the Napoleonic Wars the fall in prices called a temporary halt, but from the 1830s to the 1870s prices were sufficiently high to maintain the profits in sheep-farming. The introduction of sheep occasioned some evictions and has roused much anger, partly through concentration on a few areas, where the worst effects were evident, even more through a misapprehension of the grinding poverty which existed before the sheep came and which impelled emigration, sooner or later, unless the Highlands were to be left in squalor. Overall perhaps only 20 per cent of the land went out of cultivation to make way for sheep, and even where the area was greater, as in the areas of greatest notoriety, such as the straths of Sutherland, the process was more gradual than has sometimes been assumed. Nevertheless the introduction of sheep was an explosive force in the life of the Highlands. It was a new agricultural enterprise which required new men. The Highlanders had neither the capital nor the requisite technical skill. It also implied bigger farms, restrictions on hill grazing, and fewer people. Population pressure was increased still further in areas without sheep and where fishing was either impossible or inadequate. But sheep-farming was not the cause of the clearances and of emigration. In certain areas there was emigration without sheep. It is the tragedy of some of the clearances, especially of those in Sutherland, which has caused sheep-farming to be blamed. Yet even in Sutherland, the introduction of sheep only occasioned the change. The prime cause was the rejection of the conception that the land should support the largest number of people irrespective of their standard of living. For that reason the stimulus to emigration was there, and took place from certain areas without the introduction of sheep. In others the new agricultural enterprises precipitated it.

NOTES

1. For further information see R. M. Mitchison, 'The movements of Scottish corn prices in the seventeenth and eighteenth centuries', *Economic History Review*, second series, vol. 18 (1965).

2. Sinclair, *Analysis of the Statistical Account*, vol. iii, p. 376.

3. The export figures are from the Report on Scotch Distillery Duties, 1798. British Parliamentary Papers, 1803, XI, p. 431. In evidence in the same Report two London distillers gave much higher figures of Scottish exports to England (1781-2, 257,544 gallons; 1782-3, 245,700 gallons). Comparison of these with their statistics of production over the same years leads to the improbable conclusion that consumption in Scotland must have declined from 1780 until 1783, when it became negative, a reflection of illicit distillation.

CHAPTER X

An Industrial Society

Population

A simple but striking change in Scottish society in the nineteenth century was its increased numbers. Sinclair's estimate in the *Old Statistical Account* was of a population of 1,526,492 in 1795. From 1801 the census figures provide more reliable data:

POPULATION OF SCOTLAND (000s)

		Percentage increase			Percentage increase
1801	1,608.4	–	1841	2,620.2	10.8
1811	1,805.9	12.3	1851	2,888.7	10.2
1821	2,091.5	15.8	1861	3,062.3	6.0
1831	2,364.4	13.0	1871	3,360.0	9.7

Any discussion of demographic change in the first half of the nineteenth century is hampered by the absence of reliable statistics until the introduction of compulsory registration of births, deaths and marriages in 1855.[1] An adequate statistical foundation is available only after the census of 1861. If, as a rough measurement, a rate of natural increase of ten per cent is assumed to apply to the earlier decades, the actual increase exceeded the natural increase in all of the first half of the nineteenth century. After 1861, when changes may be calculated reliably, a net loss by migration was recorded in each decade, though always less than the natural increase until the First World War. How many of those who left Scotland went to other parts of Great Britain and how many went overseas is uncertain. From 1825, and more reliably from 1853, the number who left Scotland for non-European destinations is known, though subject to qualifications. Using this group as a basis for rough calculations, it may not be far wrong to suggest that in the later nineteenth century one in every two went overseas. Many Scots certainly went to other parts of the United Kingdom and overseas even when the population was rising rapidly at home.

The apparent readiness of Scots to move out of Scotland was partly a reflection of the greater mobility of the Scots at home. One of the most dramatic accompaniments of the industrial growth of the nineteenth century, now an accepted part of Scottish social life, was the redistribution of the bulk of the population towards the central belt. The movement was both cause and consequence of industrial growth. The growth of industry in the central belt relied on the elastic supply of labour from rural Scotland, and the industrial growth attracted the excess population from the countryside. The move is evident in the various censuses from 1801 and can be linked to Webster's census of 1755. The proportions of the population of Scotland living in the ten central counties of Ayr, Clackmannan, Dunbarton, Fife, Lanark, Renfrew, Stirling, West, Mid- and East Lothian increased from 35.2 per cent in 1755 to 40.8 per cent in 1801 and to 57.5 per cent in 1871. The proportion in the four west-central counties of Ayr, Dunbarton, Lanark and Renfrew grew from 14.3 per cent in 1755 to 20.6 per cent in 1801 and to 37.0 per cent in 1871. By contrast rural counties recorded peak populations from the middle of the nineteenth century: in 1831 in the counties of Argyll, Kinross and Perth; in 1841 in Inverness; in 1851 in Kirkcudbright, Ross and Cromarty, Sutherland and Wigtown; in 1861 in Berwick, Caithness, Orkney, Roxburgh, Zetland.

Since the place of birth of all inhabitants in Scotland is given from the 1841 census onwards, it becomes possible to demonstrate the course of the movement of population within Scotland more clearly thereafter. The statistics derived from the census give only a minimum measurement of movement. They do not include semi-permanent or seasonal migrants, if they happened to be in the county of birth at the date of the census, nor those who may have made several moves in the decade between the censuses, but the general pattern is not affected. At mid-century the main area of reception was Glasgow and its neighbouring counties. The only other reception area was Edinburgh and the Lothians. In Aberdeen and the north-east the population movements balanced each other. In 1851 other areas in Scotland sent more of their natives to other parts of Scotland than they themselves received the natives of other parts. The two reception areas, however, differed from each other. Glasgow gained a net inflow from all other regions, even from Edinburgh, the only instance of such a contribution from the capital. Glasgow also absorbed a greater proportion of emigrants than Edinburgh from all regions except the Borders, though the latter's contribution to Edinburgh was more than counterbalanced by the movement from Edinburgh to Glasgow. The movements of population within Scotland were supplemented by movements into Scotland, particularly from Ireland. In 1871, 6 per cent of the total population, or 207,770, were Irish-born, but the proportion varied considerably throughout Scotland. Some counties had practically none, but in Lanarkshire about 14 per cent of the population was Irish-born in 1871, in Renfrewshire about 13 per cent.

The attractions of industrial growth explain why immigrants moved to particular districts, above all to Glasgow and the west of Scotland, but not why people were willing to move in the first place from the rural areas of Scotland and from Ireland.

Seasonal migration within Scotland, especially from the Highlands to the Lowlands, was an old practice, most migrants finding employment in agriculture, though some gained openings in industry, as in the bleachfields of the Vale of Leven. It was a means which enabled many Highlanders, and the

Highland economy as a whole, to postpone the worst effects of demographic pressure on limited resources in the eighteenth century. In the nineteenth century, while seasonal migration persisted, more permanent settlement in the Lowlands grew. Until the displacement of the handloom weavers by the use of power-driven machinery around the 1820s, such permanent migration, whether within Scotland or overseas, was generally from the land because of new agricultural practices. In both Highlands and Lowlands, the basic factor underlying rural change was the end of an old social structure, but from the 1780s a perceptible difference can be noted. The Highlands provide the best illustration, but the Highland problem was not unique. Its experience was shared by other areas of rural depopulation. Unless a district achieved 'solvency through reform',[2] there was no alternative for an increasing population but emigration. The extent of 'solvency through reform' depended in turn on natural conditions or on industrial development. In the south-east the growth of the woollen industry, combined with the region's traditional fertility, did not produce the same pressing problems as in the south-west, troubled by its lack of industry, by the conversion of arable land to sheep-farming, and by a continuous, and occasionally rapid, influx of Irish.

Though the Irish represented only a small part of the movement into the central belt, their contribution to its social life was unique. There had long been traffic, both ways, between Ulster and south-west Scotland, but the first modern movement was initiated by the Irish rebellion of 1798, and the number of Irish-born inhabitants of Scotland increased after 1815. The Irish potato famine of the 1840s initiated a second phase of migration, quantitatively greater than anything experienced earlier and qualitatively different. Until the 1840s the Irish immigrant was comparable to that from rural Scotland. Both were seeking higher standards of living than could be obtained at home. Blight in the potato brought a difference. 'Self-improvement was the impulse that transported him to Scotland in pre-famine days. Self-preservation was the urge that drove him onwards in the black night of pestilence.'[3] The tendency for the Irish immigrant in Scotland to be much poorer and more desperate than his predecessor before the famine was increased by a further factor. Since most preferred to go to the United States, for which the fare was £4, only the poorest stayed in Scotland. Most immigrants came from Antrim by the shortest and cheapest route to Portpatrick. At the beginning of the nineteenth century they settled in Galloway, Dumfriesshire, and Ayrshire to work as farm labourers. By the 1840s, when the type of migrant changed, Galloway had few opportunities left for Irish labourers, and so the new migrants had to seek employment elsewhere, though they continued to use the traditional route. The way of the majority lay, therefore, across agricultural Galloway and south Ayrshire to the developing industrial areas of north Ayrshire, Renfrewshire and north Lanarkshire, where most remained except for a small number who reached Dundee. After 1830, when the heavy industries were established, and especially in the 1840s, when the type of Irish immigrant changed, the drift of the Irish was to the ironworks and to the coalmines, where they could find unskilled, unpleasant tasks requiring little or no training, which the native Scots were not anxious to accept.

The influx helped offset movements of Scots overseas in the first half of the nineteenth century, but the high rate of natural increase was the more important factor leading to the rise in population. It was concentrated in the areas of industrial development, especially in the new growing towns, where an industrial society was first formed.

An industrial society

The larger cotton mills established in the later eighteenth century were such a contrast to anything which had gone before that they can be taken to represent the first moves towards the emergence of an industrial society. Their mere size — New Lanark employed 368 people in 1791 and about 1,700 in 1820 — alone made them unique, comparable in their influence on industrial organisation only to the earlier example of Carron Company in the iron industry. Their influence was great because they were unrepresentative, but their problems were shared by others. One which determined much of the subsequent form of development of many mills was the inadequacy of the supply of labour. Even the larger mills in existing centres of population were not assured of an adequate supply, but the difficulty was more acute in the remote establishments, in those larger mills placed in sparsely populated districts to exploit natural advantages and which, until the advent of steam power, had no alternative but to remain near adequate water supplies. The costs of construction were such that mills remained in the initial location even when steam power was used in them. They met their labour requirements in various ways: by using pauper children supplied by parish poorhouses, and by using emigrants. Pauper children were not used extensively in Scotland. Carron Company found them troublesome, and New Lanark was one of the few cotton mills in which they made an important contribution to the labour force. Emigrants were the major source of supply of labour. They came from rural Scotland and from Ireland. Preferences varied and, when expressed, cannot always be considered reliable. One employer who had no doubt of his preference was Henry Houldsworth, who had mills at Anderston and Woodside in Glasgow. He commented in 1833 that they were 'almost full of Irish; we can scarcely get a Scotchman for a partner or a watchman'. Houldsworth was highly, almost offensively, critical of some of the local labour which he had first encountered when he had come to Glasgow from Manchester at the beginning of the nineteenth century:

> At that period the spinning trade was extremely limited; there was not, I believe, more than one mill or so at Glasgow; at that time the hands employed were principally highland men, and all the attempts that were made to induce those men to work hard and live better were of no avail, and I had to get Englishmen to show them an example of industry before I could stir; for the first six months I could not

get them to earn more than 12s. to 14s. a week; they would rather live upon meal and potatoes than exert themselves, but they were much more sober than they are now.[4]

Overcrowding and squalid conditions accompanied the concentration of industrial population, but conditions varied. In larger concerns — New Lanark, Catrine, Deanston and elsewhere — a new way of living was evident, yet not necessarily in increasing squalor. The housing, though differing from what many had previously experienced, was an advance on earlier standards. In Catrine, for instance, the stone-built, two-storeyed, slated houses were better than what was common in adjacent country districts. In even sharper contrast, some attempt was made to organise social services in most of the larger establishments. At Catrine a church, schoolhouse, gardens and pasture for cows were provided, while, in an early effort to supply police measures, even though aimed chiefly at ensuring the security of the mill and the proprietors' property, the gates at both ends of the main street were locked every night. The existence of such social provision warns against assuming that greatly increased squalor was introduced by the larger examples of the new industrial order. Squalor and harsh industrial discipline were found more often in the smaller concerns. The distinction runs through the reports of the various parliamentary investigations of the time. Various commissioners were often unduly impressed, perhaps by conscious design on the part of the mill-owners, by some melodramatic features of the new industrial enterprises, as at Rothesay, where a band of workers 'serenaded us while there, and from the work to the pier, where we reimbarked [sic]',[5] but throughout all their reports they stressed the adverse and inhuman conditions of those smaller mills, especially on the east coast, which continued producing linen. The favourable reports of the Factories Inquiry Commissioners in 1833 on Catrine, New Lanark, Deanston, and Stanley contrasted with those on four mills in Dunfermline, twenty-two spinning mills in Kirkcaldy and thirty-five mills in Dundee, nearly all small and engaged in the linen industry. Later, in Perthshire, after fulsome praise of the Stanley mills, the Commissioner visited a number of small flax mills around Blairgowrie, and reported that 'the small mills are uniformly ill-cleaned and ventilated, and there is more dust in the preparing rooms and less attention to the boxing in of machinery, than in large establishments'. At Stirling a number of woollen and paper factories 'are kept in a very filthy state, ill ventilated, and the machinery is not well boxed'. An exception to the absence of criticism of the larger establishments was Blantyre. To use the Commissioner's own words,

The Blantyre works belonging to Messrs. Henry Monteith and Company is the only great establishment which I have seen, situated in the country, away from the population of a town, of which it is impossible to write chiefly in terms of approbation. The buildings are most of them old, the apartments are not well cleaned, low-roofed, the passages narrow, ventilation little attended to, there are no seats for the workers, and occasionally considerable annoyance from the water closets.[6]

The Commissioner's explanation of the defects of Blantyre — that they arose through the control and direction of the mill being left in the hands of managers rather than retained by the proprietors — was hardly convincing, but, whatever the explanation, the condition of Blantyre was considered exceptional. That was the measure of its importance.

The proprietors of the larger establishments may simply have been better advocates of their case, or the commissioners unduly impressed by the great, the new, and the powerful, but, even if their better physical conditions are accepted, the larger establishments had other defects. They loomed large in the minds of the workers, though objections raised to them were frequently ignored, or regarded as examples of irrational prejudice or ignorance, by owners and official investigators alike. The objections were basically to industrial discipline, or to such social discipline as was required for the effective operation of the communities. As New Lanark was the leading example of what could be achieved in the new industrial society, its experience was viewed with special interest. Not all thought New Lanark could succeed commercially. When it did, attention was concentrated on the social arrangements which seemed to contradict many of the viewpoints held tenaciously by cotton manufacturers. They delighted when such arrangements collapsed, especially if through rejection by the workers. One example shows the opposition of some workers to better social provision under Owen's more idealistic regime. The Blantyre mill did not provide the best conditions among the larger mills, nor the most enlightened management, but its proprietor alleged in 1816 that a 'good many' workers preferred to move from New Lanark to Blantyre. In explaining why, one worker stated clearly the opposition to industrial discipline and direction even when well-intentioned:

> They had got a number of dancing-masters, a fidler, a band of music, that there were drills and exercises, and that they were dancing together till they were more fatigued than if they were working.[7]

Much of the output of yarn from the new spinning mills was woven in Scotland and so increased the demand for the services of the handloom weavers. Their number probably doubled from 1780 to something under 60,000 in 1800. From the 1780s to about 1815, while the demand for their services was high, handloom weavers earned as much as 30s. a week, or more, and became the most prosperous, the most aristocratic, and the most autocratic, of workmen. The introduction of the power loom, used successfully at Catrine in 1807 and soon afterwards at other Finlay establishments, was a direct technical challenge to their supremacy, but before 1820, when the power loom had still not been adopted extensively in cotton weaving, and but little in weaving other fabrics, the wages of weavers were falling. Competition overseas, but most of all at home, led to cuts in the wages of weavers as well as those of spinners in attempts to keep costs low. The number of handloom weavers increased to a peak of over 80,000 in 1840, when the demand for their services was faltering and their distress known. Most were in the west of Scotland, which in 1838 had over

50,000 looms, or about two-thirds of the Scottish total. Over one half of the total looms were engaged in weaving cotton goods, about one-third in linen and the remainder in the silk and woollen trades. The increase in numbers was too great and continued too long to be only a short-term failure by weavers to adjust their expectations. The apparently perverse reaction arose because handloom weaving was an easy trade to learn. In the condition of the labour market after 1815 it offered the only possibility of some form of living to many from the rural Lowlands, from the Highlands, and, recognised most of all, from Ireland. The report of Jellinger Symons, the Assistant Commissioner for the South of Scotland, to the Hand-loom Weavers Commission in 1839, summed up the situation:

> The Irish weavers are a little in advance in the career down hill, for they are the main cause of pulling the Scotch down after them. Of course they are in a slightly better condition than in their own country, which is precisely the reason why they take the lead in the career downwards, having less natural repugnance to privations which they have been previously in some measure inured to; when a manufacturer desires to lower his wages, it is ten to one but the Irish are the first to accept his terms.[8]

The comment may have attributed too much causal influence to the Irish. One estimate suggests that around 1820 only some 30 per cent of the weavers in Glasgow, and something under a quarter of those born in Scotland, had been born in Ireland. The technical change to power-weaving was not the first, or an adequate explanation of the collapse of handloom weaving, but it was the final, and most evident, cause, from which no recovery was possible. In the same way the Irish were not the sole cause of the 'career down hill', but, as an immigrant group, they were more evident, at least in parts of the west of Scotland. Many would ignore the qualifications and attribute the plight of the handloom weavers to the inevitability of technical change, worsened by Irish immigration.

Their distress forced many handloom weavers to enter other occupations. Some entered the factories, others left the textile industries altogether, others emigrated — sometimes under the auspices of the emigration societies, which were active from the 1820s among handloom weavers, though not always most successfully. In spite of its decline, handloom weaving did not end entirely. The woollen weavers in the Borders, carpet weavers in Kilmarnock, and those engaged in higher-quality woollen and silk goods were less hard-pressed, but also suffered from cyclical depression and from more protracted decline. From the woollen trade emerged the most persistent centre of handloom weaving at Kilbarchan, which around 1870 still had about 800 handloom weavers. At the same time, the woollen manufacturers of Paisley employed about 2,000 handloom weavers in busy seasons. By then most handloom weavers found an independent existence almost impossible. The mass market, on which most of the Scottish textile industries depended, gave decreasing scope for their activities. By the late nineteenth century handloom weavers could exist only if, as in Kilbarchan, they were able to work for a very high-quality market which was anxious to obtain woollen goods simply because they had been hand-woven.

The rest, almost literally, died away in abysmal conditions. In 1862 one handloom weaver, who stated that a regular day for a weaver was from 6 a.m to 10 p.m., and frequently till midnight or 1 a.m., summed up the situation:

> In town a room and kitchen above and a four-loom shop below is the most universal system, sometimes a six-loom shop, but in country districts 'a but and ben', i.e. a room with part divided off for a loom or two, is very common. Some of the shops are so damp that a fire has no effect upon them; I have seen some quite wet.[9]

The heavy industries and housing

The heavy industries brought a new way of life to many, one which was to leave a lasting physical legacy in Scotland. The tendency for industry to be localised, or concentrated, was maintained. In the eighteenth century the availability of water supplies determined the location of the cotton mills; in the nineteenth century the increasing use of steam and the large consumption of coal in the ironworks took industry to the coal measures. As well as being an age of concentration, it was the period of filth and of the destruction of the landscape. Of itself the use of water power created neither smoke nor dirt, nor did the mills using it produce great quantities of waste. A change came with the steam engine, only slowly applied in industry in the nineteenth century. With the spread of coalmining and ironworking came the bings, the pit-shafts with their desolate buildings and coke-ovens, the criss-cross of mineral railways. The transformation was mainly on the coal measures of north Lanarkshire and north Ayrshire. In some parishes, notably the Monklands, existing hamlets grew rapidly and towns, such as Coatbridge, appeared from nothing. Other towns which had first appeared, or grown to significance on the basis of textiles were changed by the middle of the nineteenth century. The part of the town which had been tacked on to the old agricultural community, when domestic weaving expanded, was interspersed and increased by Victorian tenements, while Presbyterian disputation and Irish immigration frequently brought an accession of ecclesiastical buildings.

The social problems of the heavy industries were not novel. The mining areas had a long-standing tradition of harshness, evident in the ancient serfdom of the Scottish miners, who until 1775 were bound for life to a certain colliery. An Act of 1775 offered freedom through a Sheriff Court process to those who, after a period, were able to provide apprentices to follow them. An Act of 1799 finally freed Scottish colliers completely. Previously freedom was not gained easily. Miners were presumed bound unless they could prove the contrary and could be recalled even if they had been clearly dismissed. Legal records show vigorous attempts to enforce the law by the owners of the collieries being successful. Sparse information in the records of the owners shows another side to the enforcement. Colliery owners made a pretence of unity, and some were willing to support each other's actions. Whenever a bound collier fled, possible employers were frequently warned to refuse to engage him, while any who had actually engaged such a man were asked to dismiss him. In spite of such co-operation, there was much squabbling, and attempts were made to attract colliers from one pit to another. Sometimes such disputes arose through doubts over the legal ownership of the men. More important were cases where the overseers in charge of the mines did not follow the policy of their masters, even when the latter favoured strict adherence to the law. Generally the law was applied rigidly when any large-scale trouble or defection among colliers was feared, and, therefore, of course, only when the need to apply it was greatest. In sum, the recall of bound miners probably depended both on who was being recalled and on who was recalling. If a collier who departed was regarded as troublesome, fairly persistent efforts were usually made to have him returned to his lawful owner. The Act of 1775 lessened the number of actions for recall. Only the masters who had previously been most stringent in enforcement continued to try to exercise their powers. Personalities, both on the side of the masters and on the side of the men, were important before 1775; they were even more so afterwards.

The restrictions of the old social order were most felt, most resented and lingered longest in the east, even late in the eighteenth century when the needs of the domestic consumers in Edinburgh and the salt trade in the Forth increased the demand for the output of the collieries on both sides of the Forth. On the other hand the first rapid expansion of the coal industry in the west of Scotland was based on a more modern, typically nineteenth-century, social structure. The difference was clear in the investigations which formed the basis of the Report of 1842 on the employment of women and children in collieries. The employment of women was unknown in the west but common in the east and continued, though not always with the consent or knowledge of the colliery owner, after the Act which forbade their employment. Again, before the legislation of 1842 children employed in the pits in the east of Scotland were generally two or three years younger than those employed in the west. Conditions could hardly be described as better in the west; they were only different. While the remnants of an old social order lingered in the east, the west possessed the most dramatic examples of a new social order, but one equally characterised by brutality and vice. The reason for the distinction is simple. The coalfield of the west witnessed the most rapid expansion of the nineteenth century. It suffered from the worst effects of rapid immigration and concentration of population in previously agricultural communities. In these areas, especially in parts of north Lanarkshire and north Ayrshire, the harshness and inadequate social provision of the new settlements was evident. To Thomas Tancred, visiting the Monklands parishes, it seemed that:

> This vast and sudden accession of population consisting for the most part of irregular and dissolute characters from all parts — from Wales, England, Scotland and Ireland — has produced a state of society, upon the existence of which, in a civilized country, we cannot reflect without a deep feeling that it manifests something essentially defective in our religious and educational institutions. . . .

Everything that meets the eye or ear tells of slavish labour united to brutal intemperance. At night, ascending to the hill on which the Established Church stands, the groups of blast-furnaces on all sides might be imagined to be blazing volcanoes, at most of which the smelting is continued Sundays and week-days, by day and night, without intermission. By day a perpetual steam arises from the whole length of the canal where it receives the waste-water from blast-engines on both sides of it; and railroads, traversed by long trains of waggons drawn by locomotive engines, intersect the country in all directions, and are the cause of frequent accidents, into which, by the law of Scotland, no inquiry is made.[10]

The most lasting single legacy of this phase of expansion of mining was the miners' row, which gives the best example of the defective housing standards in some areas between 1830 and 1880. The miners' row was squalid and remained so. Even during the First World War the Royal Commission on Scottish Housing could still refer to 'the present foul congeries of middens, ashpits and coalsheds'[11] in front of the older rows, and to the 'ramshackle brick survivals of the mining outbursts of seventy years ago in the mining fields, monotonous miners' rows flung down without a vestige of town-plan or any effort to secure modern conditions of sanitation'.[12] 'Flung-down' was the most appropriate description of their planning. The exact location of a row was determined by the need to be convenient to the mine. Little attention was paid to the nature of the soil or the subsoil, amenities or exposure, and the possibly short life of a mine, combined with the tendency to regard the houses as an unproductive form of capital investment, absorbing resources which might well have gone into the mine itself, militated against good construction. For long the proportion of small houses — of one or of two rooms — was higher in the mining areas than elsewhere. Improvement was not easy because of the reluctance of many miners to pay much rent; in the expansion from around 1830 housing was frequently a perquisite. When this changed, miners seem to have paid out a smaller proportion of their income in rent than other groups of workers. Even if the rents paid were all that the houses were worth — as may well have been so — a solution required not only the provision of better houses, but the occupation of these houses by tenants willing to pay a higher rent. Unfortunately the experience of poor housing became so ingrained in all Scots, but especially in the miners, that they became satisfied with poor conditions and unwilling to pay for improvements. The problem could be solved only by official action which meant that in practice little could be achieved in the nineteenth century.

To many contemporaries a barrier to improvement, and the cause of the degradation being most marked in the mining communities, was the advent of the Irish. One contemporary writer commented:

they have . . . eaten up our public charities, filled our prisons, crowded the calendar of crime, and destroyed the appearance and character of many an old Scots village. Dark shadows marked the advent of the Irish among those scenes of peace and prosperity — shadows, which have darkened into sullen, gloomy clouds.[13]

More accurately, the explanation was the overcrowding which followed the rapid influx of people into an area with no, or inadequate, social provision. Many, but by no means all, of those who came to such areas were Irish, but their number, rather than their nationality, was the prime cause of the problem. The criticism of the Irish was not simply exaggeration or an example of racial intolerance, especially after the appearance of the post-famine immigrant. To these later immigrants squalor was, if possible, less obnoxious than it was to many native Scots, since, as the minister of Whithorn dramatically and precisely recorded, 'they are possessed of nothing but a number of naked, starving children'.[14] They were more ready to accept squalor. Only to that extent had their nationality any effect on the degradation.

The squalor and filth of the mining areas had a less devastating effect on public health than might have been expected. The presence of ample fresh air was a chief preventive of many pulmonary diseases. It was used to explain the relative mildness of the incidence of tuberculosis in Edinburgh and Leith compared with other towns, and its supply was certainly ample in the exposed situation of many of the rows, as in the villages south and east of Shotts, such as Breich, or in another area, the valley of the Doon, where the miners, especially if they were Irish, were 'balloted out among the hills in distinct communities by themselves'[15] to mitigate their baneful social influence on others. Even today the desolate ruins of some of the mining villages yield a useful insight into the social fabric of nineteenth-century Scotland. The degradation and squalor of the rows reflect the position the miners occupied in Scottish society for years after their legal emancipation. The ethos of the mining community can be explained only if the extent of their physical segregation and desolation is first understood. Their living alone led the miners to regard themselves as a race apart, as a gathered community, which, of course, they were. A tour of the old settlements, in all their bleakness and primitiveness, shows how such sentiments could continue even when the grounds for them had gone.

The housing of miners may have been entitled to the unenviable distinction of being the worst of all in the nineteenth century, but others suffered similarly. The *Reports on the Sanitary Conditions of the Labouring Population* of 1842, while concluding that colliers were worst housed, demonstrated the general nature of the problem. In the same year, while some of the Reports, especially that on Tranent, suggested that the condition of the houses of agricultural workers, especially the hinds, was superior, a description of the housing of the same type of rural labourer in the Borders suggested otherwise.[16] The difference between the collier and the rural labourer, and it was a material one, was that, while the miner did little to improve his squalid position, the rural labourer, especially the permanently employed hind, sometimes did. In the countryside condemnation could be passed much more unequivocally on those who provided the houses. Conditions varied, and it was only in the more backward parts that the housing conditions of the eighteenth century remained unimproved into the nineteenth. Whatever the improvements in some areas, there was no doubt that generally throughout Scotland there was overcrowding in the nineteenth century in the new industrial areas and in the old rural communities, and that it became worse.

In 1801 there were 546 persons to every 100 houses, most of which were extremely small; in 1851 there were 780 persons to every 100 houses. In the following census, that of 1861, fuller information was requested to ascertain Scottish conditions. It was then revealed that 226,723 families, or one-third of Scotland's population, were living in houses of one room; 7,964 of them were in single rooms without windows. The worst examples of such overcrowding were in the towns, where the population increased through migration. In the towns, too, other factors worsened the already abominable conditions. Houses and tenements were frequently subdivided, an ominous sign indicating that an area had fallen on evil days, and one which, because it did not affect the exterior, did not come under the control of the Dean of Guild until 1891. Even thereafter the inability to determine when an alteration was taking place, if the structure was unaffected, made control difficult. Immigrants took in lodgers, often from their native districts, though not on a scale sufficient to provide for all who required accommodation. For them, too, the number of lodging-houses, virulent sources of infection, grew as their quality declined.

Much of the inadequacy of housing, arising from a rapid accession and concentration of population, was not uniquely Scottish; but one problem more peculiar to Scotland was the rapid multiplication of the tenement, especially in the spreading towns of the mid-nineteenth century. Though the tenement had advantages, many of those erected in the nineteenth century were inadequately lit and ventilated. Worst of all, they had the common stair, which, being no one's responsibility, was, in the words of Glasgow's first medical officer of health, 'just simply a mass of chaos and confusion, with no one to keep order'.[17] The effect was worse when the landings had long passages or, worst of all, a T-passage, off which the doors to the various houses branched. Frequently, too, the tenements produced other defects, such as underground dwellings, which at best were the lowest flats of good tenements built on sloping ground. The defects of the tenements lay less in their construction than in the gross overcrowding of so many of them. Hence came the almost indefinite proliferation in them of box-beds, 'cubicles of consumption', and the widespread sub-letting and sub-division. Overcrowding rather than construction had to be controlled, as was indeed recognised after an outbreak of typhus in Glasgow in 1866, when an attempt was made to control the numbers occupying a house by the system of 'ticketing'. The ticket stated how many people could be accommodated in a house, but gave rise to obvious difficulties in enforcement. Its use as a means of preventing overcrowding lay only in a later period.

Disease and destitution

The social conditions had a direct influence on the incidence of disease, attributed by one Glasgow doctor to the total want of cleanliness among the lower orders of the community; to the absence of ventilation in the more densely peopled districts; and to the accumulation, for weeks or months together, of filth of every description in our private and public dunghills; to the over-crowded state of the lodging-houses resorted to by the lowest classes; and to many other circumstances unnecessary to mention.[18]

The only remedy was to be rid of such filthy, squalid conditions; a palliative, which did not exist, was better medical facilities. The rudimentary beginnings of a hospital system had been provided in the eighteenth century with the foundation of the first infirmary in Edinburgh in 1729 and the Edinburgh Royal Infirmary in 1741, of the Aberdeen Infirmary in 1742, of the Dumfries and Galloway Infirmary in 1776 and of the Glasgow Royal Infirmary in 1794. Asylums for the insane were founded somewhat later — in Montrose in 1779, in Aberdeen in 1798, in Edinburgh in 1807, and in Glasgow in 1814. The first public dispensary was in Edinburgh in 1776. The impact of such institutions in curing patients was slight. It could not have been otherwise when the Edinburgh Infirmary started with accommodation for only six patients, while the Royal Infirmary opened in 1741, with accommodation for only 228. The Glasgow Royal Infirmary had originally 150 beds, increased in 1816 to 230. In any case the cures for many diseases — among them the most deadly — simply were not known. The greatest contribution of the new hospitals was, therefore, to medical education and the training of doctors.

The inadequacy and general ineffectiveness of hospital provision was highlighted during periods of epidemic, as, for instance, in the cholera outbreaks of 1832, 1848 and 1855. Public dispensaries had to bear the brunt of combating epidemic disease. Since they were ill-organised and inadequate, general hospitals had to assist them, with disastrous consequences for the general hospitals' primary functions, through the possibility of the infection being passed to others. The public authorities acted only when a particular epidemic had become virulent, and usually when it was too late for action to be fully effective. The position in Glasgow was typical. In emergencies the magistrates set up a Board of Health and the parochial authorities opened special premises. In Glasgow during an outbreak of typhus a temporary fever hospital for 200 patients was opened in March 1818 and closed in July 1819; in 1827 the infirmary re-opened this hospital for five months; in 1828 a 'temporary booth' was erected for 68 patients in the infirmary grounds; in 1832 a fever hospital was opened and closed at Mile End. Though they could never be effective, it was long before such short-term expedients were superseded as the Town Council of Glasgow provided a permanent municipal fever hospital only in 1865, while acceptance of patients remained subject to qualification until 1881, when the corporation accepted full responsibility.

Reliance on such temporary and inadequate provision for the victims of an epidemic placed a greater strain on normal hospital facilities. In Glasgow the sudden increase in the number of fever (which usually meant typhus) cases treated at the infirmary shows the problem:

PATIENTS TREATED IN GLASGOW ROYAL INFIRMARY,
1816 to 1836

	Total	Fever			Total	Fever
1816	1,511	399		1827	2,725	1,084
1817	1,886	714		1828	3,133	1,511
1818	2,289	1,371		1829	2,321	865
1819	1,861	630		1830	2,010	729
1820	1,570	289		1831	3,183	1,657
1821	1,454	234		1832	2,974	1,589
1822	1,596	229		1833	3,082	1,288
1823	1,759	269		1834	3,879	2,003
1824	2,091	523		1835	3,260	1,359
1825	2,438	897		1836	5,130	3,125
1826	2,317	926				

Source: R. Cowan, *Vital Statistics of Glasgow* (Glasgow, 1838), p. 8.

Even those sent to the infirmary, or accommodated in the temporary provision, did not represent the total number of fever cases. Many remained at home, so spreading the danger of infection further, as is evident in the cases of paupers treated by the District Surgeons in Glasgow:

CASES OF FEVER TREATED BY DISTRICT SURGEONS
IN GLASGOW, 1827 to 1836

	Total	Sent to infirmary
1827-28	1,281	281
1828-29	1,730	390
1829-30	485	135
1830-31	898	306
1831-32	1,428	336
1833	681	294
1834	936	538
1835	542	215
1836	1,359	643

Source: Cowan, *Vital Statistics of Glasgow*, p. 10

The major obstacle to improvements in public health was the almost total absence of preventive medicine. It was difficult to make headway in the eradication of disease, as one usually replaced another. The history of smallpox provides an illustration. The first attempt to combat it by inoculation was probably not as successful as some of the sweeping claims made on its behalf suggested.[19] The position changed with the introduction of vaccination with calf lymph, though perhaps not so dramatically as to suggest that

up to the very moment of small-pox inoculation being superseded by cow-pox the mortality is immense, and the instant the latter is employed, the mortality becomes trifling in comparison.[20]

Vaccination was adopted on a widespread scale in the nineteenth century. In Glasgow in 1801 the Faculty of Physicians and Surgeons began vaccinating the children of the poor free of charge and in the next ten years vaccinated 14,500. In 1818 others not connected with the Faculty began vaccinating at the Cow Pock Institution. The effect was undoubtedly beneficial. The low incidence of smallpox among the Irish, which contrasted with the high incidence of typhus, was attributed, at least in part, to the prevalence of vaccination among them, especially when it was discovered that the reverse incidence prevailed among the city's Highlanders, a group which tended to neglect vaccination or which had been vaccinated in the Highlands with impure lymph. But the failure of such successes to lead to a marked improvement in public health was demonstrated in two ways. First, the place of smallpox as a killing disease at least among children was taken by measles, though it struck less frequently and less severely. Given the inadequate concern with preventive medicine, another disease simply took the place of the one being eradicated. Second, smallpox itself was not wholly eliminated, but remained an important disease among children, especially during periods of industrial distress. It accounted for over 5 per cent of all deaths in Glasgow in the late 1830s and could not be classified as a minor killer disease until after the introduction of compulsory vaccination in 1863:

CAUSES OF DEATH OF CHILDREN UNDER 10 IN GLASGOW,
1801 to 1812

	Total	Smallpox	Measles
1801	1,434	245	8
1802	1,770	156	168
1803	1,860	194	45
1804	1,670	213	27
1805	1,671	56	90
1806	1,629	28	56
1807	1,806	97	16
1808	2,623	51	787
1809	2,124	159	44
1810	2,111	28	19
1811	2,342	109	267
1812	2,348	78	304

Source: R. Watt, *Treatise on Chincough* (Glasgow, 1813), pp. 375 ff.

Under such conditions improvement in public health was slow. Even where the means of preventing a disease was known, as was the case with smallpox, a general reduction in the death-rate could not be achieved. In spite of vaccination and other advances, the death-rate in the cities rose in the early nineteenth century. One writer of the nineteenth century drew attention to conditions in Edinburgh where the crude death-rate in the first two decades of the nineteenth century was just over 25 per thousand and in the 1830s had risen to 29 per thousand. A modern study shows an even more alarming situation in Glasgow, where the death-rate crept up from 25 per thousand in the early 1820s to almost 40 per thousand in the late 1840s, with only a slight drop earlier in that decade.

Death-rates were highest among young children and in the lower social classes. In Glasgow in 1841 the age-specific death rate (i.e. deaths per 1000 living in the same age group) for those under five was 112.8; in 1861 it was 96.4, and in that year 54 per cent of deaths in Glasgow were of children under ten. Death-rates fell sharply after the early years of life. The variation by social class was well illustrated by an analysis of Edinburgh in the early nineteenth century. For every 1,000 deaths in the highest class, only 72 took place under one year of age; in the lowest class there were 241 deaths in the same group. In the highest class the mean age of death was 47.22 years; in the lowest it was 25.88. Half the highest class died before 51.5 years of age; half the lowest before 17.5 years of age.[21] Frequently the high death-rate in the lowest social classes, and especially its tendency to rise again in the nineteenth century, was explained by the influx of the Irish, but this viewpoint was sometimes challenged, most of all by medical opinion. The challenge was justified. The death-rate was highest, not among the immigrants themselves, but among their children and the children of others of similar social status.

Preventive medicine required measures for public health, such as better water supplies and better drains. It also required better nutrition. Very pertinently the writer of the sanitary report on Inveresk commented in 1842, 'where fever is prevalent it will often pass by those who are in the habit of being well fed, well clothed, and particularly if they are cleanly in their habits'.[22] To achieve such ways of living was difficult in an urban society. Even nutritional standards may have declined, as choice and income grew, with the rejection of oatmeal which had long been the leading item in the diet of rural Scotland.

The high death-rate was the ultimate characteristic of the new industrial and urban society. Many others both caused and were the consequences of the social turmoil. Drink and drunkenness were the most commonly cited as the great evils of the industrial society. The alcoholic tradition had, however, been inherited from rural Scotland. The difference lay in the increased social disapproval, partly because of the emergence of different drinking habits among different groups and because drunkenness caused greater economic dislocation in an industrial society which could not accommodate the long periods of drinking possible in a rural society. In the eighteenth century the imposition of the malt tax hastened the decline in the consumption of ale and helped the growth of whisky drinking in Scotland, which became the form of alcoholic consumption characteristic of industrial Scotland. The apparently sharp rise in consumption in the 1820s is misleading. Reliable statistics were only then becoming available, and the reform of the system of taxation led to the decline in illicit distillation. Of the Scots' alcoholic consumption there is no doubt. In

Glasgow in 1832 there was a spirit dealer to every 14 families. In 1841 the Scots drank 23 pints of spirits annually per head of population; the Irish, 13; the English, seven. The legislative attack on drink started with the Forbes Mackenzie Act, which came into force in 1854, and which abolished the sale of alcohol in grocers' shops for consumption on the premises; closed public houses, though not specially licensed hotels, from 11 p.m. to 8 a.m; and stopped Sunday drinking, except in hotels by lodgers and *bona fide* travellers.

The excessive consumption of alcohol was partly the cause of another characteristic of the industrial society, the need for credit. In the words of J. Hill Burton, 'credit is a national peculiarity from the bank-note and cash credit system, down to the grocers' passbook held by the mechanic'.[23] This peculiarity persisted although, from the foundation of a savings bank in the rural parish of Ruthwell by the minister, Henry Duncan, in 1810, Scotland witnessed the successful growth of similar ventures and had in the City of Glasgow Savings Bank an institution with the rare distinction, especially significant in an industrial area such as the west of Scotland, of having a wide range of social and economic classes among its depositors. Of the chronic need of so many of the lower-income groups for credit there were many examples. Pawnshops grew rapidly in the nineteenth century. The first was opened in 1806, and from the 1830s the numbers increased. In 1865 in Edinburgh there were 33 licensed pawnshops and 219 'wee pawns' or brokers, who were unlicensed and so not subject to control. The 33 licensed shops had 1,381,200 pledges in the year, and of pledges under 10s., 12 per cent (165,744) were forfeited. A striking and socially harmful need for credit was in the mining areas. In the nineteenth century in most Scottish collieries and ironworks, especially in the developing areas of the west, the time between pays was commonly two weeks to a month, though exceptionally, as at the lead mines in Wanlockhead, it was a year. Many workers had to obtain credit in some form, generally through an advance of wages. The most satisfactory solution would have been to increase the frequency of pay-days, as had long been the practice of some of the older Scottish coalmasters, but even with long-pays there would probably have been little complaint if a worker had been able to obtain a cash advance as and when he wanted it. The real dispute was over the conditions normally attached to them. When some colliery owners advanced cash they charged 'poundage', a fee of approximately 1s. in the £, ostensibly to cover the additional costs incurred. In almost every case the employee was then free to spend the remainder where he wished. More commonly an advance was given on condition that at least part was spent in the stores which the mining companies had to start in the rural areas in which they operated, though in some cases all employees were expected to spend their total earnings there. The employers argued that the men were free to spend their advances where they pleased; the men disagreed; and pressure — ultimately of dismissal — was extended to force them to the store, where goods were sometimes inferior and more expensive than elsewhere.

The employers' objections to more frequent pays, which were recommended by such observers as the Inspectors of Mines, were the supposed administrative difficulties involved and that, by lengthening the period between pays, the absenteeism which resulted from drunkenness on the Mondays after pay-days was reduced. Forcing the workmen to spend any advances in the stores was also supposed to reduce their consumption of alcohol, somewhat specious reasoning when some stores sold alcohol too. These arguments provided the basis for the suggestion that the system was the only means by which the pattern of expenditure of the profligate and the drunkard could be determined in a more desirable fashion. But the group which required advances was not composed wholly of such people. As the Truck Commissioners pointed out in 1871, 'large families, ill health, bad times, accidental misfortunes, swell its numbers'. The truck system made the unfortunate still more so. The system declined quickly only in the 1870s so that, when further legislation against it came in 1887, it was unnecessary in practical terms. If its ill effects weighed heavily on the miners, they suffered less than others from the effects of the law by which wages could be arrested or attached to meet debts due to third parties. One reason advanced in favour of truck, or of the company store, was that it prevented arrestment. Proceedings for arrestment were instituted mostly by the agents of menages (clubs), which were most common in Glasgow and district, and among colliers on the east coast, where the truck system did not operate. Such agents generally issued tickets against which goods could be obtained on credit. Any failure to meet the payments due, a common occurrence, led to actions for arrestment. In Glasgow at any time in the middle of the nineteenth century about 6,000 actions for arrestment were being prosecuted by menages, in addition to similar prosecutions by small traders, particularly by grocers. Since the payment of the sum advanced through the issue of the tickets by the agents of the menages was often jointly and severally guaranteed by others, any failure to meet the appropriate payments involved even those who had not received the goods. From 1838 workers had to be left with a sum sufficient for subsistence before wages could be arrested, but the allowance was inadequate to provide the margin above subsistence so urgently required to eliminate, or even simply to palliate, the prevailing destitution.

Drunkenness, pawnshops, truck and arrestment were just symptoms of destitution. Its main cause in the industrial society of nineteenth-century Scotland was unemployment. In the industrial system, of which for the first time many were finding they were a part, a trade depression left many operatives without any means of support, and frequently in a large town where there was no possibility whatever of any subsistence. These cyclical depressions had the worst influence on health and mortality. Robert Cowan, the Glasgow doctor whose careful researches provided posterity with a number of valuable statistical series, always supported the connection between good trade and good health, and between bad trade and bad health. He felt the relationship between changing economic conditions and the death-rate from fever was most adequately demonstrated in the boom which culminated in the spring and summer of 1836:

DEATHS IN GLASGOW FROM FEVER, 1835 to 1837

	Total	To total deaths	To total population
1835	412	1 to 15	1 to 570
1836	841	1 to 10	1 to 290
1837	2,180	1 to 5	1 to 116

He concluded that

> the mortality bill of 1837 exhibits a rate of mortality inferring an intensity of misery and suffering unequalled in Britain; and not surpassed in any city we are acquainted with on the continent of Europe.[24]

The conditions of life in the industrial society which appeared in Scotland in the nineteenth century needed reform.

NOTES

1. Much of the information which is available is in M. W. Flinn *et al*, *Scottish Population History* (Cambridge, 1977).

2. M. Gray, *The Highland Economy, 1750-1850* (Edinburgh, 1957), p. 223.

3. J. F. Handley, *The Irish in Modern Scotland* (Cork, 1945), p. 1.

4. *Select Committee on Manufactures, Commerce and Shipping*, 1833, Q. 5288.

5. *Factories Inquiry Commission*, 1833. First Report, p. 19. BPP. 1833. XX.

6. *Factories Inquiry Commission*, 1833. First Report, A.1. Northern District, p. 92.

7. *Report of the Select Committee on the State of Children employed in Factories*, 1816, p. 167. BPP 1816. III.

8. *Report of the Assistant Hand-loom Weavers Commissioner*, 1839 (South of Scotland), p. 19. BPP. 1839. XLII.

9. *Children's Employment Commission*, 1864. Second Report, p. 227. BPP. 1864. XXII.

10. *Report of Commissioners to Children's Employment Commission on Employment of Children in Mines and Colleries*, vol. ii, 1842, pp. 311 ff., paras. 12 and 13. BPP. 1842. XVII.

11. *Report of the Royal Commission on the Housing of the Industrial Population of Scotland Rural and Urban*, 1918 (Cd. 8731), para. 822. BPP. 1917-8. XIV.

12. *Ibid.*, para. 2232.

13. R. Wylie, *Ayrshire Streams* (London, 1851), p. 15.

14. *New Statistical Account*, vol. iv (Wigtownshire), p. 60.

15. Wylie, *Ayrshire Streams*, p. 92.

16. W. S. Gilly, *The Peasantry of the Border* (London, 1842, new edn. 1973), pp. 6 ff.

17. W. T. Gairdner, *Proceedings of the Philosophical Society of Glasgow*, vol. vii (1870-1), p. 254.

18. R. Cowan, *Vital Statistics of Glasgow* (Glasgow, 1838), p. 12.

19. See p. 18.

20. Cowan, *Vital Statistics of Glasgow*, p. 28.

21. J. Stark, *Contribution to the Vital Statistics of Scotland* (London, 1851), p. 44.

22. *Reports on the Sanitary Condition of the Labouring Population of Scotland*, 1842, p. 133. BPP. 1842. XXVIII.

23. *Report on the Arrestment of Wages*, 1854, p. 43, BPP. 1854. LXIX.

24. Cowan, *Vital Statistics of Glasgow*, pp. 37 and 45.

CHAPTER XI

Social Reform

The poor law

Three different ways of tackling the problems of the new industrial society can be distinguished. First, the traditional provision for dealing with destitution, the poor law, was adapted, with varying degrees of success, to an urban society; second, medical reform tried to eliminate the worst effects of ill-health and disease; third, those who suffered raised their own protests.

Two distinct features of the Scottish poor law had governed its effectiveness in dealing with destitution in an industrial society. The first was that, though assessment was legal by an Act of 1574, the poor should be supported by voluntary contributions in the parish churches and by such subsidiary sources of income as fees for the hire of the parish mortcloth and from legacies or mortifications; the second was that relief should not be given to the able-bodied.

Financing by voluntary means placed an obvious limit on the effectiveness of the poor law, but criticism of its success, or suggestions that it was harshly administered, can be levelled as much at the rigid interpretation of those who were entitled to relief, and in particular at the law's failure to provide for the destitution which arose from unemployment. Recent writings on the history of the Scottish poor law have rightly stressed the harsh interpretation of this provision in urban societies and have suggested that it represented a change of policy from the eighteenth century. In one sense it did, for the problem of urban unemployment on a large scale did not exist earlier. In a rural society the problems of the able-bodied poor were very different both quantitatively and qualitatively. The earlier statutes gave a rigid interpretation of those entitled to relief, but by the end of the seventeenth century a looser interpretation was appearing, encouraged by local diversity. With modification it could have gone some way to meeting the problems of an industrial society. In 1693 the Privy Council decreed that kirk sessions should make over one-half of church collections to support the regular poor; by implication the other half could be applied to the relief of the occasional poor. The regular poor were those recognised by an Act of 1579[1] as entitled to relief — defined more fully in 1661 as all 'poor, aged, sick, lame, and impotent inhabitants . . ., who (of themselves) have not to maintain them, nor are able to work for their living, as also all orphans and other poor children . . ., who are left destitute of all help'; the occasional poor were those who were suffering from some temporary and exceptional misfortune. The regular poor were granted periodical allowances permanently and as of right; the occasional poor were to be relieved only out of the charity of the parish. The difference was in the right to relief. Though the distinction drawn was important, it could be suggested that in a properly administered parish, where each case was considered on its individual merits, all deserving cases would be met. Failure arose from deficiencies in the implementation of the system, especially from an increasing insistence on permanent disablement for relief, and from its variety, rather than from the system itself.

The reluctance and refusal of help to the able-bodied poor cannot be separated from the other main problem of cost. A general concern over cost is neither surprising nor particularly Scottish, but when it was combined, as in Scotland, with an extreme reluctance by the heritors to levy an assessment to be disbursed by the kirk session, a strong economic incentive was at hand to exploit any underlying moral stimulus to refuse help to the able-bodied poor. Even such a powerful combination was insufficiently strong to ensure complete neglect of their plight, especially with the onset of depression in the manufacturing districts. In 1839 the General Assembly reported 'that the situation of people destitute of employment was not to be overlooked, and that many cases might occur in which men of this class ought to obtain temporary relief in times of occasional sickness or unusual calamity, although not as a matter of right'.[2]

Although with each period of depression the more affluent public were encouraged to augment their existing poor law contributions with further help,[3] such assistance was usually inadequate, spasmodic, and depended on charitable impulses. Destitution was not relieved. Hence in 1843, following depression in the manufacturing districts, a Commission was appointed to review the system of poor relief in Scotland. The Commissioners interpreted their terms of reference stringently. They held they were not asked to suggest anything completely new but only to devise ways of making the existing laws work more efficiently. Typically, on the leading issues of the granting of help to the able-bodied poor and of assessment, the Commissioners were unwilling to recommend any changes of consequence, and in Lowland rural parishes judged it 'the veriest wantonness of innovation to interfere'.[4] They were optimistic, believing that, even in industrial areas,

> Unless . . . it is held, that the experience of late years has proved that the destitution arising in times of great commercial and manufacturing distress, cannot safely be left to be supplied by the spontaneous efforts of public and private benevolence, which the recurrence of such times may be expected to call forth, we must deprecate recourse to any less provisional fund of relief. But no such proof has been given; for if we except the individual cases of hardship incident to the commencement of periods of depression, for the relief of which a temporary assessment is obviously as inadequate as a voluntary contribution, no evidence from medical men, as well as others, countenances an opposite conclusion.[5]

Not surprisingly, therefore, section 68 of the Act of 1845, which followed the Commission's report, reiterated the existing Scottish practice. It permitted the use of an assessment levied for the relief of the occasional as well as of the regular poor, always 'provided that nothing herein contained shall be held to confer a right to demand relief on able-bodied persons out of employment'. The restriction was unrealistic in an industrial society and had to be modified. In its third report of 1848 the Board of Supervision, which had been instituted to control poor law administration, initiated a major change — probably because the exigencies of the potato famine had rendered any other action impossible — and, after taking legal advice, argued that section 68 did not preclude granting occasional aid to the able-bodied poor, even though they had no right to assistance. This interpretation — comparable to that adopted by the General Assembly in its Report of 1839 — caused the Board of Supervision to issue instructions that parishes might use funds raised by assessment and half the collections at the church door for the temporary relief of the destitute able-bodied unemployed.

In this way the administration of the Scottish poor law was forced to adapt itself to a new environment, but so reluctantly and inadequately that it could not produce satisfactory solutions. Some of those most concerned with the administration of the poor law failed to take account of the social and economic changes that had taken place; others, in haste to avoid English practice, favoured retaining Scottish ways irrespective of their merits; others uncritically advocated the adoption of the new English system. There was some approach to unanimity only in the analysis of the situation. The example of the old English poor law, which under the Speenhamland system had supplemented wages, and above all popular interpretations of the warnings of Malthus on the dangers of over-population, led a varied group of people to the same conclusion. Any proposals to improve the condition of the poor, and so encourage them to increase their number, were unlikely to command widespread acceptance, especially when many of those who accepted such Malthusian fears also supported an equally popular interpretation of contemporary economic theory which upheld the principles of voluntary assessment. They regarded legal assessment as a means of providing for, indeed encouraging, a larger population. But for many Scottish parishes the possibility of continuing to rely only on voluntary contributions was an academic question, and, no matter how distasteful, legal assessment was increasingly adopted. Though cost seemed high, especially when legal assessment was introduced, it was lower in Scotland than in other countries. In England, even under its new poor law after 1834, a greater proportion of the population was being relieved and at a greater cost per head. The international comparison failed to satisfy all critics. Some reiterated the basic assumption of the Scottish poor law, that it authorised aid only as a supplement to assistance given by members of the family and other sources, and that generosity was encouraged by the absence of legal assessment. To them, as to the General Assembly in its Report of 1818, legal assessment was 'a national calamity'. Most people still judged the success of the poor law by the degree of economy achieved, and so their interest in the effectiveness of its administration easily gave way to complacency.

To uphold the voluntary principle was a formidable task in the industrial areas. By the middle of the eighteenth century an *ad hoc* administration had to be erected in the larger cities. In Edinburgh a special committee managed the affairs of the poor after 1740 and a Poors' Hospital was built. In Glasgow the Town Council, the Merchants' House and the General Kirk Session provided a Town's Hospital in 1733. Though the aim of the hospital was the optimistic one of the gradual extinction of pauperism by the profitable employment, virtuous education and frugal maintenance of the inmates, outdoor relief of an allowance of meal was granted from 1774 and was later converted to cash. The hospital benefited from such assessments as were made but required additional voluntary contributions to make ends meet. Its resources were continually under strain, especially during extensive or prolonged industrial depression, when many could no longer subsist even on the highest pensions granted by their kirk sessions and so came under the hospital's care.

Heritors, who would have had to meet any assessment, were likely to support the voluntary principle to justify their failure to provide kirk sessions with adequate funds for their ministrations to the poor; others advocated its retention through their belief that the moral obligation of Christian charity to care for the poor should be in the context of a Christian community without any support from assessments, whether voluntary or legal. The leading adherent of this point of view was Thomas Chalmers, a parish minister in Kilmany and Glasgow and latterly professor at St Andrews and Edinburgh. The widespread nature of his proposals was well summarised by the directors of Glasgow's Town's Hospital:

> to confine the legal assessment to the existing generation of paupers; to apply the disengaged fund to the establishment of churches, — and then, to invigorate the impulse of voluntary collections for the new cases; to multiply the number of parishes; to narrow the field of superintendence; to cement the intercourse between the administrators and recipients of charity; to increase the personal influence of the ecclesiastical overseers; and to extend the benefits of moral and religious information.[6]

The crux of Chalmers' analysis was to encourage Christian charity and to do nothing to destroy either its spontaneity or the moral resilience of the recipients. Chalmers feared that compulsory assessment would be the worst possible solution to the problem of destitution in times of industrial depression. 'What in fact is the best defence of a people against the evils of a state of fluctuation? Their own providential habits, and these are what a compulsory provision goes directly to extinguish.'[7] He also believed that a compulsory assessment would increase the number of regular poor, so increasing the difficulty of providing for the occasional poor, among whom were the victims of unemployment. Lastly, he thought compulsory assessment made the wealthy less willing to support special appeals in times of depression. 'The distress arising from fluctuations of trade ought in fact to be committed to those impulses of public benevolence, which the occurrence of such fluctuations is ever sure to awaken.'[8]

Another stream of criticism produced an analysis of the existing situation, not unlike Chalmers' in some ways, but advocating the radically different solution of a compulsory legal assessment. Its supporters envied the greater expenditure on the poor in England, or in countries overseas, and held that the poor were far from being demoralised wherever a legal assessment was in force; that indeed they were often improved, even if only because they were cleaner. The chief exponent of this school of thought was W. P. Alison, medical professor at Edinburgh. While Alison accepted many of Chalmers' recommendations, two of his comments show the force and pertinence of his standpoint. Negatively, he pointed out that

> while there has been much disposition to relieve the sick poor, there has been a very general discouragement of the institutions for the relief of *mere poverty*, — of the unemployed poor, the aged or permanently disabled poor, and the widows and orphans of the poor.

Positively he suggested that

> the kind of assistance to the poor, which all medical men know to be of the utmost importance for the *prevention* of many of their most formidable diseases, has been as much as possible withheld.[9]

Where Alison gained over Chalmers was in the way in which he had acquired his knowledge of the condition of the poor. So many of Chalmers' ideas had been formed in his earlier years in the intimate society of a rural parish, where the traditional method of poor relief could operate successfully. He wanted to apply these ideas to the city. Alison fully understood the benefits of a rural parish and provided a description of its advantages which can hardly be bettered:

> In a perfectly simple, and at the same time educated and civilized state of society . . . where all the higher orders who are to give, and all the lower orders who are to receive, are aware of their duties, and are known to one another, and, as long as the proprietors are resident, of charitable disposition, and attentive to their duties, the burden may be sufficiently equalized among the former, and the benefits sufficiently secured to the latter, without intervention of the law; or if the law interfered, it will be only to sanction, or sometimes to define, and partially extend the present practice.[10]

Alison also believed it was impracticable to transplant such ideals to the new industrial urban society. His medical experience was more bitter. 'These repeated and severe visitations of fever . . . are not merely the occasions of much and widely spread suffering and destitution but . . . *the indication and test* of much previous misery and destitution.'[11] To Alison, and to other pioneers of social medicine, sheer practical considerations of self-preservation, apart from any demands of Christian charity, demanded action. The strength of Alison's position and achievement lay in his refusal in practice to accept the popularised versions of Malthusian ideas, whatever he may have said about their theoretical importance. To him

> the whole secret of the preventive check appears to me to consist in the growth and support of *artificial wants* among the poor.[12]

Or again, realising the importance of a higher standard of living in limiting population,

> nothing short of a legal enactment can be relied on for uniformly and permanently securing such comforts during youth, as are essential to sustain these habits; and counteract that real *bounty of population* which accidents and misfortunes, and consequent destitution and degradation, would otherwise continually and inevitably bring on numerous families in every season and in every district of the country.[13]

Alison's propositions, especially his advocacy of legal assessment, savoured of the new English poor law to many. There were differences, notably in Alison's sympathy for the 'deserving poor', for whom he advocated outdoor relief; but even he failed to understand fully the nature of industrial unemployment, which could produce a large number of deserving able-bodied poor. Chalmers recognised the existence of such people and made provision for them — inadequate though it may have been — through exceptional private charity. Alison, like most of his day, feared the growth of a large number of work-shy people and broke from the Scottish tradition of outdoor relief by advocating relief for such able-bodied only in the workhouse. By doing so, Alison failed to provide large-scale help to the able-bodied poor and virtually failed to provide a solution to the main problem which had led him to consider the need for amendments to the poor law, the problem of how the destitution, disease and epidemics, to which depressions gave rise, could be alleviated. The tragedy is that the two points of view were set at variance and not reconciled as they might have been. The individual care and inspired service of Chalmers on the one hand, when allied with the more generous financial provisions of Alison on the other, would have produced a system of social provision in Scotland far in advance of its time. The failure of both to provide an analysis which accepted the new poor of the industrial unemployed within the framework of the old Scottish poor law without qualification left a gap in social provision which became increasingly dangerous. It was one which, not surprisingly in view of the presuppositions of its members, the Poor Law Commission of 1844 did little to fill. The way was then left open for the ideas of the English poor law to infiltrate and eventually to dominate.

The early reports of the Board of Supervision show the gradual infiltration of English ideas. The long-standing tradition of outdoor relief, with all its advantages, declined. Though in its first report the Board of Supervision stated that it 'had no power to sanction the abolition of outdoor relief in any parish, and that they must judge of the propriety of refusing to relieve a pauper otherwise than by admitting him into the poorhouse', in a few years the Board's report, its fifth, contained a perfect exposition, with commendation, of the function of the English workhouse as a means of testing the genuine nature of applicants for relief. Not only were the number of unassessed parishes declining; all traces of the Scottish poor law were being removed. The extent of the problem was too great to be met any longer by private philanthropy even before the Disruption of the Church of Scotland in 1843 finally made the system unworkable.

The result of the protracted and learned controversy over the poor law may seem negligible. Yet the complacency, which so long inhibited any action except over cost, was eventually roused by the medical arguments raised in the poor law controversy. Provision for the sick poor had always been approved and encouraged in Scotland. Partly for this reason, partly reflecting the force of current medical criticism, the most interesting and effective conclusions of the Poor Law Commission of 1844 were in the medical provisions it suggested. Even they had flaws by failing to stress the relevance of preventive rather than of curative medicine. A change of opinion, forced in large measure by the desire for self-preservation induced by epidemic, was necessary.

Sanitary reform

The interest shown by medical reformers, and the time taken to change the poor law in Scotland, led to its reform being associated with improvements in the physical environment. The emphasis was evident in 1842 in the reports on Scottish sanitary conditions. They were compiled to satisfy a request for information from the English Poor Law Commissioners and showed that the majority of Scottish reporters, while admitting and deploring the sanitary conditions of the towns and countryside, suggested that improvement required a reduction in the incidence of personal destitution. Such concern produced a race of humane medical reformers, possessed of a scale of values in which strict sanitary reform supported the relief of the individual.

The main barrier to sanitary reform in Scotland was not, however, the diversion of the interests of medical reformers to changing the poor law but public and private opposition or lethargy. Until their reform in 1833 the town councils were rarely amenable to any projects for reform. In any case, in the late eighteenth and early nineteenth centuries the expansion of towns beyond the original burgh boundaries meant that many councils' political authority was not always coextensive with the need for sanitary supervision. As sanitary reform remained in the hands of local authorities until the 1860s, they had to take the necessary action. The first attempts were made through local acts appointing police commissioners to deal with sanitary problems. The first, for the southern suburbs of Edinburgh, was in 1771; the first for Glasgow was in 1800. Even where a Town Council, or a Police Commission, wanted to act, it was usually obstructed by private opposition. Scots law placed difficulties in the path of the sanitary reformer through a corporate body, such as a town council, being unable to bring an action for the abatement of a nuisance. Action had to be taken by a private individual, who had to prove personal damage. Worse still, it was possible to achieve a permanent right to create a nuisance through its use during a prescribed period. The classic legal impasse was the case of the Meadows in Edinburgh which were irrigated by sewage. Though undoubtedly a nuisance, the practice could not be stopped through a right to create such a nuisance being obtained by its exercise during the period of prescription. A possible solution was that the Meadows, being near Holyrood, might have been harmful to the Queen, who was excluded from the rule of prescription. In the face of strong protection of property the town councils had a hard task, even when they became conscious of the problem and active in its solution. The need for sanitary reform was so great and so widespread that any attempt to meet it immediately ran foul of a variety of vested interests. Once again Edinburgh provided a conspicuous example when in 1846 the Town Council promoted a Sanitary Improvement Bill, which was opposed successfully by some of the groups whose interests would have been affected: the owners of the irrigated meadows to the east of the city; the mill-owners on the Water of Leith; the spirit trade; the owners of private slaughterhouses; the pawnbrokers; the dealers in second-hand goods; and others.

The extension of sanitary reform rested essentially on the wider acceptance of preventive medicine. There was little evidence of its efficacy in the eighteenth century. When all lived together, all were subject to the same physical or sanitary conditions, and there was little distinction in the incidence of disease. In the late eighteenth century, when segregation increased, different locations had their own physical and sanitary conditions. The old and new towns of Edinburgh provide an illustration.[14] Such moves represented an acceptance of the belief that refinement was not a luxury but a necessity, even though initially it was thought it need be confined to only some in the community. That even removal to the New Town could not give immunity from the filth of the Old Town needed a demonstration from the epidemics of the nineteenth century to bring home the need to improve the lot of those who remained. The motives behind the actions inspired by the epidemics were often blatantly selfish; they were probably more effective for being so.

Cholera was not as prevalent and it did not kill the numbers who fell victims to tuberculosis and typhus, the other scourges of the industrial society, but the nature and incidence of the cholera epidemic of 1832 first broke through much of the indifference to sanitary reform. The breach was made effective in mid-century by an outbreak of typhus in 1847 and by two of cholera in 1848 and 1854. The effective reform movement may be dated from the passing of the Glasgow Corporation Water Works Act in 1855. It marked the approval, after twenty years' opposition, of an early proposal of the reformed Town Council that it should take over the private suppliers of water. The way was then opened for the step, most fruitful for posterity, of inaugurating the waterworks at Loch Katrine. Thereafter sanitary reform spread. The Nuisances Removal (Scotland) Act, 1856 enabled Glasgow Corporation to form a Committee of Nuisances. In 1859 the Corporation produced a scheme for the sanitary reform of the city and its proper inspection and enforcement, which was authorised in the Glasgow Police Act, 1862. In the following year the city's first medical officer of health, W. T. Gairdiner, was appointed. The Glasgow Improvement Act, 1866 gave the necessary powers for the removal of the worst slums in the city.[15] Action in Edinburgh came more slowly, but was precipitated more dramatically in 1861, through the collapse of an old tenement in the High Street, resulting in the deaths of thirty-five people. The following year Henry Littlejohn was appointed the city's first medical officer of health. His work led to the Edinburgh Improvement Act, 1867.

In spite of the opposition and inadequate financial support, a new era in public health was beginning by the 1870s. Increasingly, initiative became central rather than local. The Public Health (Scotland) Act, 1867 ensured that the earlier spasmodic action, both local and central, was replaced by bodies responsible for continuous supervision. By about 1870, public health measures were accepted in Scotland, even though they were not always acceptable in all circles. Preventive medicine was at least accorded a place. Its achievements still lay in the future.

The workers' protests

Those who suffered most from its defects advanced their own remedies to change the fabric of the new industrial society. Even when the remedies advocated were similar to those suggested in England, they were conditioned by legal differences, as in the poor laws of the two countries. More subtle distinctions arose between the two countries because of their contrasting economic development. In Scotland the boundaries of pronounced social discontent were sometimes more limited both geographically and occupationally. The simple remedy of emigration adopted in the major areas of distress in the Highlands did not give rise to any consequential problem in one sense. The Highlanders moved to other parts of Scotland and overseas but, having adopted the simple remedy of leaving the adverse social conditions in which they lived, most made no further contribution to attempts to solve the problem left behind. The handloom weavers were the most conspicuous group displaced by factors operating occupationally. They too tried to adopt the same despairing remedy of emigration, though with less success. Few other distressed groups emulated the example of the Highlanders or the handloom weavers and sought a remedy in emigration.

The acceptance of the new way of life was made easier for most members of the new industrial society in Scotland by one factor of overriding importance. Their economic prosperity was dependent on the success of a complex of industries, which, fortunately for Scotland, were buoyant until the last quarter of the nineteenth century. The stagnation of the cotton industry was offset by the rise of the heavy industries, and both offered employment opportunities of some kind in roughly the same areas. In the centre of industrial Scotland there was no long-term stagnation of employment and, apart from the Highlands and the handloom weavers, there were no depressed areas or industries in Scotland in the middle of the nineteenth century. Yet distress, notably cyclical, was sufficient to justify much protest, and if from time to time a high level of demand alleviated, or perhaps entirely removed, much of the economic unrest temporarily, social stress still remained.

Two aspects of the workers' own protests in Scotland in the nineteenth century warrant recognition. First, the protests experienced phases of violence, as in Glasgow among the weavers in the attempt to call a general strike in 1820, and among the cotton spinners in the 1830s, but they were also marked by orderly activity and at times by elements of idealism. Second, the miners made a major contribution to various social protests through the existence in their ranks of a number of able leaders.

The idealism was evident in the co-operative movement, though always combined with hard practical economic calculation. An early co-operative venture (it cannot properly be dignified by the name of a society) was at Fenwick in 1769, when the weavers bought oatmeal jointly and where the sum invested in provisions rose from four guineas in 1770 to £40 in 1800. As far as is known, the first which justifies the designation of a society was the Govan Victualling Society, which carried on business from 1777 to 1909. Next, in 1812, came the Lennoxtown Victualling Society. Both the Govan and the Lennoxtown Societies were founded by weavers. The precursors of the more famous Rochdale society differed from it chiefly in the method of paying dividend. In the early Scottish societies the dividend was not related as strictly as at Rochdale to the purchases made. Tradition claims that the Cambuslang society paid dividends according to purchases made even before Rochdale, and Alexander Campbell, one of the chief advocates of Owenite co-operation in Scotland, claimed that he devised the system at least as early as 1822. Their claims cannot be fully substantiated and, in any case, the Rochdale society gave the method its greatest publicity.

The degree of idealism behind the early ventures is difficult to determine. Though three of the twelve Fenwick weavers who signed the original agreement in 1769 were unable to write their names, the early societies were the product of action by the highest grade of labour in contemporary Scotland, but it is difficult to conclude that the founders were motivated by ideals any more lofty than the desire to meet economic difficulties caused by increasing prices. The economic objective was firmly in mind at Lennoxtown, where wartime inflation, and the attraction of selling goods on the neighbouring Glasgow market, kept prices at a level as high as in the city, though wages were lower. Since the weavers were generally more intelligent, independent and enterprising workers, they devised a remedy. They were the pioneers, less because of their idealism, more because, unlike many others, they were not sunk in such squalor that they could not, or would not, make an effort to ameliorate their position.

The great advocate of idealism in co-operative thought in Scotland was Robert Owen. He was more concerned with the establishment of a co-operative community than simply a co-operative store. A co-operative store was merely a palliative of the existing social system. Owen devised schemes for its total reformation. He was also a paternalist employer. Whatever the achievements, and whatever the benefits the workers gained there, Owen did not surrender control to his workers in any way. The ideals of the society at New Lanark were imposed from above; the employer knew best what actions should be followed. Owen's actions at New Lanark were restricted by his fellow partners. In light of his attitude towards the only major attempt to implement his principles, at

Orbiston, near Motherwell, it is difficult to judge either how far New Lanark was conducted in accordance with his views or whether his views were simply less far advanced than they became later. Though he first purchased Orbiston, Owen did not participate in the experiment. He had become attracted by ventures in the United States and considered the views of the chief promoters — James Hamilton, younger of Dalziel, and Abram Combe, a wealthy Edinburgh tanner — too restricted, especially in their refusal to recognise equality and community of property between members. The scheme continued without Owen and was a failure.

Owen's brand of revolutionary co-operative idealism made little permanent impression on the practical growth of the co-operative movement in Scotland. His idealism received greater and more successful publicity in Scotland from the work of his disciple, Alexander Campbell, who, unlike his master, was able to work through the existing societies, even when trying to infuse them with his ideals. His greatest achievement was in the first Glasgow society in 1830, when he instituted a bazaar, at which goods were received from the workers who had produced them, their value being determined by the cost of the raw materials and the time spent on producing them. The goods were exchanged by what was in effect a system of barter for goods of equal value, estimated in the same way, or for notes issued by the co-operative society, and which were accepted in exchange for groceries and other goods by the store. The scheme was not acceptable to many members, and the Glasgow Bazaar's existence was as brief as that of the Orbiston community, though Campbell continued to make a major contribution to the co-operative movement, especially by encouraging the formation of societies in the west of Scotland.

The early societies were pioneers and, as with many of their kind, their casualty rate was high, especially from 1840 to the mid-1850s. The first Glasgow society foundered, rent by disputes between those who favoured Owenite idealism and those who did not. Revival came between the mid-1850s and the mid-1860s with the foundation of a number of societies which provided the basis for the new and modern co-operative movement in Scotland. The origin of the new movement was in Glasgow, where Alexander Campbell again appeared in the 1850s as leader of the second Glasgow society, and in Edinburgh, where St Cuthbert's Society, founded in 1859, became one of the most successful societies in the east of Scotland. From these two centres, in west and east, branches spread into surrounding districts. The culmination of the successful movement came in the 1860s with the beginning of a national movement, indicative of a new-found unity. In 1863 the first co-operative journal, *The Scottish Co-operator,* was published and the Glasgow Society proposed the institution of a wholesale society for Scotland, similar to that being formed in England. Progress was arrested in 1864 by the collapse of the Glasgow Society, even though some of its branches were able to carry on as independent societies. The proposals for a wholesale society did not die, and, after suggestions for a form of union with the Co-operative Wholesale Society were rejected, the Scottish Co-operative Wholesale Society came into being in 1868. Other ventures in co-operative production followed, among them the United Co-operative Baking Society, founded in 1869. The successful trend in consumers' co-operation, which had been temporarily interrupted by the failure of the second Glasgow Society in 1864, was reasserted by the formation in Glasgow of the Kinning Park and the St George's Societies in 1871. By the 1870s the Scottish co-operative movement was well established in all its branches.

Trade unions differed from the co-operative movement by representing an attempt to remedy the problems of the new industrial society through action within industry itself. The co-operative movement drew much of its inspiration from the problems, thoughts and aspirations of the weavers; the strength and initiative of the trade union movement in Scotland in the nineteenth century owed much to the miners. They were among the most degraded elements in Scottish society. If the degraded position of the miners called for exceptional protest, the extent of that degradation made the protest more difficult and produced turmoil and ferment far removed from co-operation.

The state of the law and its interpretation in the courts influenced early attempts at association. Repression was at its worst in the 1790s — illustrated in the sentencing of Thomas Muir, the radical advocate, to fourteen years' transportation — but was moderating by the end of the decade. The Combination Acts of 1799 and 1800 brought several associations to an end. The Acts were drawn up in English terms and, according to the best legal opinion, did not apply in Scotland, but the illegality of combinations under the common law of Scotland had been well-established earlier in the eighteenth century. The position of the individual worker was also weak legally. If he left his employment without notice, he could be imprisoned by summary warrant. The slow change to a more favourable legal environment did not lead to a major growth of trade unionism in Scotland. Though many of the early industrial activities in Scotland produced some form of union, few lasted. Inadequate communications and poor leadership led to the disintegration of much of the effort of the unions into local ventures. Of these early attempts perhaps the best-known and most representative was the Association of Cotton Spinners of Glasgow and neighbourhood, the activities of which were illustrated in 1838 in the trial for violence and sedition of Glasgow cotton spinners, who, though acquitted on the major charge, were transported for seven years for the minor offence. The aims of the union were simply to retain as secure a monopoly of labour as possible. Since Glasgow spinners were generally paid higher rates than operatives elsewhere, others were attracted to Glasgow. Employers preferred them because of the restrictive actions of the Glasgow spinners. From this explosive situation the violence of which the spinners were accused — the throwing of vitriol — could easily arise. The Glasgow association was the main one in the neighbourhood. Other, more local unions appeared, as at Campsie, where the block printers had a union with funds of over £6,000. Opposition to all was so strong that, whenever they risked their resources in action, be it strike or not, defeat was certain, and they stagnated thereafter. Since many of the activities of the cotton industry were widespread, Glasgow alone had a sufficient concentration of operatives, employed by relatively few firms, to make an effective union possible, but in Glasgow the work of any association was greatly weakened by the trial of the cotton spinners in 1838 and thereafter by the beginnings of stagnation in the cotton industry.

A variety of similar local unions appeared — notably in the building trade — but the miners could claim the best-organised association of the period. The first attempt on a national scale was in the Miners' Association of Great Britain and Ireland, formed at Wakefield in 1841 and active in Scotland in the 1840s. As the strikes it called had little success, the movement collapsed, as with much similar activity, in 1848. Thereafter the achievement of constructing the miners' organisation belonged chiefly to Alexander McDonald, who, from entering the pits at the age of eight, earned for himself a university education and became the leader of the British miners and a somewhat controversial figure. McDonald's first attempt to build a general association on the shifting sands of racial and religious jealousies came in the mid-1850s. A strike in 1856 was a major trial for the new association, from which McDonald grew to appreciate the dangers of the local unions still more, and so to stress the need for greater centralisation of both funds and organisation. His efforts were not conspicuously successful at the time. The next move towards greater organisation came from the local level. In the 1860s Lodges of Free Colliers, modelled in ceremonial and procedure on masonic lodges, appeared. They were mainly social in character and combined an unusual mixture of nationalist sentiment, opposition to Irish Catholicism, and tentative but largely unsuccessful attempts to enrol employers. More important was the progress around 1870, which was aided by the buoyant demand for coal of those years. An eight-hour day was started in Fife, Lanarkshire and the Lothians, and gatherings of miners led to the acceptance of an Association of Confederated Miners of Scotland in 1873. The changing economic conditions brought the short period of successful consolidation to an end in 1874 in a turmoil of wage cuts, inter-district rivalries and strikes, which dissipated funds and organisation. The activities of a dedicated local organisation could be merged and made widely effective only briefly during periods of prosperity. Disintegration accompanied depression. When McDonald was elected member of parliament for North Staffordshire in 1874, his parliamentary duties absorbed an increasing amount of his time and he had to leave much of the subsequent growth of the Scottish miners' movement to others. His insistence on the need for a centralisation of organisation and finance, and on the value of propaganda and of parliamentary action, were lessons which the miners and other associations of Scottish workers grew to appreciate.

In the middle of the nineteenth century Scottish trade unionists had still to learn the value of unity at a national level, but its merits locally had long been appreciated in what were in effect nascent trades councils. They expressed the views of members on a variety of topics, ranging from the strictly industrial to the social, philanthropic and political. Such associations, which existed from about 1830 at least, had only a shadowy existence and were frequently called into being only to deal with a specific problem, as to assist the accused in the cotton spinners' trial. A permanent body was formed in Glasgow in 1858. In Edinburgh, though an antecedent body, if not the council itself, had been in existence from about 1853, the Trades Council was formally constituted only in 1867. In Aberdeen and Dundee the history of the trades councils was similar: earlier associations gave way to modern councils in 1868 and 1885 respectively.

NOTES

1. *Acts of the Parliaments of Scotland*, III, pp. 139-42.

2. *Report by a Committee of the General Assembly on the Management of the Poor in Scotland*, 1839, p. 7. BPP. 1839. XX.

3. Some details of the assistance given are in the *Sanitary Reports*, 1842, pp. 166-7.

4. *Report of the Royal Commission on the Poor Laws*, 1844, p. xlviii. BPP. 1844. XX.

5. *Ibid.*, p. lviii.

6. *Report of the Directors of the Town's Hospital of Glasgow on the Management of the City Poor* (Glasgow, 1818), p. 39.

7. *Ibid.*, p. 45, quoting reply by Chalmers to the directors.

8. *Ibid.*, p. 47.

9. W. P. Alison, *Observations on the Management of the Poor in Scotland* (Edinburgh, 1840), pp. 21-2.

10. *Ibid.*, p. 58.

11. *Ibid.*, p. 10.

12. *Ibid.*, p. 54.

13. *Ibid.*, p. 55.

14. See p. 15.

15. For details, see p. 229.

Part Three

Economic Pressure, 1870s to 1939

CHAPTER XII

Industry to 1914

Shipbuilding

For almost half a century after 1830 the rise of the iron and related industries helped to draw attention from the less rapid growth of the once leading cotton industry. Thereafter the place of the leading sectors in the economy was surrendered to shipbuilding and heavy engineering, which were linked in turn to modern steelmaking. They differed in a number of ways from the cotton and iron industries. Their output was specialised, ensuring that competition was less directly and exclusively linked to cost and included ability in design, delivery and servicing. The consequential differentiation of their products gave some control over the market. Less favourably, their growth was potentially discontinuous because it depended, not on relatively stable domestic consumption, but on the demand for investment goods, part of which came from overseas and part from the public sector. Problems produced by such dependence were easily surmounted before 1918; they still placed much of Scottish industry in a precarious position for the future.

The shipbuilding industry showed such characteristics clearly when it came to make a major contribution to the country's economic development from the 1870s. Its modern growth was concentrated on the Clyde. Initially the river had few special advantages over other similar waterways, and Glasgow's earliest trade with America was conducted in vessels built elsewhere, first in Holland, then latterly in America. The main rise of the industry on the Clyde was encouraged by changes in methods of construction (wood, iron and steel) and changes in methods of propulsion (sail, steam, diesel). Those in the first group are behind suggestions that the rise of the iron and steel industries in the west of Scotland provides an adequate explanation of the rise of shipbuilding on the Clyde, but it is possible that changes in methods of propulsion were of even greater importance and made the adoption of new constructional materials more effective. If the latter interpretation is valid, the rise of the iron and steel industries becomes a second, though not necessarily a secondary, factor in the growth of Scottish shipbuilding.

The contribution of Scottish marine engineers to the development of the three chief methods of propulsion (the steam engine developed from Watt's ideas, the steam turbine, and the diesel engine) varied. The earliest experiments in steam navigation took place in 1788 on the loch at Dalswinton in Dumfriesshire under the supervision of the inventive laird, Patrick Miller (the patron of Burns), and James Taylor, a private banker from Edinburgh, with technical assistance, though of disputed importance, from William Symington, the engineer in the mines at Wanlockhead. In spite of further experiments by Symington with the *Charlotte Dundas* on the Forth and Clyde Canal, full success in Scotland came only in 1812, when Henry Bell launched his *Comet*, built by Woods of Port Glasgow, and engined by John Robertson of Glasgow, and with the boiler made in the foundry of David Napier. By 1820, 42 vessels of 3,200 tons had been built on the Clyde, more than half of the British total, a share that was lost temporarily until the marine engineers on the Clyde regained two-thirds of the output of steam tonnage by the 1840s.

The widespread adoption of the steamship rested on the solution of two problems: first, the need to improve the efficiency of the boilers, frequently limited to 5 lbs. per square inch above atmospheric pressure or even less, as their weakness restricted attempts to gain increased power by increasing steam pressure; second, the need to improve the efficiency of the engines, as the expansion of higher-pressure steam within one cylinder led to considerable losses in the initial condensation and subsequent re-evaporation and so led to heavy coal consumption. Improvements in both engine and boiler were complementary to each other until a reasonable degree of success in solving both problems was achieved in the 1860s. The simple engine, still basically the early adaptation of Watt's design, was superseded by the compound engine, in which the steam was expanded in stages. An increase in boiler pressure followed, sometimes to as high as 100 lbs. per square inch, more commonly around 60 lbs. per square inch, but progress was neither quick nor easy, nor was the achievement even then complete. When pressure was low, boilers were approximately in box form, or tank boilers, but higher pressures could be resisted only by cylindrical-shaped boilers, at first by a type of small diameter, known as 'water-tube' boilers. Progress with the new boilers was sometimes hesitant. In 1857 Scott's of Greenock experimented with a water-tube boiler at a pressure of 125 lbs. per square inch but reverted to half that pressure. In 1862, James Howden established his firm and developed successfully a cylindrical 'tank' boiler, which was the prototype of the 'Scotch boilers' used until the First World War. The next step forward came with an improvement in the engine in the 1870s, when, in response to an order for a boiler to work at a pressure of 150 lbs. per square inch, A. C. Kirk of Napier's devised the triple-expansion engine, which, with its expansion of steam in three stages, could operate with steam at higher pressures without leading to losses similar to those which were experienced earlier with the simple engine. The first triple-expansion engine was unsuccessful, and mastery came in the 1880s, again on a prototype of A. C. Kirk, but with a boiler made of steel, which, because of its resistance to higher pressures, made many boiler improvements feasible. Later, the quadruple-expansion engine completed the development of the steam engine from Watt's model. By then the common practice was to use Scotch boilers working at about 180 lbs. per square inch for triple-expansion engines and at about 220 lbs. per square inch for the less common quadruple-expansion engines.

A second line of development in mechanical propulsion came with the steam turbine. Though the quadruple-expansion engine marked the culmination of a phase of development, it left one problem unsolved. In the reciprocating engine the transference of the linear motion of a piston within the cylinder to the rotary motion of a shaft results in considerable loss of power through friction, so the chief mechanical problem by the end of the nineteenth century was to achieve the rotary motion direct from the engine. It was achieved by C. A. Parsons' steam turbine, first patented in 1884. The *King Edward*, which plied on the Clyde for half a century, was the first merchant vessel powered by steam turbine, with Denny's as builder and Parsons as engineer. The early steam turbine left another problem to be solved. For maximum efficiency the turbine had to rotate at high speed, while the propeller had to rotate at only a low speed. The solution lay in gearing. Sir John Biles, the Professor of Naval Architecture in the University of Glasgow, claimed that he suggested the innovation to Parsons, and the first ships were designed and built with geared-turbine machinery at Fairfields in 1912.

The third major advance in propulsion in the century before 1914 was the invention of the diesel engine, first patented in Britain in 1892, and which was similar in design to the steam engine. The first seagoing diesel vessels were built in Italy and Holland in 1910 but they were designed for only short voyages. The first ship for long voyages was built in Denmark in 1912. In the same year Barclay, Curle and Company built its sister ship, the *Jutlandia*, on the Clyde. The advent of the diesel engine marks a significant change in the history of Clyde shipbuilding. In the development of the steam engine and to a lesser extent of the steam turbine, Scottish engineers played a vitally important part but not in the development of the diesel engine. The Clyde never produced its own model, the Doxford from Sunderland being the only large British engine. If the Clyde's shipbuilding fame rested on its engineering abilities, its lead was being lost.

At certain stages the success of marine engineering depended on the prior development of some of the new methods of construction, but the order is significant. Marine engineering came first; shipbuilding came later. When the *Comet* sailed in 1812, twenty years before the rise of the new Scottish iron industry, the first step was taken towards the establishment of the Clyde's reputation. Since ships built elsewhere were then sent to the Clyde to be engined, it was a short step to having them built on the Clyde. In short, it was the substitution of steam vessels for sailing ships that, in the words of John Scott of Greenock, gave 'a very large impetus' to Clyde shipbuilding.[1] The Clyde was active when other areas were not. In 1833 Alexander Stephen, then still building ships on the east coast, recorded in his diary that shipbuilding had been remarkably flat apart from the construction of steamboats on the west coast. He was already casting his eyes towards Linthouse, where his firm was later to make its main reputation. Even later, when the Scottish iron industry had grown, and when Clyde yards were building iron ships in increasing numbers, the early contribution of marine engineering was not forgotten. In 1852 the Town Chamberlain of Greenock wrote a report on the past and present of his town for the Town Council. In it he spoke of the increasing demand for Clyde-built ships from foreigners and pointed out that:

> our superiority in producing engines has hitherto been the cause of these potentates preferring the work of our artisans to that of any others. But, now that iron is superseding timber and becoming the principal component, not of the engine only, but also of the hull, our power to excel is vastly increased.[2]

The first iron steamship in Scotland was the *Aglaia*, of 30 tons, built by David Napier to sail on Loch Eck. The beginning was hesitant. In 1831 four iron vessels, at least two of which were for the Forth and Clyde Canal, were built, not in Scotland but in Manchester. One was an experimental vessel; the other, the *Lord Dundas*, plied for several years between Port Dundas and Lock 16 on the Forth and Clyde Canal. Also in the year 1831 John Neilson of the Oakbank foundry in Glasgow launched the *Fairy Queen*, the first iron vessel to ply on the Clyde. Some of the engineers, who had previously made a reputation as shipbuilders, quickly adopted the new material for their hulls. One of the best known, Robert Napier, launched his first iron vessel, the *Vanguard*, in June 1836. But the most significant development on the Clyde came with the appearance of new firms, formed specifically to build iron ships. The most important was founded by two ex-foremen of Robert Napier, David Tod and John McGregor, who started a yard of their own at Govan to build iron ships and launched their first vessel, the *Vale of Leven*, in 1835.

Most of the early steamships were built of iron. Of the 247 steam vessels launched on the Clyde between 1846 and 1852, only 14 were wooden. Since the iron vessels were often larger, the Clyde's share of tonnage launched in Britain grew. The use of iron was restricted by prejudice and by Lloyd's reluctance to produce any insurance provision for iron vessels until 1855; but its benefits could not be ignored and were increased by its ability to withstand the vibration of the screw propeller which came to displace the paddle-wheel. The 1850s saw the virtual extinction of construction by wood. The last wooden Cunarder, the *Arabia*, was built in 1852, and in 1859 the last wooden ship of any considerable size was launched from Scott's of Greenock. In the twenty years to 1870 over two-thirds of Britain's iron tonnage was launched on the Clyde.

Wood survived as a material in 'composite' construction (that is, wood was placed on iron frames and beams), a method used in the 1860s for the clippers, the best-known of which was the *Cutty Sark*, launched at Dumbarton in 1869. Their history demonstrated the ability of sailing vessels to survive even after the victory of steamers. Until the opening of the Suez Canal in 1869, the difficulties of coaling vessels enabled sailing vessels to compete on the long routes to Australia and China, and thereafter, until the isthmus of Panama was breached in 1915, on the long route round Cape Horn. Their operation was not confined to specialised routes. In times of depression the cheapness of operating the sailing ship was an obvious advantage over its more expensive, though technically more efficient, steam-propelled rival. Consequently, even after the opening of the Suez Canal, there were times when the proportion of tonnage of sailing vessels launched on the Clyde rose. In 1868 it was 45.1 per cent of the total; in 1871 it was 4.7; in 1877 it was 44.6; in 1879 it was 5.7; in 1885 it was 51.7. The pattern was broken only with the increase in output after the adoption of the steam turbine in the 1890s. After 1896 the proportion of sailing vessels rapidly became insignificant.

Just as iron displaced wood in shipbuilding, so it was displaced in turn by steel after the adoption of new methods of steelmaking in the second half of the nineteenth century. The first successful experiments on the Clyde were in the late 1870s. In 1877 John Elder built two steel paddle-steamers at Govan for service on the English Channel. Then, most important of all, in 1879 William Denny, who had previously launched several small steel vessels, built the *Rotomahana*, the first ocean-going vessel to be built of mild steel. Denny's action was an example for others to follow, especially when he became a leading protagonist of the new metal. In 1879 almost half of the 18,000 tons of steel shipping launched on the Clyde came from his yard. Initially cost limited the use of steel, but its use spread as price fell with the adoption of cheaper methods of production during a period when prices generally were falling. In 1879, when Denny launched the *Rotomahana*, only 10.3 per cent of the tonnage launched on the Clyde was of steel, the remainder being of iron and wood. The position was reversed ten years later when 97.2 per cent of the tonnage launched was of steel. The use of steel in construction and of the steam turbine in propulsion combined to provide the basis from which Scottish shipbuilding yards were able to respond at the end of the nineteenth and beginning of the twentieth centuries to rising demand, helped greatly by naval orders in some yards. From the 1870s output was maintained; from the 1890s it increased until in 1913 an all-time record tonnage of 756,976 was launched on the Clyde. From the 1870s until the First World War shipbuilding was a growth point of the Scottish economy.

Steel

For all practical purposes the Scottish steel industry dates from the adoption of the new steelmaking processes of the second half of the nineteenth century: the Bessemer converter and the Siemens-Martin open-hearth furnace, with their initial fundamental defect that they could use only low-phosphorus irons, remedied in the 1880s by the Gilchrist-Thomas basic process. Since the success of the new technology in Scotland depended on the demand from the shipyards, steelmaking was an integral part of the complex of industrial specialisation which appeared in Scotland at the end of the nineteenth century.

Two long-term and two short-term determinants of the industry's growth help to explain its dependence on shipbuilding. The first long-run determinant was the structure of the older Scottish iron industry which specialised in the production of pig iron and was relatively little concerned with subsequent processes. High costs of production bore hard on the profit margins of the malleable iron manufacturers, who had to find new methods and outlets to survive, but those who produced pig iron only were more favourably placed and, though less secure than a few decades earlier, still enjoyed reasonable profits and so did not have the same incentive as the malleable iron manufacturers to introduce the new steelmaking processes. The greatest concern of all, William Baird and Company, did not do so, even though the Baird brothers, who were by then no longer active, were followed in the direction of the firm by men of comparable ability and energy. Their chief rival, Merry and Cunninghame, made the change at Glengarnock.

The second long-term determinant was that the first introduction of the new processes in Scotland was unsuccessful and blighted many thoughts of emulation. The lack of success was chiefly because local supplies of iron were unsuitable for the new processes. The first attempt to use the Bessemer process in Scotland was by Thomas Jackson at the Coats Ironworks at Coatbridge, then, more seriously, by Dixon at Govan. Unlike Jackson's home-made plant, Dixon's was properly erected, and the experiments were under the supervision of Bessemer. His attempt was given every chance of complete success, but it failed, as at the Coats Works, and Bessemer returned the money paid for the licence. The reason was the common one, which was beginning to show the limited applicability of the Bessemer process: ordinary Scotch pig iron was an insufficiently low-phosphorus iron and as such was unsuitable for the Bessemer process. Since the difficulty was unexpected, and its cause at first unknown, the disappointment was greater. Even when it was recognised, and the need to use low-phosphorus or hematite ores understood, immediate success did not follow. Though hematite pig iron was used, the introduction of the process at the Atlas works in 1861 encountered difficulties, and until the converters were dismantled in 1875 the Atlas works was the only successful producer of Bessemer iron in Scotland. The next main technical development in steel production, the Siemens open-hearth furnace, had much to commend its use. It gave greater opportunities for control of the process and it could use scrap, of which Scotland was to have a generous supply from her shipbreaking yards for many years, but it too required low-phosphorus iron for successful operation. Technically, it became possible to use ordinary Scotch iron only when the Gilchrist-Thomas basic process, first developed in the 1880s, could be applied to either the Bessemer converter or the open-hearth furnace and free the new processes from their dependence on non-phosphoric iron, which had to be imported to Scotland. Yet it was on the basis of the older method — the acid, not the basic — using especially the open-hearth furnace, that the modern Scottish steel industry first grew.

The first attempt at the large-scale production of steel in Scotland came in the early days of these disappointing experiments, in the establishment of the Steel Company of Scotland in the early 1870s. Its origins were exceptional. They were in another line of industrial development, in attempts by Charles Tennant of St. Rollox and others to circumvent the inadequate indigenous supplies of non-phosphoric ore by using 'Blue Billy' or 'purple' ore, the residue after copper and silver had been extracted from the iron pyrites which was then displacing pure sulphur as a raw material in the production of sulphuric acid, and of which the Tharsis Sulphur and Copper Company had acquired a large quantity. Tennant and his associates envisaged producing steel directly from ore (in this case it was hoped direct from the 'Blue Billy') without the necessary intermediary of the blast furnace. The Company was incorporated in 1872 and the site of its works was fixed finally at Hallside. Furnaces specially designed by C. W. Siemens were erected, but, though good puddled iron was made from an equal mixture of 'Blue Billy' and ordinary iron, costs were so high that the process was stopped and standard open-hearth furnaces were installed. The unusual attempts were brought to an end and the Steel Company of Scotland came to rely conventionally on external supplies of pig iron and scrap.

The restrictive influences on steelmaking of the existing, satisfied position of many already in the iron industry and the inadequacy of supplies of suitable ore, unless imported at additional cost, were reinforced by two less permanent short-run factors. The first arose from the lack of contact between Scottish ironmasters and the market in the shipyards to which much steel production was to go. The demand for steel rails was strong, and at first the Steel Company of Scotland specialised in producing them, but, since Scottish ironmasters had never specialised in their manufacture, this early demand came from a market with which they did not have strong links. The Steel Company of Scotland soon demonstrated a more successful specialisation. It diversified its output and began to produce steel for shipbuilding and other constructional activity. The Company was given its first Admiralty order in 1876 and, not altogether a coincidence, it then made its first profits. Expansion followed. Blochairn was purchased in 1880 and was quickly turned to steel production. The second short-term restrictive influence was that the 1870s, when the opportunities of the new technology appeared, were mostly a period of depression and low prices, when ironmasters and others were naturally reluctant to venture from a still reasonably stable position into the risks of new enterprises. If economic pressure increased, the ironmasters always had the alternative of renovating their techniques in iron production itself, an alternative they adopted.

The exceptional nature of the foundation of the Steel Company of Scotland meant that in its early years in the 1870s it was not in the main stream of growth of the Scottish iron and steel industry. Absorption came after about 1880 with the appearance of other Scottish steelmaking concerns in two distinct groups. First, Scotland's relatively few malleable iron manufacturers transferred to steelmaking. In 1879 William Beardmore began to transform Parkhead Forge into a steelworks. In 1880, as the rate of expansion increased, and as the Steel Company of Scotland bought Blochairn and extended Hallside, David Colville built four Siemens furnaces at his malleable ironworks of Dalziel. Second, an exceptional few of the iron smelters followed the lead of the malleable ironmakers, notably Merry and Cunninghame, who erected Bessemer converters to use the basic process at Glengarnock in 1884-5. Later they added some Siemens open-hearth furnaces, but Glengarnock remained unusual among the larger Scottish works in producing basic Bessemer steel. Open-hearth acid steel was much more common, and by 1885 Scotland had ten steelmaking firms with 73 open-hearth furnaces producing 240,000 tons, or 42 per cent of the British make of open-hearth steel.

The expansion of the early 1880s cannot be explained by any general increase in prosperity, nor by the introduction of a new technology. Existing Scottish producers, of both pig and malleable iron, were attracted to steel production at the time because of the operation of new factors. The early history of the Steel Company of Scotland shows what they were. It did not provide a profitable example for others to follow. It had difficulties and was not especially profitable in its early days. When profits did come, even though only slight, they were in part derived from sales to the shipyards. The 1870s witnessed the increasing use of steel in shipbuilding. The Admiralty was satisfied and placed orders with the Steel Company of Scotland. In 1877 Lloyd's issued its first set of rules for steel vessels. The growing demand for steel for shipbuilding was the factor which brought the Scottish steel industry into being in the early 1880s and which continued to maintain it.

The close connection between the two industries explains the Scottish steel industry's preference for the open-hearth furnace. When Lloyd's banned the use of Bessemer steel in shipbuilding in 1887, those few Scottish concerns, such as Merry and Cunninghame which had built Bessemer converters faced considerable difficulties. Chiefly for that reason, Merry and Cunninghame built open-hearth furnaces beside their existing, and quite new, Bessemer converters at Glengarnock. The criticism that the steel industry failed to develop the production of Bessemer steel is misplaced in so far as it is applied to Scotland. It concentrates on one section of the industry alone. In Scotland the production of open-hearth steel did not decline, but increased, as that of Bessemer steel fell, to meet the demand from the shipyards. Fluctuations there were, but they originated in fluctuations in the demand for ships.

Industrial decline

The success of shipbuilding and marine engineering, and their consequential benefits to steelmaking and other ancillary industries, depended on the superior skills which engineers and others in Scotland brought to their work. The success of the older textile and iron industries depended instead on their ability to compete on the basis of low costs and price.

As their ability to do so lessened, prosperity came to depend on how far they were able to exploit some specialist field of production. The cotton industry was least successful and its contraction, which accelerated from the 1870s, spread from spinning to weaving in the 1890s. The jute industry was in a similar position, and in the thirty years before 1914 the consumption of jute remained almost stationary. There were several explanations, but one was particularly important. Jute had been adopted as the staple fibre of the Dundee textile industry in the process of successive substitutions of inferior raw materials for the flax originally used. During subsequent depressions various adulterants (such as tow and hemp) were used to keep costs down, but no experiments with new fibres seem to have been made in periods of relative prosperity. The policy enabled the industry to survive before 1914; in the inter-war years, when the policy of substitution could be followed no longer, the range of possible action was severely limited. More than thirty years of stagnation could not easily be overcome. By contrast, the woollen industry retained its competitive position because some branches established reputations for specialist production. In 1892 a representative of the South of Scotland Chamber of Commerce reported that 95 woollen manufacturers of the Chamber's 142 members had 'fairly regular trade' and that 'work is fairly plentiful', statements which contrast with much gloomier comments from other textile areas. In 1907 Scotland produced 10 per cent of the United Kingdom's output of woollen cloth. In some fields Scotland's share was even greater: it was 31 per cent of the United Kingdom's output of woollen carpets in 1913.

Other branches of textile production survived through combining new commercial practices with the growth of an independent specialisation. The best example is probably the Paisley thread industry which met international competition successfully until 1914. Scottish firms were international pioneers and set up mills in the United States in the 1860s: Coats at Pawtucket and Clark at Newark. When the two firms amalgamated in 1896, a large part of the world's thread industry was controlled directly from Paisley, while the remainder was influenced by a central pricing policy. But Coats' Central Agency, which controlled sales and prices, was more a commercial achievement, perhaps the most striking in Scotland in the nineteenth century, and less a sign of industrial success. Though control of the Coats empire continued to be exercised from Glasgow, production in Paisley became increasingly overshadowed by production overseas. The manufacture of thread in Scotland was unable to maintain its position internationally. In the textile finishing trades commercial reorganisation proved less beneficial for Scotland. Calico printing and dyeing, especially in the Vale of Leven, showed the same independence in growth and the same tendency towards amalgamation as in thread manufacture. By 1868 Turkey Red dyeing in the Vale of Leven was concentrated into three firms, which gained from the exploitation of the Indian market following the coming of the railways there. Calico printing gained less. Towards the end of the nineteenth century both suffered from competitive price-cutting. Again amalgamations followed. In 1898 the three Turkey Red concerns merged into the United Turkey Red Company, and in 1899 the calico printers formed the Calico Printers' Association. The resulting concentration of the industry, especially when the headquarters of the Calico Printers' Association was in Manchester, led to a neglect of Scottish interests. Scotland gained from commercial concentration in the thread industry; it lost in the finishing trades. Unemployment was high, especially among calico printers in the Vale of Leven at the end of the nineteenth century.

The iron and coal industries gained some benefit from the successes in shipbuilding and steelmaking, but their own lack of specialised production led them to suffer the same effects of competition as in the less specialised textile manufactures. Local iron industries expanded overseas and the United States and Germany, which had previously been among Scotland's leading customers, quickly achieved a high degree of technical competence. Scottish ironmasters also faced competition from rivals at home within their own special field of the production of foundry pig iron. Iron production increased rapidly in the Cleveland area around Middlesbrough between 1850 and 1870. Costs of production were so low that pig iron was delivered in Coatbridge below the price at which local production was profitable. From the late 1860s Cleveland pig iron entered Scotland in increasing quantities, especially in years of depression. With the exhaustion of the best seams of blackband ironstone, thinner seams, or the less valuable clayband and slateyband ores, had to be worked at a time when the advantages of the native ores had declined in any case because of the need of the new steelmaking processes for pig iron from non-phosphoric, or hematite, ores, which were not found in any quantity in Scotland. Scottish ore production, which was 3,000,000 tons and more in the 1870s, was less than 600,000 tons in 1913. Ore had to be imported, chiefly from Spain, and so costs of production rose. Supplies of coal generally remained adequate, but those of particularly valuable grades, such as the important splint coal of Lanarkshire, and supplies adjacent to the ironworks, did not. The experience of the iron industry had repercussions on coalmining. The iron industry had not consumed a major proportion of Scottish coal output but it had provided the demand behind the industry's growth and exploitation, especially in the west of Scotland. From the early 1870s the connection between the two became less close and the coal industry's fortunes grew to be determined by other, and less stable, factors. The great boom in the coal industry between 1872 and 1873 marked the beginning of a new age, for it as for other sectors of the economy.

As the indigenous base of the iron industry diminished, Scottish ironmasters changed many of their traditional practices in iron-smelting. The change was much needed. Some critics averred, with justification, that Britain was technically inferior to foreign countries in the production of iron and that Scottish performance compared unfavourably with that of other areas in Britain. Natural resources were so abundant that Scottish ironmasters could afford, for a time at any rate, to follow a policy of 'suicidal prodigality'.[3] In Scotland about 30 cwt. of coke (or about 55 cwt. of coal) were required to produce a ton of iron, against about 20 cwt. or, under the best practice, even less, in spite of the charge with the fuel in the furnace in Scotland being only about two tons of ore and limestone, though it was about four tons in Cleveland. Accordingly, the average productivity of a furnace in Scotland was low: about 165 tons of pig iron a week compared with nearly 500 tons a week in Barrow, where the hematite ore was nearest to the blackband in its iron content.

The most striking features of Scottish blast-furnace technique were the small size of the furnaces, the lowness of the temperature of the blast, and the failure to utilise waste gases from the furnaces. Heightening the furnaces did not offer an obvious improvement. Considerable difficulty was experienced in keeping the hearth clear of solid matter with furnaces of the normal Scottish height of from forty to sixty feet. For similar reasons raising the temperature seemed impossible; a high temperature softened the materials more and choked the furnace. At some works, such as Shotts, the problem arose even with the splint coal, but not at others, such as Summerlee, where the temperature was raised. Whatever the future possibilities of improvement along these lines, the most obvious advance in blast-furnace practice in the nineteenth century in Scotland was the utilisation of the gases which escaped from the open-topped furnaces. When raw coal is used as a fuel, as it was in Scotland, the coal is coked near the top of the furnaces and consequently the furnace gases are mixed with coal gas. Instead of trying to conserve and use these gases and their heating power, the ironmasters allowed them to escape and additionally to pollute the atmosphere. One estimate suggested that a Scottish furnace exuded twice as much heat into the atmosphere as was used. Attempts at conservation by some Scottish ironmasters in the early 1850s were soon abandoned because of the abundance of cheap fuel in Scotland. The need to conserve resources, and consequently the need to use waste gas, was taken seriously only in the early 1870s. The accumulated neglect of decades could not easily be remedied, and the lessened comparative advantages could never be regained, but the Scottish iron industry tried in the last quarter of the nineteenth century to solve its problems through greater technical efficiency.

The iron industry's counterpart, coalmining, needed similar measures of adaptation, though not uniformly in all sectors. A notable feature of the Scottish coal industry from the mid-1870s was its division into two sections, the prosperity of each being determined differently. The first indication of the need for adaptation came in the late 1860s, when the ironmasters began to sell coal on a large scale. After the boom of the early 1870s, they were forced to do so again with the decline in the prosperity of the iron industry in the west of Scotland, where by then about 80 per cent of Scotland's coal was produced by nearly 74 per cent of its miners. In the east, and especially in Fife, which was increasingly dependent on export demand, there were no comparable problems. Export prices for coal were slightly higher and the east-coast collieries gained until 1877 when, for the first time in the decade, they suffered from a fall in both the value and volume of exports. In 1878 some collieries in Fife were closed. In the 1880s inter-district competition, not only in Scotland but from the north-east of England as well, inhibited revival. In the west the depression in the iron industry forced producers to restrict output; in the east, increased exports, especially in 1885, failed to lead to any increase in price. Lastly, to complete the industry's difficulties, supply increased from collieries sunk because of the high expectations of the boom of the early 1870s. Adaptation in the coal industry in the last quarter of the nineteenth century was difficult because Scottish coalmasters, in trying to find new markets, were simply competing with each other; the one hope for more stable, and more universal, prosperity lay in expanding sales overseas into new markets.

Though coal sales to Ireland, not recorded as exports in trade statistics, absorbed part of the output of the west-coast collieries, foreign demand was of major importance only in Fife, where nearly half of the output went overseas by the beginning of the twentieth century. The experience of Fife was exceptional. At the end of the nineteenth century the proportion of Scottish output exported was only slightly higher than for the whole country. From 1895 to 1900 nearly 19 per cent of Scottish output was exported, compared with nearly 18 per cent of the output of the United Kingdom. The difference was too slight to place the Scottish producers in a unique position in the late nineteenth and early twentieth centuries, but was still the chief variable determining the industry's prosperity as the demand from the ironworks had done in the middle of the nineteenth century. Most Scottish exports went to a few countries — to Denmark, Germany, Norway, Russia and Sweden — and about the turn of the century Scotland generally contributed from 25 to 50 per cent of their imports from the United Kingdom. The growth of Continental production, especially in Germany, affected directly the prosperity of the eastern collieries of Scotland, and, indirectly through inter-district competition, affected the prosperity of those in the west. The coal industry was therefore forced to rely on foreign markets during years of increasing international competition. Some attributed the severity of the industry's difficulties to internal characteristics as well as to external competition. Exporters blamed the coalmasters for failing to produce the type of coal required by the overseas customers, and the greatest Glasgow exporter of the day, D. M. Stevenson, asserted that the British consumers encouraged such conservatism. Other criticisms were applicable to Scotland. It was asserted that the tendency of Scottish miners to regulate their output inversely with wage fluctuations, so that they would be assured of a given income, inhibited increases in output to meet rising demand. The greater cost of railway transport in Scotland, compared with other parts of the country, and notably with Wales, was alleged to lessen the competitiveness of Scottish coal in more distant markets. The exact relevance of such criticisms cannot be assessed easily. Their importance is more as symptoms of the changed position of the coal industry from the 1870s. No longer able to rely on the underlying demand from the ironworks, the industry was being forced increasingly to try to meet the requirements of new, and often foreign, markets. Such adaptation was not easy, but without it the industry's prosperity was bound to decline.

New industries

A continuing strand in any explanation of industrial decline in the later nineteenth century is the diminution in Scotland's natural advantages of coal and iron ore. At the same time, or a little later around the time of the First World War, Scottish wage rates and earnings, which had been relatively low, converged with those of the United Kingdom as a whole without clear evidence of a compensating increase in productivity. Specialist producers were not affected to the same extent by such an erosion in cost advantage, and the later nineteenth century saw the emergence of a range of new industries with great promise of economic success for those able to carry out the technical processes involved. Achievements were evident in many fields, but it is possible that the Scottish educational traditions, even the nature of Scottish scientific education, inhibited the exploitation of their full potential.

The source from which achievement in a whole range of new industries could have grown was the tradition of Scottish engineering. Its origins were diversified. Some early engineering establishments made machinery for their own requirements. The Houldsworths met the mechanical needs of their cotton mills in their foundry at Anderston. Another group manufactured specialised machinery, generally for export. Blair Campbell and Maclean, Duncan Stewart and Company, and the Mirrlees Watson Company, founded in the late 1830s, made sugar-manufacturing machinery though sometimes extending their work to general engineering. Both groups supplied the machines required for Scottish industrial activities or for the country's overseas trade. The steam engine introduced new engineering requirements through its own demands for means of transport by land and sea. Marine and locomotive engineering, at first frequently combined, began to be separated from the 1850s. Neilson and Company, founded in 1836 by a son of the inventor of the hot-blast, first specialised about 1843 at the Hyde Park Works by beginning the manufacture of locomotives and survived to become one of the three firms which merged to form the North British Locomotive Company in 1903. The use of new metals brought further specialisation. Steel encouraged structural engineering, especially bridgebuilding, which, with shipbuilding, became the main market for open-hearth steel in the west of Scotland, and in which the success of Sir William Arrol and Company in building the Tay and Forth bridges was the best-known achievement.

Such successes were part of the tradition of Scottish heavy engineering, of which shipbuilding was the most notable example, but much of the future lay, not in heavy, but in light engineering. Again achievements can be recorded. In electrical engineering an important contribution came from the firm of Kelvin and White, in due course to become Kelvin and Hughes, which was founded by James White in mid-century. Through its connection with Lord Kelvin it began the manufacture of electrical instruments and made an important contribution to the laying of the first Atlantic cable. Other firms followed its lead until by the beginning of the twentieth century Scottish firms were manufacturing electrical appliances of all kinds and for all purposes of power and lighting. Some began to specialise. In 1885 Mavor and Coulson supplied the city of Glasgow with electricity from the first supply station in Scotland, and, while still carrying on its general engineering work, increased its output of electrically driven coal-cutting machinery after 1897, and specialised entirely in its manufacture from the 1930s.

Early efforts in the motor-car industry left a less permanent legacy. The pioneer of the industry in Scotland was George Johnston, who devised the first all-Scottish car, modelled on the Daimler, and had it put into commercial production in 1896 by the Mo-Car Syndicate, later the Arrol-Johnston Company. In 1901, when the Company's Glasgow works were destroyed by fire, production was transferred to Paisley, and again, just before the First World War, to Dumfries, where it continued until the 1920s. Other concerns followed the lead given by the Arrol-Johnston Company. For years William Beardmore and Company manufactured their own taxi-cab in the old Paisley works of the Arrol-Johnston Company; the A.B.C. Company, with which George Johnston was connected, did likewise in Bridgeton for a few years after 1906; the Bergius Company was more successful when it surrendered car production but used its engine to produce the Kelvin engine for boats. The two concerns which made the most striking contribution to the growth of the car industry in Scotland were, however, the Albion Company, famous and lasting, and the Argyll Company, also famous but not lasting. The Albion Company outlived the other pioneers but specialised from 1913 in the manufacture of commercial vehicles. It did not meet the new mass consumer demand which provided the basis for the success of the modern car industry. In Scotland an attempt to do so came from the unsuccessful Argyll Company. The Argyll car was designed and engined by Alexander Govan, who first gained his ideas when assembling the French Darracq car in Bridgeton. Govan opened a new factory at Alexandria in Dunbartonshire. Its opening in 1906 was symbolic of Govan's hopes. He had grasped the modern conception of producing for the mass market, and his new factory was designed after an international study of the latest means of production to reap all possible economies of scale. Unfortunately Govan died, aged only 39, shortly after the opening of the new factory, and its financial burdens led the Argyll Company into partial liquidation in 1908. Subsequently the Company developed the single-sleeve-valve engine, invented by a Glasgow engineer, Peter Burt, whose own firm, the Acme Engineering Company, later became the Acme Wringer Company. The fruits of this technical achievement were nullified by litigation over patent rights, especially with the inventors of the double-sleeve-valve engine, used by the Daimler Company. Though the Argyll Company won the actions in 1913, the cost of development and litigation forced it into liquidation in 1914. All the Argyll rights and designs were acquired and a new company formed to manufacture the car at the Hozier works in Bridgeton, where Govan had first assembled the Darracq car. Production there ceased in the 1920s.

In aeronautical engineering early developments were not consolidated, though the early successes were sporadic. First, in 1895 Percy Pilcher, a lecturer in naval architecture at the University of Glasgow, made the first glider flight in Britain at Cardross in a model he had built, and was far advanced in the development of a power-driven aeroplane when killed while demonstrating a glider in 1899. Second, on the basis of Burt's sleeve-valve engine the Argyll Company designed an aero-engine which won a prize at Farnborough in 1914, in spite of the breaking of the crankshaft. Finally, Beardmore's pioneered aero-engines before 1914, and during the first three years of the war the Royal Flying Corps flew more hours with Beardmore engines than with any other.

The reason why many of the early successes in light engineering failed to be consolidated is complex and emerged only after 1918 and sometimes only after the efforts had come to an end. Before the war the ventures were often too new and experimental to guarantee success. Even then many of the pioneers in light engineering industries followed the path of the heavy engineers by producing specialised goods for specialised customers. The future for many of their products lay in exploiting mass consumer demand, but that was not a market to which an engineering tradition nurtured in shipyards and heavy engineering workshops could adjust easily.

The manufacture of chemicals and allied products was another field which opened out new industrial prospects in the later nineteenth century. The prospects were clouded by diminished natural advantages. From the 1870s the Leblanc method was superseded by the Solvay process in alkali production. The Solvay process depended on the action of ammonium bicarbonate solution on strong brine, and was more suited to the natural resources of Cheshire, where brine could be pumped direct from the saltbeds, than to Scotland, where, indeed, the Solvay method was never adopted. Second, the electrolytic process for the direct conversion of common salt into caustic soda and chlorine worked similarly against alkali manufacture in Scotland. Subsequently alkali production suffered from amalgamations which led, as in the dyeing and calico-printing industries, to the closure of Scottish works. About 1890 the Irvine Chemical Company, the Eglinton Chemical Company, and the St. Rollox works joined with others to form the United Alkali Company. The outcome was the end of alkali production in all Scottish works of the combine, and only one Scottish concern manufactured caustic soda. All was not loss. Two examples in the chemical and allied industries showed the possibilities. The first, the shale-oil industry, originated earlier in the nineteenth century in the work of James Young, who pioneered the preparation of paraffin as a commercial article from mineral sources at Bathgate in the 1850s and later at Addiewell. When Young's patent expired in 1864, others entered the industry, and by the 1870s it was estimated that Scotland produced annually about 1,000,000 gallons of refined burning oil in addition to crude solid paraffin, naphtha, lubricating oils and other products giving employment to about 6,500 men. The second began in 1873 when Alfred Nobel established his works for the manufacture of nitroglycerine and dynamite at Ardeer in Ayrshire. It grew to be among the world's largest explosive works and produced a wide range of chemicals.

Nobel's entry into Scottish industry was significant. Other foreigners were also doing so and, ominously for Scotland, some of the more successful branches of modern industrial growth originated in foreign enterprise. In 1856 the North British Rubber Company set up Scotland's first vulcanised rubber factory in Edinburgh with American capital, management, machinery and workers. Even after ownership passed to British interests in the late 1860s Americans remained influential in company policy. In the early 1880s Singer's, which had shortly before had a factory in Glasgow, established their large sewing-machine factory at Clydebank. Lastly, the British Babcock and Wilcox Company, formed by its American parent in 1891, started its first British works at Renfrew in 1895 and subsequently spread to Dumbarton.

The first stirrings of what later generations were to dub the science-based industries were obviously not insignificant, but there were signs that Scotland no longer offered an intellectual and educational background as helpful to their growth as it had been to some of the industrial endeavours of the eighteenth century. The pioneers of the heavy industries which dominated so much of the industrial life of the west of Scotland had no great reputation for scientific achievement. Some of the managers of the ironworks, notably Ferrie of Monkland, were technically competent, but as the Professor of Natural History in the University of Glasgow maintained, 'a very small number indeed' would have passed an 'elementary examination in science'. The masters were little different. Professor Young encountered 'exceptional liberality' in Lanarkshire but 'not a sufficient appreciation of the benefits of scientific education'.[4] Yet their liberality was insufficient to keep the Mining School in the Andersonian University in Glasgow open for more than five years, even though James Merry, of Merry and Cunninghame, was the chairman of its first committee.

The failure may have had roots in the educational system, perhaps especially in the universities. In the eighteenth century, their contribution lay mainly in the provision of an education which was not specialised, but which encouraged the growth of the application of scientific method to all forms of human effort, and less in the provision of an abstract, specialised branch of knowledge. The bias of the Scottish educational tradition, reflected in the success of the Scottish engineers, was a bias which met many of the requirements of the earliest phases of industrialisation. The abstract, scientific background was not unimportant, as in chemistry, but it was certainly possible to gain many of the advantages of the application of science to industry from an educational background which was not specialised. The requirements of the later period were different, and to meet them the scientific, and more precisely the mathematical, attainments of the Scottish educational system were inadequate and inappropriate. Until they had been improved, it was somewhat premature to suggest that the fault lay in the inadequate application of science to everyday problems.

NOTES

1. *Royal Commission on Depression of Trade and Industry*, 1886. Q. 11,903. BPP. 1886. XXIII.

2. John Adam, *Greenock as It Was and Is*, p. 18. (Copy in Glasgow University Library.)

3. F. Kohn, *Iron and Steel Manufacture* (London, 1860), p. 3.

4. *Royal Commission on Scientific Instruction and the Advancement of Science*, 1872. Qs. 9603 and 9602. BPP. 1874. XXII.

CHAPTER XIII

Industry, 1914 to 1939

Industry under pressure

The high level of unemployment in Scotland between the wars left a lasting social and political, as well as economic, legacy. Its incidence varied. In the 1930s the unemployment rates of every southern and eastern county from Aberdeen to Wigtown were, with the exception of the Dundee area, below the national average. By then, when the contraction of the coal industry had removed some of the more persistent pockets of unemployment on the east coast, certain districts, especially those near Edinburgh with a high proportion of service and light industries, had unemployment rates as low as in the English Midlands. The east and south were not immune from depression, but, though sometimes intense, it was more localised, in the jute industry of Dundee, the linen industry of Dunfermline, the fishing and granite trades of Aberdeen, and the herring fishing in the Moray Firth. Further west in West Lothian, dependent on such heavy industries as engineering, ironfounding, coal- and shale-mining, the industrial structure became more comparable to the western counties of Ayr, Dunbarton, Lanark and Renfrew, and unemployment rates became higher. They were highest of all in the industrial areas of the four western counties. The effect of unemployment on life and thought in these areas was intensified because they had enjoyed some of the greatest industrial success of the previous century. The change in their prosperity, which seemed to arise more suddenly to contemporaries than in retrospect, was a blow to the confidence and self-esteem bordering on complacency which had characterised much of the industrial west of Scotland until 1914.

The post-war disorganisation of foreign trade contributed to the industrial difficulties of the inter-war years but does not explain them adequately. It does not seem possible to suggest that the severity of the depression arose from Scottish industry being more dependent on foreign customers than was the industry of the entire United Kingdom. First, export demand did not absorb a major part of Scottish industrial output. About 20 per cent of the output of Scottish coal, slightly less of new ships, and about 35 per cent of whisky was exported from Scottish ports.[1] Second, though exports from Scottish ports amounted to 16.3 per cent of the Scottish national income, total exports from the United Kingdom equalled 15.4 per cent of its national income, too close — especially in view of their possible error — to substantiate the suggestion that Scottish industry was exceptionally export-orientated. Whatever the degree of dependence, the volume of Scottish exports between the wars tended to fall earlier, fall to a greater extent and rise again more slowly than that of the entire

United Kingdom. Between its lowest point in 1931 and 1938 the volume of exports from the United Kingdom rose by 29 per cent; the volume of exports from Scottish ports — probably, of course, a minimum figure — rose by 13 per cent. The lack of buoyancy is evident from an examination of the figures for the individual heavy industries on which so much of Scotland's prosperity depended. In 1930, 243,000 tons of new ships, or 46 per cent of the total Scottish output, were exported; in 1933, 9,000 tons of new ships, or 16 per cent of total Scottish output. In 1929, 650,000 tons of iron and steel goods were exported; in 1933, 234,000 tons; in 1937, 339,000 tons. Taken together, the proportion of output exported by three groups — ships, iron and steel products, and textiles — was 23 per cent before the depression, fell to 21 per cent in 1932, and at the peak of the recovery of trade in the 1930s was as low as 17 per cent. In brief, basic Scottish export industries were not recovering fully. Even those which sent specialised products to markets throughout the world in the years before 1914 suffered.

Though the prosperity of the pre-war years was lost, and most industries shared the stagnation of the times, individual experiences varied. Many of the difficulties, and the variations between industries after 1918, perpetuated those of the pre-war years. The contrasting experiences of the three major textile industries of cotton, jute and wool can be linked to their history over a longer period. The worst affected was the cotton industry. The cotton manufacturers of Scotland were more apprehensive than those of Lancashire about their prospects at the end of the war and did not immediately respond to optimistic plans for expansion. Even when the transition to peace was accomplished more easily than any had expected, they remained apprehensive of competition from overseas and to a lesser extent from Lancashire. Their apprehension was soon justified. Comparative costs were high, and by the end of 1922 only those producers of the highest-quality coloured cotton goods were well employed. Others could only strive for higher-quality production to try to obtain a similar prosperity. In the mid-1920s, when the manufacturers of white cotton goods found they could no longer meet competition from India, China and Lancashire, they tried to diversify output by introducing fabrics of varied colours and designs and by using artificial silk with cotton. Quality adequate to offset higher costs could not easily be achieved, and between the wars the final liquidation of the industry, at least as it had been known in Glasgow and the west of Scotland, became a stark reality. Amalgamations, useful before 1914, became increasingly necessary after 1918. Small-scale producers with limited resources could not withstand the pressure on profit margins and gradually disappeared, among them the job weavers — once common in Glasgow's east end, to whom merchants had given material to be woven according to certain specifications — and many small firms which had specialised in one process of production, such as warping. Soon the only survivors of this once flourishing sector of Scotland's industrial past were exceptional mills, such as those at Deanston and Catrine, or specialised producers, such as the thread industry of Paisley.

Stagnation in the manufacture of jute was similar, relieved periodically between the wars when the industry was able to meet overseas competition, especially from India, though more through the diminution of foreign competition than from any successful internal changes in the industry. Examples were in 1922, when Indian manufacturers could not meet the demand for bags from the Cuban sugar trade or from importers on the river Plate, and in 1927, when low stocks of hessian in Calcutta encouraged such speculation that prices in India rose. In both cases demand from importers on the river Plate was diverted to Dundee. The insecure foundations of the occasional prosperity of the 1920s were confirmed after 1929. Any bursts of prosperity became even rarer and arose less from the occasional inability of Indian manufacturers to meet demand because their output was fully absorbed elsewhere than from their inability to do so because mills were closed, sometimes by agreements aimed at restricting competition, sometimes by strike. As in the manufacture of cotton, so of jute, foreign competition was not new, only more intense, after 1918. Retained imports of raw jute to Dundee, which were stable from 1896 to 1913, declined thereafter. Output of jute yarn exceeded that for 1912 only in 1938. Just as the industry's difficulties had accumulated over years, so the possibilities of remedying them were limited by the industry's own action of combating depressions by substituting various adulterants for jute. The crux of the depression of the 1930s in the Dundee jute industry was that, in the face of Indian competition, there was no inferior fibre which could be used to produce a cheaper, coarser article. In the 1930s Dundee's method of meeting depressions had reached its limit. The situation was not without its advantages. It brought an increasing awareness of the need to tackle the industry's problems in a different direction by attempting to reorganise its mills.

The woollen industry continued to follow a different path determined, as it had been before the war, by its concentration on the manufacture of higher-quality goods. The difference was clear in the export of woollen goods and carpets after 1918. The pattern of distribution of exports changed and, being quality products often competitive with domestic manufactures in the countries importing them, they were a favourite target for tariffs and other impediments in the restrictive trading conditions of the 1930s. Before 1914 Germany was the most important overseas market; after the war it was surpassed by new Continental markets and by the United States, which absorbed 35 per cent of all direct exports of Scottish tweeds by 1928. The 1930s were less prosperous than the 1920s chiefly because of trade restrictions. Though foreign markets were lost, especially those in Italy, Holland and Austria, the woollen industry provided relatively stable employment for its workers in both decades. The numbers employed at the Censuses of Production in 1907 and 1924 were almost identical at just under 28,000; in 1930 the total fell to 24,000, but in 1935 it rose once again to 25,000. The manufacture of carpets, a specially successful branch of the woollen industry, illustrates the adverse influence of tariffs in the 1930s. Overseas markets were the basis of the industry's buoyancy in the 1920s. After 1930 increased tariffs in the United States and Canada and financial difficulties in Australia, which had become the largest overseas market for British carpets, all limited exports and led some factories to work at less than full capacity. The industry had high hopes of the Ottawa conference on imperial preference in 1932 but was disappointed. The Canadian market was not re-opened and a special tariff was not imposed on Indian carpets, the main source of competition. In spite of considerable exports to Australia and South Africa, the improvement in the industry's prosperity from 1933 to 1937 was based mainly on increased domestic demand as the economy, and especially housebuilding, recovered. Home consumption could not easily replace overseas markets, and at the end of 1937 some carpet factories in Scotland were working short-time once more. Exports, which had increased since 1933, fell in 1938 and, with falling prices, Scottish carpet manufacturers estimated that their net return was the lowest since 1916.

The competitive decline of some branches of the textile industries, especially cotton, was evident to contemporaries before the war in a way any problems of the heavy industries were not. The latter's difficulties were revealed only retrospectively. Even so, a distinction may be drawn, as in textiles, between the coal and iron industries, which extracted Scotland's natural resources and provided only basic raw materials for subsequent processing, and the shipbuilding, heavy engineering and supporting steel industries, which supplied extensively manufactured, skilled products, and so competed in quality and design as much as in price. Though the slackening of the connection between the two industries of coal and iron was forcing the coal industry to rely increasingly on more volatile markets overseas, the ironworks still provided a major source of demand, especially for the collieries in the west of Scotland. The coal industry was then affected by the continued decline in the national and international competitiveness of the iron industry. A fundamental cause of the increased costs of production of Scottish iron arose from the exhaustion of some of the best of Scotland's geological resources of iron ore and coal. After the First World War Scottish ore production became negligible; in 1913 less than 600,000 tons were mined, in 1920 less than 280,000 tons, in 1929 a mere 25,000 tons, against the 3,000,000 tons and more in the 1870s. Since the blast furnaces produced mainly hematite pig iron for the acid process in the steelworks, the exhaustion of home supplies of phosphoric ores was less important than it might have been. The major geological concern of the iron industry between the wars was over the supplies of coal, particularly good coking coal, which were so limited that the Balfour Committee in 1928 sweepingly decided that 'Scotland has no good coking coal'. This dictum was disputed by the Scottish ironmasters and steelmakers, because there were adequate supplies of semi-coking varieties, though they could be used only at increased cost. The consequences of the worsened position of the iron industry were widespread. Production of pig iron declined to just over 600,000 tons in 1929 and to less than 500,000 tons in 1937. After the First World War the character of the Scottish pig iron trade was completely changed. The decline in its international importance, which had started before 1913, continued after 1918, and by 1930 foreign shipments of pig iron were negligible. In 1931 and 1932 only one furnace was in blast at times. The duty of 20 per cent on foreign iron did not help because of imports from England and from India. The furnaces in blast rose from three in 1933 to a peak of 15 in 1934 but fell to 13 by the end of the year. The increased domestic demand from the economic recovery was met by iron brought into Scotland from elsewhere.

The coal industry had to find additional markets to compensate for the continued decline of the traditional consumption from the ironworks. Exports had also been cut during the war from about 10,000,000 to 7,500,000 tons, including all bunkers. As became clear in the 1920s, overseas markets could be entered only when, for one reason or another, foreign competitors were unable to provide adequate supplies. As in the jute industry, Scottish coal producers sold abroad after the First World War often by default of their competitors than by their own achievements. By implication, the need for a renovation of the industry for the maintenance of more stable exports was demonstrated. The competitive weakness of the coal industry in Scotland in comparison with other districts of Britain was partly hidden by the system of government control which survived the war until 1921, and which ensured that Scottish coalfields were supported by the surpluses of other districts. Even in the prosperous year of 1920, Scotland incurred a deficit of over £5,250,000 (allowing 2s. 8d. per ton for guaranteed profit, depreciation and interest). In January 1921 (with the allowance for profit reduced by one-tenth) the loss was £1,023,700; in February it was £918,723; in March it was £1,155,800. Two periods of relative prosperity confirmed this post-war weakness before the strike of 1926. The first began in 1919, when restocking at home and overseas led to high export prices. The gains accrued mainly to the eastern collieries, above all to those in Fife, from which nearly 30 per cent of the output was exported in 1919. The second began in late 1921, by which time the Scottish coal industry could no longer gain from the pooling of earnings which had served it so well immediately after the war. In the last four months of the year coal exports from Scottish ports increased by about seven times over those in the same period of the previous year. The peak came in 1923 and was a result of the political dislocations following the French occupation of the Ruhr. Once again prosperity came to the industry from exceptional conditions overseas. Political stabilisation in Europe in 1924 led to a sharp fall in prices. The downward trend continued into 1925. Shipments fell by about 20 per cent, revenue from them by nearly twice as much.

Since such periods of easy access to foreign markets were fleeting, the Scottish coal industry was engaged throughout the inter-war years in a competitive struggle to replace the stagnant, if not declining, demand from the heavy industries. For some years after the General Strike, when foreign producers were able to displace British coal in overseas markets, and even to send it to Britain, Scottish exports lagged behind those from the rest of the United Kingdom. The rewards in the struggle did not always seem inviting. The average price of Scottish coal free on board in 1925 was 16s. 8.92d. per ton; in 1927 it was only 15s. 6.89d., the lowest since 1914. Great difficulty centred on gaining access to the traditionally important Scandinavian markets, which were penetrated in the late 1920s by Polish Silesian coal-owners, who had previously sent most of their output to mid-Germany. As a result, between 1930 and 1931 British exports to Norway fell by 50 per cent and those to Sweden by 45 per cent. Some improvement came in 1932, when greater consumption of British coal in Scandinavia increased the volume and value of exports from Scotland, even while those from the United Kingdom as a whole fell. The confidence of producers was less easily regained. Scottish output continued to fall and in 1932 was the lowest since 1897. Fortunately, pessimism was belied. Exports were maintained, not only to Scandinavia, where they were helped by an agreement on marketing between British and Polish coal-owners, but to Canada, after the Ottawa agreements of 1932, and to the Irish Free State, after the conclusion of the agreement to trade in coal for cattle. In 1934, the peak year for the 1930s, exports reached almost 6,000,000 tons, of which over 4,500,000 tons went from the east coast.

Fortunately Scotland suffered much less than England and Wales from interruptions to the coal trade in the 1930s. Trade agreements with Scandinavian and Baltic countries ensured readier access to established markets. The dislocations following the Spanish Civil War, and the imposition of quotas on imports to France, fell more heavily on England and Wales. In spite of the importance of the export trade in the 1930s, especially to the eastern collieries, its contribution to the improvement in the industry's fortunes could not outweigh the contribution of increased home demand, and the increase in production to over 32,350,000 tons in 1937 was a response to greater domestic consumption. The fall in production in 1938 reflected the failure of home industrial demand rather than of overseas sales. One consequence was that the incidence of depression was not spread evenly over the Scottish coalfield. The numbers employed in the industry increased in no area between 1913 and 1931, and in some the fall was drastic, notably in Lanarkshire where the labour force was reduced by about 50 per cent. The pattern of production was similar, though in Clackmannan and the Lothians output increased between the two years. The decline was in the older areas, where the link with the heavy industries was closest; the areas of expansion were in the east, in the Lothians and Fife, where success depended on foreign sales and where the only expansion and capital investment of the 1920s and early 1930s was recorded.

Though the continued decline of the coal and iron industry which followed the exhaustion of the best natural resources in Scotland could not easily be offset, the two industries would have suffered more rapid decline but for the continued competitive ability of the specialised heavy industries. Shipbuilding and steelmaking provided such support before 1914 when their supremacy seemed unchallenged and secure. The flaws in their prosperity, which are clear in retrospect, gradually started to become evident to contemporaries after 1918.

The relatively more secure position of shipbuilding in Scotland between the wars arose because it was competitive with other parts of the United Kingdom and stood to gain from any increase of demand at home or overseas. This advantage was offset by two adverse influences. First, the policy of naval disarmament, prosecuted unflinchingly in the 1920s by both Conservative and Labour administrations, and only gradually relaxed in the 1930s, denuded some firms of orders on which they had relied for a quarter of a century and led them to try to attract others. Second, the civilian market became less secure between the wars when many foreign yards offered more attractive terms than they had done before 1914, and when British shipowners had to face fierce competition, sometimes against subsidised foreign shipping. Freight income was often so low that building was unattractive. The second of the unfavourable influences was less severe throughout the 1920s. Scottish shipyards were active not only when some fortuitous events overseas diverted more orders to Scotland, but, in contrast to the years before the First World War, fear of foreign competition was a live possibility immediately the war was over, especially fear of competition from American yards, with their superior methods and apparent absence of demarcation. Such forebodings were submerged in the immediate post-war boom, when the Clyde in particular gained from a replacement demand for tramp ships. Of the 422 vessels of 646,154 tons launched in 1919, 90 were cargo steamers of 378,512 tons. The high demand continued into the early months of 1920, when many hoped the tonnage launched would exceed that of 1913.

The post-war boom was ephemeral, not the beginning of a new age. Few orders were placed later in 1920; in 1921 Clyde yards were working at only about half of their capacity; output fell until 1923. That the industry could not easily achieve a new level of stability became clear in the later 1920s. An increase in output for 1924 became assured late in 1923, when work was restarted on some vessels on the Clyde and three yards, which had been closed for periods of up to two years, were re-opened. The revived activity raised the Clyde's output for 1924 about three times over that of the previous year. The weakness of this achievement lay in the continued depressed state of shipping freights. The increased orders, especially on the Clyde in late 1923 and 1924, were therefore orders which could no longer be delayed, or were, at best, a recognition of the reduction of shipbuilding costs to a level which, many thought, could only be temporary. Consequently, in 1925 output was lower in all Scottish shipbuilding areas except the Tay where there was a slight increase. In the same year orders fell off sharply and the Clyde was left without a liner on the stocks. The unsatisfactory nature of the prosperity was more evident in 1927. Output continued its downward trend into 1926, when a reduced tonnage was launched in all Scottish shipbuilding areas except the Forth, where the increased output was wholly the consequence of the good performance of the Burntisland yard. The reduction was caused partly by the difficulty of obtaining adequate supplies of steel during the coal strike, so the tonnage launched in 1927 and in 1928 (with the exception of the Aberdeen area) was greater than in 1926. The boom of 1927 was largely the result of the completion of work held up in 1926, and by the end of 1928 there were few signs of more orders. In the early months of the year shipowners were reluctant to place orders for new vessels. Their lack of confidence, engendered basically by depression in the freight market, was further enhanced by uncertainty over the most appropriate form of propulsion to adopt. By the end of the year the absence of orders for new tankers was almost complete. Fortunately, the delay of some owners of cargo vessels to place orders, a delay which lasted until September, came to an end at the close of the year with the ordering of some general-cargo steamers, but not for motor-ships. The inability to postpone orders any longer enabled the tonnage launched in Scotland in 1929 to be almost the same as in the previous year and the number of vessels launched to be maintained.

The output of steel did not match the pronounced decline in that of pig iron. In some years it was greater than in 1913, being 1,582,000 and 1,895,000 tons in the two relatively prosperous years of 1929 and 1937, but these were lower shares of the total United Kingdom output than before the war. The declining competitiveness of the coal and iron industries left the steelmakers less able to obtain adequate supplies of their materials at prices comparable to those of their competitors. Though imports of cheap steel, which were beneficial to the shipbuilders but a direct threat to the steelmakers, were always a live possibility under such conditions, the fluctuations of the two industries were closely linked. Because of the immediate post-war boom in shipbuilding, Scottish steelmakers were able to charge higher prices than their English rivals in 1920. Thereafter prices fell, forced down especially in 1921 by the suspension of naval orders. For the next decade Scottish steel producers were engaged in a price war, especially against foreign rivals, whose products ensured that reductions in costs of coal, transport and scrap in 1922 failed to stimulate demand with the result that the industry did not benefit from the mild revival in shipbuilding in 1924. Further reductions in price did not provide any remedy. In March 1925 a cut (of 5s. in plates and 10s. in angles), aimed at attracting orders from the shipbuilders, brought little response. Thereafter, in a period of keen competition, the weaknesses of the steel industry were evident. As prices fell, many steelworks were closed rather than operate at prices considered unremunerative, though it was only at such prices that home-produced steel was competitive with imports from the Continent. Imports of foreign steel continued, but Scottish steelworks were active once more in 1927 when the shipyards were meeting orders accumulated during the General Strike, and again in 1929 with another revival of shipbuilding.

The activity in the shipyards in 1929 was the culmination of the decade's relative prosperity. Thereafter shipbuilding, and with it steelmaking, encountered problems comparable to those already experienced by some of the longer-established industries. Shipbuilding's fortune after 1929 must, therefore, be examined closely.

The tonnage launched during 1930 hides the absence of new orders, except for the new Cunarder from John Brown's, but that success was ephemeral, as work was suspended on the vessel in 1931. The unfinished hull of what was to become the *Queen Mary* became symbolic of the state of Scottish industry in general, and of Clyde shipbuilding in particular, and it was felt that confidence would return only with the resumption of work on the vessel. Until then, the overall output of ships continued to plunge. Only high output from a few yards, generally for exceptional reasons, prevented a complete collapse. In 1932, when foreign yards were also suffering from a reduction in the orders which had kept them engaged longer than those in Britain, the tonnage launched on the Forth increased, entirely through the achievements of the Burntisland Shipbuilding Company, which also obtained ten orders in the year. On the Clyde, Lithgow's output, especially of vessels for J. and C. Harrison, provided a base. Such varying performances were typical of the 1930s. Orders were so sparse that one or two could affect output significantly. In 1930 Barclay, Curle and Company topped the output figures for Scottish yards by launching ten vessels of 64,714 tons, but in 1931 it launched only two vessels of 3,226 tons. In 1931, two P. and O. liners, the *Corfu* and the *Carthage*, kept Stephen's of Linthouse moderately well employed. On the upper reaches of the Clyde at the end of 1932 the only ship on the stocks at Govan was a small steamer being built by Harland and Wolff, Ltd. for Bombay owners; on the north bank, between Pointhouse and Whiteinch, Barclay, Curle's had the only vessel on the stocks, a small motorship; at Scotstoun the Blythswood Shipbuilding Company were building a small tanker; Yarrow and Company were constructing two Portuguese destroyers. Generally such prosperity as the Clyde enjoyed in the early 1930s was concentrated in the lower reaches, especially at Lithgow's at Port Glasgow. In turn Lithgow's prosperity owed much to the orders they received for Harrison vessels. A good example of this trend came in 1933, when only five firms in the world launched vessels of more than 20,000 tons in total. Lithgow's was the only British yard among them. Four out of the five vessels were for Harrison's, these four being the only vessels of over 5,000 tons gross launched on the Clyde that year.

The only ray of hope in 1932 was the trickle of naval orders, though small by any standard; in 1933 the government gave help towards the completion of the Cunarder (No. 534). In 1934 its launch, as the *Queen Mary*, increased the Clyde's output sharply, but the performance was impressive more by comparison with the very low level to which output had fallen in earlier years. The type of work was exceptional and was not what the Clyde was entirely accustomed to. The *Queen Mary*, the *Orion*, and a few tankers and refrigerated motor-vessels accounted for more than 40 per cent of the shipbuilding; warships in the larger yards accounted for about 20 per cent more; the remainder consisted of trawlers, coastal and other smaller vessels. Consequently, the revival on the Clyde in 1934 was accompanied by the continued absence of orders for general cargo steamers and tramp tonnage. Without a revival of this demand, on which the Clyde had so often relied, a lasting recovery did not seem possible. The government's scrap-and-build policy provided little incentive to British shipbuilders to place new orders, but in 1935 some came for vessels of around 9,000 tons but not for high-class liners. That year the reduction in output on the Clyde, though not on other Scottish rivers, was misleading, being the result of the launch of the *Queen Mary* in the previous year, and though

Brown's launched nothing in 1935, the fitting-out of the *Queen Mary* made it one of the busiest yards on the Clyde. More ominously, in 1935 Britain launched only 35 per cent of the world's tonnage, compared with 50 per cent in 1934. The timing of the launch of the *Queen Mary* was not the only explanation; so too was foreign competition. Not only were foreigners ceasing to order from British yards; British shipowners were also ordering overseas, especially when for some that became the only method of obtaining a return on debts due to them from Germany. For that reason Aberdeen trawlers were built on the Elbe rather than on the Dee.

Though orders from foreign shipowners remained absent, those from British owners spread in 1936 to other fields, including passenger vessels. Government policy in a variety of different aids to the shipbuilding industry and, much more important, in increased expenditure on naval construction, was responsible. Without the increased naval work — which continued to provide a basis for activity in some shipyards throughout the later 1930s — the reduction in foreign orders would have had more severe repercussions. Once again, in 1938, though output remained high, especially because of the launching of the *Queen Elizabeth*, orders were so reduced that it was estimated that only one merchant ship was ordered for every four launched. The position seemed similar to the early 1920s. The industry was exhausting its order book and there were no new orders to follow. British costs were too high, and so many British orders were going to Continental yards that there was an adverse balance of shipbuilding orders in 1938. It was too soon for the output to reflect the adverse position. It would have done so later, as orders were completed, but, before that position had been reached, Admiralty orders increased with wartime demand and any excess capacity was fully absorbed.

Disputes and remedies

Cracks in the solid prosperity of much Scottish industry were identified only by the most perceptive before 1914. After the end of the post-war boom they were evident to many more. Whether any drastic action was needed to deal with them was another matter, and one bound to be seen in different lights by contemporaries and by later historians. The need for adaptation to meet the requirements of peacetime was expected at the end of the war but not any need for a radical alteration of the structure of pre-war industry. Even a period of depressed trade, such as followed the post-war boom, was something to which much of Scottish industry was not unaccustomed. Such fluctuations were part of commercial life, and the well-established methods of dealing with them were by drawing on reserves or by cutting overheads in ways or to an extent which did not jeopardise the firm's future well-being. Serious problems emerged only if a firm's financial resources were insufficient to meet the period of depressed trade. The response to the problems of Scottish industry between the wars must be judged as that of industrialists whose outlook and attitudes had been moulded by such conditions before 1914. The greater the degree of industrial adjustment required in the uncertain conditions of the post-war world, the greater the attraction of being able to retain the security of continuing to tackle industrial depression by traditional paths. In these circumstances the most reasonable policy to follow was that of trying to obtain orders of any form which were available. To later commentators that may seem to have been clutching at straws, but not to those whose livelihood had been removed apparently by political decisions, which led directly to the disruption of world trade and to disarmament, and to whom any reversal of that policy, always a live issue, particularly after 1931, held out the prospect of some form of recovery.

Inaction may be explained; it can be defended as a desirable policy only if decline in demand was short-term and not the response to defects in the ability of a firm, industry, or economy to supply what was required. Its danger was that it neglected the need for internal change. For such change there was great need. The fundamental problem was that stagnation had spread through industry since the 1870s, and in Scotland the relative sparseness of population and the absence of certain necessary raw materials, or semi-processed goods, limited the extent to which established industries could be renovated and re-equipped to withstand competition or be reorientated and diversified to produce more for the home market.

Though the emergence of new industries is too easily neglected, they did not eliminate excess capacity or antiquated equipment and practices in the older industries. Doing so was the central problem which faced the Scottish economy between the wars at a time when government made its first tentative moves towards accepting responsibility for directing economic policy. The political implications of the economic problem were even more acute when most people lived in west-central Scotland, where the need to modify the old industrial structure was greatest and where a new sense of political activism appeared. In the 1920s the extent of the modification required was not always appreciated; in the 1930s such adaptation as took place was frequently restrictionist rather than expansionist.

The problem was evident in coalmining, which gave rise to the main industrial and social unrest of the 1920s. The issue which faced coalmining after the First World War was that, given the level of demand, costs had to be reduced or the industry had to contract. The dilemma was more acute in Scotland where the exhaustion of the better seams was indicated by the size of the losses incurred before the industry was decontrolled. Immediately after decontrol the dispute between employers and employees flared up as the employers attempted to remedy Scotland's adverse competitive position by cutting wages. The coalowners thought that doing so was the only way of reducing costs. Wages were a large component of total costs; they could be cut speedily; and output per man had fallen sharply since before the war. To the men, who looked for salvation in improved methods and efficiency, it was the least satisfactory solution. The men pointed to the lowness of their wages; the masters to how, even at these low wages, they were failing to make a profit. In 1921 it was agreed that wages in Scotland were not to fall below a minimum of 110 per cent above the level of 1888. The minimum was reached in March 1922, when the level of wages, though not of earnings, was down to 8s. 4.8d. per shift. An increase of 2½d. was granted in April, but the minimum returned the following month and continued until December. By any standards the rate was sufficiently low to explain the miners' grievances. On the other hand the masters pointed out that from the resumption of work after the strike on 1st July 1921 until October 1922 the average profit per ton of coal sold was only 5.44d. In 1913 it had been 1s. 8d. per ton.

Such standpoints were not reconciled by subsequent negotiations. After an exceptional increase in wages and employment following the occupation of the Ruhr, a new wages agreement was concluded in 1924. Under the wages agreement of 1921 every £100 of proceeds was distributed in the ratio of £84 6s. to wages and £15 14s. to profits; in the 1924 agreement the distribution was £87 8s. 9.6d. to wages and £12 11s. 2.4d. to profits. At the same time the minimum wage was raised from 20 per cent to 33⅓ per cent above the pre-war standard. The gain to the men was minimal by any standards, but in the masters' eyes was enough to explain the reversal in their fortunes. The fall in prices after the occupation of the Ruhr was a more accurate explanation of the loss per ton (calculated by independent accountants) in the first month of the agreement, May 1924, a loss which became the normal practice. In April 1925, at the end of the first year of the agreement, the total loss in Scotland was £348,934, or 2.51d. per ton; if various interest payments were added, it became £765,434 or 5.51d. per ton. When the agreement came to an end in July 1925, the aggregate loss for 15 months was £1,346,254 or 7.96d. per ton. Apart from a temporary break in 1927 the position was unchanged after the long-protracted strike of 1926. In 1928 there was a debit balance per ton in Scotland every quarter, and in 1929 a credit balance only in the first quarter. The cumulative deficiency under the wages agreement continued to rise, to £6,175,374 in September 1929 and to £7,663,718 in September 1930. In such circumstances there was no cessation of the pressure by the masters to reduce wages. In November 1926 work was resumed on the basis of an eight-hour instead of a six-hour day, and a temporary agreement divided proceeds in the ratio of £87 to wages and £13 to profits, with a minimum wage of 9s. 4d. a day. A permanent agreement, which came into force in April 1927, accepted the same distribution, but with a minimum wage cf only 8s. 4.8d. The strike brought no benefit.

The wages dispute in the coal industry in the 1920s reflected the difficulty of reducing costs. An alternative was to seek greater efficiency in methods of production. Mechanisation in Scotland, where almost 60 per cent of the coal was obtained by mechanical cutters in 1928, was more advanced than in the rest of the United Kingdom. When attempts were made to increase it, they led generally to advocacy of the concentration of production on more efficient units. Too easily such a policy became an attempt to restrict output. Restriction of output, or controlled marketing, was adopted extensively in the coal industry in the 1930s. Doing so was easier than in the 1920s. Voluntary movement from the industry had left fewer people to be displaced through any schemes of amalgamation and restriction, and in the 1930s the government began to assist the reorganisation of the industry. The attitude of the masters then seemed to indicate that, having failed to achieve a reduction in costs through lowering wages, the only alternative left was to reduce output. As a result, though the coal-owners and the government agreed on the aim, they frequently disagreed on the means. The coalmasters first suggested that inland prices should be 20 per cent higher than export prices, the surplus being used to help exporters, a scheme aimed at controlling marketing without any provision for ensuring greater efficiency, not even through the then popular method of amalgamating coalmines. The coalmasters opposed any large-scale amalgamation, even when aimed at obtaining some limited improvements in marketing. The only amalgamations acceptable were those of individual firms with interests in the same area, as when the coal interests of William Baird and Company and the Dalmellington Iron Company were merged into Bairds and Dalmellington Ltd., in 1931. Consequently, the industry was split in its approach to the two parts of the Coal Mines Act of 1930. The first part, which attempted to introduce a quota system to restrict production and so, it was hoped, lead to a rise in price, was acceptable to the owners; the second part, which set up a Coal Mines Reorganisation Commission to assist in amalgamation schemes, was not.

The relative stagnation of coalmining in the 1930s suggests that the attempts to reduce wages, and the bitter conflicts which followed, did not lead to any salvation for the industry. The information on labour costs in the 1930s shows that, while the Scottish coalfield had a degree of profitability after 1932 which it had not experienced earlier, its labour costs were slightly higher than those for the whole of Britain. The 1930s demonstrated that the industry was able to operate profitably when prices could be increased, which was possible in face of declining consumption only by restricting output. The improved conditions of the industry in the 1930s can be explained by the success in doing so, as well as by the beginnings of more general economic recovery. There was a price to be paid in the diminishing scale of the industry's operations. Compared with the overall performance of the United Kingdom, Scotland's share of production and employment, though fluctuating, did not change significantly, but total output and employment fell. The peak output between the wars in Scotland was 38,500,000 tons in 1923, less than in any of the pre-war years since 1905, and a recovery of output in the 1930s led only to a peak of 32,261,000 tons in 1937. Employment fell even more dramatically. The all-time record of employment of 154,500 men was in 1920; in 1933 only 81,600 were employed and even in 1937, the peak year of the 1930s, only 90,600. Whatever the achievements of the industry, it was in decline. The stability of the 1930s could not remove that harsh fact.

In the 1920s similar disputes and remedies emerged in shipbuilding and its dependent steelmaking, though neither experienced the acute difficulties of coalmining. In 1921 Sir James Lithgow put forward the need to reduce wages:

under present conditions suggestions that our prosperity as a shipbuilding country can be regained at anything like the present level of wages are the purest humbug, and those who make them are doing our men an ill-service in fostering hopes which the hard logic of events is bound to blast.[2]

A year later Lord Maclay, writing as a shipowner, offered a different way of salvation by accusing the shipbuilders of failing to adopt the most efficient production:

There has been very little improvement on the tramp type of steamer since the introduction of triple expansion engines over thirty years ago. Many orders would be immediately forthcoming if shipbuilders and engineers could produce a steamer which would show any real economy over old vessels. There are many owners anxious to build if they could see reasonable hope of a very modest return for their money.[3]

The words of Lithgow and Maclay represent two different points of view. Maclay looked to greater economy in operation through the construction of more efficient vessels, Lithgow was more concerned with reducing costs for vessels whatever their design. Neither interpretation offered a complete explanation. In the 1920s shipbuilding was not inherently uncompetitive; it seemed simply to need too large a share of the market to use the capacity in the shipyards which its expansion, especially during the war, had produced. In the 1920s the belief that British shipyards could never again expect to build the tonnage of former years began to gain ground, leading to acceptance by some that the industry had to be rationalised. The shipbuilders made the first move themselves towards the objective of reducing capacity in the shipyards with the formation of National Shipbuilders Securities Ltd. The purchase of Beardmore's yard at Dalmuir dominated the early activities of NSS. It accounted for 13, or almost half the value of the 46 berths purchased on the Clyde or more than one quarter of the value of the 99 berths purchased overall by November 1932. British shipbuilders maintained their policies more widely. In 1937 they were instrumental in the establishment of the International Shipbuilding Conference to try to obtain some collaboration and control of international competition. It is practically impossible to determine whether the avowed aim of reducing costs was achieved, but the plan did not lead directly to any significant revival in the industry. The revival which did come owed much to defence expenditure. The industry stressed its high cost level as the explanation of its lack of competitiveness. In spite of the recovery of the later 1930s, the future outlook was considered to be so unpropitious that the industry felt no longer able to meet its problems unaided and required government assistance. From any possibility of immediate disaster it was saved by the onset of war.

Steelmaking was a bridge between the two types of industrial specialisation which characterised the Scottish economy. It gained from the demand for the skilled products of the shipyards and engineering workshops but was not immune from the problems which faced the coal and iron industries as their natural resources became exhausted. As the output of pig iron fell while that of steel rose, supplies from the Scottish blast furnaces could not meet the needs of the steelworks. The Scottish practice of using a large quantity of scrap in the open-hearth furnaces provided some relief, but it was estimated that Scotland would have had to produce about 1,000,000 tons of pig iron annually, or about double its then current level of production, to be self-sufficient in the inter-war years. The problem was intensified for the basic steel producers, whose output was increasing, since the Scottish ironworks continued to specialise in the production of hematite iron from imported ore. In 1937, 198,000 tons of hematite pig iron and 117,000 tons of basic iron (also 182,000 tons of foundry and forge pig) were produced, when only 466,000 tons of acid open-hearth steel and 1,392,000 of basic open hearth (also 37,000 tons by other processes) were made. The problem of bringing supplies of pig iron into Scotland was, therefore, greater for those steelmakers using the basic process, who were placed at a peculiar disadvantage against their Continental competitors with ample supplies of basic ores.

The most striking economies, particularly in fuel consumption, lay in the integration of production. Integration was lacking in Scotland, because the extensive use of scrap, and the use of imported pig iron, made cold metal practice the normal method of Scottish steelmaking. As the scrap ratio declined, so the need for, and advantages to be derived from, integration increased. If the lack of integration was the most conspicuous example of failure to obtain the highest degree of technical efficiency, it was not the only one. The pig-iron production per furnace in blast in Scotland, which was only 16,000 tons annually in 1915, was only 33,000 tons·in 1937, the figure reached by the whole United Kingdom in 1915, while even the United Kingdom's performance compared adversely with that of other countries. Scottish coal may have been partly responsible for the difference, but can hardly have accounted for such a striking lag in technical efficiency. Whatever the relative importance of these various possibilities of internal reform through technical change, the steel industry was more concerned after the war with the elimination of surplus capacity, much of which was the result of expansion undertaken at the behest of the Ministry of Munitions. The wartime legacy, on which future expansion had to be built, did not initiate moves towards greater integration, but a fragmented piecemeal development, and one which contributed least successfully to curing Scotland's long-standing weakness in smelting and in fuel consumption. After the war shipbuilders on the Clyde and in Belfast purchased steelworks in attempts to ensure supplies of steel on the erroneous assumption that demand would outstrip supply. The move was to sustain the position of the shipyards, but was another barrier in the way to integrated production. The owners, being consumers of steel, and owning steelworks for that purpose, were reluctant to accept the need to devote resources — especially when under financial pressures themselves — to the reorganisation of a steel industry in which their concern was marginal in any case. More fundamental were the moves which led to the creation of Colvilles Ltd. David Colville and Sons absorbed Clydebridge and

Glengarnock, in which the increase of capacity in wartime did little to alter their inability to achieve efficient production. The next move by Colvilles was an even more obvious example of the absorption of firms which were no longer able to exist and to produce profitably. James Dunlop & Co. were in a parlous financial state, and were taken over and fused with David Colville and Sons to form Colvilles Ltd. in 1931.

The underlying locational difficulties of the Scottish steel industry became more widely apparent in 1932 by the decision of Stewarts and Lloyds to move from Mossend to Corby. Stewarts and Lloyds originally used iron-tube hoops and strips and were supplied with necessary materials from the puddling furnaces and rolling mills of the area. Steel tubes and strips used basic steel, because of its suitability for rapid welding. Though basic steel was not made extensively in Scotland, the disadvantage was partly offset by local firms re-rolling Continental billets and slabs. The relief was only temporary, and gradually the material was brought direct from the Continent. That supplies were never likely to be obtained again from Scotland was made clear in 1932 when depreciation and protection forced the use of British, but not of Scottish steel, as basic Bessemer steel had not been produced in Scotland since the closure of the plant at Glengarnock in 1920. By 1932 it was not available anywhere in Great Britain, and acid Bessemer, which could be used, was made only in England. The position facing Stewarts and Lloyds was, therefore, quite simple. They had to supply their works with cheap basic Bessemer steel, and that could be done effectively only at Corby. Such advantages as Scotland could offer were no longer adequate to arrest the movement south to the raw materials.

The move of Stewarts and Lloyds to Corby had more implications than being a sign of the loss of Scotland's relative advantages. It showed that newly designed plant was more likely to improve the competitive efficiency of the industry than were piecemeal amalgamations. In Scotland the tendency towards amalgamation, confirmed by the formation of Colvilles Ltd., was well established by 1933. In the early 1930s the closure of the Mossend and Calderbank steelworks began to concentrate steelmaking in the hands of Colvilles, which, at the beginning of 1934, absorbed the steel-plate rolling section of Stewarts and Lloyds. Apart from Colvilles, with works at Motherwell, Cambuslang and Glengarnock, the other main steelmaking concerns in Scotland by then were the Steel Company of Scotland, with works at Blochairn and Newton, the Lanarkshire Steel Company, with works at Motherwell, and the Scottish Iron and Steel Company, mainly engaged in wrought iron, with works at Coatbridge. In 1934, when government and Bank of England pressed for the completion of the scheme to reorganise steel production, the amalgamation continued with the purchase of the Steel Company of Scotland by Sir James and Henry Lithgow. By 1936 the process was virtually complete. Both the Steel Company of Scotland and the Lanarkshire Steel Company were controlled by Colvilles. Colvilles were then virtually synonymous with the Scottish steel industry, apart from those who undertook specialised work. In particular they were the suppliers of the needs of the shipyards. Being in such a dominating position, the form of Colvilles' plans determined how the Scottish steel industry would grow.

Growth became more evident in the later 1930s though its form was determined by the amalgamations which had taken place earlier. Towards the end of 1936 a modern wire, rod and bar mill, with appropriate increases in melting capacity, was completed at Motherwell; reorganisation at Glengarnock aimed at producing an additional 2,500 tons per week of semi-products and sections; at Parkhead Beardmore's had a scheme in hand to yield another 50,000 tons a year. In the spring of 1937 Colvilles announced their major plan for renovation: a scheme of expansion at Clydebridge and Clyde including the erection of a battery of coke ovens, modern blast furnaces and steelmaking plant, and an additional plate mill, all of which provided the basis for the future by leading to a semi-integrated plant. The expansion still left Scotland without a wholly integrated steelworks. Some thought the improvements introduced by Colvilles, especially the changes at Clydebridge, were likely to impede more radical moves towards new locations. In the 1930s the decline of the availability of indigenous natural resources gave rise, not to doubts about the survival of the steel industry, but to reservations about the desirability, or even the possibility, of survival on its existing location in the older areas of coalmining and iron manufacture. The strength of the locational argument was not easily accepted. Poor comparative performance could neither be ignored, as producers became aware of more competition and of the possession of less assured markets than in the past, nor dismissed, as was the failure to produce basic Bessemer steel as a response to consumer demand. The danger in many of the improvements made and advocated was that they could stand in the way of the relocation of the industry because of the decline in the original endowments of natural resources. The adoption of large-scale integrated production did not eliminate the significance of the locational problem; it coalesced into it in a way that is fundamental to an understanding of the problems of Scottish industry.

In the 1930s the steel industry faced a dilemma. The steelworks were being improved on their existing inland sites, but to reduce the costs of transporting the ore, which was mostly imported, the blast furnaces had to be located on the lower reaches of the Clyde, and to gain the advantage of fully integrated production, the steelworks had to go with them. In 1929 a plan was advanced for a new location downriver. If implemented, it was alleged that the cost of slabs would have been lowered from the then current average of £6 12s. a ton to £5. For a variety of reasons, the scheme was not adopted. Effectively the choice of an inland location had been made in the formation of Colvilles and its plans for expansion in the 1930s.

Expansion and new developments

The restructuring and especially the reduction in the scale of operation of any industry is always painful and draws attention to its difficulties, especially when political thought attributes an increasingly interventionist role to government in economic affairs. It is not surprising, then, that the toils of the staples of Scotland's industrial past received much attention from contemporaries and subsequently. The displacement of labour and the reduction in output which frequently followed industrial rationalisation did not suggest a promising future. Some looked with greater hope to the displacement of the old through the emergence of a new economic structure, with its own vigorous growth, though they often neglected, or underestimated, the changes — occupational, industrial, geographical — which its growth implied, and the possibility that the Scottish economy was no longer as able, or as willing, to adapt to new challenges as it had once been.

The belief that such an infusion of new industries was essential for the country's economic salvation was not extensively adopted until the 1930s. Until then it was hoped that the key to prosperity lay in the revival of the heavy industries. In one sense that was still true, but in the 1930s the expectation of imminent recovery, characteristic of the previous decade, evaporated. The change in attitude had a favourable effect in leading to a greater appreciation of the need for new industries in Scotland. No longer were they regarded as interesting, faintly exotic growths, indeed almost luxuries, but as necessities, as important as the heavy industries for the future prosperity of the Scottish economy. Two factors were particularly influential in leading to the adoption of this position. First, the east and south of Scotland were more prosperous than the main industrial belt and they had a higher proportion of light industries. The decline in Scotland's major industries overshadowed the successes in a variety of others: papermaking in Aberdeenshire; printing and publishing in Edinburgh, Dundee and elsewhere; the preservation of fruit and vegetables near the Carse of Gowrie; rubber manufacture in Edinburgh; the production of a variety of foodstuffs, especially in Edinburgh. Second, the need for new industrial development was given a special political dimension by comparison with England. A popular and influential work shows how the difference was seen:

> There are . . . important industries in which, between 1924 and 1930, production and employment in England has made great strides but *where no Scottish production exists at all*. Aircraft employed 11,735 in 1924 and 21,322 in 1930. Aircraft are not made in Scotland. In others, Scottish production is trifling. Motors and cycles gave work in England, 185,576 in 1924 and 233,176 in 1930. But in Scotland the numbers at work were only 6,105 and 7,077. Silk and artificial silk; in England, 39,932 in 1924, and 58,905 in 1930; in Scotland, no figure exists for 1924. The employment in 1930 was 971.[4]

All this was grist to the mill of those who demanded some measure of political independence for Scotland. Earlier demands for greater independent control of Scottish affairs, especially from the 1880s, were based more on political theories of self-determination or on injured pride. Whatever political or cultural motives may have dominated the leaders of the movement, such popular support as it had in the 1920s, and especially in the 1930s, was based largely on economic considerations. How far any measure of home rule would have provided an effective answer to the country's economic problems is doubtful. Few believed that the severance of union with England would lead automatically to economic salvation. More common, and more justifiable, was the belief that the effects of adverse international economic conditions could be mitigated by the adoption of certain economic policies which a United Kingdom parliament, concerned with much wider interests, was less likely to adopt than a parliament in Edinburgh.

The basic objection to the existing union with England was that it prevented Scotland adopting the economic policy most suited to the country. Even those who actively opposed any change in the parliamentary union — and most of Scotland's leading industrialists were among them — came to advocate policies devised specifically for Scotland's needs. As government came to accept some slight responsibility for the direction of the economy, no matter how tentatively, the existence of a separate framework of law and administration, and of a series of Scottish-based, non-political organisations, led almost automatically to policies being devised for Scotland's specific needs. The likelihood of Scotland's problems being accorded recognition and solution independent from those of other parts of the United Kingdom grew between the wars as increasing legislation required more Scottish statutes and particularly when much of the Scottish administration moved physically from London to Edinburgh immediately before the war. The replacement of the Calton Jail with St Andrew's House may have done more to focus the economic case for nationalism than the institution of the modern Scottish Office in 1885 because of the time when it took place, but it was not enough. While welcoming the planned move late in 1937, Walter Elliot, the then Secretary of State, feared the changes 'will not in themselves dispose of the problems upon whose solution a general improvement in Scottish social and economic conditions depends . . . It is the consciousness of their existence which is reflected, not in the small and unimportant Nationalist Party, but in the dissatisfaction and uneasiness amongst moderate and reasonable people of every view or rank — a dissatis-faction expressed in every book published about Scotland now for several years'.[5] Elliot had identified the source of discontent in the 1930s. As govern-ment began to play an increasingly interventionist role in the economy, it became easy to advocate a nationalist remedy to ensure that it was in whatever was deemed Scotland's interest.

The failure of new industrial development in Scotland lent apparent support to these analyses. William Beardmore and Company had moved during the war from the production of components for motor cars to making three models, at Glasgow, Paisley and Coatbridge, and were considering the possibility of adding another plant to these three; a new model of the Argyll car — embodying the famous single-sleeve-valve engine — was planned for marketing early in 1920; at Dumfries Arrol-Johnston specialised in a new model of the 15.9 h.p. car with which they had achieved distinction; earlier, the Albion Motor Car Company produced a new 30 cwt. chassis and Halley's Industrial Motors a six-cylinder engine; Carlaw and Sons planned to market a 20 to 30 cwt. industrial vehicle entirely of their own design and manufacture; the Caledon Company brought out a passenger vehicle chassis fitted with an Argyll-type engine; Barr and Stroud adapted the single-sleeve-valve engine to a motor-cycle. Few of these portents bore much fruit in the 1920s. Most of the ventures started after the war continued, with varying degrees of success, throughout the decade, but by the early 1930s all had been eliminated or diverted to other activities except the Albion Company, which continued to manufacture commercial vehicles.

The problems of Scottish industry between the wars reflected those which can be seen in retrospect to have been emerging before 1914. While major industries were declining, especially in their international competitiveness, insufficient industrial growth was appearing and being maintained to take their place. The gleam of hope in Scottish industry after 1930 was that the problem was being analysed and attempts made to find a solution. Many of these attempts had a possible defect. They assumed that new industries should be encouraged in Scotland, but it is possible that, no matter how successful these industries were (and their success, as it transpired, was not wholly unqualified), they could do little to alter the structural balance of the economy, and so could do little else but touch the fringe of the problem. Consequently, any attempt to alter the structural balance of the economy could succeed, if at all, only in the long run. If so, more important than the need for diversification was the need for existing firms to innovate within their own fields; in short that they should attempt reform through expansionist, not restrictionist, solutions. Though it might be held that there were two remedies for the problem of Scottish industry — diversification through the introduction of new industries and innovation in the traditional fields — they were complementary; but the relative stress placed on the remedies over the years reflected a changing analysis of the problem. Its more ardent advocates saw diversification as the only way of dealing with the permanent labour surplus which they feared was emerging from the inexorable decline of the traditional industries; the less ardent advocates saw it only as a useful addition to the policy of increasing the competitive ability of the basic heavy industries without leading to a radical change in the industrial structure. On the whole the depressing view of the first group predominated. Many accepted the possibility of revival in the heavy industries in the 1920s, but only their permanent depression in the 1930s. *The Industrial Survey of the West of Scotland*, compiled by members of the staff of the University of Glasgow in 1932, envisaged a permanent surplus of male labour, an expectation the *Report of the Investigation into Depressed Areas* thought confirmed in 1934. Even in 1937, when some revival had come to the heavy industries, Sir Steven Bilsland wrote that 'no conceivable expansion of these industries *[the heavy industries]* is likely to absorb all the surplus labour which remains'.[6] This view led many to look with suspicion on the revival of the heavy industries in 1936 as having no substantial basis. The desire to diversify cannot be criticised in itself; the danger was that undue stress on its importance led to failure to recognise that the encouragements given to the new industries might more appropriately have been given to the old. A broader industrial base was necessary, but that could never have been achieved by the neglect of the older industries.

Diversification had probably more success on the morale of Scottish industry than in producing a solution to its worst problems. Attempts at self-help, in the form of encouragement to new industries to settle in Scotland, came in the 1930s. A Development Board for Glasgow and District was set up in 1930. In the following year the Scottish Development Council was formed to encourage, and to indicate possibilities of, industrial development throughout the entire country. Until the Scottish Council on Industry was formed in 1942 to consider the industrial future of Scotland, it remained the most important body assisting new industry. Government aid came after 1934 in the policy for the Special Areas. Its effectiveness was limited by inadequate and severely restrictive financial provision; by a very limited geographical designation of the areas to be helped; by concentration on such social improvements as sewerage schemes, which, however desirable in themselves, contributed only marginally and indirectly to economic change; and by readiness to withdraw support once the level of unemployment had been reduced even though no significant change in the industrial structure had been achieved. The policy's most lasting contribution towards diversification was in the establishment of the industrial estate at Hillington, in which the Scottish Development Council co-operated with the Commissioner for the Special Areas. In 1938 the same ideas, which many thought offered the greatest prospect for diversification, were extended to smaller sites at Carfin, Chapelhall and Larkhall. The success of such ventures, though welcome, was limited. In 1939, while the industrial estate at Hillington accommodated 75 firms employing about 1,500 workers, it gave employment to only about 3 per cent of the estimated surplus of labour. Moreover, the employment in the new firms was frequently for females, while the surplus labour was chiefly of males. It did show that light industries could succeed in the west of Scotland in the way many had already succeeded in the east. Remoteness from the main markets in the south, which militated against the large-scale expansion of the production of consumer goods in Scotland, unless the country could offer other compensating advantages, was shown not to form an absolute barrier to that form of industrial growth.

It was still necessary to overcome serious barriers raised by resistance to change. The industrial structure remained tied to its origins. The production of consumer goods in Scotland was inhibited by the refusal to adopt the mass-production methods essential for success. Before 1939 only the clothing trade had made much progress in that direction. Although according to one estimate, between 80 and 90 per cent of the Scottish demand for cheap furniture, for the manufacture of which mass-production methods were necessary, was met in Scotland, the furniture trade adopted such methods only under enforced wartime standardisation. As important, new industrial growth itself required innovation in the heavy industries, not such as would ensure their traditional international competitiveness, but innovation which would also enable them to supply the raw materials required by the consumer durables industries, the materials for light constructional activity — tinplates rather than ship plates. That was a problem which had to wait for attempted solutions until after 1945. The basic dilemma, about which direction industrial development should take, was as unsolved in the 1930s as in the 1920s, but in the later decades more people were aware that such a dilemma existed, even if they did not know what the solution was.

NOTES

1. Exports from Scottish ports are the only statistics available. They are almost certainly minimum figures, as English goods exported from Scottish ports would probably be more than offset by Scottish goods exported through English ports. See M. W. Flinn, 'The Overseas Trade of Scottish Ports', *Scottish Journal of Political Economy*, vol. XIII (1966), pp. 220-37.

2. *The Glasgow Herald Trade Review*, 1921.

3. *Ibid.*, 1922.

4. G. M. Thomson, *Scotland, That Distressed Area* (Edinburgh, 1935), p. 47.

5. Scottish Record Office. DD10/175. Scottish Office: Special Areas Inter-Departmental Committee. Memorandum on The State of Scotland, 18 December 1937.

6. *The Glasgow Herald Trade Review*, 1937.

CHAPTER XIV

Agriculture, 1870s to 1939

1870 to 1914

By the 1870s Scottish agriculture had developed various specialisations which continued to provide the basis of its activities until 1939. Its history from then until the Second World War is one of adaptation to a changing pattern of supply and demand nationally and internationally.

The changing environment became evident in the later 1870s. Many difficulties could be attributed to the severity of the weather, which was at its worst in the winter of 1878 to 1879, but one matter showed that the problems were not confined to the short-run influence of the vagaries of Scottish weather. The reduced output of some crops — the yield on wheat was down by about 20 per cent — failed to lead to any significant increase in price. The explanation, though simple, had far-reaching repercussions. Imports of foreign produce were beginning to make a major contribution to the British food supply, and in years such as 1879, when American crops were good and British ones were poor, the British farmer could no longer rely on high prices compensating for low yields. The opening of new lands, especially the grain-producing regions of America and Russia, combined with the cheapening in transport costs which the railways and better shipping facilities brought, became the crucial factor determining much agricultural prosperity from the 1870s. As its fortunes were increasingly influenced by what was happening overseas, Scottish agriculture came to occupy a position similar to that occupied by Scottish industry for a century, but with a difference. The international connections of Scottish industry were formed through its success in penetrating foreign markets; those of Scottish agriculture were formed through its inability to prevent foreign produce entering its markets at home. Comparative international costs of production were in favour of industry but against agriculture. Scotland retained some measure of international agricultural leadership from the 1870s only by dint of great enterprise and ability on the part of its farmers.

Scotland gained from the varied incidence of foreign competition. The worst effects were felt by wheat producers. In the two decades from the mid-1870s to the mid-1890s wheat imports to Britain almost doubled to nearly 100,000,000 cwt; barley imports more than doubled to 26,000,000 cwt., the increase being concentrated in the decade from the mid-1880s. But the relative proportions of home to foreign produce consumed in Britain were more important in determining the prosperity of the home farmer than the absolute level of imports. The proportion of consumption of wheat met by foreign supplies rose from about 50 per cent in the mid-1870s to about 75 per cent by the mid-1890s;

of barley, from 20 per cent to 45 per cent; of oats, a constant proportion of about 20 per cent. This was the differential impact from which Scottish agriculture gained. Except in the Lothians and parts of the centre and east, Scottish agriculture was not primarily arable, and among the typical Scottish cash crops — wheat, barley, oats, potatoes — wheat was least important. Scotland had no areas so wedded to wheat as were the clay soils of East Anglia and the Midlands. In those districts in the east where wheat was most commonly grown, its cultivation was combined with barley, oats and potatoes; on many farms it was virtually a joint product with potatoes, being sown after the potatoes had been lifted and its straw used to cover potato pits. Consequently, even on the arable farms of east Scotland the price of wheat was not the sole consideration in deciding whether to cultivate the grain, as it was in parts of England; the profitability of barley, oats and potatoes, crops which did not suffer so adversely from competition, was equally relevant. All, of course, suffered some falls in price until the 1890s, but, while that of wheat fell by about 50 per cent during these years, those of barley, oats and potatoes fell by only about one-third and the fall was concentrated in the period after the early 1880s.

Though the price fall had less drastic effects on arable farming in Scotland than it had in England, it still provided a similar, though less pronounced, incentive to move away from the less profitable crops. Between 1880 and 1914 the acreage under wheat in England and Wales fell by about one-third to just over 1,800,000 acres, but in Scotland it fell during the same period by only about one-fifth to just over 60,500 acres. The Scots had already made their major move away from the production of this crop, which they had never cultivated extensively in any case. The fall in the acreage under barley was similar in the two countries: in England by about one-third to just over 1,500,000 acres; in Scotland by about two-sevenths to 194,000 acres. The cultivation of oats differed significantly. The acreage under oats in England and Wales in 1914, almost 1,930,000, was 10 per cent greater than in 1880; in Scotland during the same period the acreage fell by almost 10 per cent to about 920,000, the level of the mid-1850s. The proportionately greater acreage under oats in Scotland reflected the traditionally greater emphasis always given to the crop; the increase in the English acreage was partly the result of the movement away from the cultivation of wheat to that of other cereal crops, such as oats, which had become relatively more profitable. Though there was a reduction in the less profitable cereal crops on the marginal lands in Scotland — as in the less fertile upper reaches of the valleys of the Tay, Dee and Don, into which the improvements earlier in the century had caused cultivation to extend — there was never the same pressure to switch from wheat to oats. In both countries the overall effect of the changes in arable cultivation was for a smaller acreage to be cultivated and for more pasture to be laid down to permanent grass. English permanent pasture was nearly 16,116,000 acres in 1914, almost 3,000,000 more than in 1880; in Scotland in 1914 permanent pasture of nearly 1,500,000 acres was 330,000 acres more than in 1880.

The arable crops in Scotland reflected the continuing importance of livestock husbandry in the country's agriculture, a specialisation which mitigated some of the effects of foreign competition in the later nineteenth century. Livestock husbandry suffered less and later from foreign competition. It gained from the changing dietary habits of the British people, as a rising standard of living brought some commodities within the purchasing power of a greater number of people. Wheat consumption dropped slightly from the 1870s. The consumption of potatoes, traditionally a diet associated with a lower standard of living, and therefore popular much longer in the Highlands, as in Ireland, fell more drastically. In Scotland gross production per head of the population was 5.8 cwt. in 1867; in 1939 it was 4.1 cwt. Since a large, almost certainly increasing, proportion of the crop left Scotland as seed, the decline in consumption was even greater. In place of bread and potatoes the British public wanted more meat and dairy products. They also wanted more fruit and green vegetables, but generally over the entire country, and more particularly in Scotland, with its different dietary habits, the preference was for meat and dairy products.

The demand for perishable products, unlike that for cereals, could not be met from overseas until later in the nineteenth century. The evidence of Scottish witnesses before the two Royal Commissions on Agriculture of 1881 and 1896 shows the later and lesser effect of imports on Scottish farmers. Complaints on many matters appear in the evidence to both Commissions, but livestock farmers did not attribute their problems to foreign competition in the 1880s, and, though it was a more common cause of complaint fifteen years later, dairy farmers advanced it only with qualifications. By the end of the century it was a significant determinant of prosperity of livestock husbandry. New methods of preservation, especially the introduction of refrigeration, almost doubled meat imports in the two decades to the 1890s. Dairy farmers also suffered, sometimes directly from competition from the new lands, as from imports of American cheese, more commonly they suffered indirectly, through the exploitation of the grain-producing regions of the new world forcing some European countries, notably Denmark, to specialise in dairy and poultry products, for which the unprotected British market provided a ready demand.

As they had done when exposed to greater competition after the Napoleonic Wars, Scottish farmers responded to the relative opportunities offered by livestock husbandry and by arable cultivation. From the dairying south-west and the cattle-rearing north-east farmers moved to succeed, sometimes even as arable farmers, in areas whence those used to easier market conditions had fled. Aberdeenshire breeders moved to the arable areas along the Moray Firth or further south to the Mearns; Ayrshire dairy farmers moved into the Lothians. The migration spread to England, especially in the late nineteenth century when a number of Ayrshire dairy farmers moved to the Essex clays, on which arable cultivation had been surrendered, but which they transformed into successful dairy farms by exploiting the adjacent urban market and using imported feedingstuffs.

Both north-east and south-west Scotland enjoyed several favourable factors, which enabled them to confirm their earlier successes based on the Aberdeen-

Angus and the Ayrshire breeds of cattle. In both the dominance of family farms reduced money labour costs to a minimum, though the real costs, always impossible to estimate, were high. Unavoidable cash expenditure was kept low, an essential for success in a period of falling prices. Again, the farmers of both districts, following unwittingly the same path to success as in industry, adapted to the new international economic situation by specialising in quality, rather than cheap, products. Farmers in the north-east improved the Aberdeen-Angus and beef Shorthorn breeds, generally by empirical methods of breeding and feeding, backed by successful arable cultivation in seed selection and manuring, to ensure an adequate supply of winter fodder, especially of turnips. The result was the production of the highest grade pedigree animals, though in general the north-east breeders were more dependent on producing good commercial animals. In the south-west, after some years of itinerant instructors, a permanent dairy school, which eventually became the Dairy School for Scotland, was founded at Kilmarnock in 1889 in an attempt to improve the quality of the butter and cheese. At the same time the south-west pioneered better dairy practice by introducing milk recording, by trying to eliminate bovine tuberculosis, and by devising the first satisfactory milking machines. In both areas success in livestock production depended on the state of grassland husbandry. As permanent pasture increased, many farmers on both sides of the border found that an ordinary seeds mixture used in some rotation was inadequate to maintain satisfactory grass for long. The problem was more pressing in England — where the seed was often of short-lived plants suitable for a hay crop for one year — than in Scotland, where the ordinary mixture ensured a reasonable quantity of grasses and clover for two or three years. The result was increased attention to the choice of grass seed and to its cultivation, towards which Scots — and Scots in England — contributed.

Better grassland husbandry is an improvement in arable cultivation, though one aimed at supporting livestock. In those branches of arable farming which had no such connection, improvements were less striking. The greatest success was in the cultivation of the potato, the price of which did not fall as those of most other arable products. The maximum acreage under potatoes in Scotland, 189,161, was reached in 1881. Though it had fallen to 152,318 acres by 1914, the Scottish seed potato trade grew throughout the period. Scottish seed was acceptable primarily because of its relative freedom from disease, one of the few benefits of the Scottish climate to Scottish farmers, because greenfly, which carry many of the worst diseases to the potato, do not exist so easily in the cooler and windier conditions of Scotland. Even before the 1870s English growers used Scottish seed potatoes, and throughout most of the nineteenth century Scottish growers held a monopoly of the seed potato trade in Britain. In the 1890s the trade took a notable step forward, when, especially with the introduction of the Up-to-date variety, it began to sell seed potatoes overseas, notably in South Africa. The seed potato crop was mainly exported; the ware crop was largely consumed in Scotland. The fortunes of the two varied. The seed trade gained from the increased demand which followed the entry into overseas markets; the ware trade supplied a market in which consumption per head was declining in the half-century before 1914. Only the south-west maintained a profitable share in the ware trade by specialising in the production of early potatoes on the Ayrshire and Wigtownshire coasts. 'Boxing', or sprouting of the seed, encouraged the growth of the early potatoes in Ayrshire from the early 1880s, while the Epicure, first marketed in 1897, proved the most successful variety and provided the basis for an export trade in early potatoes, especially to the north of England.

The success of the cultivation of the potato was offset by failures in arable farming in two other directions. First, the period was not one of marked improvements in machinery, comparable to the first development of the milking machine and of cream separators in dairying. The most striking were in potato harvesting. The rotary spinner lifter, patented in 1855, was tested, rather unsuccessfully, by the Highland and Agricultural Society in the 1870s and subsequently adapted satisfactorily. In potato lifting the adequacy of the labour supply, especially of seasonal labour, delayed the development of a more efficient machine until the elevator digger was adopted in the 1920s. In other arable operations the basic form of the implements used remained unaltered, or they were simply continuations of those of earlier periods, as in the extension of the use of the reaper, which led to a decline in the labour force used in grain harvesting. More important, the yield on grain crops failed to show any marked improvement during the period, even though land less suited to grain crops was going out of cultivation. Yields of most crops seem to have risen in the twenty years before the 1880s, then until 1910 those of hay, oats and barley remained stable, while those of turnips and wheat rose slightly. Some care must be exercised in interpreting these figures. Yields may have failed to increase because many Scottish farmers survived the depression of the 1880s and 1890s by reducing costs rather than by forcing production to a high level. For instance, improved knowledge of manurial practice in turnip husbandry led to an efficient use of fertilisers to reduce costs rather than to attempts at increasing yields. On the other hand, in potato growing, where the same pressure to reduce costs did not operate, yields did rise, especially after the introduction of the Up-to-date variety in the 1890s.

Many improvements in all branches of agriculture were the work of tenant farmers or of owner-occupiers. An example was John Spier of Newton, near Cambuslang. Many of the causes he advocated — notably milk recording — were later accorded international recognition. Such improvers of the late nineteenth century, who have been neglected by agricultural historians, differed from those of the late eighteenth century. In the fifty years before 1914 landlords as a group did not show the interest and ability in agricultural matters which their ancestors had shown in the fifty years before 1815, but they provided a system of landholding which encouraged those tenant farmers who could exploit agricultural opportunities. Contention between them and their tenants continued on such old issues as the provisions in leases for fixed rotations of cropping and the need to consume crops on the farm, especially necessary in days before artificial fertilisers, but some slackening in the rigid enforcement of these provisions was evident and they were surrendered on some estates. More difficult to solve was the thorny question of compensation for improvements, including the residues of fertilisers with long-run effects, which came into greater use in the late nineteenth century. Since the problem was especially acute for improvements undertaken by tenants in the closing years of a lease, negotiations for its continuation began on some estates sufficiently long before its end to give the tenant the security needed. Another well-established source of friction — the level of rents — assumed a keener edge in the late nineteenth century. Rents increased in the leases concluded in the years of prosperity in the 1860s and early 1870s and became more onerous in real terms as prices fell. Over-renting was a common complaint of the late nineteenth century, but one which gave inadequate recognition to the allowances given to the tenants towards meeting their rents, and to the way in which they were allowed to fall into arrears, which were often written off, even when the formal reductions in rent were not so common as the landlords' critics desired. The consequences of fixed rents in a period of falling prices led to the introduction of shorter breaks in leases and to the beginning of the end of the long lease of nineteen years or thereabouts, which had been so common in Scottish agriculture. Such aid from the landlords did not absolve them from political criticism. Increasing intervention by the state was evident in agriculture with a series of measures which instituted a policy of restricting their rights, which, when accompanied subsequently by increased taxation, led in due course to the virtual end of a system of land tenure which had served Scottish agriculture well. The legislative measures were widespread. A series of Acts from 1875 to 1906 tackled the need for compensation for improvements; in 1880 hypothec was virtually abolished; in the same year the Ground Game Act allowed those who were tenants for periods of more than one year to kill hares and rabbits on their ground.

The tenant farmers or the owner-occupiers, to whom the responsibility for agricultural improvement was passing, faced the need for some formal scientific training if they were to make the best use of the knowledge which was becoming available. Success attended those who, even without such training, still adopted the rudiments of scientific method in their investigations. Often the work of such empiricists only exploded long-accepted theories but did not provide satisfactory alternatives. Its negative approach did not commend itself to contemporaries, especially when, as was inevitable with pioneers, the advice given to other farmers was not always correct. The extension and dissemination of formal agricultural education was necessary. To that need another can be added. Scottish farmers could not easily adopt many more advanced agricultural techniques and more modern implements because of the small scale of their operations, and for the same reason they could not easily obtain commercial advantages in buying and selling. In this case the remedy suggested was co-operation.

The tradition of agricultural education in Scotland was of long standing. The

H

chair of agriculture was founded in the University of Edinburgh in 1790. The University of Aberdeen planned to have one from the same year, though the intention took effect only in 1840 in the creation of a lectureship. Throughout most of the nineteenth century responsibility for agricultural education lay mainly with the Highland and Agricultural Society. In 1816, after its attempts to establish veterinary education in the University of Edinburgh were rejected, the Society encouraged William Dick to begin the lectures from which the Edinburgh veterinary school emerged. In research the Society was equally active. In 1848 it appointed a chemist who helped with his successors to adapt many experiments to local conditions. In 1858 it instituted examinations for diplomas in dairying and agriculture. On the other hand the Society, though pressed to do so from the days of Sir John Sinclair, was reluctant to establish an experimental farm, but eventually started experimental stations at Pumpherston and Harelaw. On this educational foundation private and public effort built in the later nineteenth century.

The private effort was based on the three centres of higher education at Edinburgh, Glasgow and Aberdeen. Edinburgh instituted a degree in agricultural science which, though of little direct relevance to the average Scottish farmer, produced some of the country's leading agricultural scientists. Aberdeen started a full degree course in agriculture in 1895. Glasgow remained backward until the late 1880s when the Technical College assumed responsibility for teaching agriculture. Then in 1899 Glasgow took the lead, when, mainly through the efforts of some local directors of the Highland and Agricultural Society, an agricultural college was established and experimental work carried on at the old dairy school at Kilmarnock. Following this example, the East of Scotland Agricultural College was founded in 1901 and the North of Scotland Agricultural College in 1904. All three colleges awarded diplomas and prepared students for the National Diplomas in Dairying and Agriculture, which had been started in 1897 and 1900 respectively. The agricultural colleges provided a more popular form of agricultural education aimed at the ordinary farmer, education of a type which the universities could not provide. Public provision for agricultural education began at the end of the century, when local authorities were given grants-in-aid to supply technical instruction. The southwest led. Full-time instructors were appointed in Kirkcudbright and Lanark, and the dairy school at Kilmarnock received help. Help from public sources remained limited until 1912, when the effectiveness of official interest in Scottish agriculture was increased by the creation of a Scottish Board of Agriculture from the Board of Agriculture which had been founded, for a second time, in 1889.

Co-operation in Scottish agriculture was less successful. It first appeared in the depression of the 1880s, when the Farmers' Supply Association was formed at Leith in 1884, to be followed in 1905 by the Scottish Agricultural Organization Society. The movement made slow progress, though about fifty societies were in operation by 1910. In spite of the closure of a few societies, major catastrophes were avoided in Scotland. The main limiting factor was the individualism of Scottish farmers. The value of co-operation was outweighed by that of education.

1914 to 1939

The First World War provided a temporary respite from the foreign competition which had been a leading determinant of agricultural prosperity since the later nineteenth century, but some of the attendant benefits were offset in the early part of the war by shortages of labour, fertilisers, implements and horses, many of which were commandeered in 1914. In 1916 the grain harvest was lower than in 1914; the yield of potatoes, then a vitally important food, at just over half a million tons, was only about half of what it had been. In 1917 the announcement of guaranteed minimum prices for wheat and oats was a direct attempt to encourage the cultivation of some permanent grassland. In Scotland the main grain crops acreage was 1,175,000 in 1914 (61,000 in wheat; 194,000 in barley; 920,000 in oats); 1,224,000 in 1916 (63,000 in wheat; 170,000 in barley; 991,000 in oats); 1,476,000 in 1918 (79,000 in wheat; 153,000 in barley; 1,244,000 in oats). The acreage under potatoes also rose from 152,000 in 1914 to 169,000 in 1918, though it had fallen to 130,000 in 1916, but, reflecting the emphasis on the production of food for human consumption, the acreage under turnips declined steadily from 431,000 in 1914, to 414,000 in 1916, to 397,000 in 1918. The switch from grass to arable cultivation was easier in Scotland than in England. No areas in Scotland, with the potential for alternative use, were so pre-eminently suitable for grazing as were some of the finest permanent pastures in England. Much of the grassland ploughed up in Scotland was only temporary grass, which would in due course have been brought into cultivation in any case, though perhaps not quite so soon. If the process had been continued for long, adverse repercussions on agricultural practice might have followed, but not in the short run. In England the problem could not be dismissed so lightly.

Government's intervention and agriculture's response led to the expectation of greater support after the war, especially to ensure that agriculture would not be sacrificed so readily to foreign competition. The expectation was given substance by the Agriculture Act of 1920, which promised a firmer basis for prosperity than the price rise of 1919 and 1920. Its central feature was a guarantee of the prices of wheat and oats, but its most permanent legacy came from the provision which gave tenants greater security of tenure.

The expectation that government action would transform the condition of agriculture proved to be unfounded. Agricultural prosperity ended suddenly in 1921 and 1922. The price of wool fell first, to be followed quickly by those of wheat and oats, until by 1922 all were at least half, and often less, of what they had been only a short time before. Though livestock prices remained higher, the fall in the price of wool led to a fall in those for sheep. The explanation was much the same as in the 1880s and 1890s: foreign produce again entered the still-unprotected British market, the situation from which the farming community, with memories of the earlier decades, expected to be protected by the price guarantees of the Agriculture Act of 1920. The government thought differently, and conceived the Act chiefly as a measure to maintain a high level of grain production and not one to compensate for the effects of a policy of free trade. When the cost of implementing the price guarantees would have amounted to about £20,000,000, the strategic benefits the Act offered seemed to justify the cost no longer. It was repealed in 1921.

With the removal of the promised support, agriculture was once again at the mercy of world food prices. They fell until 1923, then steadied until 1929, when there was an even sharper drop. The explanation was simple. After the fall in price in the early years of the 1920s world stocks of wheat remained around 635 million bushels throughout most of the decade; in 1931 they were 900 million bushels; in 1934 they were 1,140 million bushels. Imports kept British prices in line with those elsewhere. In 1931 wheat prices in Britain were only 75 per cent of what they had been before 1914; those of all cereals were down by similar proportions, though the fall in barley was less steep than those of wheat and oats; the price of store sheep fell by 40 per cent between 1930 and 1931; when there was a good crop of potatoes, as in 1929 and 1931, all could not be sold or fed to stock and so often rotted in their pits.

Once again Scottish farmers had to adapt their policies to competitive international conditions. The only difference, a major one, from the half-century before 1914 was that their short experience of government aid during and immediately after the First World War led many, as in other sectors of the economy, to continue to hope for economic salvation through its reappearance. The hope was realised, at least in part, only in the 1930s.

During the first period, the ten years following the Corn Production (Repeal) Act of 1921, official aid was sporadic and contributed little towards solving the overriding problem of meeting the continuing danger of more foreign imports, but covered many fields. Two cases of aid in 1919 were peripheral to the mainstream of Scottish agriculture: smallholding and afforestation. The policy of encouraging smallholdings started with the objective of providing small but self-supporting units but by the 1930s became more concerned with helping to resettle the unemployed. Afforestation was of much greater importance especially in the long run. The Forestry Commission's relations with Scottish farmers were not always amicable, primarily through disputes over the acquisition of land for afforestation. Part of the difficulty arose through differences in the jurisdictions of the Commission and the Department of Agriculture. When the Commission's powers of acquiring land were transferred to the Secretary of State in 1945, disputes did not end.

Four statutes of the 1920s made more direct contributions to agriculture. Two of the measures were financial, two more technical. For Scotland the financial contributions were more important. They were the Agricultural Rates Act of 1923 which granted some rating relief, made more influential by the complete derating of agricultural land and buildings in 1926 and 1929; and the

Agricultural Credits (Scotland) Acts of 1925 and 1929, which granted credit to the growing number of farmers who were purchasing their own farms as landlords were forced to dispose of them. The more strictly agricultural assistance took the form of annual grants on the basis of a percentage of cost of drainage schemes; and encouragement to the sugar-beet industry in the British Sugar Subsidy Act of 1925. The drainage schemes were aimed at relieving unemployment as well as helping agriculture. Frequently they only patched old systems. Even patching was valuable. Though drainage is necessary in Scotland, given its soil and climate, its long-term benefits lead to its neglect in times of depression. The subsidy to sugar beet was less relevant in Scotland. Its production made some progress only in Fife, which had almost half of Scotland's acreage of over 7,000 in 1938. The soil was often too acid, and the climate prevented the early sowing necessary for a long period of growth and gave inadequate sun for harvesting. Potatoes were generally considered a more rewarding crop until the compulsory growth of sugar beet on many farms during the Second World War taught some farmers the best techniques for its cultivation. Even during the war the maximum under the crop was 140,000 acres in 1942.

These measures of the 1920s did not tackle the crucial issue of imports of foreign produce. They neither tried to restrict them in some way through a form of protection, made much less probable politically in any case by the electorate's rejection of any such policy in 1923, nor with the exception of the drainage grants did they try to make farmers more efficient and so more able to meet their foreign competitors. After the Corn Production (Repeal) Act, 1921, farmers were left to meet their difficulties, as before 1914, on their own resources and initiative. One difference from the pre-war situation was that the landlords were less able to help them to do so. The landlords were the one part of the agricultural community which lost by the war. Political opposition was restricting their power and privileges beforehand. During the war the burden of taxation increased. In 1921, when most of the Agriculture Act of 1920 was repealed, the retention of its provisions for greater security of tenants diminished still further the attraction of holding land to let. As in the depression of the late 1880s and 1890s, landlords were expected to help tenants to maintain profits through remission of rents, though still less able to do so. In any case in most tenancies started before the short period of wartime prosperity rents were so low that landlords were only too anxious to sell when the opportunity arose. A system of land tenure, which, in spite of its defects, had served Scottish agriculture well, especially in encouraging labourers to become tenants, was being brought to an end. Few foresaw the rigid and inflexible structure of domination by owner-occupiers which was to come about. All was not immediately well, however, for those who responded to the opportunity offered by the landlords' increased willingness to sell farms. Many of the new owner-occupiers had to carry a heavy fixed debt charge, which had to be met in spite of falling prices. They were most susceptible to bankruptcy.

Given the similarity of the farmers' problems to those of the years before

1914, it is not surprising that their reactions were also similar. The acreage under grain, which had increased especially during the last two years of the war, made way for more grass, both temporary and permanent, which rose between 1918 and 1932 by 157,000 and 266,000 acres respectively. By the trough of the depression of the early 1930s the acreage under most root and grain crops in Scotland was lower than it had been in 1914. In some cases the reduction was drastic. In 1914, 194,000 acres were under barley, but only 69,000 in 1932, and only 60,000 in 1933. Even the acreage under oats fell from 920,000 in 1914 to 867,000 in 1932 and to 777,000 in 1939. Comparison between the two periods must be qualified. Between the wars livestock husbandry did not retain its relative profitability over arable cultivation. After 1918 the price fall, which was first felt by the wool-growers, soon spread to all products, both livestock and arable. The rise in imports of dairy products from 1919 was as marked as the rise in imports of grain. Moreover, as some of the grain producers put land down to grass, they frequently specialised more in livestock husbandry and dairying, providing yet more competition for those who had long concentrated in these fields.

In the 1920s advances in agricultural practice were the increasing use of wild white clover in grasslands and more scientific poultry husbandry. Neither was new, but their potentialities were only then fully exploited. The increasing use of wild white clover improved rotation pastures and delayed their deterioration sufficiently to support more livestock. It had some disadvantages. In the short run it increased the incidence of intestinal worms in sheep; in the long run its success may have prevented many Scottish farmers from undertaking the more radical and more expensive changes in grassland management which were developed between the wars. The improvement in poultry husbandry was in an altogether different category. In spite of the measure of natural protection from foreign competition given by the perishability of eggs, poultry farming as such hardly existed in Scotland before 1914. Few ordinary farmers regarded it as a serious agricultural enterprise. The main commercial concern of specialist breeders was to produce table, not laying, birds. Scientific poultry farming in Scotland began only in 1906, when a poultry school was established at the Scottish Dairy School by the West of Scotland College of Agriculture. It spread quickly after the war, when the low prices for grain led many farmers to feed it to poultry. In the 1920s and 1930s, new methods of poultry husbandry were introduced, culminating in the 1930s in the introduction of the battery system, an attempt to ensure the maximum returns for each bird by eliminating the least productive.

Such advances of the 1920s were directed no more than the government aid of the same decade to the central problem of meeting foreign competition. In the 1930s, especially after the acceptance of tariffs, increasing government intervention in the economy generally came earlier and was more extensive in agriculture than in most other sectors. A general tariff was impracticable. Not all agricultural products suffered from foreign competition. Government action assumed mainly two forms: first, the Agricultural Marketing Acts of 1931 and

1933, and, second, a variety of measures aimed at granting aid to enterprises in particular adversity.

Generally the marketing acts aimed at satisfying the desire, commonly accepted at the time, that controlled marketing would stabilise, and probably raise, prices. The only Board set up under the first Act was for hops and of no account in Scotland. Those for potatoes, pigs and bacon, and milk, which came under the second Act, were. The most important was for milk. Under the Act of 1933 two regional boards, the Aberdeen and District Milk Marketing Board and the North of Scotland Milk Marketing Board, were formed, as well as the main Scottish Milk Marketing Board. They were not the first agencies of their kind in Scotland. In the 1920s the Scottish Agricultural Organization Society and the Scottish National Farmers' Union had tried to organise similar marketing schemes. The schemes collapsed since they could not retain the allegiance of all producers. The compulsion of the marketing Acts was clearly necessary for success, but the Boards' right to impose levies on every gallon sold by producer-retailers was successfully challenged. The organisation of the Boards, and the effects of their pricing policies on consumers, were frequently criticised. Sometimes the Board's policies had unexpected repercussions. For example, since a chief aim was to maintain the price of liquid milk, the Scottish Board so flooded the English market with milk that it was given compensation of about £100,000 annually to desist. As more Scottish cream was then sent south, and the Aberdeen Board started dumping its surplus milk in the London market, it is doubtful how effective the measure was for English dairy farmers.

The help given to enterprises in difficulty assumed various forms. The Wheat Act of 1932 guaranteed wheat prices by placing an excise duty on flour, which was made mainly from imported grain. It was of slight help to the majority of Scottish farmers, who grew little or no wheat. In 1937, partly under pressure from the Scottish National Farmers' Union, the subsidy was extended to oats and barley. Since oats, unlike wheat, was not generally a cash crop, an acreage payment was substituted for a payment on the price deficiency. In 1932 imports of meat were restricted, but proposals to form a Meat Marketing Board were not followed. Subsidies for beef, granted temporarily in 1934, were made permanent in 1937. Also in 1937 the Agriculture Act included a Land Fertility Scheme, with subsidies for lime and slag. The Scheme encouraged the liming of land in Scotland, so neglected since the 1880s that the growing of barley and other crops was difficult. On the other hand two other activities it encouraged were less relevant to Scottish conditions: one, ley farming, had been commonly practised for years, while the other, the reseeding of permanent pastures, was too expensive, even with the subsidy, to be an economic proposition in Scotland. Because of the particular specialisations of Scottish agriculture, the Milk Marketing Board held out the greatest prospects for Scottish agriculture. Its critics complained that it was insufficiently enterprising to encourage expansion Their view was a special case of a more general objection. Though the various measures represented a change in government action to give special character to the 1930s, they provided only a patchwork of assistance, one which, it could be suggested, aimed mainly at preserving the existing structure of agriculture and not at the development of one more in keeping with the modern pattern of international trade in agricultural products.

Major changes took place in agricultural education and research. Before 1914 expansion had been in the provision of formal instruction in the universities and agricultural colleges; after 1918 it was principally in the number of research stations. Three were of major importance — the Rowett, concerned with nutrition, at Bucksburn; the Macaulay, for soil research, at Aberdeen; and the Hannah Dairy Research Institute at Ayr. Though founded earlier, all made their contribution in the 1930s. Other organisations with similar aims were the Animal Diseases Research Association, the Scottish Society for Research in Plant Breeding, and the Edinburgh Centre of Rural Economy. Through these institutes, and through the Agricultural Colleges' Advisory Officers, a system of advice on the latest scientific knowledge, as it could be applied in his own area, was made available to every individual farmer. It provided a more permanent basis for the future of agriculture in the changed international trade in agricultural products of the twentieth century.

The Highlands

In the fifty years before 1914 better transport and the breaking down of linguistic barriers brought about by changes in education led to greater assimilation of Highlands and Lowlands. Though the railways did not penetrate the Highlands extensively, their influence, where they did go, was great; government assistance continued to be given to the roads as in the past; shipping was subsidised from 1891, the subsidy being converted into a payment for mails in 1897; better education came after 1872 when the Scottish Education Act placed responsibility for it on the state. The opportunities opened by such assimilation often attracted the Highlander from his native region. Population continued to fall, by about 10 per cent in the crofting counties between 1881 and 1911. The fall was concentrated in the younger age groups, which contain the potential migrants. The Highlands and Islands became inhabited by an increasingly ageing population. Such a population was less likely to be able to tackle the problem which had long faced the Highlands. It remained the struggle, by individuals and by the entire region, to earn adequate cash income to pay for essential imports. For most the natural resources were insufficient to provide adequate subsistence.

From the 1870s to 1914 the forces making for agricultural change in the Highlands were broadly similar to those elsewhere. Land was converted from arable cultivation to pasture except in areas, such as Lewis, where population pressure was intense. In the Highlands the switch had wider repercussions. The cattle trade, once such an important source of revenue for the area, retained only local customers, and sheep-farming, introduced especially in the century before the 1870s, was no longer so profitable. The decline of the cattle trade had appeared before the 1870s. The adoption of better and more modern methods gave other areas a lead over the Highlands. The loss of the sheep trade, which came after the 1870s, especially after the 1890s, was initiated by the fall in agricultural prices, but several explanations lay behind it. The pastures were unable to support as many sheep as before. The grass on the old arable land had become fogged, or choked with weeds, while restrictions placed on heather-burning and the absence of cattle-grazing caused further deterioration. The sheep, too, contributed by spending the nights on the higher and drier pastures, and so removing some of the manure which the lower grazings urgently required. About 1880 it was estimated that in some areas, such as Sutherland, the grazings were adequate for only about two-thirds of what they had supported forty years earlier. A partial remedy was to winter the animals on the fertile east coast, but doing so was more expensive. Sheepfarming was already in a precarious position when a further sharp fall in sheep prices after 1890 precipitated a social as well as an economic crisis in some areas. Deer forests had increased earlier, even at times when sheep prices were maintained, but from the 1880s their expansion gained momentum. Sheep and deer could not easily exist together. When sheep-farming became less profitable, many landlords were willing to clear land to make way for sporting rights, as they commanded a higher return from those to whom the delights of the Highlands had just been revealed by Queen Victoria. The area of deer forests rose from about 2,000,000 acres in the mid-1880s to a peak of over 3,500,000 acres in 1912. By then one-third of the land had been made over to forests in the five counties of Argyll, Caithness, Inverness, Ross and Cromarty, and Sutherland. In the same period their total number of sheep fell from a peak of slightly over 2,400,000 in 1891 to just under 1,950,000 in 1914, while the number in the rest of Scotland fell from 5,220,000 to only 5,078,000.

In these conditions initiative for any remedial actions passed increasingly into the hands of the state, especially in the 1880s when violent resistance to eviction by crofters and occupation of land forced political action. The entire Highland problem was investigated by a Royal Commission which reported in 1884. In spite of the forces which had long encouraged greater assimilation with the Lowlands, the Napier Commission found the Highlander's position very similar to what it had been a century earlier. In two respects his condition differed materially from that of the Lowlander. First, tenancies were insecure and provided no incentive to improve the land, especially when there were no proper arrangements for compensation. Second, subdivision under population pressure left many holdings too small for efficient agricultural practice. The Napier Commission suggested remedial action in both directions. First, it recommended leases designed to encourage improvements, for which compensation would be given whenever the lease was terminated. Second, it advocated the legal recognition, and, normally, the perpetuation of the township as the unit of organisation most suitable for encouraging and ensuring improvements. The Commission recognised that within the township further disintegration of holdings had to be avoided and every effort made to increase their size. It recommended that when smaller holdings fell vacant, they should be consolidated with others, and that further subdivision should be prevented. Finally, one overriding qualification to all the Commission's recommendations was its suggestion that they should be applied only to the minority paying £6 a year or more in rent. Only from this group of the relatively more substantial tenants would any improvements come; the remainder of the tenantry could not be accommodated in an improved and stable economy.

To some the Napier Commission's report was a ruthless document; to others it was realistic in its acceptance of the impossibility of continuing to maintain 'the load of tenantry', with which Highland estates had been burdened for so long. Since the report was not wholly acceptable, the legislation which followed, the Crofters Holdings (Scotland) Act of 1886, failed to implement all its recommendations. Underlying all the suggestions of the Napier Commission was the belief that the Highland economy could survive only with drastic changes. In effect the Act of 1886 rejected this assumption and virtually froze the existing structure, especially through the grant of perpetual tenancy, with the Land Court fixing rents if necessary. Unlike the recommendations of the Napier Commission, the Act of 1886 preserved rather than changed. The exception was its creation of the Crofters' Commission, which was given powers to enlarge holdings, and later the power to create new ones. Otherwise the Act assumed that legislation should protect the position of the individual crofter rather than provide the environment in which more efficient and effective crofting could become possible. The social consequences of doing so were deemed politically inexpedient.

In these circumstances it is not surprising that the problem was not solved. Another Royal Commission was appointed in 1892, followed in 1897 by legislation in the Congested Districts (Scotland) Act. The Act of 1886 granted security of tenure but failed to provide more land for crofters, except through the very limited powers granted to the Crofters' Commission. The Act of 1897 instituted the Congested Districts Board, charged to provide more land for the enlargement of holdings and for the creation of new ones, and to develop subsidiary industries, such as fishing and weaving, which would supply the necessary cash supplements to the income — mainly in kind, and in itself inadequate — which could be obtained in crofting. Though the second Act helped to remedy some of the deficiencies of the first, the guarantee of individual tenures made an overall renovation of the economy unlikely. Such security made drastic changes, always difficult to achieve in Highland society, even more intractable. In spite of the benefits given to crofters, along lines they themselves advocated, depopulation continued. From 1891 to 1911 the population of the crofting counties fell from 360,367 to 341,535. Tillage and livestock in most crofting parishes also fell.

The next statutory attempt to provide a remedy came in 1911 with the passage of the Small Landholders (Scotland) Act. Its most important consequence for the Highlands came later, and indirectly, through a peculiar legal decision of 1917.[1] Until 1914 most of the changes which affected the Highlands were only of administrative importance. The Act set up the Board of Agriculture for Scotland, which in 1929 became the Department of Agriculture for Scotland and assumed the land settlement powers previously vested in the Crofters' Commission and the Congested Districts Board. The origin of the Act lay less in the belief that the creation of smallholdings on the model of certain European countries was a way of providing the intensive cultivation which could meet the agricultural depression. In the Highlands it simply encouraged the policy first evolved in 1886. The Highland problem remained as unsolved in 1914 as it had been a century earlier. Greater security of tenure had been provided. In the eyes of those who wished to see a drastic enlargement and consolidation of holdings it was much too great, and it certainly failed to arrest emigration. The problem had to be tackled yet again after 1918, by which time a legal decision under the Act of 1911 had made a solution no easier. The decision was made in 1917 in the case of Rogerson *v.* Chilston. The Act of 1911 provided a new definition of the term 'crofter', and the courts interpreted it to mean — though the meaning was almost certainly unintentional — that crofters did not need to live on their holdings. The decision introduced a race of absentee crofters into the Highlands. Until then the various statutes and attempts to deal with the Highland problem had aimed at making more land available for the genuine crofter. After 1917 land held by an absentee was not used to give the maximum production, as it was frequently sublet to a resident crofter only for grazing, and indeed was often not cultivated at all. The absentee crofter was as harmful as any absentee landlord. He helped to ensure the continuation of the decline in cultivation, and, with the exception of sheep, in the number of livestock.

After the First World War such policies as affected the Highlands were often primarily concerned with encouraging land settlement generally, especially smallholding, then considered both an acceptable form of agricultural development and a suitable method of settling ex-servicemen. Under the Land Settlement (Scotland) Act, 1919, 1,344 new holdings were formed, and 1,179 were enlarged in the crofting counties in the 1920s, but in the 1930s there were only 234 new holdings and 238 enlargements. It was a minor, and largely ineffective, attempt to deal with the situation. The continuing decline in tillage and in population, both human and livestock, was a sure indication that the Highland problem was as unsolved in 1939 as it had been in 1914 or even in 1815. The new statutory provisions of the close of the nineteenth century provided some encouragement to Highland development, notably in the improvement of housing, which had long been a disgraceful feature of Highland society. Cattle and people all lived in squalid conditions, practically under the same roof, until security of tenure and compensation for improvements under the Act of 1886 encouraged those who could afford to do so to improve their own dwellings. Since many, especially among the cottars, could not, the medical officers of health of various crofting counties requested special aid to encourage housing improvements. Some of their recommendations were elementary precepts of public health, that, for instance, the local authorities should grant loans to help replace with sanitary dwellings those black houses whose inhabitants were infected by various diseases, and especially with typhus. The Local Government Board finally decided in 1895 that there was no possibility of national funds being made available for such purposes. Eventually only legal action against crofters at the end of the century initiated some more general improvement.

NOTES

1. See p. 223.

CHAPTER XV

Social Assimilation

Population

Though the population of Scotland continued to grow until after the First World War, the very high rates of growth of the earliest decades of the nineteenth century were not repeated. In the twentieth century the rates of increase were much lower and the population fell in the 1920s:

Population of Scotland (000s)

		Percentage increase
1871	3,360.0	9.7
1881	3,735.6	11.2
1891	4,025.6	7.8
1901	4,472.1	11.1
1911	4,760.9	6.5
1921	4,882.5	2.6
1931	4,843.0	−0.8
1951	5,096.4	5.2
1961	5,179.3	1.6
1971	5,229.0	1.0
1981	5,130.7	−1.9

As in earlier decades, the increases were achieved in spite of net losses through migration. The 1880s saw a net loss of 217,000 or 43 per cent of the natural increase. Only the 1890s were lower. In the first decade of the twentieth century the net loss was 254,000; between 1911 and 1921 it was 239,000; or 47 and 66 per cent of the natural increase respectively. After the First World War came a major change. In the 1920s the net movement outward of 392,000 exceeded the natural increase and the population fell. In the early 1930s a net inward movement from countries overseas was more than counterbalanced by net movement to England, and, as the inward movement from overseas declined in the later 1930s, the trend of the 1920s seemed to be reappearing just before the Second World War.

One change from the earlier nineteenth century which influenced the balance of migration was the decline in Irish settlement in Scotland. The 1881 census registered 219,000 Irish-born in Scotland, the largest number recorded. By 1931 the Irish had been supplanted by the English as the most important group of immigrants. At the census of that year 3.4 per cent of the population of Scotland had been born in England, but only 2.6 per cent had been born in Ireland.

The overall rate of growth was composed of very different contributions from the regions. Between 1871 and 1931 the population of the counties of Ayr, Bute, Dunbarton and Renfrew increased by 85 per cent; of the three Lothians by 61 per cent; of Stirling and Clackmannan by 62 per cent; of Angus, Fife, Kinross and Perth by 27 per cent; of Aberdeen, Banff, Kincardine, Moray and Nairn by 12 per cent. The remaining areas of Scotland registered a decrease in population: that of the seven crofting counties fell most sharply of all, by 21 per cent; of Dumfries, Kirkcudbright and Wigtown by 10 per cent; and of the Border counties of Berwick, Peebles, Selkirk and Roxburgh by 6 per cent. The increase in population in the later nineteenth century was still concentrated in central and west Scotland. The experience of Lanarkshire was, however, most striking. It maintained the increase of its population, though at a diminished rate, until the Second World War. In 1931 its population of 1,586,047 was 46,625 greater than it had been a decade earlier. In 1931 other adjacent counties, such as Ayrshire, Dunbartonshire and Renfrewshire, all of which had shared in the population rise earlier, registered decreases in population. Lanarkshire was not unique in recording an increase in population between 1921 and 1931, but among the other counties which did so — Dumfries, Midlothian, Roxburgh, Selkirk and Stirling — it was significant only in Midlothian, where the population increased between the two censuses by 19,919 to a total of 526,296, and to a lesser extent in Dumfries. The declining rate of growth of population was general throughout Scotland, even though its incidence varied. On the other hand, since the sharpest decreases were registered in agricultural areas, principally the more remote, especially the Highlands, the declining rate of growth in the industrial areas did not arrest the existing trend for Scots to become urban dwellers. The two counties which recorded the main increases — Lanark and Midlothian — had the two main conurbations. Even the small towns of the rural areas which were losing population frequently grew.

Housing

The growth of urban Scotland with its high population density gave rise to some of the worst housing in Europe, but the need for improvement was equally pressing in the mining districts and in areas of rural depopulation, such as the Highlands, where the inadequacy of income and employment brought similar dereliction to existing inferior housing. The improvement of housing standards became a leading aspect of social policy in modern Scotland. In some ways too it was unique. Scottish housing retained several indigenous features of architecture and law, which ensured a distinctive if often unenviable reputation, even when statutory provisions were determined by a British parliament according to the concepts of an increasingly comprehensive welfare state.

The problem had many facets. In several booms before 1914, tenements of three, four or five storeys were most commonly built, and into them crowded the population of the towns. Since many kept lodgers — 23.3 per cent in

Glasgow and 23.1 per cent in Edinburgh in 1871 — overcrowding increased still more. Many had small houses, or flats. In 1871, 32.5 per cent of the houses in Scotland had only one room and 37.6 per cent had only two rooms; by 1901 the proportions were 17.6 and 39.9 per cent; by 1911 they were 12.8 and 40.4 per cent. The smaller houses need not necessarily have been overcrowded, but they were. In 1911, 56 per cent of one-roomed houses had more than two persons in each room; so had 47 per cent of those with two rooms and 24 per cent of those with three. The deficiencies were more evident when compared with conditions in England, where in the First World War only 7.1 per cent of the population were living in one- and two-roomed houses against 47.9 per cent in Scotland. The difference could not be explained by the average size of room being larger in Scotland, perhaps by as much as 20 per cent, a benefit which was, in any case, offset by most English houses possessing good sculleries. The Royal Commission on the Housing of the Industrial Population of Scotland of 1918 pointed out that, if the standard of overcrowding adopted by the Registrar-General for England and Wales, of more than two persons to a room, were applied in Scotland, 2,077,277 people, or 45.1 per cent of the population, were living in overcrowded conditions. If the excess, as determined by this standard, had been removed from their existing houses, 695,842 people would have required rehousing. The result of such overcrowding was especially marked in Glasgow, where the density of persons per acre in 1911 was about twice that in Dundee and Edinburgh. Between 1871 and 1914 even Glasgow registered some improvement. The peak density, of 94 persons to the acre, was in 1871; in 1881, it was 84; in 1891, it was up again to 93; thereafter there came a sharp change, and in 1901 and 1911 the density was 60 persons per acre. Further falls between the wars reduced the densities to 54 and 36 persons to the acre in the two census years of 1921 and 1931, and to 27 to the acre in 1951.[1]

Until 1891 alterations to houses could be carried out without any possibility of control by the local authorities so long as the structure was not affected, but the worst overcrowding did not arise in the subdivision of houses, typical of areas which had known better days, but in tenements, which contained all the deplorable, and frequently criticised, features of Scottish building: inadequate light and ventilation, sunk or basement flats, box-beds, shared toilets on stairheads, and others. Several factors explain the perpetuation of the tenement, but one frequently forgotten is that it was often the form of housing chosen by many. In his evidence to the Royal Commission of 1918 a Glasgow builder, though personally not in favour of tenements, suggested they had seven main attractions: tenements were substantially constructed and so gave better protection against adverse weather conditions; they enabled their occupants to live nearer to their work; some tenants were further from damp ground and less liable to suffer from choked drains; since tenement flats did not have stairs they were more easily looked after; there were fewer burglaries in tenements, and so there was greater security for those living alone; good-sized apartments, more usual in tenements, could be let more easily; the death-rate among tenement dwellers was as low as among cottage residents. These compensatory advantages ensured the continued adoption in Scotland of a form of building which led inevitably to a high density of people. They also show that high density, without any qualifications, gives an erroneous impression of the disadvantages of Scottish housing. To some extent density was high by choice.

The acceptance of low standards helps to explain why concern over the state of Scottish housing became general only in the twentieth century. Early attempts to effect improvement through co-operative enterprise took two forms: first, the modern type of building society, more frequently and more accurately known in Scotland in the nineteenth century as property investment societies; second, associations, more literally deserving the name of building societies, which were concerned not only with the financing of the building of houses, but with their construction, whether for the members of the association or for others. The earliest of the first group, the property investment societies, date from the early nineteenth century and were often mutual societies lasting only long enough to achieve a certain limited objective. Many were encouraged to become permanent through changes in their legal status later in the nineteenth century. From the 1870s they prospered through their popularity with Scottish investors. By 1892 Scotland had some 68 societies, with total funds of about £1,000,000, though the trend which has continued, for the movement to be dominated by English societies, was then appearing. Such success was not reflected in an improvement in Scottish housing conditions. The societies mobilised small savings to encourage house-ownership rather than house-building, but not normally among the most inadequately housed. The contribution to construction of the second group, the co-operative societies of various kinds, was greater, though their effectiveness was also diminished when they came to be regarded as safe investments for small savers, and so when they ceased to be as concerned with the provision of accommodation for those who needed it most of all. In origin the early societies were mainly philanthropic ventures of the early and mid-nineteenth century and were frequently the means by which such housing reformers as Robert Cranston, or the Free Church leader, the Rev. Dr James Begg, implemented their ideas. They could be classified as genuinely co-operative ventures with the registration of the Edinburgh Co-operative Building Company, which erected buildings at Canonmills, Abbeyhill, and elsewhere in the city. Once again the contribution to solving the housing shortage lessened as they became property investment societies. Since many of them also built houses for their own subscribers or for sale, they did not provide a major addition to the stock of houses to let, which was the greatest need of the times.

Scottish public opinion was so inured to the existence of poor housing that it was not easily roused by co-operative ventures or other action. As early as the 1870s *The Glasgow Herald* campaigned vigorously against housing conditions in the mining districts. The public was impressed but little positive action resulted. Any private inactivity was not made good by public action. Less official concern was expressed over Scottish than over English conditions: the Royal Commission on Housing of 1884 ignored conditions in Scotland; at the end of the nineteenth century official plans for housing agricultural workers placed a bed in the kitchen in the Scottish plans, but not in those for England. The feebleness of official action in Scotland was also evident by comparison with the greater success in dealing with other social problems. Worse still, improvements in housing in certain areas in Scotland confirmed the ineffectiveness of action in others. Failure was most striking in the mining districts. At the beginning of the twentieth century the Scottish Miners' Federation led an agitation for improvement. Deputations met the Secretary for Scotland in 1909 and 1911, and in the following year the Royal Commission on the Housing of the Industrial Population of Scotland was appointed. Its investigations, culminating in its report of 1918, made continued complacency difficult.

Action was impeded by the disillusionment which followed the failure of some early attempts at improvement. Their basis was the Public Health (Scotland) Act of 1867, supplemented by the appropriate powers for remedial action with which local authorities armed themselves after the example of Glasgow's City Improvement Act of 1866. Edinburgh obtained an Improvement Act in the following year, 1867, and Dundee in 1871. Among the smaller burghs Greenock led by purchasing land under a Local Housing Act of 1875. The experience of the Glasgow Improvement Trust, the pioneer and with one of the most difficult situations to tackle, is most instructive. Its activities were limited by two related factors: the inadequacy of finance and the impossibility of integrating a policy of demolition with one of construction and development. Disputes appeared first, and quickly, over finance. In the first year the maximum rate of 6d. in the £ authorised by the City Improvement Act of 1867 was imposed. The opposition it engendered hindered the Trust's effectiveness, especially when after the first five years of operation the assessment was limited to 3d. The Trust had to concentrate on less expensive action and so could not link its policy of demolition to the more expensive one of construction. To demolish and not to construct was to provide only half a solution. Nevertheless, the Trust cleared nearly 15,500 houses between 1870 and 1874. Its efforts were supplemented by the Street Improvements Act of 1873 and by the railway companies' clearance of some areas, such as the widening of the Trongate for Glasgow Cross station. The result was the removal of some of the worst slums in the city. On the other hand, the demolition of a large number of properties, without the provision of adequate substitutes, increased overcrowding in the remainder. Some of the worst-housed citizens of Glasgow were displaced rather than rehoused. They spread from the old nucleus at Glasgow Cross into Gorbals, Cowcaddens and other districts, which then began to decline socially. On the favourable side, the move frequently implied better housing for the incomers, though often only at a higher rent. Worse followed. Inadequate finance kept the Improvement Trust from continuing its policy of clearance, leaving it the owner of some of Glasgow's worst slums, bought originally for demolition, and which, because of the anticipated shortness of their life, were not even maintained in the state of decay they had already reached. The limitations imposed by financial stringency became clearer after 1895, when the

Trust became self-supporting for the first time. Since its work could then expand, additional powers were obtained in a new Act of 1897.

For the years of relative failure the unwillingness of some of the wealthier citizens of Glasgow to spend must be blamed, but not entirely. Another factor contributing to the Trust's financial difficulties was the inability, or reluctance, of many of the worst-housed in Glasgow to pay higher rents to finance improvements in housing. The problem was not unique to Glasgow, but was common throughout Scotland. It offered an explanation of a striking aspect of Scottish housing, that overcrowding was common even when houses were unoccupied. In Glasgow in 1911 more than one house in ten was empty. Though the proportion varied with wages and employment, and had been under five per cent at the beginning of the century, competition for tenants between landlords inhibited increases in rents. Any unwillingness to pay more for better housing, with the resulting acceptance of poor living standards, had to be changed before any improvement could be brought about. Doing so was a major social problem, which called forth suggestions for a variety of methods of dealing with intractable tenants, from the 'licensed lodging house, the poorhouse, the lunatic asylum, the infirmary, the labour colony, [to] the jail'. It may have been comforting to the wealthier elements in society to imagine that all those who were badly housed fell into this category, but there were others, the 'decent poor', and some who were anxious to mend their ways, perhaps under supervision, to whom little help was given. Their position became increasingly difficult in the later nineteenth century, when rents did not follow the fall in most prices. Even the poor lodger was given greater help when the Improvement Trust constructed lodging-houses. The demand of poor prospective tenants for decent houses was met only in the 1890s, but not resolutely. Though Glasgow Corporation had built over 2,000 houses by 1909, only 28 per cent were reserved for the poorest class of tenant. By 1914 houses were being built as well as demolished, but they were not always the type most desperately required socially. The slums were being cleared, but decent and sanitary substitutes at low rents were not being provided.

The failure of municipal action in Glasgow was striking because of the immensity of the city's problem. By comparison, many other local authorities were even more backward. As late as 19 June 1914 the Housing Committee of Ayr County Council had only reached the stage of passing a resolution that 'privies should have doors and seats'.[2] All had to face the opposition of those who denied the responsibility, or even right, of local authorities to engage in economic enterprise, but any denial of the right of public bodies to enter into competition with private house builders was applicable in practice only in the provision of houses for those with higher incomes, and even there, where the possibilities of profitable construction were greatest, the achievements of private enterprise were not great. The majority report of the Royal Commission on Scottish Housing had no doubt on the matter:

> private enterprise was practically the only agency that undertook the building of

houses, and most of the troubles which we have been investigating are due to the failure of private enterprise to provide and maintain the necessary houses sufficient in quantity and quality.[3]

The condemnation of the private builders cannot, however, be total. The provision of working-class dwellings was not an economic proposition. Though elaborate dwellings were not required, costs could not be lowered significantly, especially in cities where land was expensive. The cost of labour and building materials rose by 25 per cent between 1905 and 1914. When the costs of construction were combined with the reluctance of many to pay a reasonable rent, the problem was virtually insoluble by the private builder. His fault was in claiming that he could solve it. On the other hand, those who advocated public enterprise underestimated or sometimes failed to see the social implications of their policy. Public enterprise could solve the problem only if allowed to levy sufficient rates to make good any deficit which might arise from the reluctance or inability of some tenants to pay an economic rent. Before 1914 the pressure to restrict expenditure made those who were anxious to see better housing for all aware of this reluctance and ready to suggest remedies, most of which were neglected after 1918 in favour of more generous financial provisions to subsidise rents. While removing the bottleneck that had inhibited much action before 1914, the new policy brought difficulties in its train. Until the 1890s, and even to 1914, slums were being demolished, but inadequate housing was provided for their former denizens. After 1918 it is not so certain that the first, and undoubtedly favourable, aspect of this judgement was as applicable.

The dispute over the ability of public and private enterprise to remedy the housing situation appeared in sharp focus in the reports of the Royal Commission on the Housing of the Industrial Population of Scotland. Its members split on the issue. The majority held that action mainly by local authorities was necessary; the minority held that all forms of enterprise should be employed, and that some form of assistance should be given to private builders. The majority realised, in a way no one had previously fully appreciated, the immensity of the problem to be tackled in Scotland, and that local authorities, though not above criticism, had been given inadequate powers. Since they considered that private enterprise had been given the opportunity to provide adequate housing before 1914 but had failed, the majority, in effect, proposed a new and radical solution. By contrast, the view of the minority was, to say the least, optimistic, but they understood some of the long-run difficulties inherent in the majority's recommendation of relying heavily on the local authorities, and even envisaged the political problems which would arise from the voting powers of municipal tenants. The difference of opinion revealed by the two reports was portentous for the future of Scottish local politics.

Both majority and minority reports shared one defect in their almost total failure to recognise the possible reluctance of Scots to pay higher rents, so that the overcrowded conditions in which so many Scots lived could be the consequence of their choice, as were the tenements in which many lived. Overcrowding was not the result of an absolute shortage in the stock of houses. Bigger and better, though more expensive, houses were available for working-class families. A general and permanent improvement in housing could have been obtained by many families if the proportion of 8 per cent of family income spent on rent in Scotland had been increased to the English proportion of 10 per cent. To rely on the efforts of private builders for an improvement in housing under such conditions was unrealistic. There was not a large and unsatisfied effective demand for housing in Scotland, and, more surprising than any failure by private builders to erect houses was their willingness to continue to do so even in the face of a surplus of unoccupied accommodation. To provide better housing for those unable or unwilling to pay a higher proportion of their incomes in rent, private builders had to allow their profit margins to be reduced, or cut altogether, which was impracticable, or public authorities had to build the houses and subsidise rents. The majority report of 1918 failed to appreciate this necessary implication of the policy of public action which it advocated.

In such conditions rent restriction worked still more against the private builder of houses to let. The peculiar system of Scottish rating, by which rates were paid jointly by owner and by occupier until placed on the latter in 1957 by the Valuation and Rating (Scotland) Act, 1956, ensured that the rent restriction Acts were more detrimental in Scotland than in England. Before 1914 owners' rates were normally passed on to the tenant through an increase in rents. On the other hand, until 1957 the rateable value was determined by the rent charged. Therefore, an owner could achieve a given increase in rent only by raising rent by a sum sufficient to give him both the desired increase in rent *and* an amount sufficient to pay for the additional rates payment for which he would become liable through the resulting increase in the rateable value of the property. The Rent Restriction Act of 1920 closed even this limited possibility of an increase by fixing the rent of a controlled house (those under £45 rateable value) at 140 per cent of the 1914 rent plus any increase in owner's rates between 1914 and 1920 only. Any later increase in owner's, though not in occupier's rates, lowered the net return to the owner. Through such legislation property owning became a still less profitable proposition, and remained so, with only slight re-laxations in restrictions, until the Second World War, when the restrictions were imposed on houses with rateable values of up to £90. Since the Scottish rating system operated adversely only after the First World War, its effect on the deficiencies of Scottish housing was limited. As the Royal Commission of 1918 amply demonstrated, the situation was bad even before 1914. Between the wars rent restriction and the rating system were only additional deterrents to private builders of houses to rent, but they discouraged the maintenance of existing property in good condition.

Between the wars responsibility for remedial action fell increasingly on public authorities. In these years the proportion of houses built by public enterprise in Scotland was greater than in England and Wales, although, per head of population, the total number of houses built in the two areas was only marginally in England's favour. Of the 337,000 houses built in Scotland between the wars, 67 per cent were built by public authorities, compared with only 25 per cent of the 4,194,000 houses built in England and Wales. By the 1970s some of the older industrial burghs — Airdrie, Kilsyth, Coatbridge, Lochgelly, Motherwell, Port Glasgow — had over 70 per cent of their population in council houses, compared with less than 20 per cent in Largs, Bishopbriggs, Peebles and Bearsden.

The scope for action by public authorities remained restricted by Scots still giving house-room a relatively low claim on their budgets. According to the Ministry of Labour's investigations into the budgets of working-class households between the wars, 9.1 per cent of the total expenditure of Scottish households was on rent and rates compared with 12.7 per cent for Great Britain as a whole. Under such conditions housing needs, as judged by any reasonable social criterion, could be met only by some form of subsidy. One other effect of the changed responsibility for the construction of houses to let was that the tenement, which had been the chief form of house construction before 1914, was built only occasionally after 1918 and in construction stone gave way to brick. Even with public action, Scotland remained the worst-housed area of the United Kingdom. By the standards of overcrowding applied under the Housing Act of 1935 almost one in every four of Scottish houses was overcrowded, compared with only one in every twenty-six in England and Wales. By 1939 housing was still Scotland's major social problem.

After 1945, when responsibility for action was assumed almost wholly by the local authorities, increased construction reached its peak in 1953, with an output of 39,548 houses, an achievement which must be modified by the recognition that it represented only a small addition (about 3 per cent) to the existing stock, much of which was being allowed to deteriorate through rent restriction rendering even the maintenance of property to let by private landlords an uneconomic proposition. While the post-war years witnessed remarkable improvements in public health — such as the virtual elimination of diphtheria and a marked reduction in tuberculosis — the state of housing remained a major social problem. Fortunately there were improvements. In 1931, 44 per cent of the people of Scotland lived in houses with one or two rooms, but in 1951 only 29.7 per cent; in the two badly housed cities of Glasgow and Dundee the reduction between 1931 and 1951 was from 55.4 to 41.5 per cent and 56.2 to 39.4 per cent respectively; to relieve the pressure in the most grossly overcrowded districts, New Towns were planned at East Kilbride, Glenrothes, Cumbernauld and Livingston, while arrangements were made for the surplus of Glasgow's population to 'overspill' into other towns. In the late 1950s Glasgow began a scheme of urban renewal. In the next fifteen years some quarter of a million dwellings were demolished, but, in spite of rebuilding, especially of high-rise flats until the mid-1960s, and a falling population, conditions in the city were low when tested by any standards. The lack of achievement since the 1950s should lead to a less critical assessment of the achievements of the past.

The poor law

As with much social policy, modern statutory provision submerged the characteristic features of the Scottish poor law in a wider framework in which English ideas and practices often dominated. The Scottish poor law may have been mean and niggardly but claimed to be concerned with all aspects of destitution. Its traditional concern with the relief of the sick had led in the work of the medical reformers of the earlier nineteenth century to more comprehensive social care and concern. In the later nineteenth century a narrower conception of relief emerged, especially when the Public Health (Scotland) Act of 1867 placed responsibility for improving public health on the Board of Supervision. The Board was more concerned with the relief of actual destitution than with its prevention or with preventive medicine in general. Its instructions to its officers in 1869, after the passing of the new Public Health Act, confirmed its priorities:

> The Board do not wish you, at present, to make such regular and minute inspection of your district with reference to its sanitary condition, as would seriously interfere with your ordinary duties as General Superintendent of Poor.

Since the peak of pauperism in Scotland, of nearly 42 paupers per 1,000 of the population, was in 1868, the Board's concern may be appreciated, but it ensured that the desire to reduce costs became a leading principle in the administration of the poor law. It, more than any reduction of poverty by better public health, or by improved nutritional standards, explains the reduction in the incidence of pauperism to about 24 per 1,000 of the population, at which level it remained until there was a further drop to about 21 per 1,000 after the removal of those who became entitled to old age pensions in 1911.

Though concern with cost was general, sometimes the lower rungs of the administration adopted a more liberal attitude to relief. The House of Lords finally decided in 1864 that neither an able-bodied man nor his family were entitled to relief under any circumstances, but it was often given by parochial boards, some of them advocating a change in the law. Again, until the twentieth century the Board of Supervision opposed granting outdoor relief to the mothers of illegitimate children, but its recommendations were often flatly ignored or rejected by parochial boards, which criticised the Board's policy for so deterring mothers from applying for relief that it implied subsequent suffering, and even death, for the children. The great bone of contention was, however, over the use of an offer of admission to the poorhouse as a test of the good faith of an applicant's request for relief. The rigidity of the Board of Supervision's policy became evident in circulars sent to parochial boards advocating this policy in 1878, 1883 and 1887, and in the Board's officers frequently trying to follow up the pressure locally, though not always successfully.

In spite of such differences of opinion the administration of the poor law in Scotland witnessed no major changes in the latter half of the nineteenth century.

Though a number of amending bills were introduced into parliament in its last quarter, none was passed, and the parochial boards continued to administer relief under the general surveillance of the Board of Supervision until 1894, when responsibility was assumed by the parish councils, and the powers of the Board of Supervision were transferred to the Local Government Board. In practice the change had little effect. In the nineteenth century parochial authorities found additional sources of dispute with higher authorities emerging through the creation of new specialised authorities, charged with the supervision of some aspect of public welfare, such as the care and isolation of those suffering from infectious diseases. The general responsibilities of local authorities hindered the effective discharge of specialised functions, which more modern conceptions of welfare advocated. The dispute foreshadowed the one which emerged in the report of the Royal Commission on the Poor Laws in 1909, when the minority recommended the dismemberment of the old poor law administration into specialised services responsible for different aspects of welfare. By then, though a few aspects of the poor law still had distinctly Scottish features, its administration, and the problems of social welfare generally, were cast in a British mould. With one major exception of housing policy, the rise of the welfare state was not a uniquely Scottish affair.

Trade unions

'The Scottish trade union movement is not, nor with a few possible exceptions, does it wish to be, completely separate and divided from its counterpart in the rest of the United Kingdom.'[4] By the later nineteenth century the truth of this statement of the early 1950s was already apparent. Assimilation became common with the growth of political action by the unions, a policy of which the Scots generally approved.

Until the end of the nineteenth century small unions, generally covering only a restricted geographical area and with limited funds, were typical of the organisation of Scottish trade unions. They were limited in effectiveness. The heavy industries employed about one-third of all Scottish trade unionists, but union membership was only 25 per cent of the possible total and was distributed among small and frequently ineffective societies. Even the well-organised and more powerful — among them the British Steel Smelters Amalgamated Association, formed in 1888, and the Associated Society of Millmen, formed two years later — failed to achieve many major gains. An increase in power and strength was accompanied by decreasing control and direction from Scotland. The British Steel Smelters Amalgamated Association extended its activities to the north of England and transferred its head office from Motherwell to Manchester, and its leader, John Hodge, became a national as well as a Scottish figure. Success implied assimilation with movements south of the border.

Once again many of the struggles, achievements and failures of the trade union movement in Scotland were illustrated most clearly by the experience of the miners. Just as the Scottish miners gave the British labour movement a leader in the middle of the nineteenth century in Alexander McDonald, so towards the end of the century they produced another in James Keir Hardie. Hardie's efforts to build up a national union followed lines similar to those laid down by McDonald, though he broke with McDonald's resistance to much state intervention and steered the miners towards specifically socialist policies. His attempts to do so seem to have attracted greatest support among the Roman Catholic miners of Lanarkshire, whose presence had given rise to the sectarian strife which had so often disrupted earlier organisations.

The incidence of the collapse of the local organisations varied after 1874. In Lanarkshire, where there was general resistance to wage cuts, the men lost ground and had to accept the cuts proposed. By contrast, in Fife a lock-out was defeated, at least in part, in 1877. Unlike the miners in Lanarkshire, those in Fife received outside support, and their action was more in accordance with the organised effort suggested by McDonald to the Lanarkshire miners, but rejected by them. By 1880 the only county union which survived was the Fife and Kinross Miners' Association.

The first step towards a united organisation came in 1886 with the formation of the Scottish Miners' National Federation with Keir Hardie as its secretary. Though the Federation was short-lived, and mainly only a propaganda body, it encouraged the formation of more local unions. Better organisations came through following English examples and by uniting with English movements until the formation in 1894 of the Scottish Miners' Federation, immediately affiliated to the Miners' Federation of Great Britain. On the basis of the new-found strength in unity, a strike was called in June 1894. It brought out most Scottish miners, even though only one in three was a member of a union, and ended completely in October, when most returned to work on the employers' terms. Its failure did not interrupt moves towards greater contact with the south and towards large-scale organisation. Both — and the tendency to use opportunities thus provided for the establishment of more direct socialist representation in political life — were encouraged when Robert Smillie, of the Larkhall Miners' Association, built up the local unions of Lanarkshire, and then of the whole of Scotland, to become by the end of the nineteenth century the first leader of the Scottish miners accepted in any way comparable to his predecessor from Lanarkshire, Alexander McDonald.

In the late nineteenth century the guiding light in the miners' struggle was the attempt to break from the sliding scale, which related movements in wages to movements in the price of coal, towards a minimum wage. Only on condition that their demand was granted were the miners willing to accept a Conciliation Board in 1899. The Board took wages in 1888 (roughly about 4s. a day) as the standard which it long remained, and accepted a minimum wage of 3¼ per cent above the 1888 basis and a maximum wage of 75 per cent above it, or 5s. 3d. and 7s. The history of the Conciliation Board was not smooth. The coalmasters sought to have the minimum wage reduced, especially when prices began to recede from their peak in 1907, a policy which to the miners amounted to a return to the sliding scale. A further grievance, which foreshadowed the more bitter disputes of the inter-war years, arose when the Scottish Conciliation Board fixed a minimum wage lower than in England. The differential stimulated trade union organisation and activity in Scotland. A threatened national strike in favour of the stand taken by the Scottish miners was only just averted and a minimum wage of 50 per cent above the level of 1888 accepted. Thereafter a sliding scale was to be adopted, with the price of coal to which the minimum wage was equated being fixed by an arbiter, and with any 'losses' incurred by the owners through the maintenance of the minimum wage, when prices were lower than that necessary to warrant it, being offset against periods when higher prices would otherwise have warranted an increase in wages above the minimum. In effect the old sliding scale was brought back, the only difference being that its adverse impact was tempered by being spread over longer periods.

Opposition to the sliding scale remained, therefore, the major concern of Scottish miners before 1914. Although they were actively engaged in the strike of 1912, the issue then at stake, the demand for a minimum wage for all miners working at the coalface, was less relevant to conditions in Scotland, where, since most miners worked on a daily basis, such exceptional interference with piecework as falls of rock could be met by transferring to a pit elsewhere. Although the Scots supported the general claim, and, proportionately, voted by a greater majority than the rest of the country for the continuation of the strike after the passing of the Miners' Minimum Wage Act, the main consequence was to confirm the suspicion of Scottish miners that they were treated harshly, because the schedule of claims for minimum wages in different districts showed that Scotland's 6s. a day was the lowest. The possibility that the Scottish coalfield was less profitable was hardly ever considered. Even before 1914 the miners were suffering from the adverse effects of the interregional and international competition which increased between the wars.

For all its varied success, the growth in numbers in the miners' organisation was steady. The Scottish Miners' Federation had about 50,000 members in 1900 and 87,200 members in 1913. Other unions showed comparable growth. According to the estimates made by the Webbs, there were 147,000 trade unionists in Scotland in 1892. In the next estimate, made by the Scottish Trades Union Congress in 1924, membership was 536,000. More strikingly, between these two dates, 1892 and 1924, the percentage of trade unionists relative to Scotland's population had risen from 3.7 per cent to 11 per cent, and though the proportions were slightly lower than for the United Kingdom, they showed a tendency to increase at a similar rate. But growth brought assimilation, and between the wars it was already difficult to speak of a Scottish trade union movement. Earlier efforts to link various local Scottish unions into one gave way to attempts to merge with United Kingdom associations. The county unions, which were common in coalmining before 1914, transformed their loosely knit Scottish Miners' Federation into the National Union of Scottish Mine Workers, a prelude, it was hoped, to one union, but a prelude which was protracted by the industry's difficulties until the Second World War. In 1944 the county unions were replaced by one union, which retained the old name of the federation, the National Union of Scottish Mine Workers, until it became the National Union of Mineworkers (Scottish Area) a year later. Assimilation was complete.

In spite of the assimilation, important Scottish unions remained. In 1924, out of a total of 227 unions with 536,432 members, 90 unions with 213,469 members could be described as purely Scottish. The proportion declined when some of the bigger unions, such as those of the miners, joined wider amalgamations. Though the proportion of Scottish unions remained high, the purely Scottish unions became increasingly smaller, local unions. Only in cases such as jute, where Scotland always had a high stake, did large and powerful unions with a completely Scottish base remain. The only way, organisationally or adminstratively, in which Scottish trade unions moved towards greater independence after 1870 was in the establishment of the Scottish Trades Union Congress in 1897. Its foundation was forced on the movement and was not a sign of rising Scottish independence. When trades councils were excluded from the British T.U.C. in 1895, the Aberdeen Trades Council convened a meeting at Dundee to protest against the decision. The following year the Falkirk Trades Council continued the protest by suggesting that a Scottish federation should be formed, and, as a result, the S.T.U.C. came into being in Edinburgh in the following year. About sixty delegates from both trade unions and trades councils were present. In 1923 the S.T.U.C. followed the example of its British counterpart by adopting a new constitution which, under the secretaryship of William Elger from 1922 to 1946, enabled the Congress to lead not only purely Scottish trade unions but all trade unionists in Scotland, as the Scottish membership of national trade unions is also affiliated to the S.T.U.C. The S.T.U.C. came to lead the trade union movement in Scotland as it became the spearhead of discussion among trade unionists on many Scottish economic problems. Indeed, one of the peculiarities of trade union history in Scotland in the twentieth century is that the greater administrative assimilation to national bodies has been accompanied by an increasing awareness of the extent to which Scottish trade unionists have to meet problems which are very different in degree, if not in kind. Without the existence of the S.T.U.C. and the focus it has given to such discussion, it is doubtful if the development would have taken place. To that extent an independent Scottish trade union movement has continued, but in the organisation of trade unions generally in Scotland, even with the existence of the S.T.U.C., as strengthened after 1923, the dominance of British thought and policy became increasingly evident.

The co-operative movement was the field of working-class activity which remained most distinctly Scottish, however, though, in contrast to the trade unions, primarily so only in organisation. Its problems arose, and had generally to be considered, on a national basis, even though Scottish co-operators often adopted a distinct viewpoint. Like their brethren in the trade union movement, they favoured direct political action more than their English counterparts. The Scottish co-operative movement, which was established in its modern form by about 1870, frequently met opposition from those who disliked its principles, as when, in an attempt to combat co-operative propaganda, the Scottish Traders' Defence Association was formed in 1888 and was especially active in the mid-1890s. One instance of opposition was when meat salesmen in the Glasgow Meat Market refused to accept offers by co-operative buyers until the Corporation, as landlords of the Meat Market, insisted that all tenants of public stances should accept the highest offers. Such opposition was generally ineffective as the progress of the co-operative movement in Scotland in the late nineteenth century was virtually uninterrupted. The sales of the Scottish Co-operative Wholesale Society showed a steady upward trend from its foundation in 1868 to 1914. In 1868 they were worth £9,697; in 1878, £600,590; in 1888, £1,963,854; in 1898, £4,692,330; in 1908, £7,531,126; and in 1914, £9,425,384. In 1886 the S.C.W.S. bought the Shieldhall estate between Glasgow and Renfrew, on which it set up a whole range of manufacturing activities. The retail societies showed a similar growth. Progress came, too, in the institution of federal retail societies to provide services which were beyond the resources of the smaller retail societies. In 1886 the Drapery and Furnishing Society was formed by a number of Glasgow societies, when the wholesale society announced that it could no longer deal with the expanding retail trade in these two fields. Such federal societies existed only so long as societies or branches could not maintain their own departments in these fields. Their growth was interrupted as constituent member-societies became able to provide their own departments, but such interruptions were signs of the movement's general growth.

NOTES

1. Exact comparison is difficult because of changes in boundaries.
2. *Report of the Royal Commission on Housing*, 1918, para. 931.
3. *Ibid.*, para. 1,937.
4. J. D. M. Bell, 'Trade unions', in A. K. Cairncross (ed.), *The Scottish Economy*, p. 295.

Part Four

Economic Uncertainty, from 1939

CHAPTER XVI

Since 1945: Retrospect and Prospect

The period from 1945 cannot be regarded simply as a postscript to earlier years. It has a character of its own but one so fashioned by the evolution of Scottish industrial society that an assessment of its problems needs the long-term perspective of the historian. Interpreting more recent years has its own difficulties and complexities. The historian's judgement is more likely to be influenced by prejudice and personal experience and less by the detached wisdom of hindsight which the passage of time allows him to enjoy in assessing events of more remote periods. Another and somewhat paradoxical source of confusion is the enormous bulk of evidence which is available for the years from 1945, much of it of an official or semi-official nature. Its quantitative precision can be deceptive. It leads to neglect of the assumptions on which it is based, of the revisions to which it is often subject, and of its margin of error.

In the years before 1914 the economic, and especially the industrial, achievements were often attributed with some justification to domestic advantages, sometimes indeed to the innate ability of the Scots. Their achievements easily engendered a feeling of national complacency and self-satisfaction, which had lasting effects on Scottish attitudes to both explanations of the industrial past and prospects for the future. Between the wars complacency waned but was not removed. In the early 1920s the difficulties of many once successful industries and firms were thought to be temporary consequences of the short-term disruption of war, or removable through improving competitiveness by reductions in costs of production, usually by cuts in wages. By the 1930s the improbability of any general re-establishment of the international competitiveness of the staple industries at their former level, and so the need for a change in the industrial structure, was increasingly accepted. The depth of the conversion to the new analysis is more doubtful. The changes in the industrial structure which were advocated before 1939 were hedged with reservations which impeded the adoption of more radical policies and which persisted into the different conditions after 1945. Few recognised adequately the social stress involved in the process of industrial change, that it required not only the expansion of new industries but the substantial reduction, in some cases even the elimination, of old industries and the rejuvenation of whatever legacy of them which remained, and that success in any field — old or new — could be secure only if based on indigenous advantages comparable to those which had brought about the earlier industrial successes. Though the need for change was diagnosed before 1939, it is questionable if its scale and magnitude had been recognised generally. For some years after 1945 it was still possible to continue to minimise, even to ignore, ominous portents with complacency.

Scottish economic and social life was transformed after the war, and the prospects for future prosperity seemed brighter than for many years.

Many indicators of the transformation were available. Attention was directed to those most characteristic of the highly industrial, urban society which Scotland had become in the nineteenth century. There was a special reason for their prominence. With the emergence of a mass electorate the problems of the Forth-Clyde valley, rather than those of the periphery, were kept in the foreground of political activity and stamped their character on Scottish history generally in the twentieth century in such a way that much political discussion in Scotland seemed to be confined almost exclusively to the area dubbed west-central by the planners. Any solution to its apparently intractable difficulties in the inter-war years and thereafter was thought to offer a way of economic salvation to all. After 1945 visual evidence of a transformation was widespread even in some of the worst instances of social degradation. Scotland's notorious housing was improved by the building of over 564,000 houses (over 86 per cent of which were in the public sector) in the twenty years after 1945, an increase of some two-thirds over the construction between 1919 and 1939. In the first half of the 1970s, around 30,000 were built annually; the number declined sharply in 1978 when the total constructed in the public sector was 3,000 less than the private sector's 14,400. Another improvement in a related field in which Scottish experience had long compared unfavourably with elsewhere was in the death rate, especially in infant mortality. The peak of infant mortality — of just under 130 per 1,000 live births in the last years of the nineteenth century — fell steadily to over 75 in the later 1930s and to over 14 in the later 1970s. The expectation of life of males at birth in the depths of the depression between the wars (1930-32) was 56 years and of females 59.5 years; fifty years later (1980-82) the expectation was 69 and 75.2 years respectively. A significant indicator of the diminished hazards of infancy was that, while in the early 1980s the expectation of life was slightly lower at the end of the first year than at birth, the high death rate in the first year of life in the 1930s led to a higher expectation of life for those who survived it than at birth, by another four years for males and two years for females.

Of the economic indicators of the transformation after 1945, the most popularly used was the rate of unemployment, however defectively calculated or applied. In contrast to the period shortly after the First World War, the rate did not rise rapidly and substantially but settled at a level which would have seemed impossibly low in the 1930s. In the twenty years from 1950 the percentage of the workforce registered as unemployed exceeded four per cent in only two years: in 1959, when it was 4.4 per cent, and in 1963, when it was 4.8 per cent. In six of these years it was below 3 per cent: in 1951, 1954 to 1957, and in 1966. A sharp reversal began only in the 1970s, especially in the second half of the decade. The change is understood more easily by examining the total numbers registered as unemployed. In 1955 just over 50,000 were registered; in the mid-1970s over 100,000; in the early 1980s over 200,000, and over 300,000 in late 1982, though the total number of employees, which was fairly steady throughout the mid-

1970s, rose to 2,100,000 in 1979 and fell by around nine per cent to 1,931,000 in 1982.

The appearance of many new statistical series after 1945 supplied wider evidence of the economic changes. Since many series date only from the years after 1945, an extended evaluation of what happened before 1939 is not always possible. One series which may be taken back to 1924 is estimates of Scottish national income. It shows a slow increase to 1939, though with fluctuations. More detailed information is available after 1945. In 1954 the Gross Domestic Product (GDP) at factor cost was £1,429 million, and in 1979 it was £14,299 million in current prices; in 1975 prices the figures are £5,841 million for 1954 and £8,905 million for 1979. Though not the doubling of the standard of living in a generation which was heralded in the 1950s, the increase was slightly over 50 per cent in real terms. Changes were also sufficiently notable and widespread in the industrial structure to seem to support until the mid-1950s and later the high hopes and expectations of economic transformation characteristic of the decade. The dependence on the heavy industries had increased during the Second World War. They employed almost a quarter of the insured population in July 1945, compared with just under 16 per cent in July 1939. Thereafter their experience differed from the inter-war years and accounted as much as anything for the greater post-war prosperity of the Scottish economy. The post-war histories of coalmining and of shipbuilding show the contrast. Much general industrial growth after 1945 was thought to require adequate supplies of coal, so the industry did not face stagnant demand as in the 1920s and 1930s; instead it was developed and was encouraged to produce to the maximum. Occasional scarcity of orders in shipbuilding, as in 1949 and 1953, indicated that its prospects were not wholly certain, but the tonnage launched was usually around 500,000 annually until the later 1950s. Even more encouraging was the apparent success of the complementary policy initiated in the 1930s of trying to broaden the industrial structure by encouraging new industrial growth, its objectives being widened after 1945 to try to save dollars and to meet defence requirements. The most apparent evidence of success in this direction was the establishment of subsidiaries of several American concerns in Scotland, so reversing the process of earlier years when Scottish firms set up branches in the United States: National Cash Register came in 1947; Honeywell Controls in 1948; Burroughs in 1949; Euclid in 1950. Between 1950 and 1975 over one-quarter of the 230,000 jobs which grew from industrial openings in Scotland were in overseas-owned concerns, and at the end of the 1970s about 100,000 were employed in them. The policy of modernising the old industrial structure reached a peak in the later 1950s. In 1958 it was announced that a semi-continuous strip mill was to be built at Ravenscraig at Motherwell and a cold strip mill at Gartcosh. In 1960 the British Motor Corporation decided to establish a plant at Bathgate to manufacture tractors and heavy commercial vehicles and the Rootes Group to produce motor cars at Linwood. Output started in 1961 and 1963 respectively, and it was estimated that each plant would employ more than 5,000. The three projects were described in 1960 as 'the largest economic advance made in Scotland during the century',[1] a comment typical of the optimism with which many portrayed Scotland's economic future at the time. The complacency of the earlier years of the century had not evaporated.

In light of such achievements, critical qualifications and questionings may seem unwarranted. Usually they were based on comparisons — often made possible only because of the growth of statistical evidence — with achievements at other times and other places, comparisons which were normally adverse to present-day Scotland. They showed that, while the Scottish economy shared in the general growth of the United Kingdom until the mid-1950s, a lag in performance began from 1954 and became more general from 1958. Improvement in the relative position of Scotland in the U.K. was evident again from 1964. Scottish income per head as a percentage of U.K. income per head, which had been over 90 per cent in the mid-1950s, fell below that level from 1958 to 1968 and rose to a peak of 96.5 per cent in 1976. The rise was even more notable in income from employment, which fell to 85.4 per cent of the U.K. figure in 1961 and was 97.2 per cent in 1978. The fluctuations suggested that even the successes in Scotland were unstable and fleeting, and, since the performance of the U.K. was relatively poor in many of the international comparisons which were commonly being made at the time, the lack of achievement on any permanent basis in Scotland was still more disturbing. The adverse comparisons assumed greater force, and were recognised more generally and more popularly, as some of the staple industries which had enjoyed a decade of peacetime prosperity suffered increasing international competition from the mid-1950s. Rivals, eliminated by war and post-war disruption, reappeared; traditional markets, notably in the Empire and less well-developed countries, which had been retained with difficulty between the wars, were lost. The consequence was the beginning of the decline, and in some cases of the end, of many concerns which had earned an international reputation for Scotland in the nineteenth century. The elimination of the great names in shipbuilding and heavy engineering in the west of Scotland is perhaps the best example of the changed conditions, which for many obliterated the solid contrasting evidence of industrial successes after 1945.

The significance of the comparisons made so freely can be exaggerated. The differences they revealed, especially statistical ones, were often small, and became significant only when several pointed consistently towards the same conclusion. Nor is there any fundamental reason why Scotland's economic performance should be as successful as the entire United Kingdom's. Sometimes debate based on comparisons leads to advocacy of the untenable position that no region should be below the national average. Unpalatable as the possibility is, Scotland may be a region which cannot attain the same level of economic achievement as some others, or as it once enjoyed itself. Retrospective support for such a pessimistic interpretation is possible by identifying weaknesses even in some of the achievements of recent years. One notable achievement was the increase in the productivity of labour in Scotland which followed the diminution in the difference between the lower GDP per worker in Scotland than in the U.K. in the 1960s and 1970s. Its weakness was that the improvement was accompanied by increased earnings, which diminished the favourable effect of the increased productivity on Scottish costs of production. The need to avoid any such loss was more pressing because of the need to improve Scottish labour productivity to match that of the U.K., which itself did not stand up well to international comparisons. Another example of a weakness in an achievement was of more general relevance. The concern, especially politically, with the tribulations of the heavy industries has tended to distract attention from the changes which were taking place in the industrial structure. Agriculture, mining and manufacturing accounted for almost half the GDP in the early 1950s but for only one third in the late 1970s. Construction and the public utilities increased their share slightly from less than ten per cent to over ten per cent. Change was greatest in the increase in the service industries, but their increase revealed a weakness to those who feared for the future of an economy which had lost its base of manufacturing industry. Some of the more apprehensive assessments of the rise of the service industries may be doubted. Their output is as useful as tangible commodities. Nevertheless, the changed structure indicates the existence of problems of adaptation which should not be minimised, especially a need for labour, and perhaps for geographical, mobility. It also poses the political question of how far the increase in the service industries reflects the desires of a society when a substantial range of them are available to the public free or at less than their full cost. If there is any possibility that these services would not have been chosen if sold at their full cost, then the public might well have found their provision less satisfying. Their relative dissatisfaction as consumers could then have influenced their assessment of the economic achievements.

Even the more popularly recognised achievements of the appearance of investment from overseas and the exploitation of offshore oil were flawed. Investment from overseas was in the form of the takeover of existing firms as well as in the establishment of new plants, with the result that 2.8 per cent of employment in Scotland was in American-owned firms in 1950 and 12.3 per cent in 1969. Foreign investment was welcomed at first as it assisted the desired change in the industrial structure. Disillusionment followed, especially from the later 1970s as many firms which had started operations in Scotland almost a generation earlier began to restrict their scale of operation and in some cases to pull out of Scotland completely. The failure of most international concerns to put down permanent roots led to little research and development being undertaken in Scotland, which restricted their influence on the technology and methods of management of the established concerns which were in need of improvement. The exploitation of oil resources highlighted problems experienced more generally with foreign enterprise. The number employed in companies wholly related to the North Sea oil industry was over 5,000 in 1973 and grew to over 41,000 in 1979 as exploration moved on to production. In 1976 about 30 per cent of the employment was in the construction of platforms and modules; by 1978 its share had fallen to 13 per cent as that of services rose. The success was qualified. The need for technological aid from elsewhere limited its direct influence on the Scottish economy. The benefits were concentrated in the north-east, especially as employment in servicing increased. Over two-thirds of the total employment wholly related to the North Sea oil industry was in Grampian Region in 1979. More ominous still for the future: unless there is some striking growth of gas processing, the activities in the North Sea may have passed their peak and the numbers wholly employed in them will decline.

Failure to perceive that faults in the industrial successes might possibly be indigenous was evident in the response to some of the closures of the old-established firms and to the retreat of the new, a failure made more probable and reinforced by the publicity which accompanied them and which was often accompanied by simplistic analysis of complicated issues. Past achievements impeded the acceptance of pessimistic, even of realistic, assessments of the prospects of the economy and led to resentful responses to criticism and to a lack of perception of impending crises and of the need for early remedial action, notably among those who were subsequently quick to denounce any remedial action designed to retain some legacy of the past successes, often simply because it involved change. The resentful response and implacable opposition to many of the industrial collapses since the later 1960s revealed the deep-seated strength of the complacent inflexibility of so many in Scotland to its economic problems. An appraisal of the diminished prospects of a firm and suggestions for its reorganisation, sometimes under different management, did not catch the public imagination and support in the same way as outright opposition to a possibility of closure. The public response had its first major exposure by modern publicity at the threatened closure of Upper Clyde Shipbuilders in 1971. At each successive threat to a major firm thereafter a similar dramatic and emotional outburst has followed; it has usually appropriated the credit for any restructuring which followed, though the opposition frequently hindered as much as helped the restructuring.

The emotional outbursts rarely draw attention to the most critical deficiency of all in the achievements since 1945. It was the serious absence of securely based local enterprise, evident in many of the new enterprises on which the prosperity of Scotland was based in those years. Whether offshoots of overseas concerns, or branches of British firms, many were encouraged into Scotland by a combination of sticks and carrots wielded and offered by government. The potential defect of such enterprises was that they had come to Scotland because of relatively temporary attractions and might not survive their withdrawal or the emergence of other adverse conditions. This was initially dismissed as an unreasonable fear, but as the lack of research and development in the offshoots of overseas enterprise showed with clarity, their roots were not deep. They were not to blame for that; the deficiency lay in the inability of the Scots to take their place.

The significance of this flaw was sharpened by the withdrawal of overseas enterprise from the 1970s. The gist of the criticism which has accompanied the retreat has been that overseas-owned plants remained mere outposts, with their operations controlled and determined by the needs of the centre. The analysis is valid, but has little critical force unless it can be shown that their presence displaced Scottish enterprise and, assuming domestic enterprise had been effective, that it would have been more capable of withstanding the changes in national and international competition which have been behind the withdrawal of many overseas concerns in the 1970s. Neither proposition has been proved. The belief that a nationally based concern, being more directly subject to governmental pressure or persuasion, would have overcome the international causes which have been behind many of the industrial difficulties since the 1970s, or the defects of domestic production, attributes to government assistance and intervention a degree of success which is questionable.

The deficiency of native enterprise in some of the major industrial achievements after 1945 was accompanied by a failure, as before the war, to recognise that, whatever the achievements in new industrial development, the tribulations of the old staples with their native roots remained. They were still major employers, with the result that complete closure, even if unavoidable as in some mining areas, gave rise to major social problems of adjustment. If complete closure was to be avoided ultimately in many more, the traditional industries had to become more competitive. The consequences of their failure to do so have been widespread. A number of reasons explain it: first, before the war too much attention was paid simply to a reduction of their scale of operation, understandable at the time but based on the erroneous assumption that the staple industries suffered simply from over-capacity; second, the war and the immediate post-war years gave a false impression of their long-term prospects; third, and one that underlies so much of the approach to the problems of the old industrial structure, changing established practices is much harder when reducing industrial capacity than when introducing something new, and is avoided whenever possible.

Failure to recognise the strength of the resistance to change was more damaging after 1945 compared with earlier years because of the emergence of the widely held assumption that solutions to many problems lay in some form of government intervention. Although some disillusionment with the effectiveness, and even more with the desirability of government intervention and planning set in after the war, the move to greater intervention was re-asserted as economic difficulties grew from the late 1950s.

The context within which government intervention took place had special relevance for Scotland. First, the integration of Scotland in the U.K. encouraged the belief that it was in danger of becoming a disadvantaged region on the periphery. Second, after 1945 it became easier to perceive the nature of any disadvantages in a Scottish context. Apparently disparate, they are linked, and each needs fuller exposition.

The integration of Scotland in the U.K. is not new and is evident in the pattern of trade. Scotland depends on English markets in a way that England does not depend on Scottish markets. In the early 1970s over half the Scottish output of manufactured goods and nearly three-quarters of metal and engineering output were exported. The chief market was the rest of the U.K. Much Scottish prosperity depended therefore on the prosperity of the rest of the U.K. The greater integration also encouraged the removal of headquarters of firms and of control generally from Scotland, giving rise to political opposition even against better economic judgements. The mergers of textile, shipping and shipbuilding firms and banks from the 1930s encouraged such an outlook, but they took place often because Scottish firms were no longer able to retain their independence internationally. That the moves could be justified on any rational economic criterion was not readily conceded in Scotland; they were more often interpreted as yet another illustration of the interests of the periphery being sacrificed to those of the centre.

Increased administrative independence ensured that the growing range of problems were discussed, sometimes even conceived, and certainly assessed, in a Scottish context. Even when only a modest role was attributed to government intervention in the economy, as before 1939, the Scottish Office was aware of this approach in its submissions to some of .the earliest inter-departmental discussion on the policies for the special areas in the 1930s. At the same time it was expressed vigorously both in popular economic literature and through the growth of such non-political agencies as the Scottish Development Council and the Scottish Economic Committee. After 1945 an extended Scottish administration played an increasingly active and well-orchestrated role in a nationally more active consideration of economic policy, which the public were enabled to evaluate in a Scottish context through an extended official Scottish statistical service. The desire to bring greater precision to Scottish economic affairs is evident in the reports of the departmental committee on Scottish Financial and Trade Statistics of 1952 and of the Royal Commission on Scottish Affairs of 1954, as well as in a series of academic publications of the same years. After 1945 even those who were not sympathetic to nationalism — including many who were actively hostile to it — considered economic issues in a Scottish context, none more effectively than the Scottish Council (Development and Industry), which was formed after the war through the merger of the pre-war Scottish Development Council and the wartime Scottish Council on Industry. Such bodies devised an economic policy, specifically for Scotland, not because of a new, or even a newly recognised, economic problem, but because the enhanced economic function of governments everywhere was grafted into the Scottish legal and administrative structure which had survived the Union of Parliaments and which had its status increased from the later nineteenth century, long before the economic role had been found for it. Created and expanded for reasons of political expediency, it lay ready to hand to give focus to the possibility that its further growth could solve the economic problem when it was recognised and taken to fall within the ambit of government.

The high level of employment after 1945, providing a sharp contrast to experience before the war, led some to accept that this happy state was the consequence of deliberate intervention by government, particularly through the acceptance of the view that government was able to control the level of economic activity through the influence of public expenditure on demand. One feature of the Scottish economy since the war has been the way in which it has relied on public expenditure, both local and national. Only a relatively small part was aid under whatever form of regional policy had been adopted to rectify regional imbalances. One estimate suggests that it provided only slightly over five per cent of total expenditure by central government at the end of the 1970s. Such studies as have been made suggest a link — though disagreeing on what it was and how significant — between regional policy expenditure and the improvement in Scottish manufacturing which took place from the early 1960s. The effect seemed to be less in the 1970s, perhaps because of diminishing returns to the policy as well as because of changes in the policy itself. Whatever the reasons behind the extent of public expenditure, it would seem likely to introduce an element of instability in prosperity which is dependent on it in the absence of other domestic changes. In Scotland consumers' expenditure per head of the population was less than in the U.K. generally, but expenditure per head of the population was similar in both. Scotland was then dependent on a greater proportion of government expenditure and investment in order to maintain the comparable level of total expenditure. Moreover, total expenditure exceeded the value of Scottish output, so there was some form of deficit in the balance of payments, though any reliable assessment of the balance of payments is subject to difficulties of calculation. If these two features which emerge from a study of Scottish expenditure are linked, even some of the benefits of increased government expenditure are lost through expenditure on goods brought into Scotland. The multiplier effect of government expenditure is reduced correspondingly. The weakness brings the discussion of the Scottish economy back to a feature which has already been suggested by examining the problem of the economy from another standpoint. The failure of government intervention generally, and in this case specifically the failure of government expenditure, might not have been the result of the inadequacies of government aid but because of the use to which it has been put. If so, more government expenditure may simply worsen the situation.

The belief in the efficacy of government intervention at the end of the Second World War is not surprising; what is more surprising is the way in which that belief persisted, particularly the assumption that a solution to Scotland's economic malaise lay in demand management and in the manipulation of public expenditure, and not in directly tackling the real problems of structural contraction as well as of expansion, and in the lack of indigenous enterprise. Admittedly, the barriers to change in the old industries were very great, and tackling them was unlikely to build up much political credit. The first of these barriers has already been mentioned but needs elaboration. It was the prosperity of much of the old staple industries until the later 1950s, which acted as a powerful brake on structural adjustment. After only a few years of attempts to change the industrial balance in the early 1930s, concentrated on the negative policy of reducing the scale of operation, the demand for the products of many of the traditional heavy industries appeared to be assured. After the war many of their problems seemed neither serious nor insurmountable. Characteristic of the approach of these years was a paragraph in *Industry and Employment in Scotland in 1955* dealing with shipbuilding, which stated that 'The year was a good one for shipbuilding'.[2] There were grounds for the judgement. The five largest firms on the Clyde launched gross tonnage of almost 237,000, among them such worthy examples of a reputation which was already out-of-date as the *Empress of Britain* and the *Carinthia*, and Scottish shipyards booked orders for over 800,000 gross tons. The extent of the acceptance of the need for change in many of the staples after 1945 was limited, and so drastic action of the type needed would not be adopted. Until the later 1950s, even into the 1960s, it was possible to defend that satisfied approach on a short-term analysis at least.

The second barrier to action in the old industries was the intrinsic difficulties in any policy of contraction. Their significance can be appreciated best by approaching the issue indirectly. One of the more interesting features of the considerable historiography which has grown up around the need to change the industrial structure, and which is evident in both the recommendations for change and in subsequent commentaries on them, is that the emphasis is placed so heavily on the need for the new developments. The emphasis may not be surprising but has the effect of minimising the difficulties of achieving adequate mobility out of the old structure. The failure to stress the need to make such adjustments, and to drive home to those concerned their responsibility to make them, has led to some inconsistency in policy. On the one hand change has been advocated through what may be described as the easy option of encouraging new opportunities; on the other hand what had to be done with the old structure was usually ignored. The apparent inconsistency cannot be excused by suggesting that more extensive expansion of the new opportunities would have eliminated the problems of adjustment from the old because a feature of the response in Scotland to the decline of the old industrial structure has been a reluctance by the workforce to accept the need to move to openings in other fields or other places. Admittedly, a distinction should be drawn between the public stance, adopted especially by organised labour or self-appointed representatives of the workforce, who have shown a greater degree of resistance to change, and what actually took place at a lower, more mundane and less publicised level, but the impression can easily be gained of a total resistance to change in the old structure. The resistance to adjustment had been intensified by the widespread publicity given to it rather than to consideration of why the adjustment was necessary and how it might be facilitated.

The third barrier to reducing dependence on the old industries was the fundamental difficulty of maintaining a stable basis for their prosperity, even if at a lower level of activity. Some of the advantages which had been behind their earlier growth had been lost or were greatly diminished. The most obvious example was in the decline of natural advantages. The industry most directly affected was coalmining, but the consequences pervaded all the heavy industries. The geological advantages, especially of plentiful supplies of coal and iron ore, were not the only foundations of the prosperity of the heavy industries, but, as their advantages declined, the need to offset the attendant loss of competitiveness by action in other directions was increased and the expansion of new enterprises distracted attention from this requirement. If costs were to be kept down, and the ability of the industries to meet changing conditions maintained, the decline in natural advantages increased the need to ensure that labour was cheap and flexible, as a large part of the costs of some of the old industries was labour costs. Doing so was likely to encounter the same resistance to change which discouraged attempts to restructure the old. Yet the need to be competitive in the old industries was vital if markets were to be retained. Those in the E.E.C. for heavy goods have been lost almost entirely and others retained only with difficulty.

Government intervention, especially when concerned with demand management, was least able to deal with such problems. More serious still, the weakness was not readily appreciated in much of the analysis of the function of government in the economy in the years after the Second World War. In the 1930s the decline of demand for many of the products of Scottish industry was an obvious cause of industrial depression; its resurgence during and shortly after the war provided an apparent remedy for the depression. It was then easy to assume that demand management would solve any sign of industrial depression whenever it emerged in the later 1960s and subsequently. To take such a step without qualification fails to recognise that, in so far as the stagnation of Scottish industry can be attributed to falling demand, this was not the product of short-term fluctuations but was the consequence of a secular decline in international demand for the commodities which Scottish industry had produced so skilfully and successfully in the nineteenth century. Specialist skill had enabled Scottish engineers and shipbuilders to sell their output even as their costs rose in the later nineteenth century. They could do so no longer as technical change left much of their traditional output unwanted. The direction in which future development lay was then in trying to improve the conditions of supply of Scottish industry, in both the traditional and in the new sectors. To stimulate demand, and especially to direct it towards some of the traditional industries, merely made matters still worse.

No government was likely to embrace readily policies which would give rise to the social stress which follows the elimination of an established industrial structure based on traditional skills and established reputations. A mass electorate, heavily concentrated in west-central Scotland and biased in favour of retention of the heavy industries and their traditions, added political and social pressure to an economic analysis which stressed the efficacy of demand management, and made unlikely the adoption of policies which tried to tackle the more intractable problems of improving industrial production. The objective of public policy was generally perceived to be almost exclusively the diminution of unemployment to a low level and not merely its minimal relief as in the 1930s. The emphasis was most conspicuous in the evolution of regional policy. A report from the Scottish Council (Development and Industry) in 1952 pointed out that 'The priority that has been enjoyed by the Development Areas has usually been justified in terms of the unemployment figures of those areas', then warned, 'Unemployment, however, cannot be the sole criterion of policy'.[3] Almost twenty years later the continuing emphasis on the pre-eminence of ensuring full employment was evident in an economic review in the first issue of the *Scottish Economic Bulletin* in the summer of 1971: 'The essence of the Scottish problem is to obtain sufficient investment in productive capacity to make full use of the country's labour resources. With the decline of traditional industries and the flow of labour which must, therefore, be redeployed, Scotland needs a higher level of investment in relation to the gross domestic product than the United Kingdom as a whole, if full employment is to be achieved and maintained'.[4] The stress on unemployment as the key to the regional policy was modified in the 1960s. The new policy, begun in 1960 and expanded in a White Paper published in November 1963, concentrated on those areas deemed to have the greatest potential for economic growth. The new policy was expounded by a new administration in a master plan for the whole economy. The implementation of objectives, often laudable in themselves, needed time, and time was not likely to be given much place in any policy which relied on government intervention. The immediacy of political decision-making impeded the adoption of long-term and consistent planning. Both the origins and the solutions of the Scottish economy were approached from a short-term perspective. The characteristic was not new and can be linked to the complacency to which the long-term industrial successes, and especially the immediate post-war prosperity, had given birth. Short-term action to deal with declining economic activity was justifiable when the decline was only cyclical, not when it was secular, as it was in many fields after 1918. There is evidence that diminished profits, even losses, did not lead to remedial action. Only a crisis of liquidity did so. If, however, such a crisis of liquidity could be removed by subventions from government in its new interventionist role, then further procrastination was possible. Such policies were as disastrous economically as they were politically attractive. The history of all the staple industries in Scotland since 1945 has taken this form. Such short-sightedness in keeping inefficient coalmines in production, choosing questionable locations for a steel strip mill or an aluminium smelter, perpetuating uneconomic shipyards, all welcomed and encouraged by a wide range of public opinion whose analysis was bounded by limited horizons of time, has been the most damaging feature of Scottish industrial history since 1945. Government intervention has almost certainly encouraged such a short-sighted approach.

The potential of North Sea oil has suffered from the same short-sightedness, not only the direct benefits in income and employment mentioned already but the wider ones made available through the effects of oil production on the balance of payments and on additions to tax revenue. Some of the strongest political criticism has been over the alleged failure to use the revenue for industrial rejuvenation, especially necessary against the day when the oil and other natural resources could be exhausted. The critics have argued, first, that the revenue was not being used for long-term benefits; second, that it should have been applied to Scottish and not to U.K. ends, since the revenue came from a source which was allegedly Scottish. The second criticism gives rise to complicated legal and political issues but would be more convincing if accompanied by hard evidence that the revenue would be used more effectively in a Scottish than in a U.K. context. It is difficult to believe that it would; the probability that it would not seems greater. In any case integration and the economic dependence of Scotland on the rest of the U.K. is such that Scotland may gain most of all from the prosperity of the U.K. as a whole. In that case, there may have been faults in the use to which the revenue has been directed, but there is no compelling evidence that Scotland suffers in some special way from the misdirection. It could suffer even more if Scots are more reluctant to change their industrial structure than those who live elsewhere in the U.K.

After 1945 the deep-seated problems and needs of the Scottish economy were recognised; the weakness lies in the perception of how the needs should be met and in how they have been distorted by short-term political considerations. The Scottish economy has not lacked analyses of its problems, yet too often the outcome has been prescriptions of a degree of superficiality, almost banality, which augurs ill for any effective action. Throughout industry — management and unions alike — it is uncommon to find prescriptions for actions which deal in detail with the issues of diminished natural resources, high costs of production, and old and outmoded industrial practices. New industrial practices are immediately hailed as successes, when the true test comes only after time. The subsequent history of some of the innovations is not always easily uncovered, and, if it can be traced, is not always a story of success. The widespread fault of Scottish industrial society since 1945, especially since the 1960s, has been to grasp the easy option, to propound objectives without considering fully how they are to be achieved, and their implications for existing practices. When combined with the greater belief in the efficacy, and in some quarters in the necessity, for political action to deal with almost any social or economic problem, the faith in the potential of the easy solution has been increased.

When government intervention was considered too exclusively as being chiefly a matter of increased expenditure, attention was directed away from more fundamental issues. They are internal to Scottish industry and lie in defects in its productive capacity and capabilities; they are then the fault and responsibility of the Scots themselves and particularly of those who work in Scottish industry. Instead of tackling them, resort has been made too readily to government intervention, often as another source of financial aid which could postpone the liquidity crises which have produced extensive recognition of the need for industrial change. Such tendencies to avoid difficulties until the last, often until it is too late, are hardly surprising in light of the magnitude of the tasks to be tackled, but every time one was avoided, perhaps through another injection of liquid funds, its magnitude was greater next time. In these circumstances it is not surprising that many evaluations of the prospects for the

Scottish economy, when they moved away from the immediacy of a liquidity crisis, concentrated on the more attractive aspects of the future, especially on the political economy of expansion, and not on the hard reality of the accompanying contraction and change. Expansion presents an easier view of the challenge to Scottish industry, but it engenders high expectations and encourages the passing of responsibility for failure to others. The aspects which should be stressed are defects of Scottish industry since 1945. When they are examined, discussion soon degenerates into the provision of a catalogue of defensive excuses for the failings of the Scots, suggestions that admitted faults are no worse than elsewhere, or attempts to pass responsibility for failure in the past and lack of action in the present to someone else, and since 1945 that has usually meant passing responsibility to government. In short, the discussion has soon become engulfed in irrelevant party political dogma and its petty irrelevancies.

To end on a wholly pessimistic note would provide an unbalanced interpretation of the prospects for the Scottish economy. There is a future but one which requires an acceptance of adaptation and change by all. To prove that Scotland has resources for economic success is difficult, but such attempts as have been made to do so suggest that defects do not lie in deficiencies in the supply of factors of production. If deficiencies are to be found, they must lie in some such residual influences as advances in knowledge or in economies of scale, which are even more difficult to measure, if they can be measured at all. The most notable feature of an attempt to use this type of analysis to try to explain Scotland's relatively adverse position, compared with the U.K., is that it leads to no clear indication of the difference. Certainly there seems little doubt that the fault does not lie in objectively indentifiable adverse conditions; it may be in the use to which they are put by Scots. That successful modern industrial growth is possible has, however, been demonstrated in the growth of the electronics industry. By the late 1970s the value of its output at 1975 prices was one-third as much again as shipbuilding, marine engineering and vehicles, and there were good grounds for hoping that Scotland would perform in the future as well as the U.K. as a whole and perhaps even better. The achievement shows what can be done.

The final suggestion to be made from a retrospect of the industrial society since 1945 and the prospect for future success is the need for Scots to recognise that the faults of their economy are indigenous and, it they are to be removed, success lies not by passing responsibility to government of any political complexion. Two examples of indigenous faults, and the seat of responsibility for their remedy, can be suggested by way of closing illustrations. The first concerns the supply of labour. Stress on its increased productivity is very proper, though some of its potential benefits are lost if it is accompanied by increased earnings. If Scottish industry is to be competitive, it needs increased productivity without any increase in earnings. It is symptomatic of the failure to recognise the root of the internal problem that the increased productivity is considered to provide justification for the increased earnings. The problem of the supply of labour is much wider. Scotland's industrial relations compare unfavourably with those of the rest of the U.K. in the eyes of many. The usual defensive response, that they are not as bad as portrayed or are no worse than elsewhere, only worsens the situation. Many think they are; it is therefore more necessary than ever to ensure that any grounds for the belief are removed, though doing so will be a long process. That industrial relations are often better in smaller firms provides a link to the second illustration, which is the absence of many of the smaller firms which are of considerable importance in the new industries which exploit high technology. The same absence of small and new developing units can be linked to the failures of new units to emerge to supply the components required in some of the larger units in vehicle manufacture and other concerns which were set up in the early 1960s. If labour in Scotland has defects and deficiencies, so too, it would seem, has managerial enterprise.

The flaws in industrial capacity are not easily remedied as they are influenced by deep-seated social attitudes and historical experience. Eliminating them has become more rather than less difficult in some ways, as much economic policy has assumed a political dimension and is accompanied by the belief that the defects and difficulties have a political explanation and a corresponding political solution. If action of another type is required — as has been suggested — then the stress on political explanations and solutions, of whatever type, will merely induce false expectations. When the politicians vie with each other to claim to have the one true policy, then expectations will become even more unrealistic. That is likely to spell economic disaster for Scotland. The way forward may lie in a lowering of expectations to a more realistic level and an acceptance that realising them involves harsh choices of closure and adaptation as well as happier ones of expansion. Only if the old industrial society is finally cast off can another emerge.

NOTES

1. Statement by the Executive Committee of the Scottish Council (Development and Industry).

2. *Industry and Employment in Scotland 1955*, Cmd. 9737, para. 180.

3. The Scottish Council (Development and Industry), *Report of the Committee on Local Development in Scotland* (Edinburgh, 1952), para. 70.

4. *Scottish Economic Bulletin*, No. 1 (Summer 1971), p. 3.

Bibliography

Articles have been excluded from the bibliography below, though many relevant ones are to be found in the following journals:

Business History
Economic History Review
Innes Review
Juridical Review
Northern Scotland
Records of the Scottish Church History Society
Scottish Economic and Social History
Scottish Geographical Magazine
Scottish Historical Review
Scottish Industrial History
Scottish Journal of Political Economy
Scottish Studies

The publications of the Scottish History Society are an essential source on most topics.

The Bibliography lists recent publications, most of which should be generally available. As many of the works cited are relevant to more than one chapter, they are classified under main subject headings.

1. *General*

J. Butt and J. T. Ward (eds.), *Scottish Themes* (Edinburgh, 1976).

S. and O. Checkland, *Industry and Ethos. Scotland 1832-1914* (London, 1984).

L. Cullen and T. C. Smout (eds.), *Comparative Aspects of Irish and Scottish Economic and Social Development 1600-1900* (Edinburgh, n.d.).

D. Daiches, *Scotland and the Union* (London, 1977).

———, (ed.), *A Companion to Scottish Culture* (London, 1982).

A. Dickson (ed.), *Scottish Capitalism* (London, 1980).

G. D. Donaldson and R. S. Morpeth, *A Dictionary of Scottish History* (Edinburgh, 1977).

W. Ferguson, *Scotland, 1689 to the Present* (Edinburgh, 1968).

———, *Scotland's Relations with England* (Edinburgh, 1977).

H. Hamilton, *The Industrial Revolution in Scotland* (Oxford, 1932).

———, *An Economic History of Scotland in the Eighteenth Century* (Oxford, 1963).

A. Harding (ed.), *Law-making and Law-makers in British History* (London, 1980).

C. Harvie, *Scotland and Nationalism. Scottish Society and Politics, 1707-1977* (London, 1977).

———, *No Gods and Precious Few Heroes. Scotland 1914-1980* (London, 1981).

J. G. Kellas, *Modern Scotland. The Nation since 1870* (London, 1968).

B. Lenman, *An Economic History of Modern Scotland, 1660-1976* (London, 1977).

———, *Integration, Enlightenment and Industrialization. Scotland 1746-1832* (London, 1981).

S. G. E. Lythe and J. Butt, *An Economic History of Scotland, 1100-1939* (Glasgow, 1975).

M. R. McLarty, *A Source Book and History of Administrative Law in Scotland* (Edinburgh, 1956).

W. H. Marwick, *Economic Developments in Victorian Scotland* (London, 1936).

———, *Scotland in Modern Times* (London, 1964).

R. Mitchison, *Life in Scotland* (London, 1978).

———, *Lordship to Patronage. Scotland, 1603-1745* (London, 1983).

N. Phillipson and R. Mitchison (eds.), *Scotland in the Age of Improvement* (Edinburgh, 1970).

G. S. Pryde, *Scotland from 1603 to the present day* (Edinburgh, 1962).

T. I. Rae (ed.), *The Union of 1707. Its Impact on Scotland* (Glasgow, 1974).

P. W. J. Riley, *The Union of England and Scotland* (Manchester, 1978).

———, *The English Ministers and Scotland, 1707-1727* (Manchester, 1964).

L. J. Saunders, *Scottish Democracy, 1815-1840* (Edinburgh, 1950).

A. Slaven, *The Development of the West of Scotland, 1750-1960* (London, 1975).

A. Slaven and D. H. Aldcroft (eds.), *Business, Banking and Urban History* (Edinburgh, 1982).

T. C. Smout, *A History of the Scottish People, 1560-1830* (London, 1969).

———, (ed.), *The Search for Wealth and Stability* (London, 1979).

D. Turnock, *The New Scotland* (Newton Abbot, 1979).

———, *The Historical Geography of Scotland since 1707* (Cambridge, 1982).

G. Whittington and I. D. Whyte (eds.), *An Historical Geography of Scotland* (London, 1983).

2. *Modern economic policy*

H. M. Begg, C. M. Lythe, R. Sorley, *Expenditure in Scotland, 1961-1971* (Edinburgh, 1975).

V. Bogdanor, *Devolution* (Oxford, 1979).

J. Brand, *The National Movement in Scotland* (London, 1977).

G. Brown (ed.), *The Red Paper on Scotland* (Edinburgh, 1975).

A. K. Cairncross (ed.), *The Scottish Economy* (Cambridge 1954).

G. C. Cameron and G. L. Reid, *Scottish Economic Planning and the Attraction of Industry* (Edinburgh, 1966).

D. Glen (ed.), *Whither Scotland?* (London, 1971).

H. J. Hanham, *Scottish Nationalism* (London, 1969).

M. Hechter, *Internal Colonialism. The Celtic fringe in British national development, 1536-1966* (London, 1975).

T. L. Johnston, N. K. Buxton, D. Mair, *Structure and Growth of the Scottish Economy* (London, 1971).

J. G. Kellas, *The Scottish Political System* (Cambridge, 1973).

C. Lythe and M. Majmunder, *The Renaissance of the Scottish Economy?* (London, 1982).

N. McCormick (ed.), *The Scottish Debate* (Oxford, 1970).

G. McCrone, *Scotland's Economic Progress, 1951-1960. A Study in Regional Accounting* (London, 1965).

———, *Scotland's Future: the Economics of Nationalism* (Oxford, 1969).

D. MacKay (ed.), *Scotland 1980: the economics of self-government* (Edinburgh, 1977).

D. I. MacKay and G. A. Mackay, *The Political Economy of North Sea Oil* (London, 1975).

C. Maclean (ed.), *The Crown and the Thistle. The Nature of Nationhood* (Edinburgh, 1979).

R. Mitchison (ed.), *The Roots of Nationalism* (Edinburgh, 1980).

R. Underwood (ed.), *The Future of Scotland* (London, 1977).

K. Webb, *The Growth of Nationalism in Scotland* (Glasgow, 1977).

J. N. Wolfe (ed.), *Government and Nationalism in Scotland* (Edinburgh, 1969).

3. *Agriculture, fisheries and rural society*

M. L. Anderson, *A History of Scottish Forestry* (London, 1967).

I. Carter, *Farm Life in Northeast Scotland, 1840-1914* (Edinburgh, 1979).

J. T. Coppock, *An Agricultural Atlas of Scotland* (Edinburgh, 1976).

T. M. Devine (ed.), *Lairds and Improvement in the Scotland of the Enlightenment* (Dundee, 1979).

J. Dunlop, *The British Fisheries Society, 1786-1893* (Edinburgh, 1978).

A. Fenton, *Scottish Country Life* (Edinburgh, 1976).

A. Fenton and B. Walker, *The Rural Architecture of Scotland* (Edinburgh, 1981).

W. M. Findlay, *Oats, their cultivation and use from earliest times to the present day* (Edinburgh, 1956).

E. Gauldie, *The Scottish Country Miller, 1700-1900* (Edinburgh, 1981).

W. S. Gilly, *The Peasantry of the Border* (1842, reprinted Edinburgh, 1973).

M. Gray, *The Fishing Industries of Scotland, 1790-1914* (Oxford, 1978).

J. E. Handley, *Scottish Farming in the Eighteenth Century* (London, 1953).

————, *The Agricultural Revolution in Scotland* (Glasgow, 1963).

A. Martin, *The Ring-Net Fishermen* (Edinburgh, 1981).

R. N. Millman, *The Making of the Scottish Landscape* (London, 1975).

R. Mitchison, *Agricultural Sir John* (London, 1962).

I. R. M. Mowat, *Easter Ross, 1750-1850* (Edinburgh, 1981).

M. L. Parry and T. R. Slater (eds.), *The Making of the Scottish Countryside* (London, 1980).

J. H. Smith (ed.), *The Gordon's Mill Farming Club, 1758-1764* (Edinburgh, 1962).

J. A. Symon, *Scottish Farming, Past and Present* (Edinburgh, 1969).

I. Whyte, *Agriculture and Society in Seventeenth Century Scotland* (Edinburgh, 1979).

4. *Highlands and Islands*

J. M. Bumsted, *The People's Clearance, 1770-1815* (Edinburgh, 1982).

A. Collier, *The Crofting Problem* (Cambridge, 1953).

A. Fenton, *The Northern Isles* (Edinburgh, 1978).

M. Gray, *The Highland Economy, 1750-1850* (Edinburgh, 1953).

I. F. Grigor, *Mightier than a Lord. The Highland crofters' struggle for the land* (Stornoway, 1979).

J. Hunter, *The Making of the Crofting Community* (Edinburgh, 1976).

A. Mackenzie, *History of the Highland Clearances* (Inverness, 1883; reprinted Perth, 1979).

N. Nicolson, *Lord of the Isles* (London, 1960).

W. Orr, *Deer Forests, Landlords and Crofters* (Edinburgh, 1982).

E. Richards, *The Leviathan of Wealth. The Sutherland Fortune in the Industrial Revolution* (London, 1973).

————, *A History of the Highland Clearances. Agrarian Transformation and the Evictions, 1746-1886* (London, 1982).

A. M. Smith, *Jacobite Estates of the Forty-Five* (Edinburgh, 1982).

D. C. Thomson and I. Grimble, *The future of the Highlands* (London, 1968).

W. P. L. Thomson, *The Little General and the Rousay Crofters* (Edinburgh, 1981).

J. Walker, *Report on the Hebrides, 1764* (ed. M. M. McKay, Edinburgh, 1980).

A. J. Youngson, *After the Forty-Five. The Economic Impact on the Scottish Highlands* (Edinburgh, 1973).

————, (ed.), *Beyond the Highland Line* (London, 1974).

5. Industry

A. Barnard, *The Whisky Distilleries of the United Kingdom* (1887, reprinted Newton Abbot, 1969).

J. M. Bowie, *The Future of Scotland* (Edinburgh, 1939).

D. Bremner, *The Industries of Scotland* (Edinburgh, 1869; reprinted 1969).

J. Butt, *Industrial Archaeology of Scotland* (Newton Abbot, 1967).

G. C. Cameron and B. D. Clark, *Industrial Movement and the Regional Problem* (Edinburgh, 1966).

R. H. Campbell, *The Rise and Fall of Scottish Industry, 1707-1939* (Edinburgh, 1980).

A. and N. L. Clow, *The Chemical Revolution* (London, 1952).

I. Donnachie, *A History of the Brewing Industry in Scotland* (Edinburgh, 1979).

B. F. Duckham, *A History of the Scottish Coal Industry, 1700-1815* (Newton Abbot, 1970).

A. J. Durie, *The Scottish Linen Industry in the Eighteenth Century* (Edinburgh, 1979).

C. Gulvin, *The Tweedmakers: a History of the Scottish Fancy Woollen Industry, 1600-1914* (Newton Abbot, 1973).

N. Hood and S. Young, *Multinationals in Retreat. The Scottish Experience* (Edinburgh, 1982).

W. S. Howe, *The Dundee Textile Industry, 1960-1977* (Aberdeen, 1982).

J. R. Hume, *The Industrial Archaeology of Scotland*
        1. *The Lowlands and Borders* (London, 1976).
        2. *The Highlands and Islands* (London, 1977).

————, *Industrial Archaeology of Glasgow* (Glasgow, 1974).

J. R. Hume and M. S. Moss, *Beardmore. The History of a Scottish Industrial Giant* (London, 1979).

M. S. Moss and J. R. Hume, *Workshop of the British Empire, Engineering and Shipbuilding in the West of Scotland* (London, 1977).

————, *The Making of Scotch Whisky* (Edinburgh, 1981).

N. Murray, *The Scottish Hand Loom Weavers* (Edinburgh, 1978).

P. L. Payne (ed.), *Studies in Scottish Business History* (London, 1967).

————, *Colvilles and the Scottish Steel Industry* (Oxford, 1979).

————, *The Early Scottish Limited Companies 1850-1895* (Edinburgh, 1980).

J. Scott and M. Hughes, *The Anatomy of Scottish Capital* (London, 1980).

J. P. Shaw, *Water Power in Scotland, 1550-1870* (Edinburgh, 1984).

A. G. Thomson, *The Paper Industry in Scotland, 1590-1861* (Edinburgh, 1974).

G. M. Thomson, *Scotland, that distressed area* (Edinburgh, 1935).

J. N. Toothill *et al, The Scottish Economy* (Edinburgh, 1961).

6. *Social conditions*

G. Bell, *Day and Night in the Wynds of Edinburgh* (Edinburgh, 1849; reprinted, 1973).

S. J. Brown, *Thomas Chalmers and the Godly Commonwealth in Scotland* (Oxford, 1982).

J. H. F. Brotherston, *Observations on the Early Public Health Movement in Scotland* (London, 1952).

R. A. Cage, *The Scottish Poor Law, 1745-1845* (Edinburgh, 1981).

E. Gauldie, *Cruel Habitations. A History of Working-Class Housing, 1780-1918* (London, 1974).

O. Checkland, *Philanthropy in Victorian Scotland* (Edinburgh, 1980).

O. Checkland and M. Lamb (eds.), *Health Care as Social History, The Glasgow Case* (Aberdeen, 1982).

A. C. Cheyne, *The Transforming of the Kirk: Victorian Scotland's Religious Revolution* (Edinburgh, 1983).

R. D. Cramond, *Housing Policy in Scotland, 1919-1964* (Edinburgh, 1966).

T. Ferguson, *The Dawn of Scottish Welfare* (Edinburgh, 1948).

————, *Scottish Social Welfare, 1884 to 1914* (Edinburgh, 1958).

M. Flinn *et al*, *Scottish Population History from the seventeenth century to the 1930s* (Cambridge, 1977).

D. Hamilton, *The Healers: a history of Scottish medicine* (Edinburgh, 1981).

J. E. Handley, *The Irish in Scotland, 1798-1845* (Cork, 1943).

————, *The Irish in Modern Scotland* (Cork, 1947).

————, *The Navvy in Scotland* (Cork, 1970).

I. Levitt and C. Smout, *The State of the Scottish Working-Class in 1843* (Edinburgh, 1979).

J. Lindsay, *The Scottish Poor Law: Its operation in the North-East from 1745 to 1845* (Ilfracombe, 1975).

D. F. Macdonald, *Scotland's Shifting Population, 1770-1850* (Glasgow, 1937).

N. Macdougall (ed.), *Church, Politics and Society* (Edinburgh, 1983).

A. A. MacLaren, *Religion and Social Class. The Disruption Years in Aberdeen* (London, 1974).

————, (ed.), *Social Class in Scotland: Past and Present* (Edinburgh, n.d.).

S. Mechie, *The Church and Scottish Social Development, 1780-1870* (London, 1960).

A. Murdoch, *The People Above* (Edinburgh, 1980).

M. Plant, *The Domestic Life of Scotland in the Eighteenth Century* (Edinburgh, 1952).

J. S. Shaw, *The Management of Scottish Society, 1707-1764* (Edinburgh, 1983).

A. E. Whetstone, *Scottish County Government in the Eighteenth and Nineteenth Centuries* (Edinburgh, 1981).

7. *Labour movements*

R. Page Arnot, *A History of the Scottish Miners* (London, 1955).

C. Bewley, *Muir of Huntershill* (Oxford, 1981).

K. D. Buckley, *Trade Unionism in Aberdeen, 1878 to 1900* (Edinburgh, 1955).

A. B. Campbell, *The Lanarkshire Miners* (Edinburgh, 1979).

R. Q. Gray, *The Labour Aristocracy of Victorian Edinburgh* (Oxford, 1976).

J. Kinloch and J. Butt, *The History of the Scottish Co-operative Wholesale Society Ltd.* (Glasgow, 1981).

K. J. Logue, *Popular Disturbances in Scotland, 1780-1815* (Edinburgh, 1979).

I. Macdougall (ed.), *Essays in Scottish Labour History* (Edinburgh, n.d.).
———, *Militant Miners* (Edinburgh, 1981).
I. McLean, *The Legend of Red Clydeside* (Edinburgh, 1983).
W. H. Marwick, *A Short History of Labour in Scotland* (Edinburgh, 1967).
R. K. Middlemass, *The Clydesiders: a left wing struggle for Parliamentary power* (London, 1965).
W. M. Walker, *Juteopolis. Dundee and its textile workers, 1885-1923* (Edinburgh, 1979).
A. Wilson, *The Chartist Movement in Scotland* (Manchester, 1970).
G. M. Wilson, *Alexander McDonald, Leader of the Miners* (Aberdeen, 1982).
L. C. Wright, *Scottish Chartism* (Edinburgh, 1953).
J. D. Young, *The Rousing of the Scottish Working Class* (London, 1979).

8. *Intellectual history*

R. D. Anderson, *Education and Opportunity in Victorian Scotland. Schools and Universities* (Oxford, 1983).
M. Ash, *The Strange Death of Scottish History* (Edinburgh, 1980).
K. M. Boyd, *Scottish Church Attitudes to Sex, Marriage and the Family, 1850-1914* (Edinburgh, 1980).
C. Camic, *Experience and Enlightenment. Socialization for Cultural Change in Eighteenth Century Scotland* (Edinburgh, 1983).
R. H. Campbell and A. S. Skinner, *Adam Smith* (London, 1982).
———, (eds.), *The Origins and Nature of the Scottish Enlightenment* (Edinburgh, 1982).
A. C. Chitnis, *The Scottish Enlightenment* (London, 1976).
A. G. Clement and R. H. S. Robertson, *Scotland's Scientific Heritage* (Edinburgh, 1961).
Sir Reginald Coupland, *Welsh and Scottish Nationalism* (London, 1954).
D. Craig, *Scottish Literature and the Scottish People, 1680-1830* (London, 1961).
D. Daiches, *The Paradox of Scottish Culture. The Eighteenth Century Experience* (London, 1964).
G. E. Davie, *The Democratic Intellect: Scotland and her Universities in the Nineteenth Century* (Edinburgh, 1961).
A. L. Donovan, *Philosophical Chemistry in the Scottish Enlightenment* (Edinburgh, 1975).
A. L. Drummond and J. Bulloch, *The Scottish Church 1688-1843* (Edinburgh, 1973).
———, *The Church in Victorian Scotland, 1843-1874* (Edinburgh, 1974).
———, *The Church in late Victorian Scotland, 1874-1900* (Edinburgh, 1978).
V. E. Durkacz, *The Decline of the Celtic Languages* (Edinburgh, 1983).
J. Dwyer, R. Mason, A. Murdoch (eds.), *New Perspectives on the Politics and Culture of Early Modern Scotland, 1560-1800* (Edinburgh, n.d.).
I. Holt and M. Ignatieff (eds.), *Wealth and Virtue. The Shaping of Political Economy in the Scottish Enlightenment* (Cambridge, 1983).
W. M. Humes and H. M. Paterson (eds.), *Scottish Culture and Scottish Education, 1800-1980* (Edinburgh, 1983).
C. Johnson, *Developments in the Roman Catholic Church in Scotland, 1789-1829* (Edinburgh, 1983).
D. Johnson, *Music and Society in Lowland Scotland in the Eighteenth Century* (London, 1972).
A. Kent (ed.), *An Eighteenth Century Lectureship in Chemistry* (Glasgow, 1950).
W. C. Lehmann, *John Millar of Glasgow, 1735-1801* (Cambridge, 1960).

D. D. McElroy, *Scotland's Age of Improvement. A Survey of Eighteenth Century Literary Clubs and Societies* (Washington, 1969).

D. McRoberts (ed.), *Modern Scottish Catholicism, 1878-1978* (Glasgow, 1979).

T. A. Markus (ed.), *Order and Space in Society. Architectural Form and its Context in the Scottish Enlightenment* (Edinburgh, 1982).

K. Miller, *Cockburn's Millenium* (London, 1975).

E. C. Mossner, *The Life of David Hume* (Oxford, 1954).

W. Notestein, *The Scot in History* (London, 1946).

R. Olson, *Scottish Philosophy and British Physics* (Princeton, 1975).

G. C. H. Paton (ed.), *An Introduction to Scottish Legal History* (Edinburgh, 1958).

R. Porter and M. Teich (eds.), *The Enlightenment in National Context* (Cambridge, 1981).

I. S. Ross, *Lord Kames and the Scotland of his day* (Oxford, 1972).

C. W. J. Withers, *Gaelic in Scotland, 1698-1981* (Edinburgh, 1984).

D. Young *et al*, *Edinburgh in the Age of Reason* (Edinburgh, 1967).

9. Trade and transport

T. M. Devine, *The Tobacco Lords* (Edinburgh, 1975).

G. Dott, *Early Scottish Colliery Wagon Ways* (London, 1947).

A. R. B. Haldane, *The Drove Roads of Scotland* (Edinburgh, 1952).

———, *New Ways through the Glens* (Edinburgh, 1962).

———, *Three Centuries of Scottish Posts* (Edinburgh, 1971).

B. Lenman, *From Esk to Tweed* (Glasgow, 1975).

J. Lindsay, *The Canals of Scotland* (Newton Abbot, 1968).

M. C. Reed (ed.), *Railways in the Victorian Economy* (Newton Abbot, 1969).

J. F. Riddell, *Clyde Navigation* (Edinburgh, 1979).

C. J. A. Robertson, *The Origins of the Scottish Railway System, 1722-1844* (Edinburgh, 1983).

T. C. Smout, *Scottish Trade on the Eve of Union, 1660-1707* (Edinburgh, 1963).

W. Taylor, *The Military Roads of Scotland* (Newton Abbot, 1976).

W. Vamplew, *Salvesens of Leith* (Edinburgh, 1975).

10. Banking and finance

S. G. Checkland, *Scottish Banking. A History, 1695-1973* (Glasgow, 1975).

M. Gaskin, *The Scottish Banks* (London, 1975).

W. T. Jackson, *The Enterprising Scot. Investors in the American West after 1873* (Edinburgh, 1968).

D. S. Macmillan, *The Debtors' War* (Melbourne, 1960).

C. A. Malcolm, *The Bank of Scotland, 1695-1945* (Edinburgh, 1948).

———, *The History of the British Linen Bank* (Edinburgh, 1950).

R. C. Michie, *Money, Mania and Markets. Investment, Company Formation and the Stock Exchange in Nineteenth Century Scotland* (Edinburgh, 1981).

C. W. Munn, *The Scottish Provincial Banking Companies, 1747-1864* (Edinburgh, 1981).

N. Munro, *The History of the Royal Bank of Scotland, 1727-1927* (Edinburgh, 1928).

D. Murray, *The York Buildings Company* (Glasgow, 1883; reprinted Edinburgh, 1973).

R. S. Rait, *The History of the Union Bank of Scotland* (Glasgow, 1930).

J. M. Reid, *The History of the Clydesdale Bank, 1838-1938* (Glasgow, 1938).

N. Tamaki, *The Life Cycle of the Union Bank of Scotland* (Aberdeen, 1983).

11. *Urban history*

I. H. Adams, *The Making of Urban Scotland* (London, 1978).
S. G. Checkland, *The Upas Tree. Glasgow, 1875-1975* (Glasgow, second edn., 1982).
A. Gibb, *Glasgow and the Making of a City* (London, 1983).
G. Gordon and B. Dicks (ed.), *Scottish Urban History* (Aberdeen, 1983).
A. M. Jackson, *Glasgow Dean of Guild Court: A History* (Glasgow, 1983).
J. R. Kellett, *The Impact of Railways on Victorian Cities* (London, 1969).
C. McWilliam, *Scottish Townscape* (London, 1975).
D. Niven, *The Development of Housing in Scotland* (London, 1979).
A. J. Youngson, *The Making of Classical Edinburgh* (Edinburgh, 1966).

Index